GREAT AUSTRALIAN
HISTORIC HOTELS

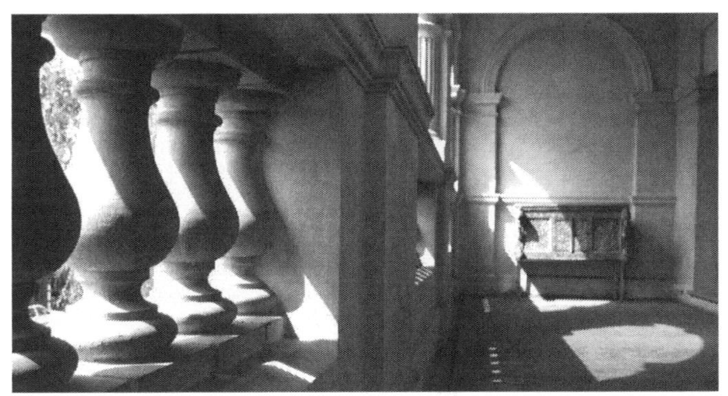

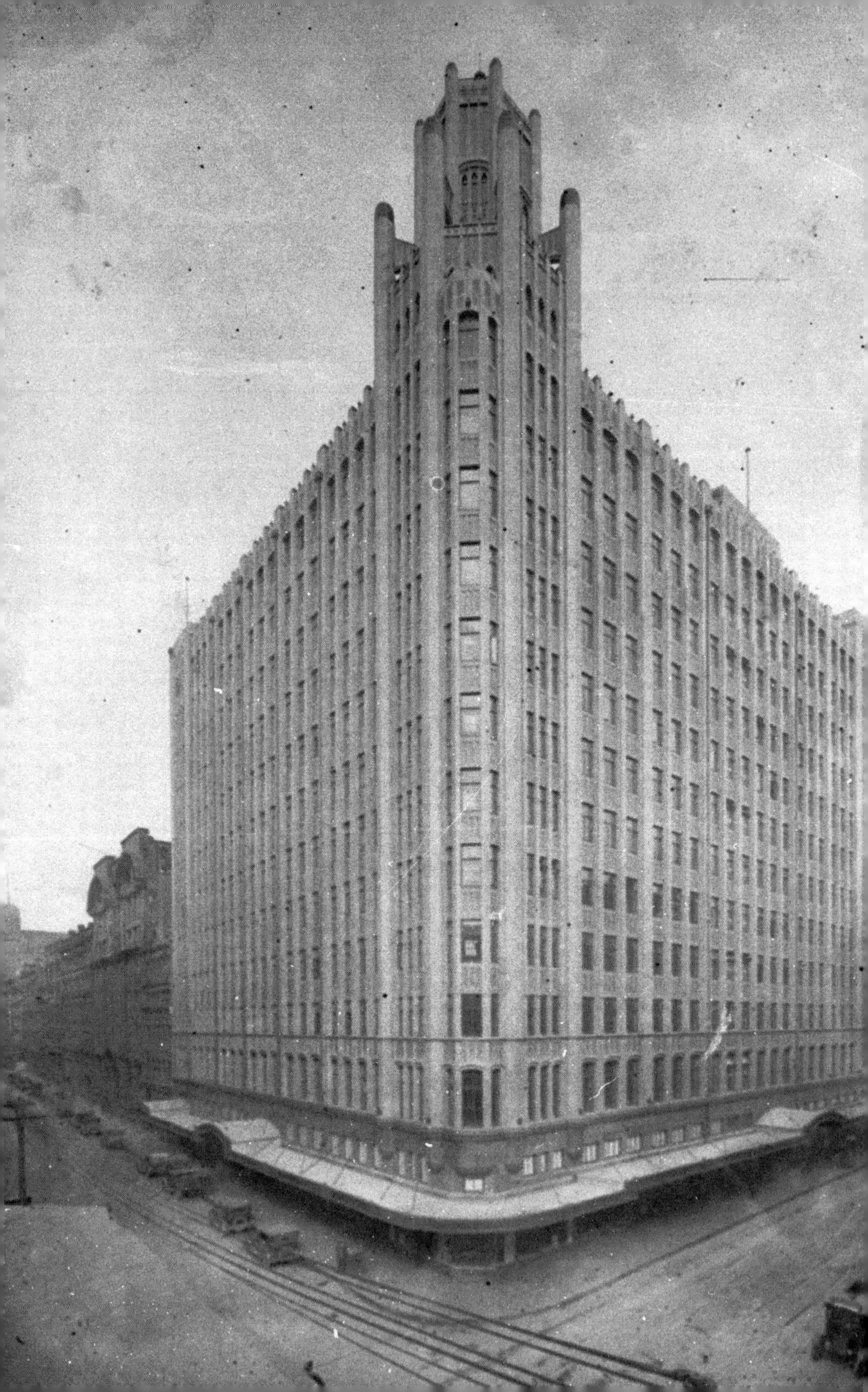

GREAT AUSTRALIAN
HISTORIC HOTELS

BARRY STONE

ALLEN&UNWIN

First published in 2010

Allen & Unwin
83 Alexander Street
Crows Nest NSW 2065
Australia
Phone: (61 2) 8425 0100
Fax: (61 2) 9906 2218
Email: info@allenandunwin.com
Web: www.allenandunwin.com

Cataloguing-in-Publication details are available
from the National Library of Australia
www.trove.nla.gov.au

ISBN 978 1 74237 408 6

Photos on prelim pages: p. i: The Hatton Hotel; p. ii: The Grace Hotel;
p. v: The Hotel Windsor's Grand Staircase

Photos on part-title pages: pp. 2–3: Boardroom, Hyatt Hotel, Canberra;
pp. 44–45: Sydney Harbour from Q Station; pp. 86–87: North Bundaleer Homestead;
pp. 122–123: New Norcia Hotel; pp. 188–189: Rupertswood;
pp. 230–231: Queenscliff Pier on Port Phillip Bay.

Internal design by Jacqueline Richards, PinchMe Design
Set in 10.5/13.5 ITC Garamond Light by Midland Typesetters, Australia
Printed and bound in Australia by Griffin Press

10 9 8 7 6 5 4 3 2 1

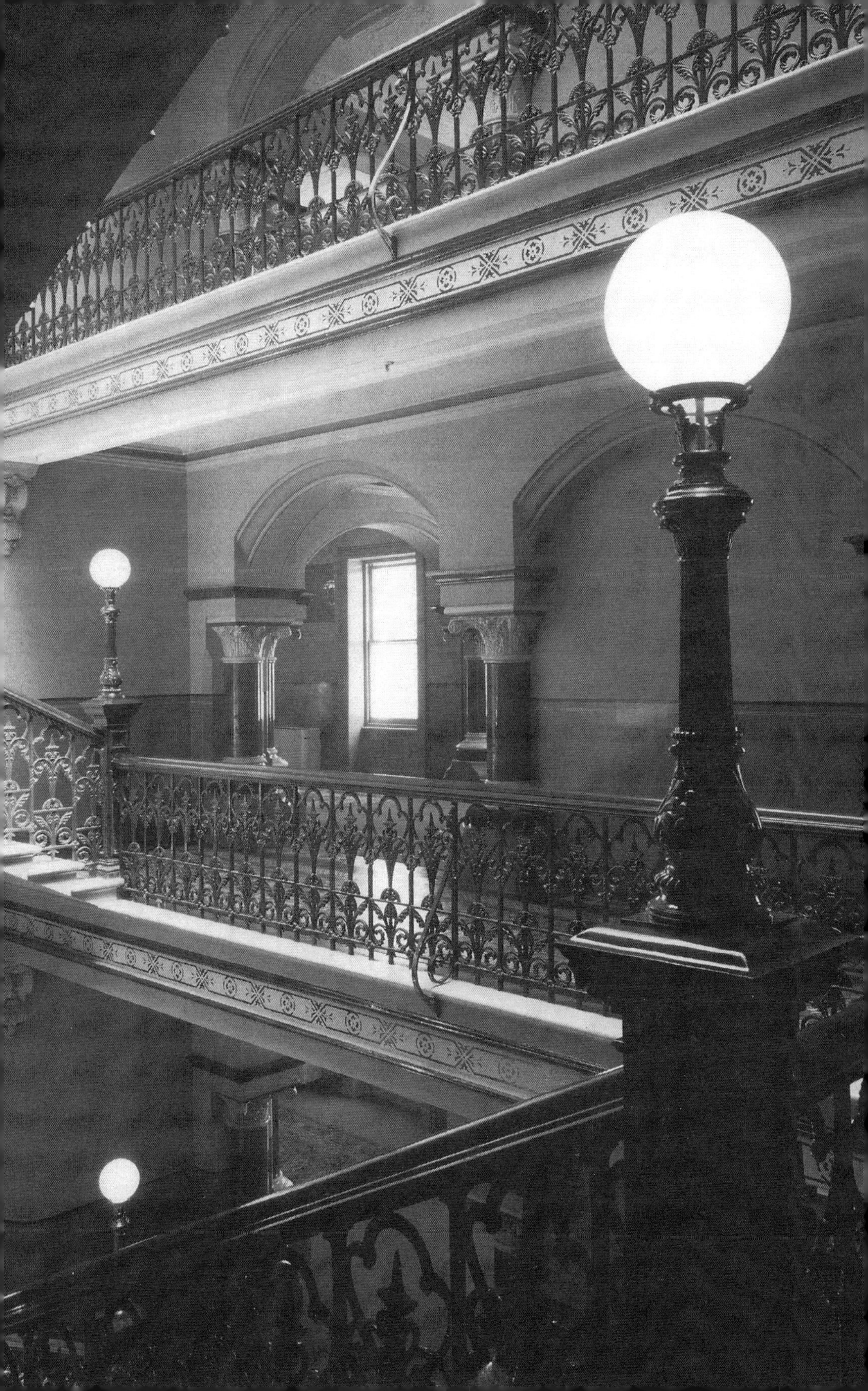

CONTENTS

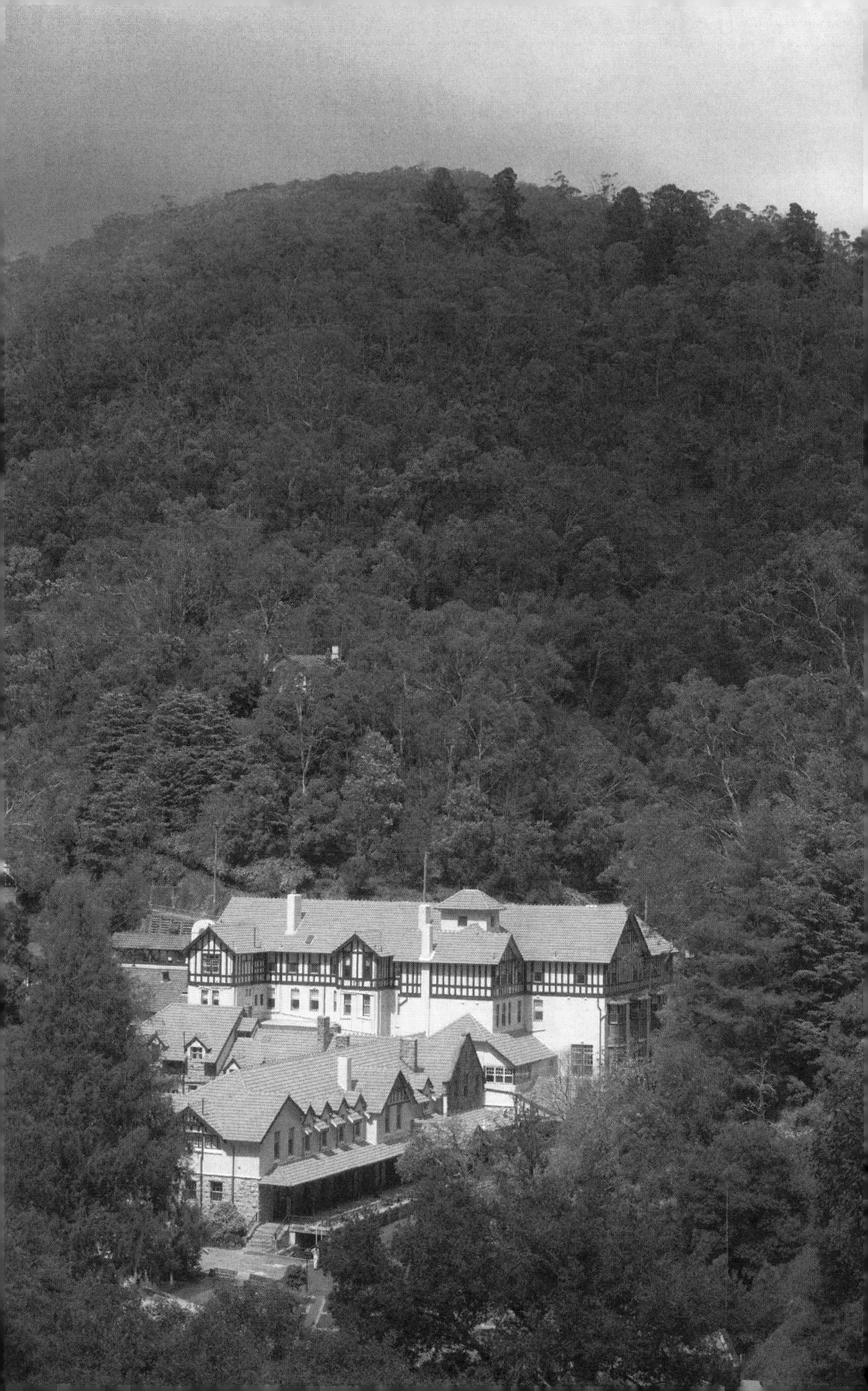

Barry Stone is a co-author of the popular books *1001 Inventions That Changed The World* and *1001 Escapes To Make Before You Die* (Quintessence, 2009), and the illustrated reference books *Historica, Geologica* and *EARTH* (Millennium House, 2008–09).

He is also the author of *I Want to Be Alone* (Murdoch Books, 2010), a compelling history of hermits and recluses both secular and religious, *Mutiny!* (Murdoch Books, 2010), an account of the famous and not-so-famous mutinies of history, and *Prison Breakouts* (Murdoch Books, 2011) revisiting some of the world's most audacious prison escapes.

In between books he likes to indulge his passion for travel writing and over the years his articles have appeared in some of Australia's leading travel publications including *Holidays for Couples, Australian Traveller*, and *DestinAsian*. He has also been a long-time contributor of travel destinations for Sydney's *Sun-Herald* newspaper.

Barry Stone lives on a quiet acre in rural Picton, an hour's drive south of Sydney with his wife Maryvonne and two boys, Jackson and Truman.

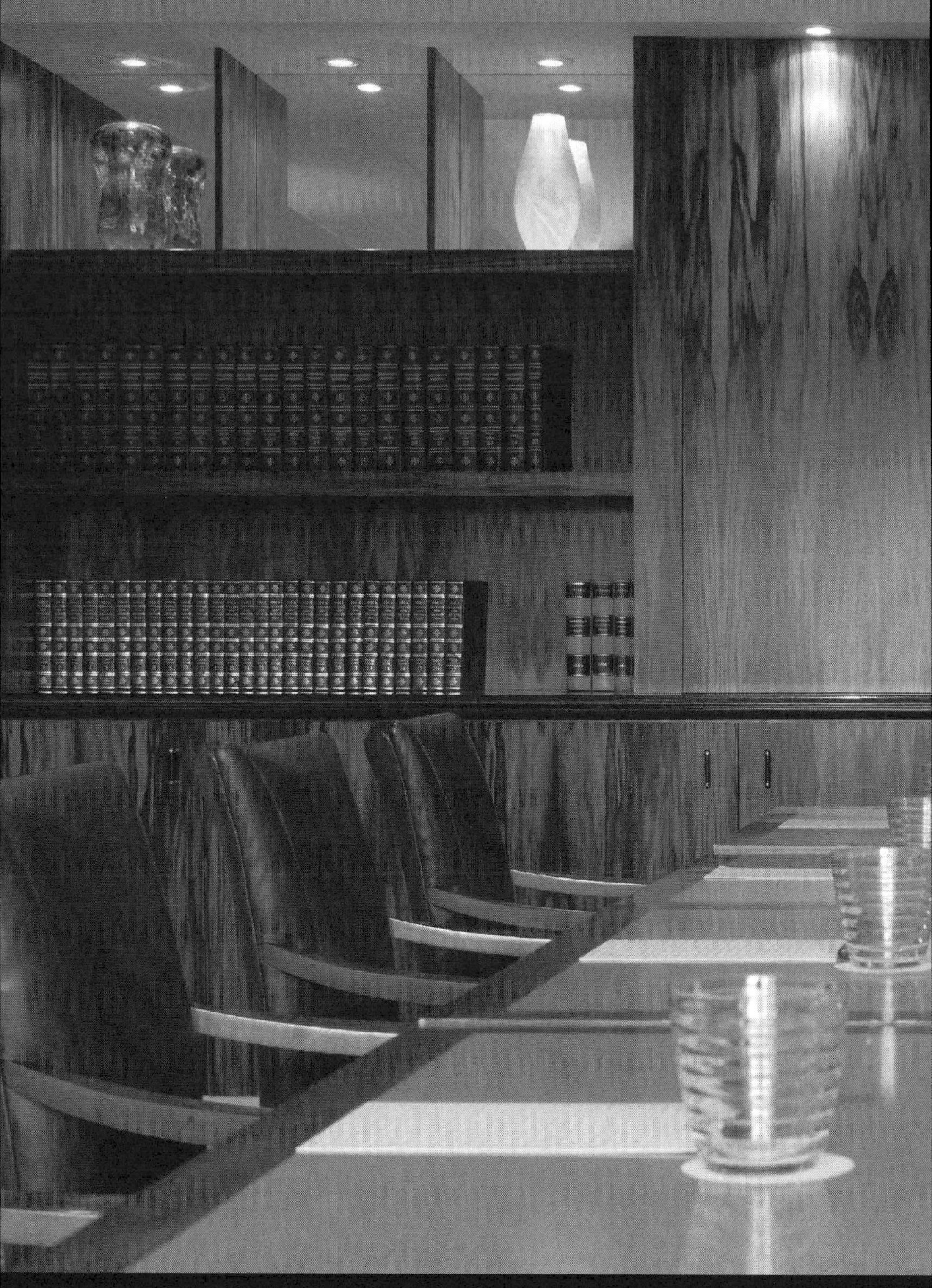
PART 1

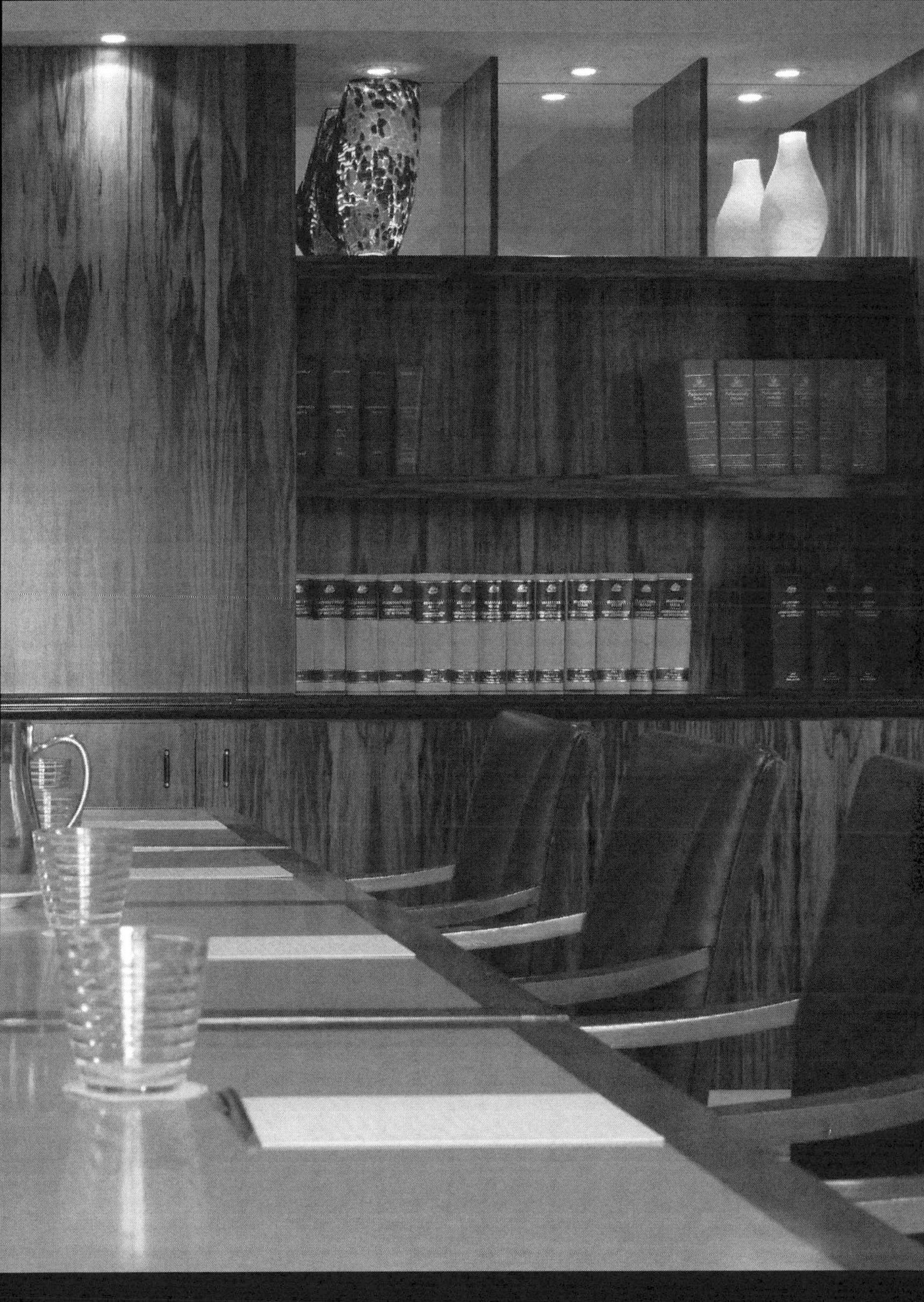

CBD Hotels

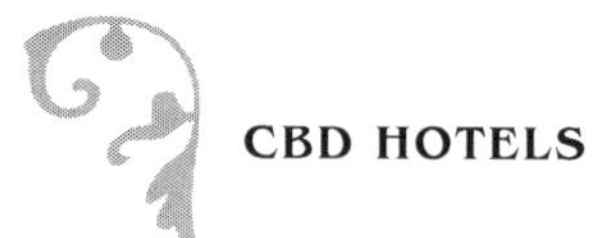

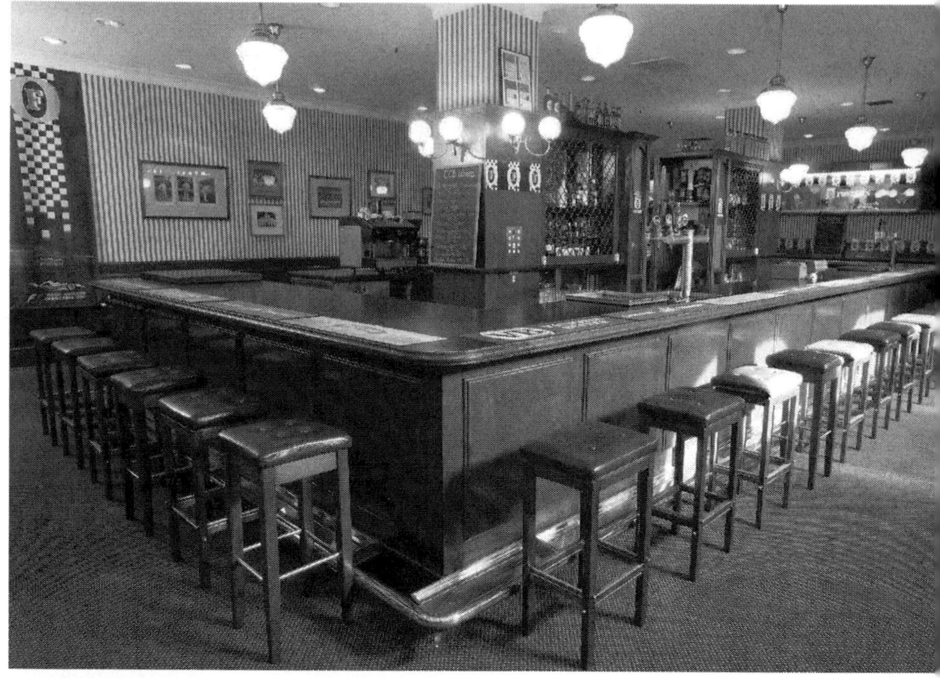

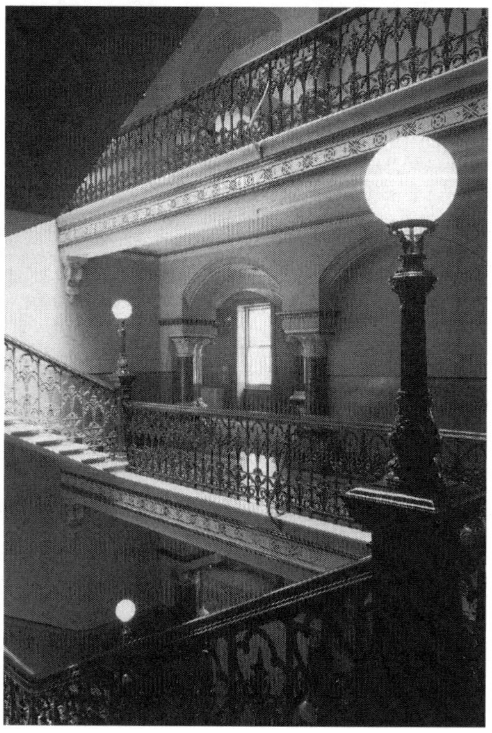

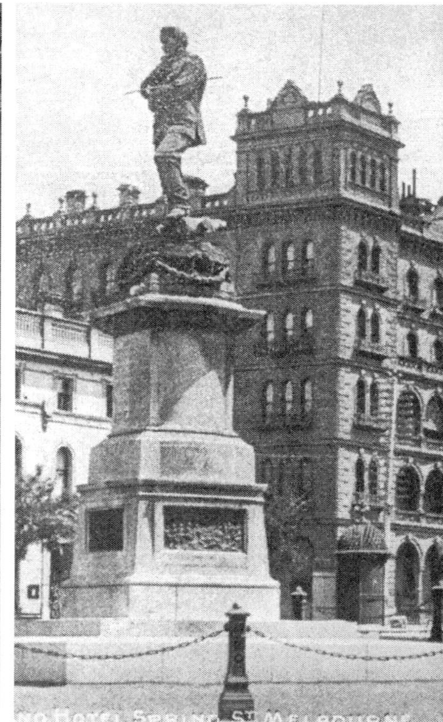

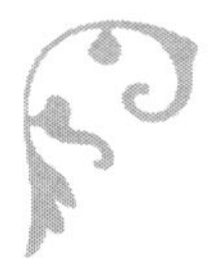

The Hotel Windsor

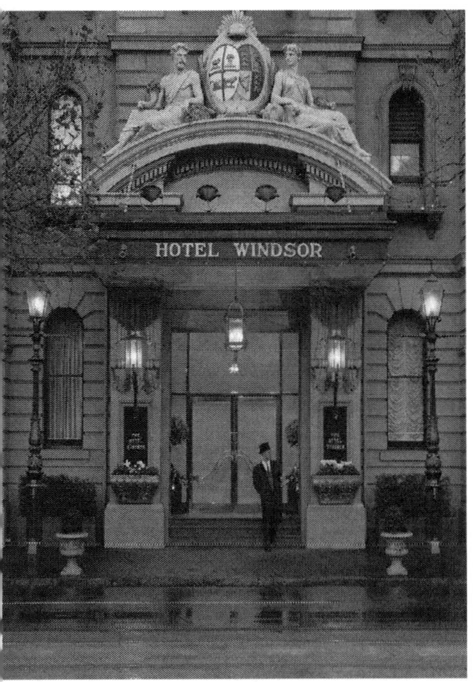

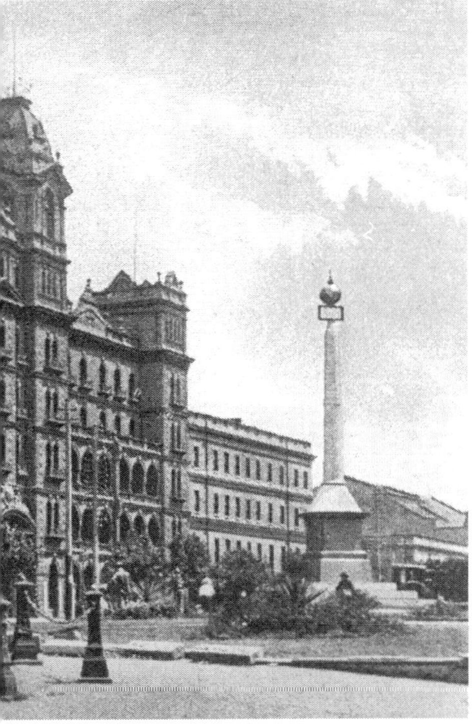

In the ten years prior to the Hotel Windsor opening its doors as 'The Grand Hotel' in 1883, the population of Melbourne had more than doubled, and its commercial buildings were the rival of any in New York or London. The city that began as an illegal settlement in the 1830s and boomed in the 1850s with the discovery of gold in the hills around Ballarat and Bendigo, had by 1890 become the 'Marvellous Melbourne' of history—the second largest city in the British Empire after London and larger than many of the capital cities of Europe, and every bit as vibrant. No single building symbolises better the brashness and confidence of late 19th-century Melbourne prior to the financial crash of 1891 better than the 'Duchess of Spring Street'.

clockwise from top left The Windsor's famous Cricketer's Bar; its ornate main entrance; its Spring St exterior with French Second Empire cupolas at centre; the Grand Staircase.

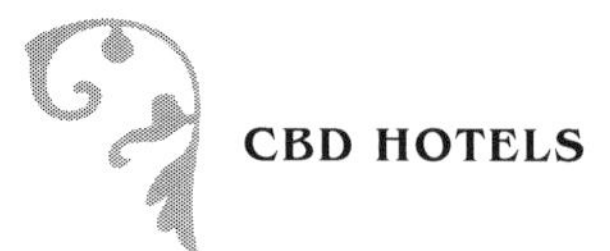

The Grand Hotel, renamed The Windsor in 1920, predated Singapore's Raffles Hotel by four years, The Savoy in London by six years, New York's Plaza by 11 years, and the Hotel Ritz in Paris by 15 years. This was no mere colonial copy of something already done well elsewhere. This building was an original, and no list of Australia's historic hotels would be complete without it.

In the mid 1970s my father had a Customs Agency business— Donald C. Stone & Co. Pty Ltd—in Melbourne's Flinders Lane, an impossibly narrow bluestone walk-up so small I still recall the carpenter having to remove the front window so my dad could get his desk inside when he moved in. Occasionally after school I'd catch the train into the city so I could spend some time in his office enjoying the privileges that came with being the boss's son: talking to whomever I pleased, doing as much or as little filing as I liked, stamping envelopes, and after work, going with Dad to the old docks area where he'd board cargo ships from around the world to meet the ship's executives while I'd become lost in their labyrinth of rooms and corridors. For me Melbourne's conservative, commercial world was not an intimidating mix of glass and concrete but more like a sort of playground. It was like the glory days of 'Marvellous Melbourne' had never ended.

The route from the railway station to Dad's office took me south down Spring Street, the thoroughfare that was, and still is, the eastern-most extremity of the CBD, right past the Hotel Windsor. But I always felt intimidated by the opulence and finery of Melbourne's Grande Dame of hotels—the one building I always wanted to enter but never did. That was more than 30 years ago. Now sitting with a coffee and a glass of chilled water in the hotel's signature restaurant, 111 Spring Street, with the hotel's Marketing Manager Grant Goodwin, I wish as a kid I'd just strolled right in and put up my feet. I've never felt so welcomed.

As it turned out, I learnt the Windsor has *always* been a sort of 'drop-in centre' for the city of Melbourne. In September of 1998 an explosion at the Esso natural gas plant at Longford in Victoria's Gippsland region killed two workers, injured eight and resulted in the entire gas supply to the state being shut off for 20 days. People that relied on gas for heating their home water systems were suddenly forced to endure almost three weeks of cold showers, a difficult prospect at any time in Melbourne but which required an extra dose

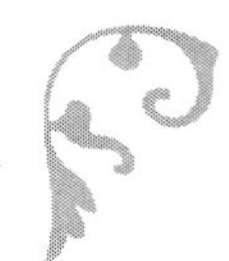

of fortitude during the city's frigid spring mornings. That is, unless you had the time to walk over to the Windsor.

The Hotel Windsor, unlike many buildings throughout the state, still relied on its old but virtually fail-safe system of oil heaters, and its guests were spared the ordeal of having to shower in cold water. Not content, however, with catering merely to the needs of its guests, the hotel announced it would open up what rooms it could, free of charge, for anyone who might be in desperate need of a shower. Lines of grateful, grubby Melburnians soon stretched around the block and were ushered one by one by the Windsor staff through the foyer to the showers in the hotel's unoccupied rooms. Everyone, I am told, had a marvellous time.

On the occasion of the hotel's 125th birthday on 18 December 2008 the hotel decided to advertise 25 rooms at 50 cents a night, the very same rate they were in 1883. The response was so overwhelming that the hotel's website and telephones went into meltdown.

Since the day the hotel's doors opened, and throughout the next 130 years, the hotel has been serving and spoiling Melbourne's mums with its famous afternoon teas, and those lucky enough to stay in its sumptuous rooms, many with unmatched views over Spring Street to the majestic colonnades of Parliament House. What the hotel's response to the disaster at Longford and events like its grand birthday celebrations continue to demonstrate is that, far from an undeserved reputation for being unapproachable, the reality is that people just can't wait for an excuse to go there. And there's no time like the present.

Just in case you might be wondering what, if anything, is happening now, whether the hotel might be becoming a little complacent, tempted to rest on its laurels and live off its history, fear not. In March 2010 The Hotel Windsor received both heritage and planning approval for a massive 260-million dollar redevelopment designed to return it to the status of one of the world's truly great hotels.

The redevelopment will see the construction of a 25-storey thin sliver of a building, described by its architects Denton Corker Marshall as a 'curtain' that will rise from behind the heritage-listed hotel and hide forever some of its less-glamorous neighbours. In addition its northern wing, a 1960s-era building which is somewhat of an eyesore, will be demolished and replaced by a futuristic, floating

cube-shaped addition with street level cafés and boutique shops that
will invite people to come in off the pavement. The two additions
will increase the hotel's capacity by 150 rooms and add a gym, a
25-metre swimming pool, saunas and wellness facilities. Also turning
the building inside-out and integrating it with Melbourne's pedestrians
will be achieved with the removal of the windows that currently fill
in the colonnades along Spring Street that now separate the afternoon
tea aficionados from the public. No more will the single front door
intimidate; The Hotel Windsor will be throwing open its doors to the
world.

In the midst of all the changes some things will of course
never change. The hotel's tradition of serving the finest afternoon
teas in town will always be an intrinsic part of its character and
really shouldn't be missed. High teas first began as more of a
light meal for European royalty who used the occasion to stave
off hunger until dinner time. Nowadays it is of course a culinary
treat, although I defy anyone to eat their way through its three
tiers of sandwiches and sweets that confront you. It is served
every afternoon from 2.30 through to 4.30, and the hotel's French-
trained pastry chef and the eight chefs that work under him
combine their skills to produce mouth-watering date scones, finger
sandwiches and assorted desserts based on 120-year old recipes,
with a contemporary twist, and which look so delicate it's almost a
shame to eat them. Our boys, aged six and ten, were well looked
after by the staff and our youngest, who has allergies and food
intolerances, was provided with specially made, pre-arranged treats
from the kitchen. There were the predictable moments like, 'Dad, I
just blew some bubbles into my drink,' through to the delightfully
unpredictable with my older boy trying a cup of Windsor Blend
tea. The whole visit was the opposite of the feared-for, anxiety-
ridden outing which is usually the result of combining children
with fine linen and silver service. In fact the entire experience was
a calorie-infested, culinary and parental delight, summed up by the
comments of a lovely elderly lady who'd been dining in the corner
with a small group of friends and who stopped by our table on
her way out to say, 'Congratulations on your two boys—if my two
granddaughters were here, they'd be running about all over the
place'. Or would they? Perhaps the Hotel Windsor would work its
magic on them as well.

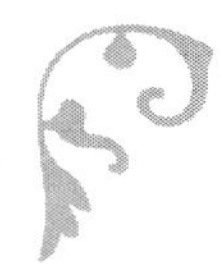

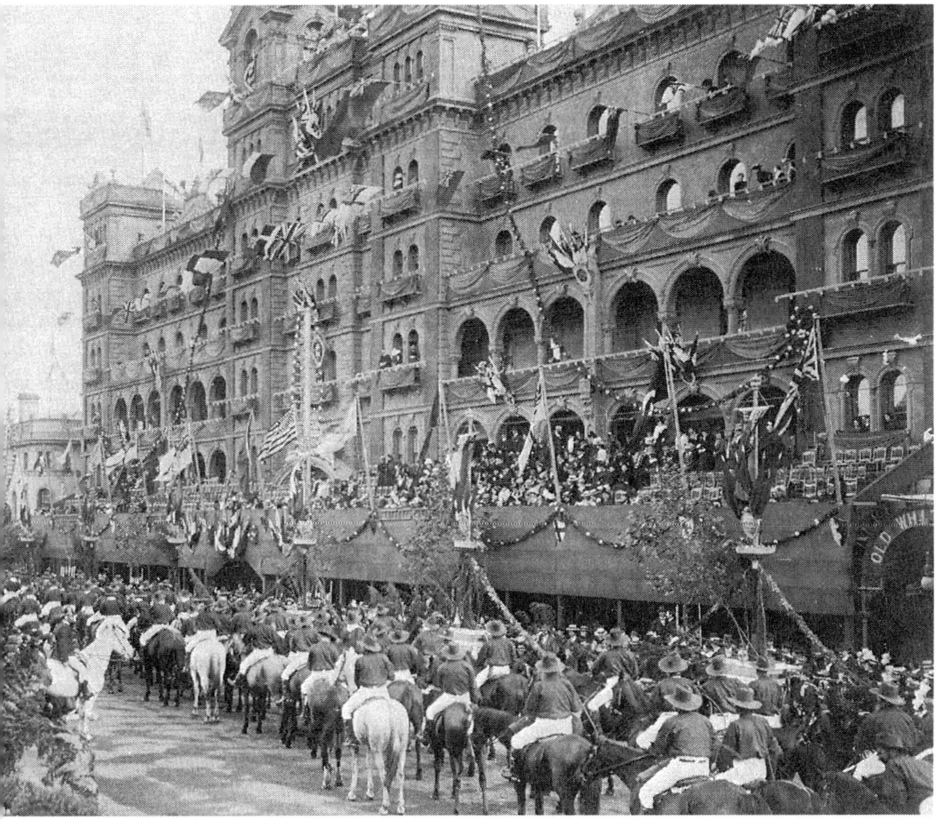

above Parade of returned World War I veterans march south down Spring St in 1919. Note the entrance to the 'Old White Hart' hotel, demolished to make way for the Windsor's extensions in the 1960s.

Wandering through its public spaces is also a treat. The hotel's two original metal cage elevators were built at a time when the elevator operator was considered, along with the concierge, to be the very heart and soul of a hotel and soon, all being well, will be again. Though not presently in operation, the elevators, which have been used in the past as telephone booths and still have an old 'telephone' sign above them, will be returned to their former operational splendour. There are, of course, more modern elevators down the hall which are invaluable to get bags to and from rooms, but you should, at least once, dispense with the elevators altogether and take to the stairs—because if there's a hotel anywhere in Australia that rewards you for simply walking its staircase, this is the one.

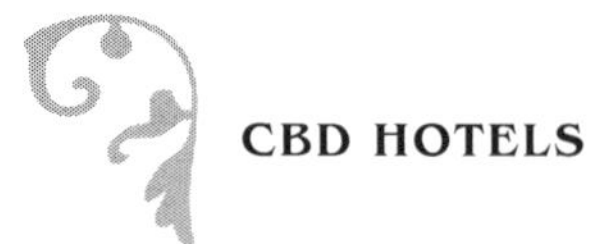

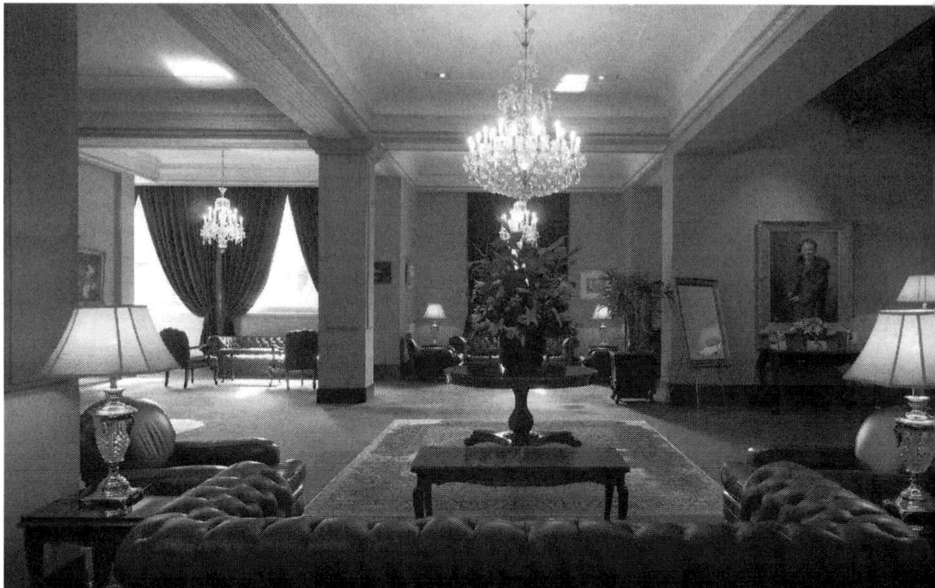

above The Windsor's opulent Royal Suite includes a dining room, a drawing room, a guest powder room, master bedroom and bathroom with claw-foot tub.

The Hotel Windsor's Grand Staircase is a monument to 19th-century craftsmanship, all the way from its tessellated tiles flown in from London to the marble of its steps designed to prevent it from burning in case of a fire and the intricate wrought iron beneath its balustrades. Overhead reinforced light-wells of stained glass flood it all with light, creating a vivid interplay of colours. You simply *have* to walk it if only to remind yourself that the best things in life don't always have to cost, and to lose a few of those calories you accumulated over afternoon tea.

You also need to see the Grand Ballroom, with its seven magnificent glass cupolas that dominate the gold-leaf encrusted ceiling allowing natural light to dance off its Belle Époque interior. Without doubt one of the most exquisite rooms in the country, it will be completely refurbished when the redevelopment begins in early 2012.

The original section of the hotel has a Royal Suite, home to kings, presidents and assorted visiting dignitaries, and seven Victorian Suites, each one individually furnished and with its own distinctive floor plan and character. Our rooms, 224 and 226, were located in the

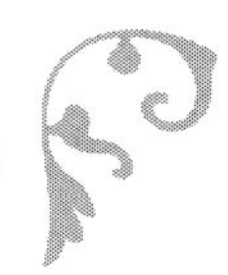

hotel's northeast wing overlooking Spring Street and connected via a common foyer which can be used as a thoroughfare between the two rooms to form a large, rambling home-away-from-home that is perfect for families. An oval sitting room off Room 224 has to be one of the finest hotel rooms in the city with State Parliament just across the road, wonderfully lit at night and perfectly framed in the room's three double-glazed sash windows. A chilled bottle of French Louis Perdrier Brut Rosé on the side table helped us appreciate it.

And you don't really appreciate the level of craftsmanship in a circular or oval room until you stay in one. Nothing sits flush against the wall. The plaster cornices are curved, and the architraves and walls are curved. Even the doors and the glass in the windows are curved. The only drawback was there was absolutely nowhere you could put a corner bookcase, and forget about telling a misbehaving child to go stand in the corner. That aside, the sheer elegance of a perfectly rounded room led me time and again to run my eye over it, marvelling at its geometric perfection. Staring at a wall was never so completely fulfilling an experience.

By virtue of its shape and its elegant furnishings, the room is reminiscent of the world's most famous oval room at 1600 Pennsylvania Avenue, Washington DC. But of course there were Australian flourishes here. A painting by Alfred Coleman (1890–1952), the early 20th-century Australian landscape artist, hung on the wall. Add the superbly comfortable leather lounges and the wool carpet beneath your feet, and it's not long before you're contemplating staying that extra night.

The northern wing of the hotel of which our rooms were a part was a 1960 addition with little to recommend itself architecturally and will be demolished to make way for the hotel's reinvention. The Hotel Windsor was saved from an appalling redevelopment with the intervention of the Victorian Government, who purchased it in 1977 before leasing it to the Oberoi Group in 1980, and who sold it to its present owners, the Halim Group, in 2005.

Now that the redevelopment has been approved we can all breathe a little easier. The Hotel Windsor is the last of Australia's great 19th-century grand hotels. All the others, the Australia and the Metropole hotels in Sydney, and the Menzies and Federal hotels in Melbourne, have gone under the wrecking ball. And their like will never come again.

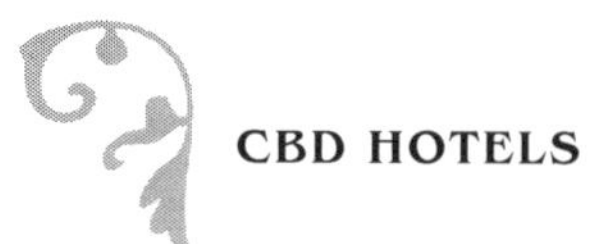

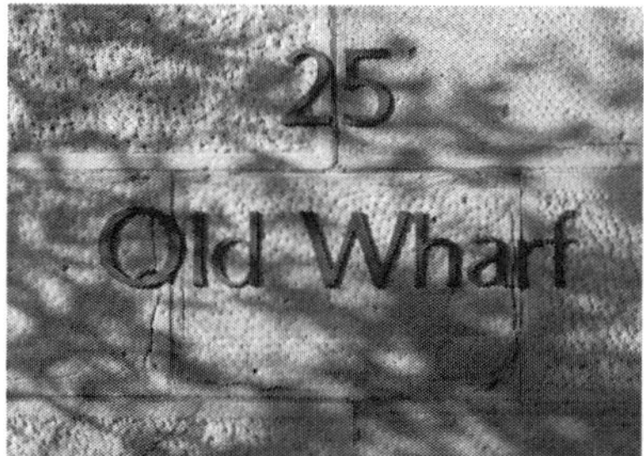

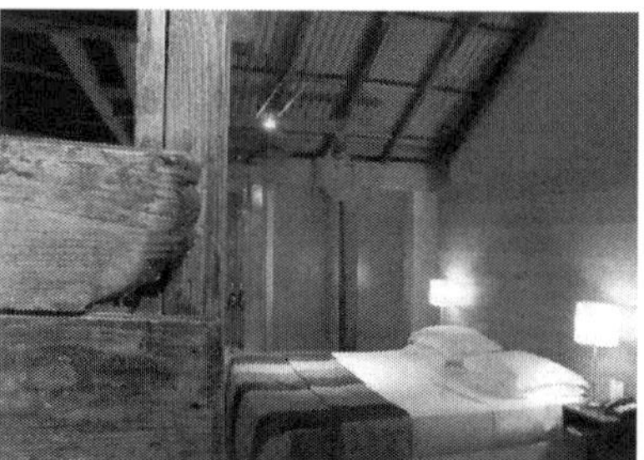

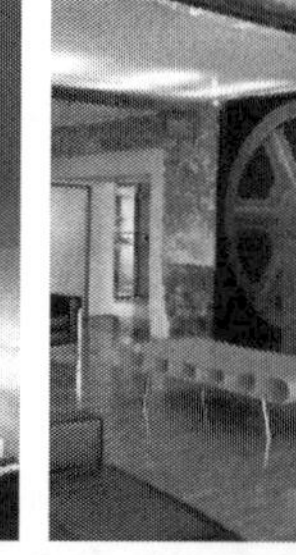

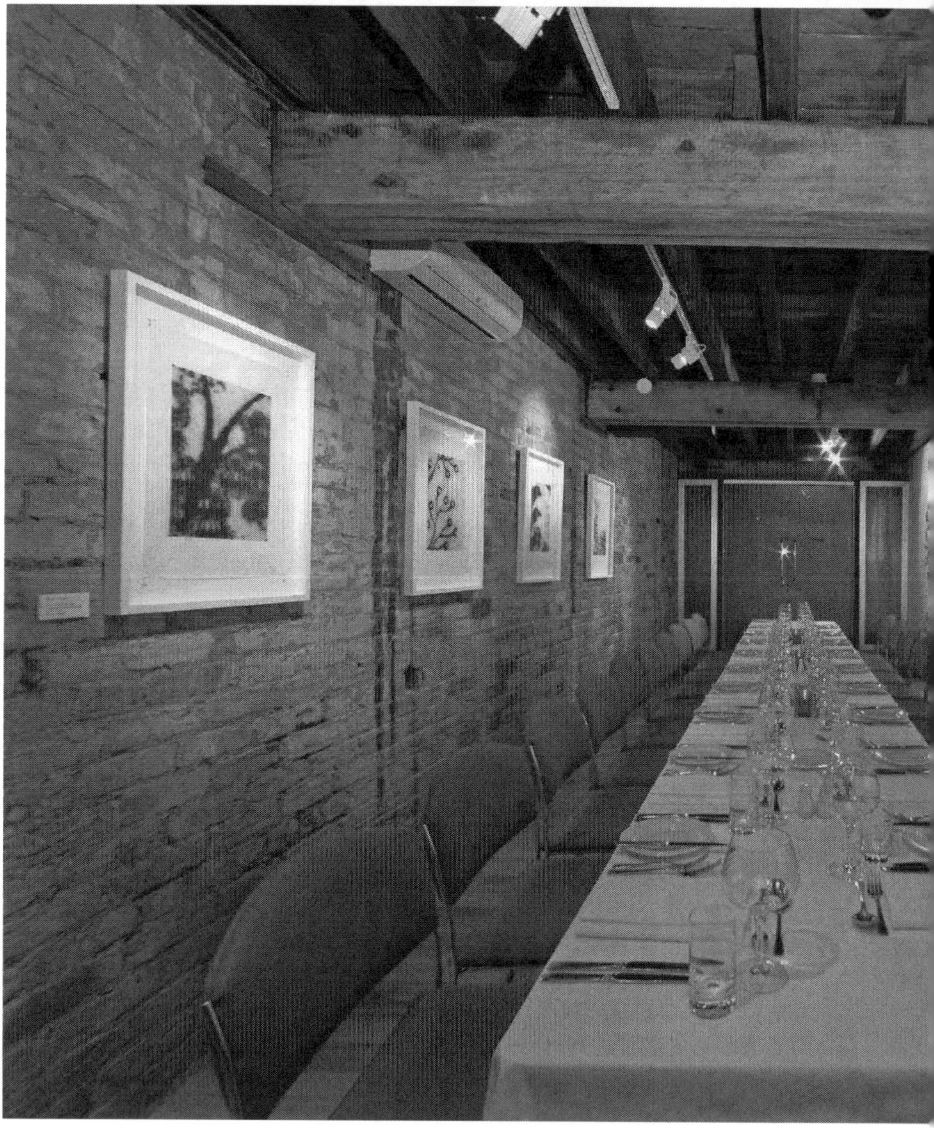

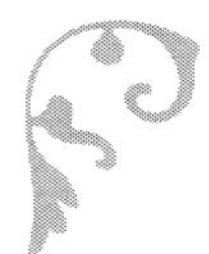

CHAPTER 2

The Henry Jones Art Hotel

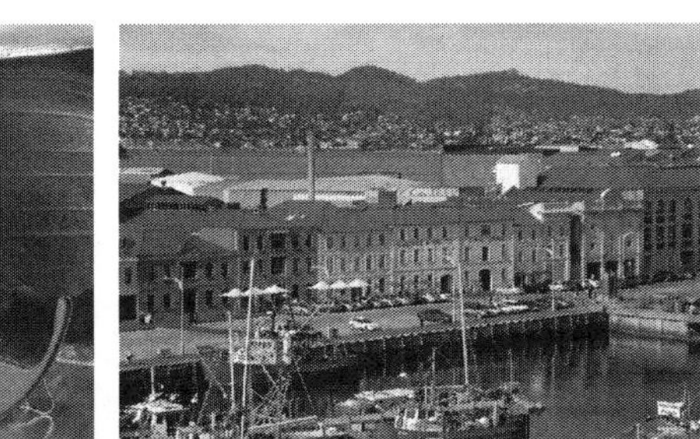

At the top of the Henry Jones Art Hotel's grand 1912 blackwood staircase can still be seen the faintest of reminders of the frugality of the building's one-time owner and founder of Tasmania's IXL Jam Company, Sir Henry Jones, known to his friends as 'Jam Tin Harry'. It's so faint, in fact, that you could walk up and down the staircase a hundred times and miss it each time if you didn't know where and what it was. I wouldn't have found it myself if I hadn't had it pointed out by Warren Glover, the hotel historian, who gets understandably excited when talking about the wealth of history that the Henry Jones Art Hotel embodies.

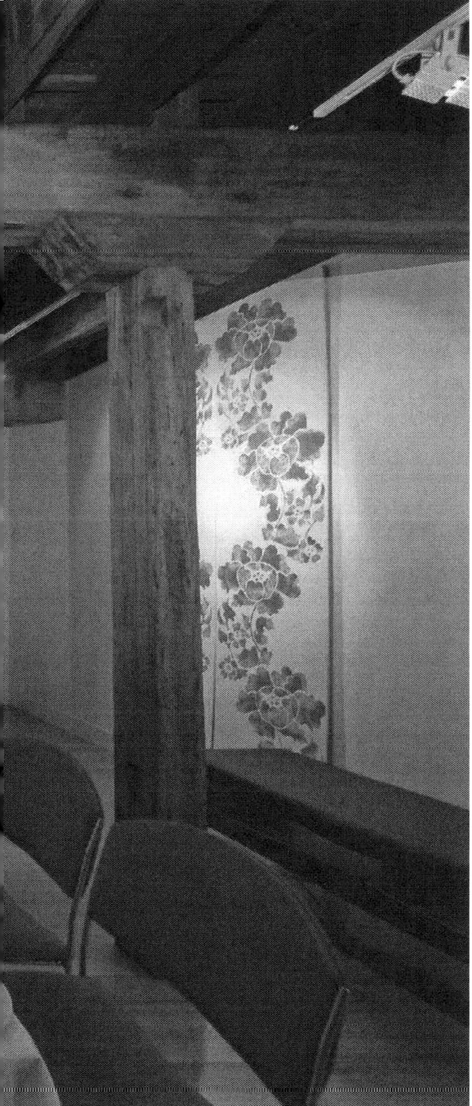

clockwise from top left 'No. 25'; rooms a seamless blend of old and new; The Henry Jones: hotel or art gallery?; Harbour-view rooms overlook Constitution Dock; the Art Installation Room.

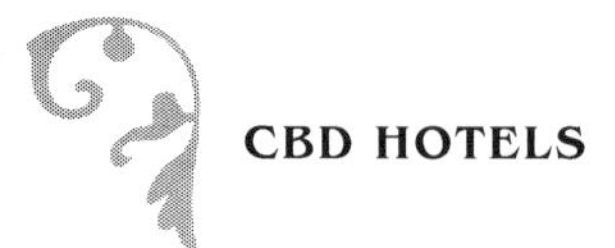

Warren is responsible for, among other things, returning to the hotel items that have been either lost or pilfered from the site over the decades and never tires of accompanying interested guests on a walk up the staircase with its elegant 'lady's waist' handrail, to show them the secret in its carved newel posts that the hotel only reveals to the very curious.

In a nod to the Arts and Crafts tradition of craftsmanship prevalent at the time, a pattern known as 'stippling' had been painstakingly etched on each side of one of the staircase's two newel posts by one of the jam factory's unskilled labourers. The employee, most likely a crate-maker whose name is now lost to history, had completed one post and was halfway through stippling the second when Henry Jones walked by. When he realised the man had not only been taken off the factory floor to do the work, but to compound the extravagance was being paid an additional wage to embellish the posts, the frugal Jones told him to down his tools and return to work, not something the labourer would have wanted to hear considering the output of the average IXL Jam Factory crate-maker was in excess of 200 crates a day.

Today the boundary where the stipple pattern abruptly ends shows us the moment in time when the employee was told by his boss to down his tools. It provides an insight into the psychology of Henry Jones, whose parents first came to Tasmania in the late 1850s and who engendered such loyalty amongst his staff that many worked in his jam factory their entire adult lives. They even had their own football team and brass band. Henry Jones went on to build an empire stretching around the world, but of course even empire-builders tend to have humble beginnings, and those of Henry Jones's can be traced to a man named George Peacock.

George Peacock was a local merchant who made jams and preserves in the back room of his grocery store at the corner of Despard and Murray Streets in Hobart in the late 1850s. He soon, however, outgrew his shop, known to locals as 'The Elbow Room', and purchased a new building on Hunter Street on the Old Wharf, on what used to be Hunter Island until it was joined to the mainland with the construction of a causeway in 1820. The site was a far more practicable one for the export of his increasingly popular jams, though at the time was anything but one of Hobart's prime stretches of real estate, with slaughterhouses upstream causing malaria and

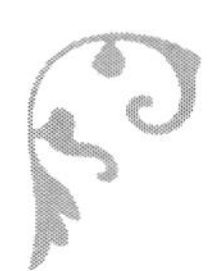

contaminated water to seep into the area's slums. Peacock's jams nevertheless grew in popularity and in 1869 he began purchasing the adjacent buildings and accumulating the Hunter Street streetscape that survives intact to this day.

In 1874 the 12-year-old Henry Jones went to work for Peacock six days a week, ten hours a day, pasting labels onto jam tins. This job pleased his mother enormously because Peacock was known for engaging his staff in compulsory hymn-singing and Bible readings every morning before work. Jones applied himself with vigour to his role and his exceptional work ethic saw him rise quickly through the company's ranks to the role of factory foreman in 1885. In the early 1890s the business began to experience financial difficulties and Jones, in partnership with Achaelen Palfreyman and George Peacock's own son Ernest, purchased the company and despite tariff wars and bank foreclosures steered it into a new era of prosperity under the name 'The H. Jones and Co. Pty Ltd, IXL Jams'.

Within five years the factory floor grew to a mammoth 140 000 square feet, an accounting office was established in the offices at the top of the grand staircase—a lovely open space now used for conferences, weddings and such—and Henry Jones's own office, now Room 103, was added. More than 2 million tins of jam were produced every growing season in copper urns weighing a tonne each and measuring 2.4 metres (8 feet) in diameter, one of which has recently been found and is in the process of being cleaned before being returned to the hotel to be placed on permanent display.

The Henry Jones Art Hotel is a stunning example of how history and modernity can be brought seamlessly together to create a space where each era needs and compliments the other. Walking its corridors and public spaces it isn't long before you come to appreciate just how much of the building's past and present are entwined. A faint tinge of green paint on the first few sandstone rises in the hotel's foyer is all that remains of an early form of dampcourse, a necessary ingredient in a building that at the time sat largely over water. As you walk in the hotel's front doors, note the bricked-in fireplace in the wall to your left, indicating the front of the foyer was once a series of small offices, each with its own fireplace. Small gaps in the existing plaster indicate where partitions and walls once stood, allowing you to imagine how it might have looked in the late 1830s during Tasmania's whaling industry when the five buildings now

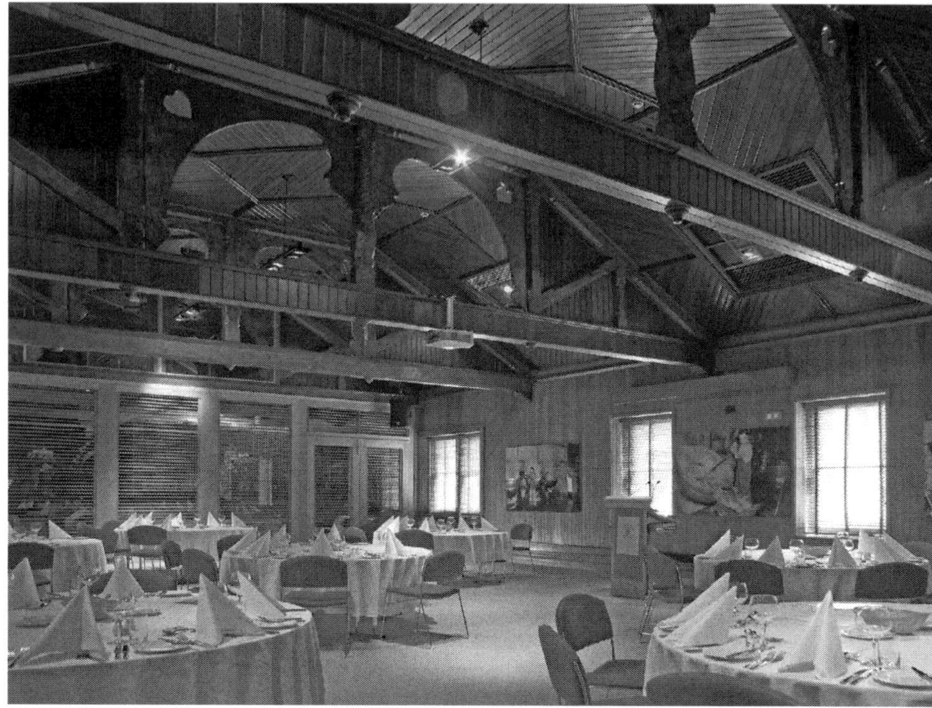

above The Jones & Co. Room, once the heart of the IXL Empire is now an event venue with seating for up to 160 diners.

associated with the hotel were filled with sail-makers, instrument-makers, boat-builders, and oil and soap factories.

The accumulation of long-lost relics and personal items is an ongoing pursuit at the Henry Jones Art Hotel. Henry Jones's granddaughter, now 84 years old and living in Hobart, still has her grandfather's pocketwatch that was stolen during a trip to Melbourne in the years after the Great War to watch a Victorian Football League (VFL) game. Pickpocketed on his way out of the ground, the 'canny' Jones didn't bother notifying the police, instead putting out an APB with the Melbourne underworld offering a reward for the watch's safe return. 'I'm not going back to Hobart without that watch,' he told his wife. His streetsmart response to the theft saw the watch returned the very next day. The watch will soon be on display inside the building where it spent its days making sure its owner was always on time for his next meeting. His rolltop Cutler desk, purchased on a trip to New York, has also been located and is due to be returned.

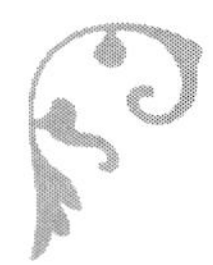

In a state where only 16 people born in 2009 could *not* claim a convict ancestry, it should come as no surprise that this hotel is so determined to reclaim and keep alive its heritage. Every staff member at the Henry Jones Art Hotel, and indeed most Tasmanians, has a very personal stake in cataloguing the story of European settlement, and as a result the state's history is being pursued and preserved by people and institutions well beyond the usual mix of museums and historical societies.

Patrons of the hotel today should take a look inside Peacock Terrace, the hotel's oldest room named in honour of George Peacock, and walk down Tasmania's oldest spiral staircase. The huge intact expanse of original 1850s wallpaper in the suite's main bedroom would most likely have been lost to the ages had it not been for the intervention in 2001 of the architectural firm Morris Nunn & Associates, who rescued the then-decaying string of buildings and initiated plans to bring them back to life. Morris Nunn & Associates were, in fact, *so* pleased with the finished product that they moved their offices into the first floor of the old Georgian townhouse behind the main buildings beneath the redeveloped atrium. The townhouse, a brick and timber structure, is supported by a network of 3-metre high hardwood posts, which are all that remain after the ground level brickwork was knocked down to create more warehouse space. It pre-dates the jam factory by several years and is Australia's oldest remaining Georgian townhouse.

Then there is the old ice works and cool store, built in 1900, the construction of which brought an end to the days of hauling down ice by horse and cart from the ice huts on the summit of nearby Mt Wellington. Now home to the hotel's Oriental Suites the building still has more than 14 miles of pipes snaking through its walls, and if you look closely you'll see that one of its external windows is set almost imperceptibly off-centre, a delightful reminder that the buildings along Hunter Street were largely the product of unskilled craftsmen.

History in this hotel is everywhere, though some aspects are more visible than others, which is why a magnifying glass and a healthy dose of natural inquisitiveness will enhance any visit as you hunt down the clues that are scattered about, daring you to find them and piece together your own individual account of the life and times of this extraordinary collection of buildings. And the slower you walk, the more you see. If you stroll through its first-floor corridors and look at the underside of the hundreds of exposed beams above your head, you'll see thousands of nail holes which at first glance seem like the remnants of some long-gone inlaid plaster ceiling. But look closer and you'll discover they were there to keep in place not plaster but leather—huge swathes of leather kept aloft just to catch the dust from the floor above and prevent it from contaminating the hundreds of bags of sugar stacked below. There are one or two telltale remnants of leather, if you know where to look for them.

One of the few casualties of the building's redevelopment was its ground floor fireplaces, though even they have left evidence of their presence in the several brick flues and vents that remain undisturbed on the hotel's upper floors, their surrounds delightfully blackened and their 150-year-old bricks loose but still intact; a testament to the honesty of patrons who refuse to souvenir them. Lengths of electrical conduit and steam and water pipes are everywhere—anything that could be left has been. Even supporting posts added out of necessity during the hotel's refurbishment have been painted bright red so they wouldn't be confused with the real thing.

The sandstone used in the building's internal and external walls is locally quarried, porous, and really not an ideal choice as a long-term, structural material, which explains why the hotel's facade has already been reworked twice since the hotel began operating. It nonetheless represents a fascinating personal record of the labourers and convicts who built it, and the dozens of cuts on the facing surfaces of each block carries the individual mark of the man who cut it. Some marks are long and shallow, others shorter but with more depth. Some cuts are closer together and repetitive while others are more scattered. Cutting tools have been used on some while others were cut using blunt or poor quality instruments. Random cuts might have been made by men carrying injuries, some were obviously left-handed, and some had received training as a stonecutter, though most had not. But they all shared one thing in common: these marks, thousands upon thousands of them throughout the hotel's corridors, rooms and public spaces, are more than just marks: they are signatures, some of the oldest to be found anywhere in Australia, each with its own style and telling its own story. For many of the men who made them, they are the only proof that they ever existed.

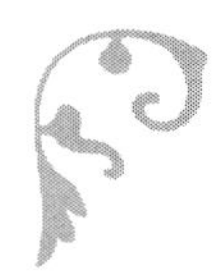

Another intrinsic aspect of the hotel—and as representative of its future as its sandstone and shingle roof is of its past—is, of course, its art. The Henry Jones Art Hotel is the only dedicated art hotel in the country, home to more than 300 individual pieces. You cannot stay here without being inspired by the constantly changing exhibitions featuring local Tasmanian artists and postgraduate work from the Tasmania School of Arts.

My room, number 119, with a view of the Hobart waterfront and Constitution Dock, was decorated with 'Dahlia, 2008', a work in black ink featuring a reclining feminine figure draped in ivy, for sale for $1800, and 'Rosie, 2008' another female figure wearing a top of flowers and petals and a 'Love' tattoo, also $1800. Tattoos are a recurring theme of the artist, Sally Rowe, who uses them to indulge herself in voyeuristic insights into the subject's personality and history. My own favourite were a pair of oils on linen by Corinne Costello: 'Becoming Reality' and 'Momentary Illusions', an abstract blend of transparent and opaque pigments resulting in heavily textured and richly glazed reds over a lime green and turquoise background, and both yours for $1500 each. Every piece seen throughout the hotel, except for two enormous, purpose commissioned canvases in the hotel foyer, is for sale. One guest recently purchased in excess of $40 000 worth.

In 1919 Henry Jones became the first Tasmanian to be knighted, though on his return to his beloved factory he gave an impassioned speech saying he hoped he would still be known by his friends and employees as 'Jam Tin Harry'. He retired in 1922, by which time he'd become the largest private employer in Tasmania, and died in Melbourne on 29 October 1926. On the day of his funeral 10 000 people filled Hobart's Cornelian Bay cemetery to overflowing, and an era in the state's history was solemnly laid to rest. To say the Henry Jones Art Hotel is part of the fabric of Tasmania is no trite statement— apricot and other stone fruit pips from Jones's factory floor were even used in the foundations of Hobart's first streets.

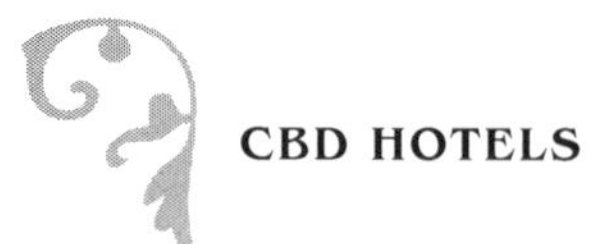

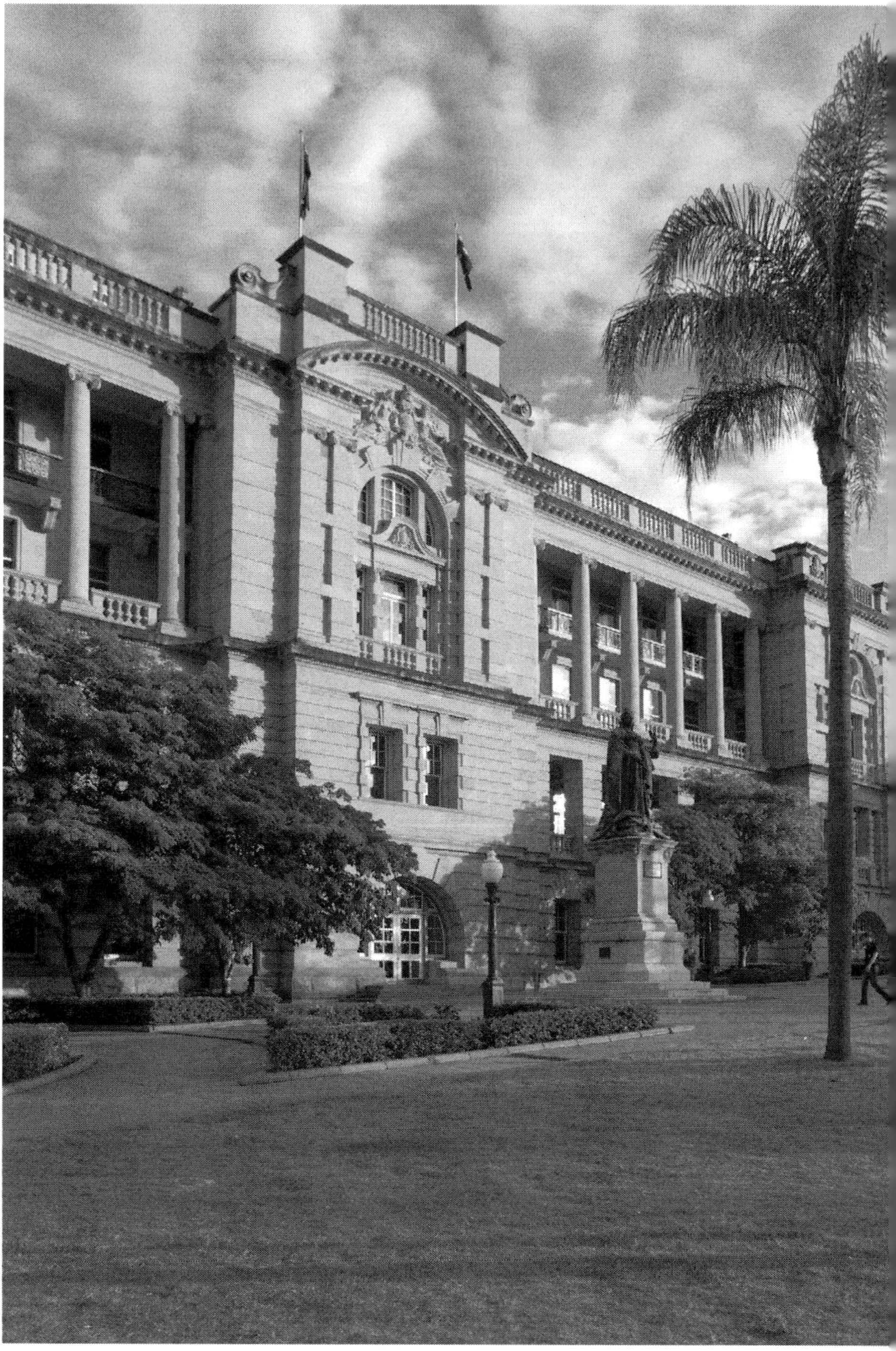

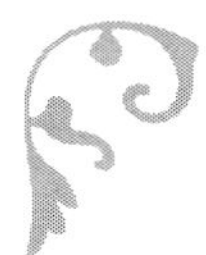

CHAPTER 3

Treasury Heritage Hotel

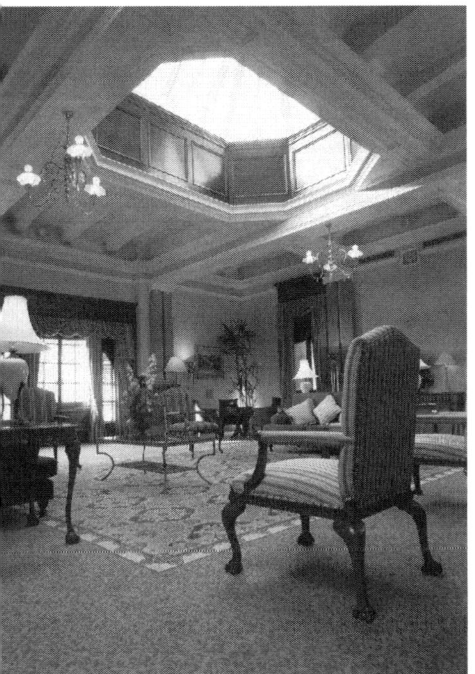

When Queensland was proclaimed a colony in 1859, there was only 5 cents in the treasury. The state was bankrupt through most of the 1860s, and then came the devastating drought of the 1870s. It wasn't until the opening of the Milton Goldfield in 1879 that the coffers of the state government finally began to fill, and by the mid 1880s, with a surplus of some 4 million dollars, it was at last in a position to think about pushing ahead with the development of major public buildings and infrastructure.

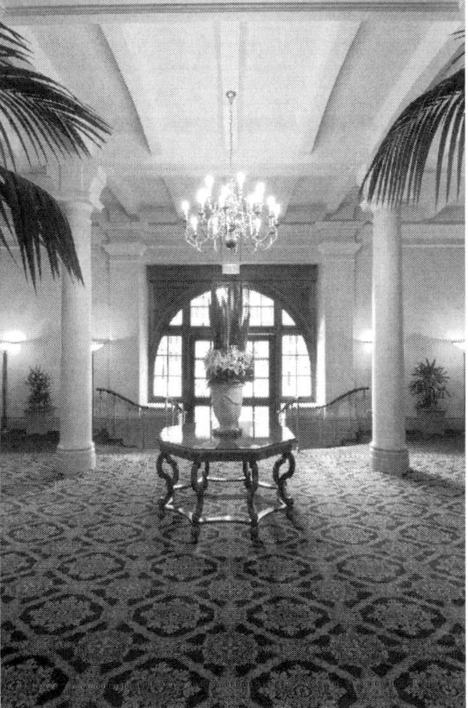

clockwise from top left Treasury Hotel overlooking Queen's Park, Court Lounge, Level 3, Treasury Hotel; Ceremonial Entrance, Ground Floor, Treasury Hotel.

In 1899, when the old Land Administration Building in nearby George Street was deemed to be obsolete, the first turning of soil occurred on the site which the new building would occupy. It would house the state's various 'Public Offices', be developed in three stages, and would not be completed until 1928. Granite brought in from nearby Mt Crosby was used in the building's foundations and its outer and colonnade walls were brown freestone from quarries near Warwick. The building had a central courtyard, and was the first building in Queensland to have expanded metal reinforcing in its concrete floors and ceilings. The building had two entrances, one on George Street for the Lands Department and the other on William Street for the Survey Office, symbolising the 'friendly rivalry' that the two departments enjoyed. The beautiful stained-glass windows above each entrance—with their images of tillers, herdsmen, sowers, reapers and pastoralists, symbolic of the state's rural economy—were designed and crafted by the Brisbane firm of R.S. Exton & Company.

From 1905 until the early 1990s the building housed the offices of the premier and the executive council, as well as the lands and survey departments. In fact the building in time became such a monumental landmark that it did more than probably any other public building in Queensland to dispel the image of the state as rough and fiercely colonial. Its scale and European grandeur rivalled the finest buildings in Sydney and Melbourne.

If you were to look at a photograph of the Land Administration Building from 1925 and compare it to a black-and-white photograph taken today from the same angle, you'd be hard-pressed to tell them apart. When it was finished the building was referred to as 'a parable in stone'. Its architect, Thomas Pye, made sure the building had every modern convenience: elevators, a ventilation system, grand staircases, gas lighting, marble fireplaces, and fireproof rooms for record-keeping, which were a big improvement over the previous records office in the Convict Barracks in Queen Street where it was once claimed a stray dog ate a number of Supreme Court documents.

The Land Administration Building is more than a building, it is an edifice, and as such lacks the informality and human scale common to many of the smaller properties in this book. At first glance it is tempting to think of it as lacking warmth. But this building wasn't put here for warmth; it was built so a colony could be more effectively governed. Nevertheless it is as interesting as any building originally

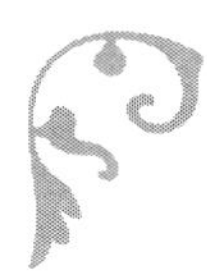

designed and built to house a government bureaucracy can be, and it does have some very interesting stories to tell.

While the building's exterior looks much as it did 80 years ago, its interior has of course been significantly altered. In the late 1960s today's reception area was a camera room for the Survey Office. Room 23 had concrete floors installed so it could accommodate two German cameras weighing 11 tonnes each. They were so large they had to be dismantled before being lifted into the building through an external window, though not before the crane managed to take a small chip off Queen Victoria's nose along the way.

The lands and survey departments took up most of level 1. Room 101 is the former office of the minister for lands and is one of the hotel's finest rooms, meticulously restored with polished cedar dados and a circular leadlight rose above the fireplace, the only one of its kind in the building. Level 2 included, until 1971, the office of the chief secretary (premier). Room 205's last incumbent was Sir Johannes Bjelke-Petersen, the Queensland Premier from 1968 to 1987.

In 1905 rooms 301 to 305 were given rent-free to the Queensland National Art Gallery and, with their soaring pitched ceilings and clerestory lights, proved ideal for the display of artworks. The gallery was opened by the state governor, Lord Chelmsford, and represented the first permanent space given over to the furthering of Queensland's cultural development. The establishment of the gallery was the culmination of a decade-long campaign by one of Queensland's most noted artists, Godfrey Rivers, to secure a permanent home, and over the next 25 years the gallery grew to include works by some of the nation's most notable artists such as Richard Randall and William Bustard. In 1906 the painting 'Light Of The World' by Holman Hunt saw in excess of 50 000 visitors pass through the gallery in just eight days. The gallery was relocated to the Exhibition Building's Concert Hall in 1930.

On level 4, rooms 406 to 408 and 414 to 416 at the Queens Park and George Street corner of the building housed the government lithographic section, headed by Jack O'Hagen, who began as a cadet draughtsman in the survey office in 1936. Stones and rocks were used to create the lithographs but the inherent humidity within the building made perfect results difficult to achieve. Nevertheless the work done here was substantial, including a complete mapping of all the then-stock routes across Queensland that took more than four years to

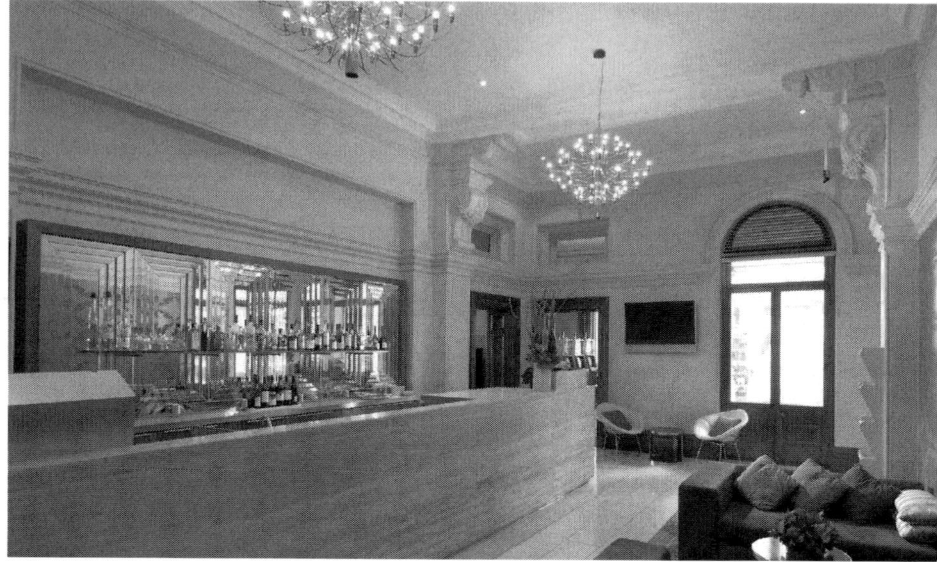

above The Treasury Heritage's award-winning Lab Bar and restaurant.

complete. Rooms 406 and 407 were also used as map mounting rooms and as storage areas for plans and survey maps. Allocated in 1905 to the Survey Office of the Department of Public Lands, three of its walls were once crammed with maps and blueprints where the public could come in, peruse what was in stock, and make purchases. A beautiful 1.2 metre-wide Australian cedar countertop, once stretched halfway across the room but is long gone now. There was also a cartography section within the Survey Office where intricate maps were drawn by hand in pen and ink.

A loft above Room 414 was once used for the storage of flags during World War II and was also used to house carrier pigeons, a war-time communications 'Plan B' should Japanese forces succeed in pushing south through New Guinea and the islands of Melanesia and threaten the Queensland coast.

In the 1930s the hotel's banquet and conference rooms were occupied by the Prickly Pear branch. A type of fleshy cactus, the prickly pear was brought to New South Wales by the First Fleet and later taken to Queensland in 1848 in the hope the plant might make a good garden hedge. By 1925, however, the infectious weed had spread over 25 million hectares in New South Wales and Queensland and the Prickly Pear branch was responsible for cataloguing its spread

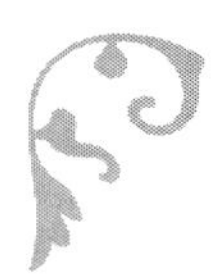

across the state. In the 1930s the cactoblastis caterpillar was imported from South America and took just six years to eradicate the prickly pear.

The building originally boasted 41 fireplaces but by 1993 only 15 were still in working order. Queensland's first radio station, 4QG, broadcast for two years from what is now the hotel's courtyard while plans were finalised for a permanent radio station on the roof of the Government Insurance Office at the corner of Elizabeth and George Streets. The hotel's foyer and guest lounge were offices of the state Forestry Department, responsible for the issuing and controlling of timber licences as well as the management of all of Queensland's forests and timber reserves.

Every room in the Treasury Heritage Hotel tells a story, but few rooms here carry the historical weight of the Cabinet Room. It was here, from 1905 to 1971, that the matters surrounding the governing of the state of Queensland were debated and decided. Dominating the room is the magnificent 5-metre by 3-metre, oval-shaped cabinet table, made from Queensland walnut, that was installed in the room during renovations in 1963–64 and restored in 1995. A series of buttons in the side of the table corresponded to each of the 13 seats that surrounded it and, when pressed, would summon a secretary from the adjoining room. The Cabinet Room also had a secondary function as the meeting place of the Executive Council, comprising the governor and three cabinet ministers, and it also bore witness to every oath of allegiance taken by governments and its ministers. On 8 August 1968 Sir Joh Bjelke-Petersen was sworn in as the premier of Queensland in this room.

On 26 March 1992 Jupiter's Limited won the contract for the refurbishment of the Land Administration Building, and its transformation into the Treasury Heritage Hotel began. Heritage architect Richard Allom and his firm Allom Lovell Marquis-Kyle were commissioned to oversee the project which also encompassed the old Treasury Building across the road and Queen's Park in between which altogether made it the largest conservation project of the 1990s. In Richard Allom's publication *The Treasury Building's Group Conservation Study* (1992) he acknowledges the building as 'the first significant example of the Edwardian baroque style in Australia and a major contribution to Queensland's architectural history'.

One of the first things to do was drape the entire building in
a protective cover to fumigate it against the West Indian termite.
Protective cladding was installed around stairways, doorways and
corridors to protect the internal timberwork and the building's delicate
lime horsehair plasterwork. Cedar doors, lights and other fittings
were removed and catalogued. Modifications made over the years
by successive governments were dismantled, numbered and taken
to the project heritage store. In Queen's Park the statue of Queen
Victoria, cast in 1906 by the English sculptor Thomas Brock and based
on the original statue in Portsmouth, England, was taken away and
cleaned, as was the Krupp field gun, the first war trophy ever given
to Australia. It was presented to the people of Queensland by King
George V in 1916 after having been captured from the Germans by
the British in 1915. The park was redeveloped in 1962 in preparation
for the visit of Queen Elizabeth II to Brisbane in March 1963.

> The public expectations of a place like this are high. The
> Treasury is a very important building and when the public
> walk in they will expect to see splendour—wonderful finishes,
> wonderful fabrics, and wonderful furniture.
>
> HARRY GREGORY, INTERIOR DESIGNER

Boarded-up fireplaces were uncovered and renewed, chipped and
shattered plasterwork was restored by hand, and layers of rust that
had accumulated on the ironwork of the building's balustrades was
stripped to make them ready for painting after scrapings determined
the original colours. The building's old red cedar doors, kickboards
and window frames crafted from Queensland's long-gone cedar
forests were removed and, where possible, replaced with cedar
from timber and demolition yards. Gold Coast cabinetmakers and
specialists in antique restoration, Charles Scale and Neil Ross, had
to imagine what each individual door was used for and return it to
its original frame so the building's heritage remained as intact as
possible. French polishers were then called upon to return them to
their bygone splendour. During the refurbishment some interesting
secrets were uncovered, such as the secret staircase that led from
the premier's office down to the street to allow him to avoid any
angry gatherings of constituents that might have been waiting for him
outside the main entrance.

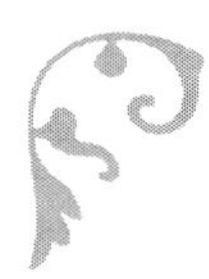

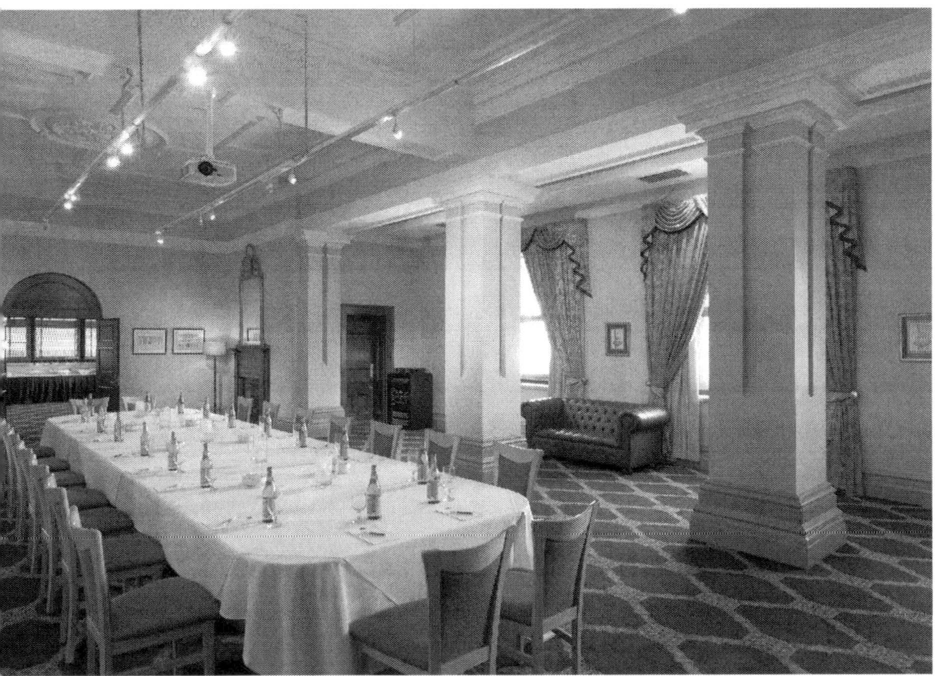

above The old Map Room is a popular choice for conferences and private dinners.

You can't but be taken by the character of the architecture internally and externally. They're grand, handsome buildings and we've changed their use from effectively former private buildings in the form of government offices now to public buildings. I think the graciousness of these spaces has been shown off beautifully with this project.

DAVID COLE, DESIGN ARCHITECT

On 11 November 1938 a typist from the Lands Department, Marjorie Norval, went missing. More than a week passed before her disappearance was reported to the police who interviewed more than a thousand people and initiated a search that extended over much of the state. A government reward of 1000 pounds was offered for any information that might lead to her return, but despite there being several reported sightings, no trace of Marjorie Norval has ever been found. Five years later, the case was closed, but sightings of her ghost wandering the corridors near the old Cabinet Room persist to this day.

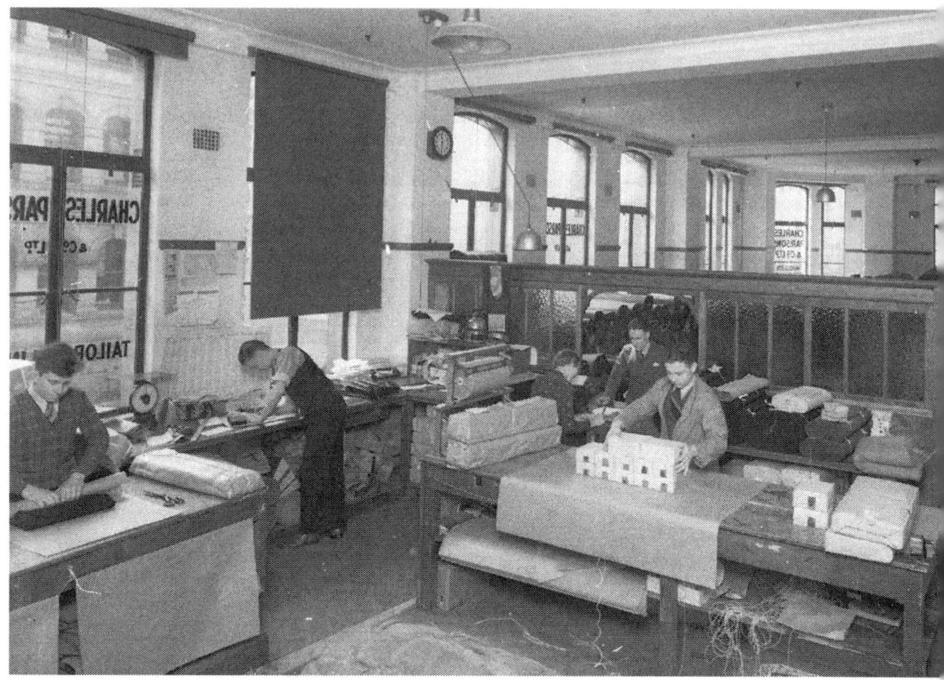

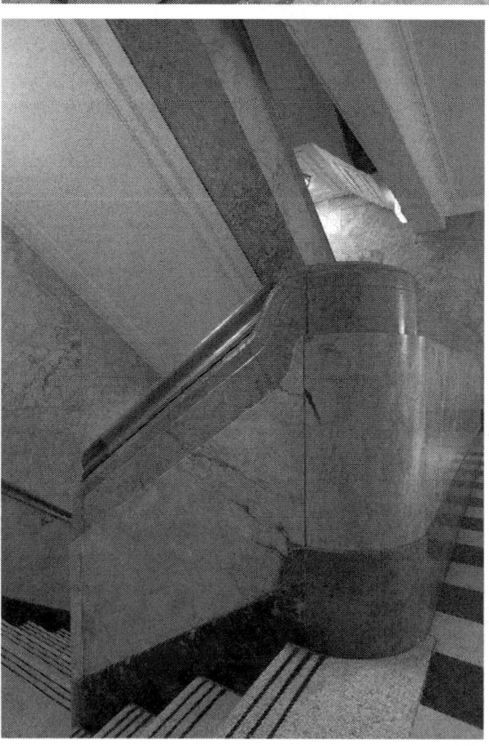

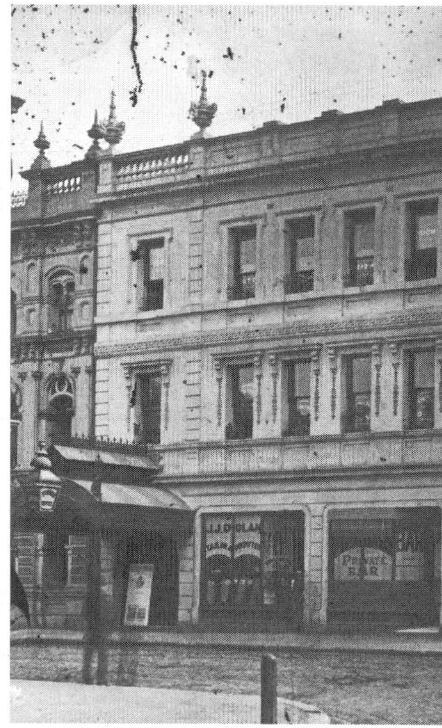

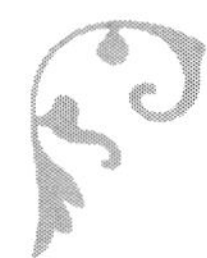

CHAPTER 4

The Grace Hotel

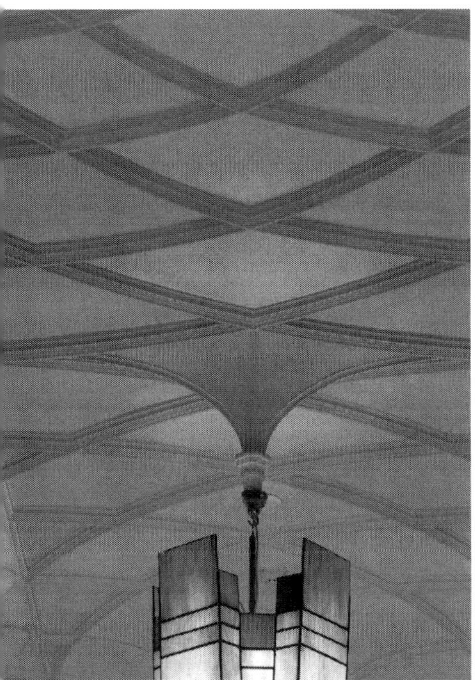

I once took my parents to a performance of Barry Humphries's *The Life & Death of Sandy Stone* at Sydney's Conservatorium Theatre. Unlike Dame Edna Everage and Sir Les Patterson, Humphries's Sandy is 'one of us'—simple, uncomplicated, melancholy, and old. With just an old armchair and a smoker's companion as props, Humphries gave us an evening of laughs, sure, and rare insights into life. As the curtain went down, my mum looked at me and through her tears said, 'How lovely. You know, Barry, nothing bad ever happens in the theatre.'

It can be funny, the things you recall while sitting in a hotel lobby.

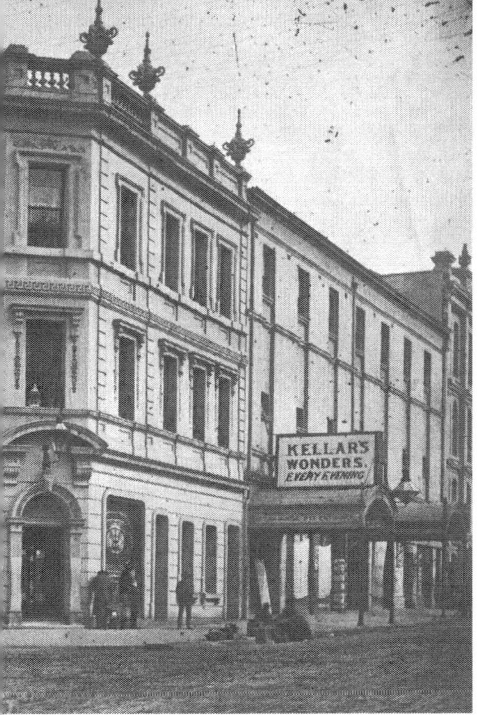

clockwise from top left The shop floor of Charles Parsons & Co. Ltd, a tailoring firm and one of many businesses who leased office space at The Grace during the 1930s and '40s; timber mouldings and Art Deco lights; the old Imperial Theatre site at the corner of King and York Streets; the hotel's magnificent marble staircase.

I *like* busy hotel lobbies. Well, large ones anyway, large ones like The Grace Hotel's, the kind with columns and atriums and lots of couches. I *like* seeing people signing in, the constant movement, the checking of watches, the cut of a doorman's uniform, the idleness of staff waiting to be asked a question and the fact that when one is asked, nothing seems too much trouble. A lobby is like a stage without a curtain, a show that never closes, and, like the theatre, is a refuge from the din and the clatter of the outside world. Lobbies have a cast of hundreds. Cameos and vignettes are everywhere. Friends greet one another, confused and disoriented guests are given their bearings. Oh, it's theatre alright. Few hotels, however, have the capacity to make me feel wistful, or melancholy, or happy or sad, or any emotion that draws on a precious, rarely visited memory. When that happens it means the lobby, and therefore the hotel, has a soul. I like a busy hotel lobby. Nothing bad ever happens in them.

If you look at photographs of The Grace Hotel's interior from the 1930s, the first thing that strikes you is that the lobby looks much bigger then, though it is still by no means a small space. The columns were thinner in the 30s, and the reception desk, though still as long today, was far narrower. So how does a lobby shrink? Well, the original columns have since been encased in fluted plaster surrounds that have increased their diameter, causing them to encroach, further, into the lobby. The reception area, too, was increased, bringing it out into the lobby. Yes, the Grace Hotel's lobby has 'shrunk' over the decades, but the encroachment is minimal, and anyway, it still has plenty of space with which to put on a grand show.

There's a 'History Walk' at The Grace Hotel just off the foyer along the corridor leading to the hotel's Clarence Street exit. Here you can find old newspaper clippings and a detailed history not only of the hotel, but of what came before it. One headline reads:

LAST OF OLD OPERA HOUSES GOES—Theaters come and go. The Life of the Opera House, at the corner of King and York streets, was from 1879 to 1899. The old opera house was a fashionable place of entertainment within the memory of many now living. Just now, what remains of the original theatre, long

---

right The Gothic splendour of The Grace Hotel, topped by a dramatic buttressed tower, was reminiscent of the great commercial buildings of Europe and America.

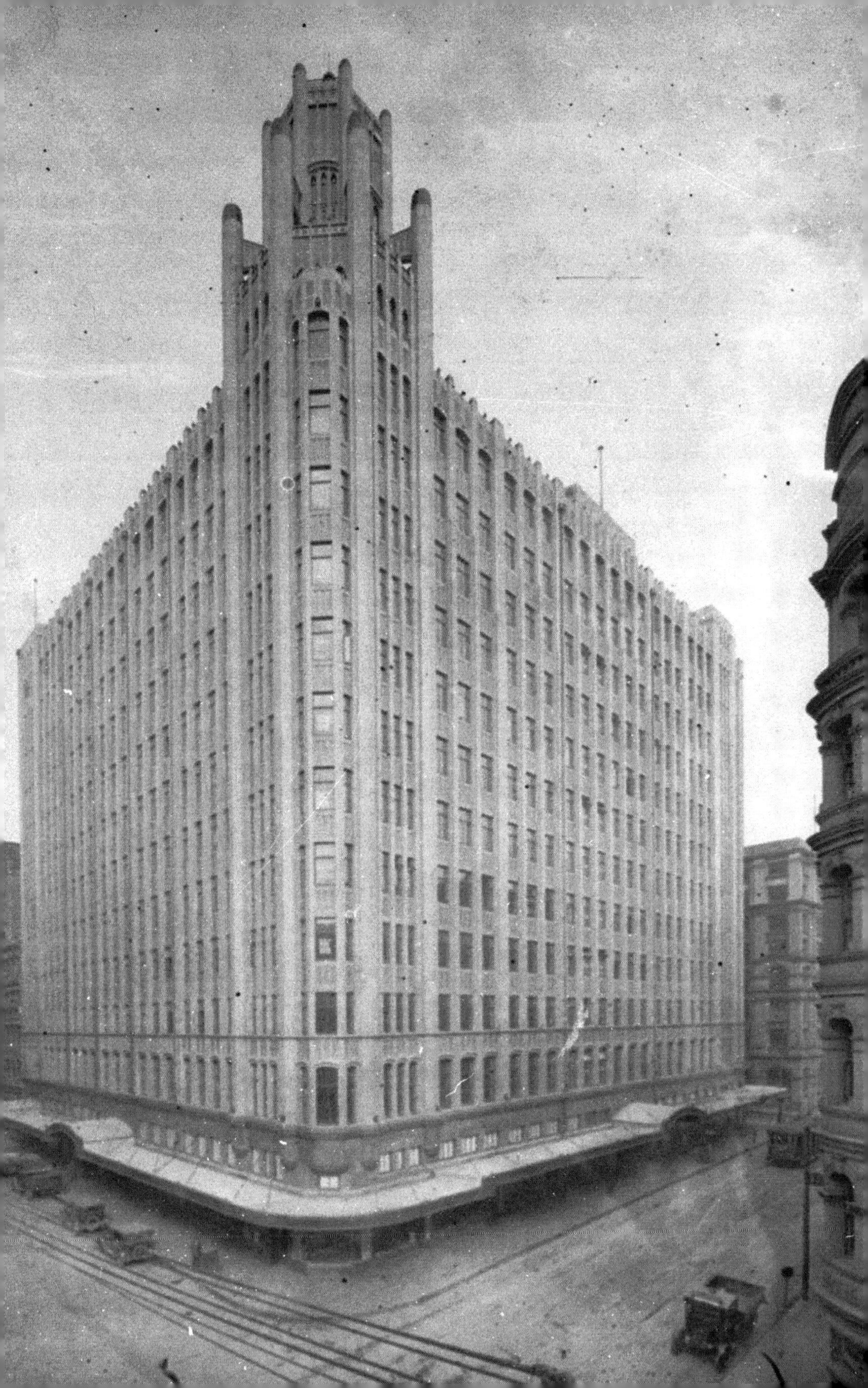

used as a warehouse by McArthur & Co. is fast disappearing for the new building that is being erected by Mr J.N. Grace.

GRACE BROTHERS

Albert Edward and Joseph Neal Grace migrated from England in the early 1880s and founded their retailing business in 1885. In 1906 they acquired a five-storey building on Broadway in the centre of Sydney. In 1926 they purchased land between Clarence, King and York Streets, and on it would build the 'crown jewel' of their retailing empire—The Grace Building. The architectural firm of Morrow & Gordon were commissioned to come up with a design for a new building, and during the last months of 1927 a warehouse that was built over the remains of the Imperial Theatre in the early 1900s was demolished, and the new Grace Building rose quickly. The basement was used for tenant and public parking and was one of the earliest underground car parks in Sydney.

Opened by the Lord Mayor of Sydney, Alderman E.S. Marks, on 3 July 1930, the building was reminiscent of the Chicago Tribune Building and New York's Woolworth Building, both of which drew their inspiration from the great gothic architecture of Europe. Notable features included a buttressed tower on its roof that was so far above street level that it threw the fire brigade into a panic as they pondered just how they'd fight a fire in a building that was dozens of metres higher than anything else in the city and beyond the reach of their ladders. The decorative corner tower rose to 213 feet above street level; it was five-storey, floodlit at night and served by an interior circular staircase. I was keen to see the tower's interior but was told the only access to the tower is through a penthouse on the top floor of the hotel which is currently being leased by the Irish consulate. Balconies outside the second floor had mullions and cusped arches that added to the decorative features. The Grace Brothers building represented one of Australia's earliest and most significant examples of the individuality of corporations being expressed through architecture.

High art motifs from the Art Deco period were featured in the retail stores that were installed in the hotel's lobby, but mostly the building was office space, typically featuring low partitions and desks located close to large windows for light and ventilation in a period before airconditioning became widespread in the late 1930s. The dominant woodwork was Queensland maple. Ceilings were fan-vaulted, a typical Gothic architectural feature, and hallways were tiled in creamy brown and olive green Australian-made terracotta tiles. Terracotta was used extensively throughout the building's interior, including in decorative flourishes on its exterior.

Terracotta tiles became a popular cladding material in the late 1920s, and the Grace Building represented a high point of terracotta use in Sydney. It was easy to mould, was sculptural, and could also be coloured. Terracotta was also practical: rain would easily wash accumulated grime off its glazed surfaces, so it would always seem clean and would last as long as it was properly maintained. It wasn't without its challenges, though. The firing process was unrefined in the 1920s and the quality varied as a result; and as time goes by the glaze is prone to breaking down and crazes, which allows in water and can cause the clay to 'explode'.

The location of the new building was carefully considered. With York Street leading directly onto the city's new harbour bridge, scheduled to open in 1932, it was hoped that the centre of the city would shift westwards away from George Street to Clarence Street and that the new building would then be at the commercial heart of the city. Unfortunately the Great Depression intervened, and by 1933 the building had become a financial liability and was significantly overcapitalised. Grace Brothers then made an historic decision. They decided they'd take retailing to the suburbs instead of waiting for the customers, who had precious little to spend anyway, to come to them, and opened their first suburban store in Parramatta that same year.

By 1939 the fortunes of the building hadn't improved. Only six floors were tenanted and it was offered for sale for $500 000 before being then acquired for nothing by the government under the wartime National Security Regulations Act in 1942. Grace Brothers received compensation for the compulsory acquisition. In 1995 the building was purchased for 'adaptive re-use as a hotel' by the Malaysian Low Yat Group and was opened by the then-premier, Bob Carr, on 1 June 1997.

The history that has been preserved here is in the building's exterior and its public spaces such as the lobby and ground-floor corridors and the marble-clad stairwell. Sadly, as is so often the case with 'adaptive re-use' projects, the interior had to be gutted to

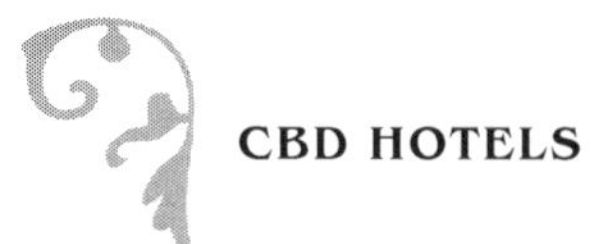

reconfigure it for use as a hotel, and walking through the hallways on its upper levels it's impossible to visualise how its interior must have once looked. Nevertheless the Grace Hotel is on every heritage list that matters—the National Trust and the National Estate, and the New South Wales State Heritage Register—which gives it real protection now and into the future.

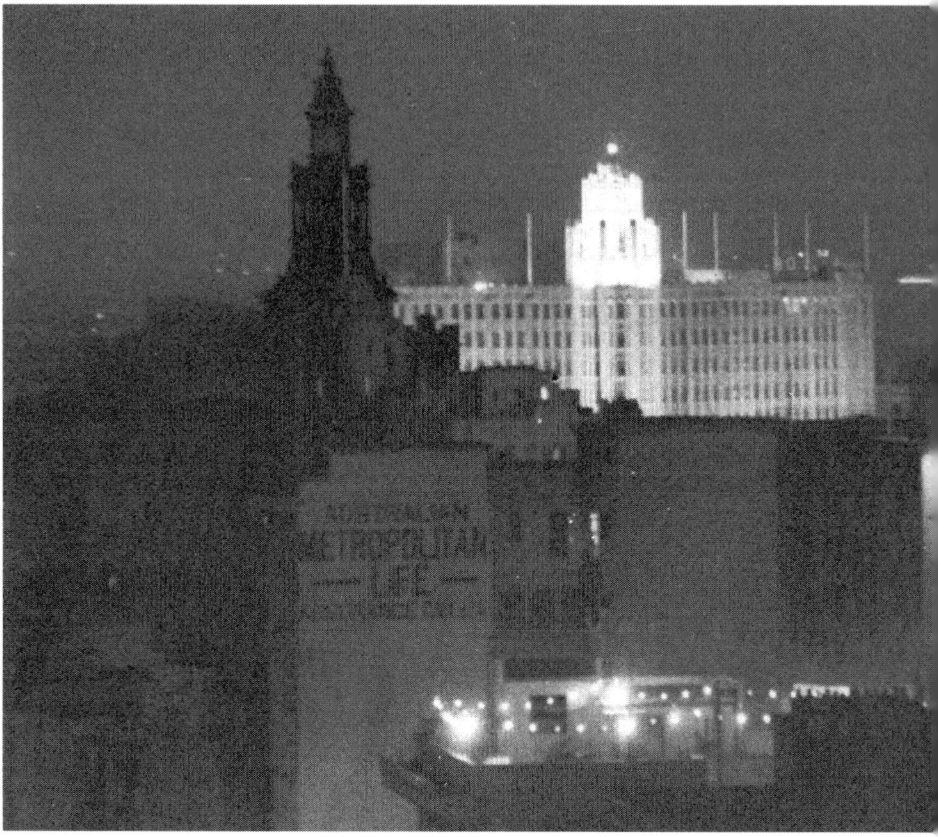

The building isn't without its myths. Like the one that General Douglas Macarthur used its rooms as a temporary headquarters during World War II. Macarthur may have visited the building, but he never worked here.

You know a hotel has a lot of serious history and takes that history very seriously when it goes to the trouble to organise a Devonshire tea complete with finger sandwiches and desserts and invites the public to a once-a-month get-together with an historian to show that history off. That is exactly what happens at The Grace Hotel.

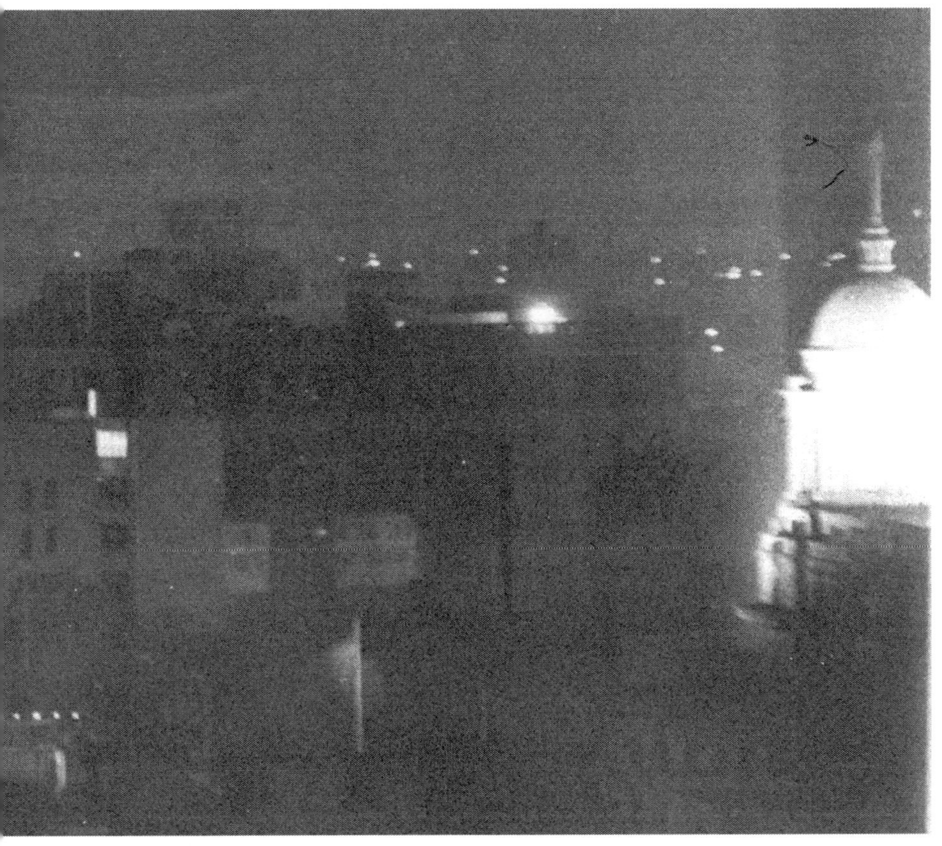

above Night views over the Sydney city skyline from The Grace Hotel's rooftop terrace.

Once every month on a Sunday afternoon from 3 p.m. to 5 p.m. Roy Lumby, a senior conservation practitioner and author of *A Spirit of Progress: Art Deco Architecture in Australia*, gives a 40-minute talk on the history of the hotel followed by a guided walk pointing out many of the hotel's architectural highlights. Descendants of the Grace family themselves have even been to one such session, which was a great honour for all concerned, provided a great sense of connectivity with the past and was an endorsement that what has happened here since the building's acquisition by the Low Yat Group in 1995 has been, all things considered, a great and ongoing success.

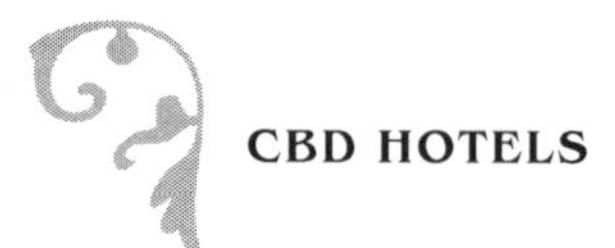

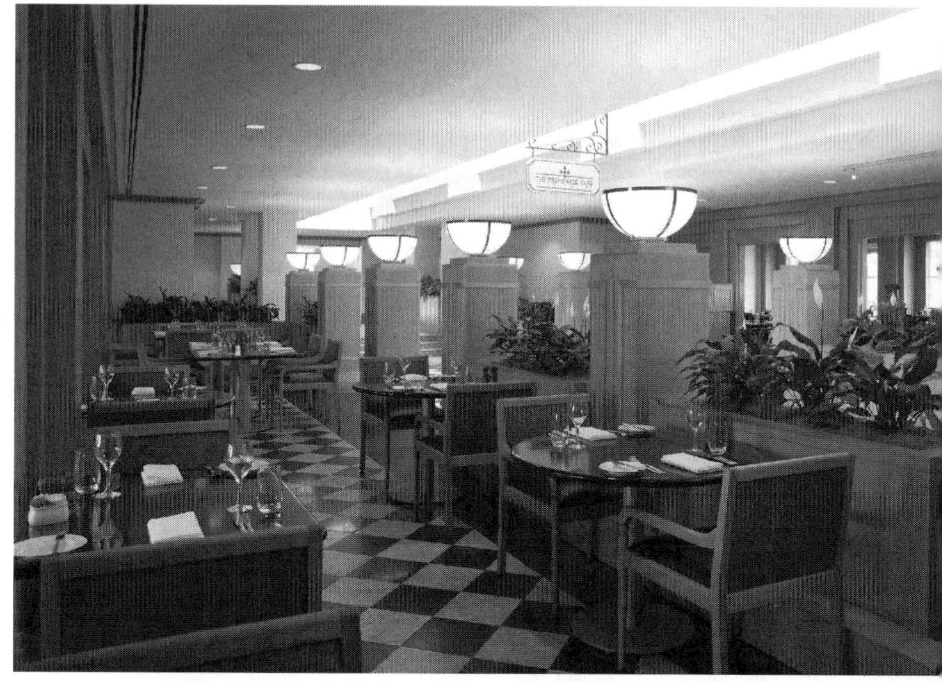

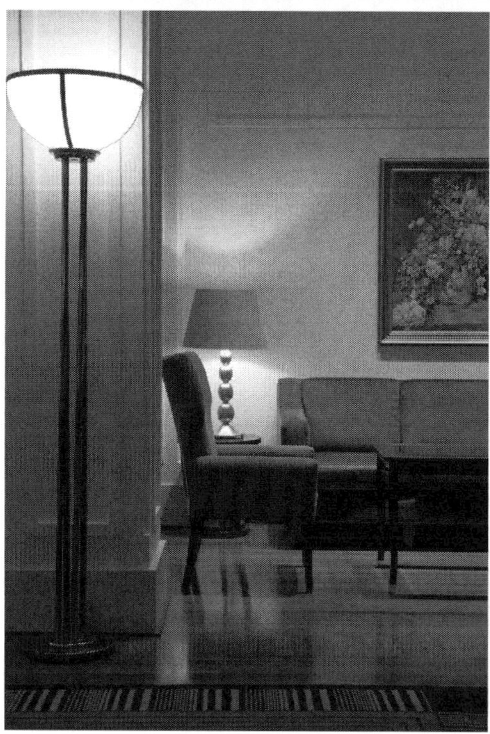

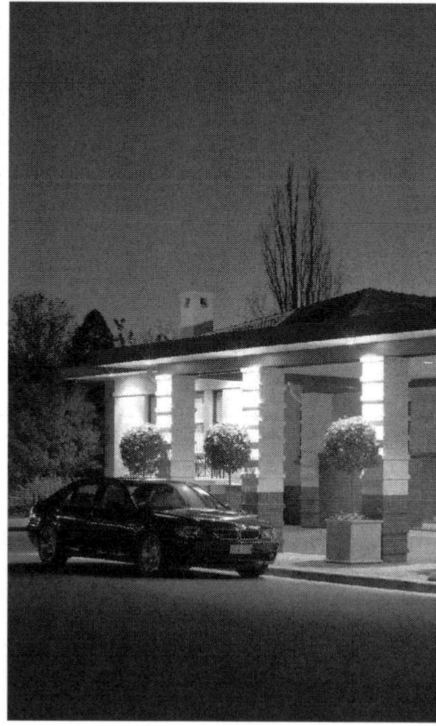

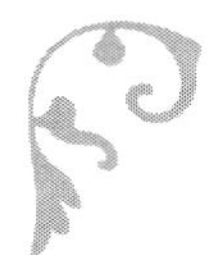

CHAPTER 5

Hyatt Hotel Canberra

It took six years to decide where our nation's capital should be built. In 1902 40 possible districts were narrowed to 23 and finally to just seven—Bombala, Albury, Tumut, Lyndhurst, Lake George, Dalgety, and Yass–Canberra. The Yass–Canberra option was finally decided upon in 1908, and in 1911 an international design competition for the proposed 'bush capital' was announced. One hundred and thirty-seven entries were received, and first prize was awarded to an American landscape architect from Chicago, Walter Burley Griffin.

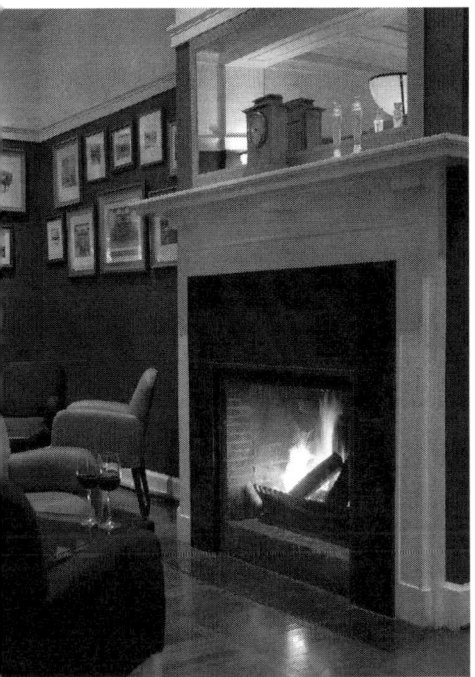

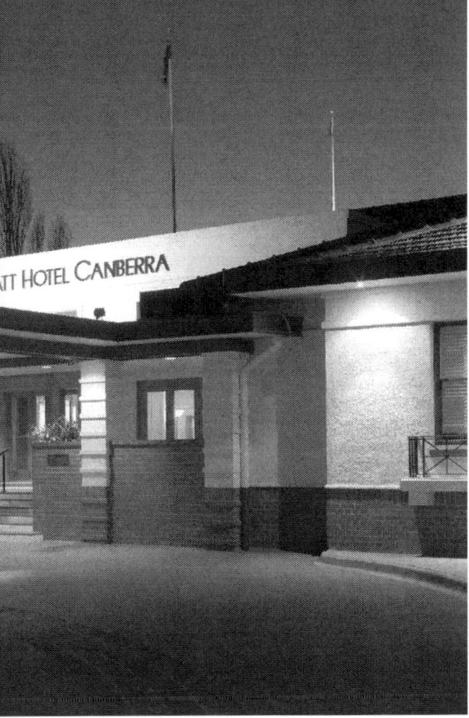

clockwise from top left The Promenade Café; public fireplaces warm chilly Canberra nights; the main entrance; a quiet nook.

Dominating his vision for the proposed city of 25 000 people was a central, manmade lake and a 'parliamentary triangle' within which would be housed all the primary government buildings and institutions. The new capital would be called Canberra, a local Indigenous word for 'meeting place'.

Buoyed by the promise of paid work, labourers arrived in their hundreds in 1912 and tented encampments soon dotted the landscape. Almost immediately there was up to a two-year wait for suitable accommodation for the families of the city's builders. A foundation stone was laid on Capitol Hill on 12 March 1913 and Griffin himself arrived in October to personally oversee construction. The advent of World War I diverted attention and funding away from the city's growth, and its development, under the eyes of the Federal Capital Advisory Committee, was slow. In 1914 a railway was diverted from nearby Queanbeyan, a power station at Kingston was constructed, and a brickworks established at Yarralumla. After the war the layout of road networks and sewerage continued, and small shopping centres were built at Manuka and Kingston. In 1914 a competition was announced for the design of a suitable parliament for the new capital, construction of which began in August of 1923, and the Cotter Dam was completed in 1915. The capital was slowly taking shape, and soon a throng of politicians and bureaucrats would be making their way there to continue the business of running the country. And they would all be needing a place to stay.

Canberra's early hotels weren't referred to as hotels because the city laboured under a ban on alcohol that wasn't lifted until 1928. Instead, they were known as 'hostels'. The first hostel built in the city was, appropriately enough, Hostel #1—constructed to house 200 government officials and administrative staff and their families as well as visiting dignitaries and members of parliament in an atmosphere of 'sophisticated simplicity'. The new hotel facing Commonwealth Avenue between Coronation Drive and Kaye Street would be a collection of ten single- and double-storey pavilions built around two garden courtyards. Glazed verandas would link each pavilion to a central administration block complete with accommodation and dining options.

The new hotel opened its doors to the public on 10 December 1924 and its first guest was Walter Geoffrey Duffield, the inaugural Director of the Solar Physics Observatory at Mount Stromlo on the outskirts of Canberra. In 1927 the hostel changed its name to the Hotel Canberra.

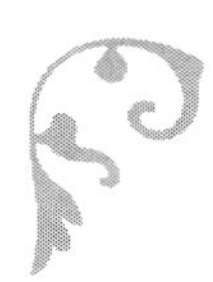

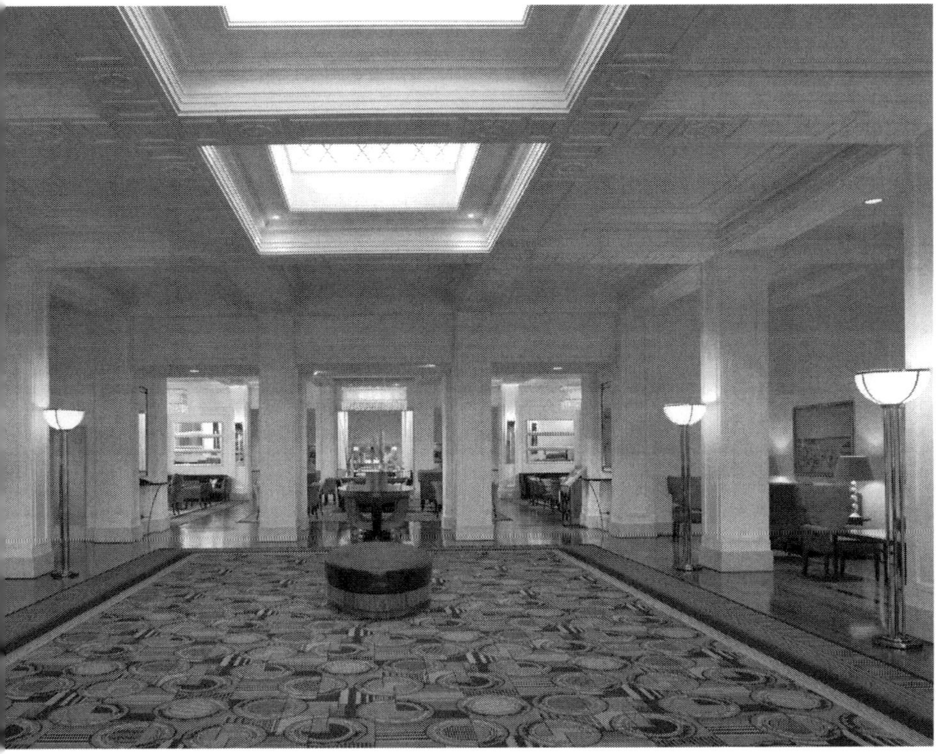

above The original main foyer area, looking towards the hotel's heritage-listed tea lounge.

When the ban on alcohol was lifted in 1928 it was granted a 24-hour liquor licence, and a bar was added to the back of the hotel.

The first two government departments transferred to Canberra early in 1926. Typists, mostly females, were accommodated in Gorman House and in hostels in Ainslie and Acton, as well as the Hotel Kurrajong. In early 1927 ten government departments with staff totalling in excess of 37 000 people arrived in Canberra. Single women required separate accommodation which was still in the process of being constructed. It wasn't until 1928 that freestanding brick homes were available for purchase, with public servants able to buy a home with a 100-pound deposit, and cottages could be rented for between 1 and 3 pounds a week. The depression began to bite, and almost ten thousand Canberra residents signed a petition claiming they were disenfranchised and demanded to be more humanely treated. It was a hectic period. And half of the nation's public service were still to come.

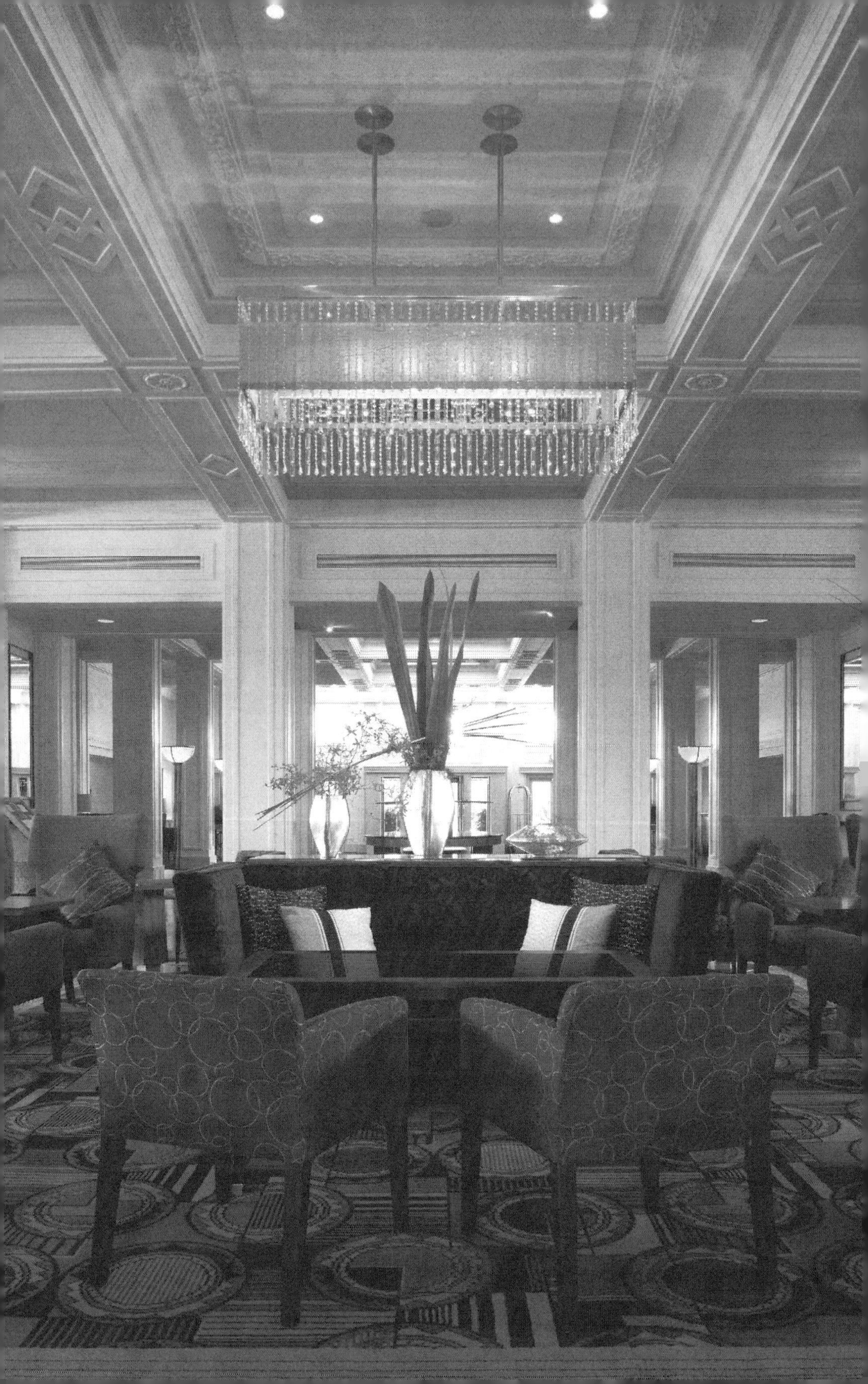

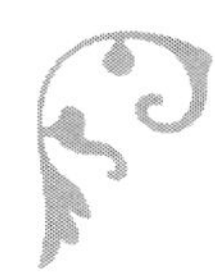

Few hotels had the sort of connectivity to their community of the Hotel Canberra. From the day it was built, it has always been a part of the social and political fabric of the city. What would one day become Canberra's only five-star hotel was designed by the Scottish-born Commonwealth architect John Smith Murdoch, who modelled it after the Imperial Hotel in Tokyo, which had been designed by the doyen of prairie-style architecture, Frank Lloyd Wright. It is one of the most aesthetically pleasing buildings in the country, similar in style to the provisional (Old) Parliament House, another of Murdoch's numerous Canberra designs. The Hotel Canberra was, and still is, a masterpiece—with its long-slung, exaggerated eaves, hipped roofs, and the grouping of external windows in horizontal bands characteristic of the prairie style, with a network of corridors linking the main building to other, smaller brick pavilions located throughout the hotel's landscaped gardens.

The hotel was initially designed to house 180 guests; although almost from the moment it was finished, sections of the hotel were used as government office space and for storing instrumentation for the Mount Stromlo observatory while the facility was under construction. For a few years the hotel was also the only truly 'secure' building in the city, and so was used as a courthouse, jury room and lock-up for criminals prior to their transfer to prisons in Goulburn gaol and elsewhere. A section of the hotel was made into a temporary dance hall in the 1930s, when partitions and a tallowwood floor were added that saw the hotel become the hub of the Canberra social scene. All the early Canberra hotels struggled to make a profit. Administered by the Federal Capital Commission (FCC), they were funded by public taxes and staffed entirely by government employees. Tariffs were determined according to an individual's ability to pay, and the hotels were staffed year round, despite the fact that their patronage was mostly confined to when Parliament was in session.

The hotel was also the scene of much political skulduggery over the years. In October 1929, as the Wall Street stock market was beginning its infamous crash, the labor government of James Scullin was elected to office and was almost immediately caught up in the chaos of the worldwide depression. Scullin led a frugal administration

---

left The Hyatt Hotel Canberra's heavily coffered ceilings are just one of its many architectural highlights.

and even announced to the press that 'this was no time for luxuries'.
He decided that he would set an example to the country. Instead
of living in the 18 000 square-metre, 40-room prime ministerial
lodge in the nearby suburb of Deakin, Scullin and his wife took a
number of rooms in the Hotel Canberra, where he lived more or
less as an ordinary guest—except for those occasions when he'd go
to the cashier's desk, exchange some notes for several handfuls of
coins, then go out the front of the hotel and toss them to passers-
by. In fact such was the hotel's reputation as being the de facto seat
of government that it gained the nickname the 'second Parliament
House'.

On 29 August 1941, in the wake of the resignation of Prime
Minister Robert Menzies, the United Australia Party (UAP, predecessor
to the Liberal Party) turned the leadership of the party and thus the
country over to the leader of the then-Country Party, later the National
Party, Arthur Fadden. Two independent MPs, Arthur Coles and Alex
Wilson, who just happened to be residing in the Hotel Canberra at the
time, were unhappy with the unceremonious way in which Menzies
was dumped and were threatening to vote against the coming Fadden
budget. The hallways of the Hotel Canberra quickly turned into
a diplomatic battleground as members from both sides of politics
courted the votes of the two independents. The independents stuck to
their convictions, however, and Fadden's reign as PM came to an end
on 7 October. He would later joke that he resembled the flood of the
Old Testament, having 'reigned for 40 days and 40 nights'. Menzies
himself was very fond of the hotel and would often be driven there
with a police escort and be greeted in the lobby with a glass of his
favourite drink—a double Gordon's gin and Noilly Prat with a twist of
lemon.

Eleanor Roosevelt stayed at the Hotel Canberra during an official
visit as First Lady in 1943, as did various ambassadors while patiently
waiting for embassies to be completed. Today, if you stand in the
driveway and look at the building's front facade it's easy to cast your
mind back to the war years when the now-enclosed verandas were
open to the elements and acted as 'sleep-outs' for overnight visitors
who couldn't afford to pay to stay inside. The government continued
to manage the Hotel Canberra until 1950, when it was taken over by a
subsidiary of the Sydney-based brewer, Tooheys.

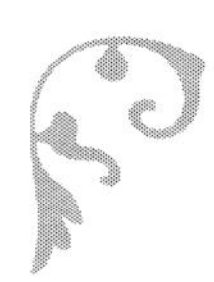

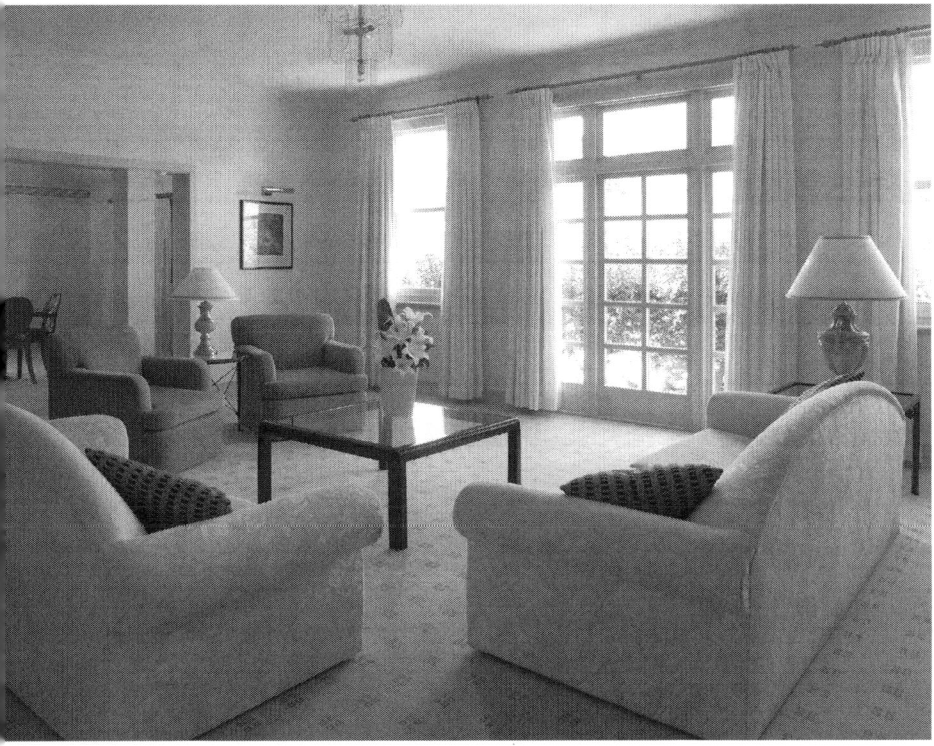

above The living room in the hotel's Diplomatic Suite, with separate butler entrance and two balconies.

Its life as the Hotel Canberra came to a premature end on 13 May 1974 when it closed its doors after almost 50 years. It then lay idle until 1976 when it was utilised by Parliament House as a storage facility and office space. In 1986 the architect Daryl Jackson added banquet halls, restaurants and a contemporary accommodation wing to the back of the hotel, all coming off a soaring top-lit galleria that extended along the hotel's principal axis and opening up towards Lake Burley Griffin. The substantial renovation helped maintain the hotel's reputation as the city's premier five-star hotel when it re-opened, as the Hyatt Hotel Canberra, under the management of Hyatt International in 1988.

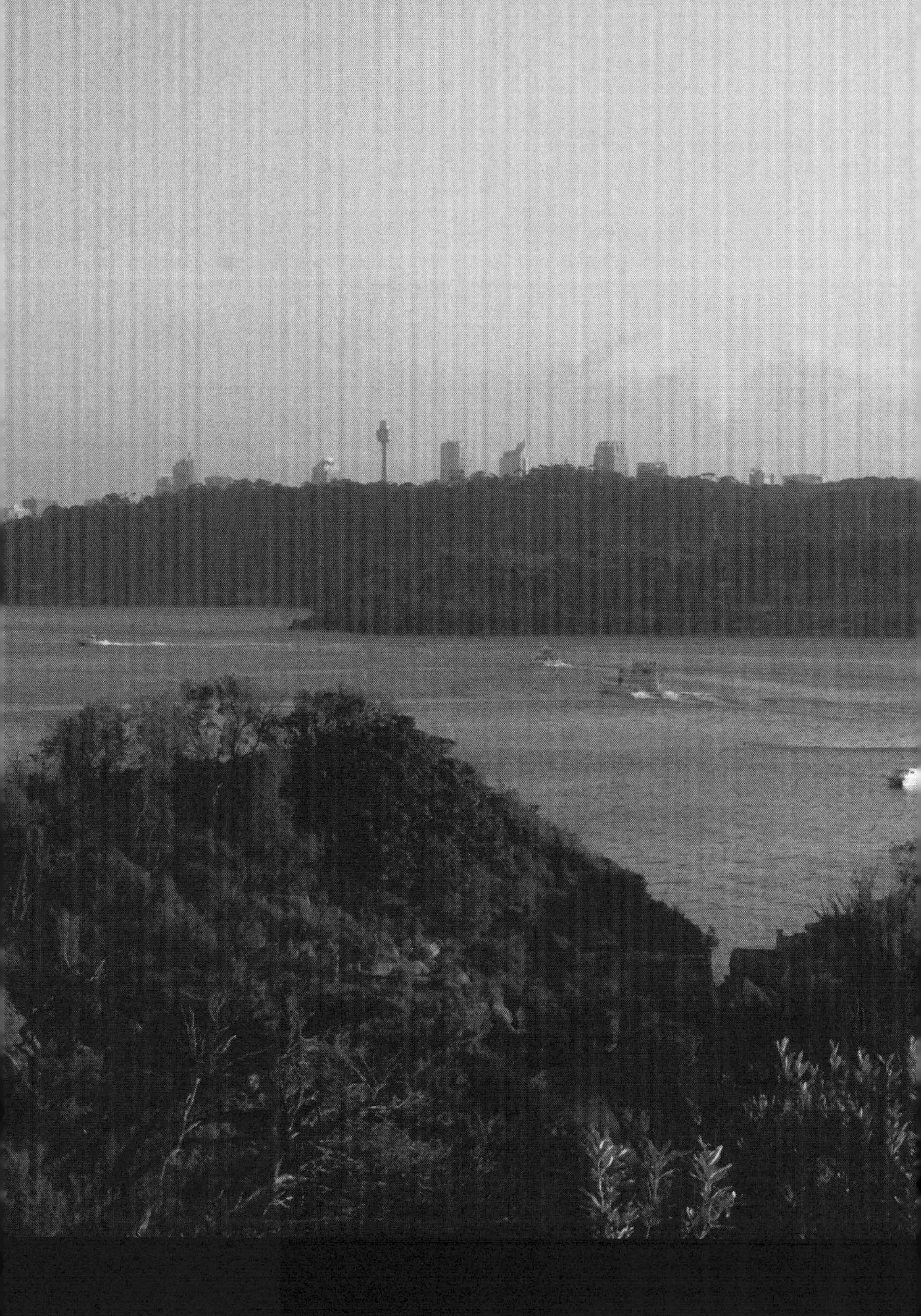

PART 2

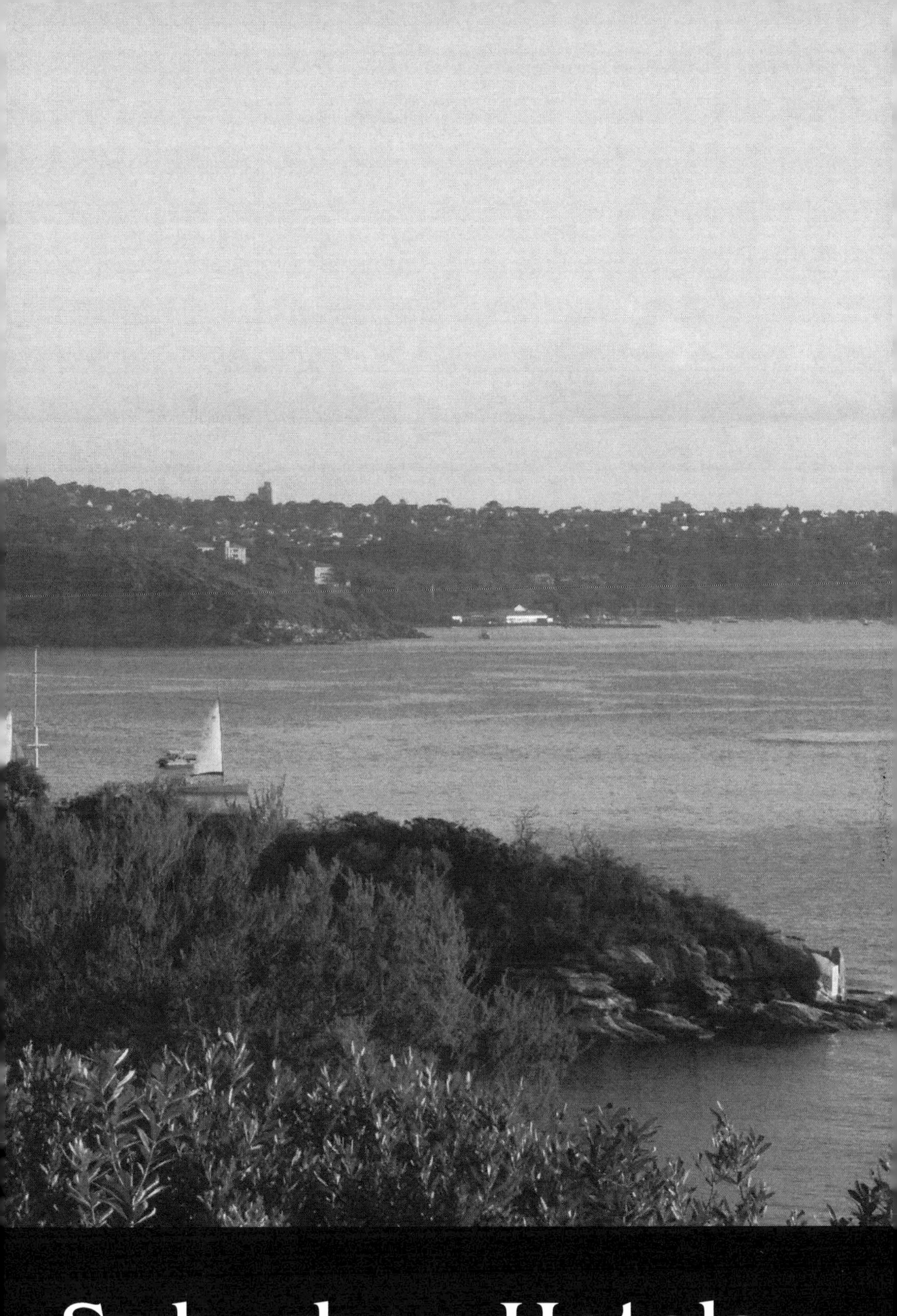

Suburban Hotels

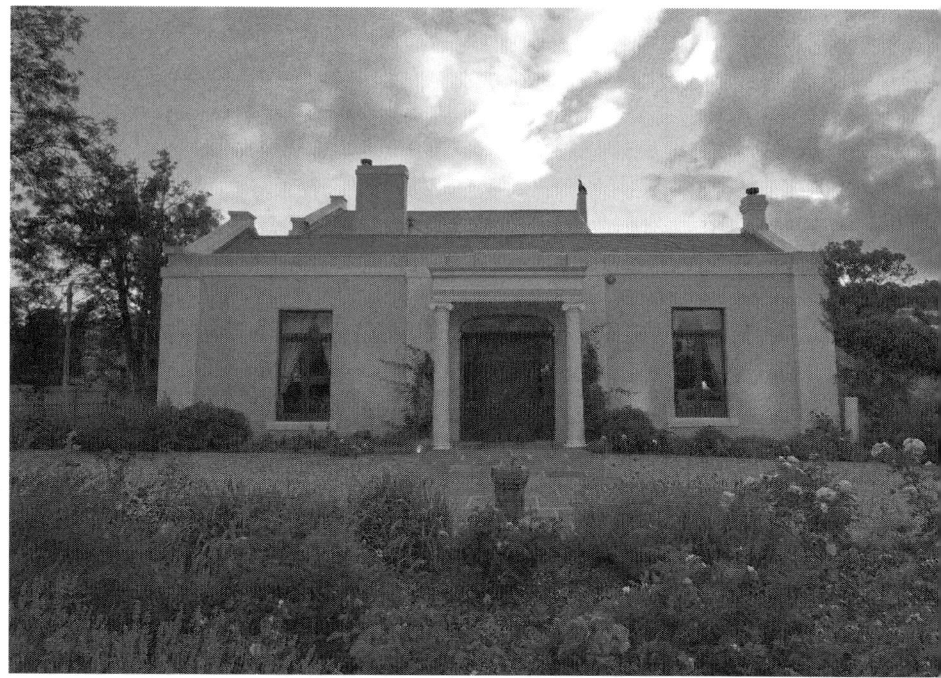

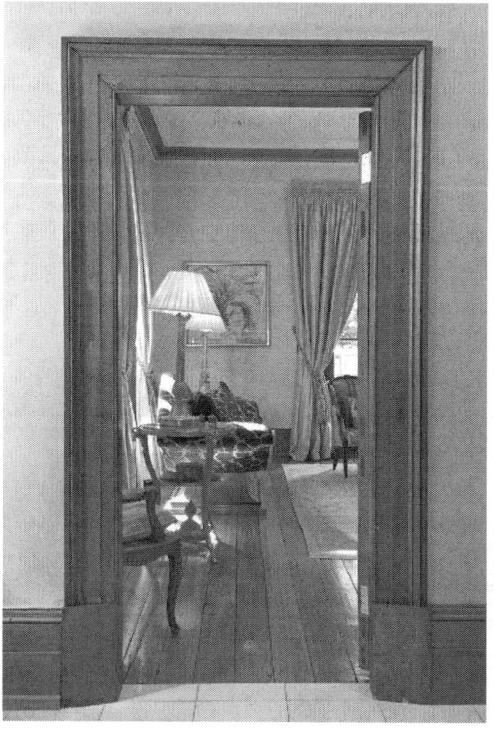

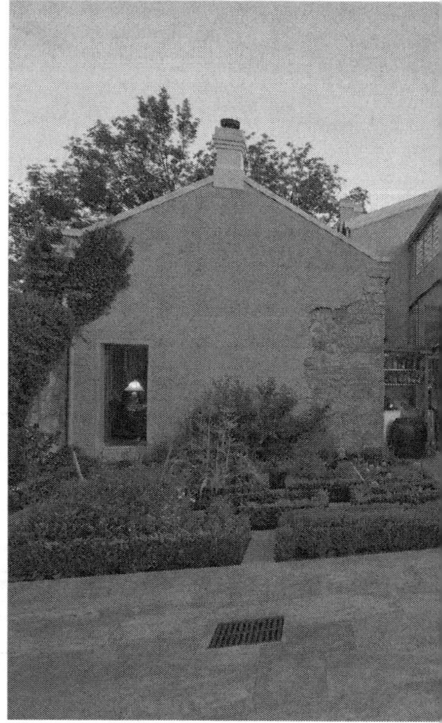

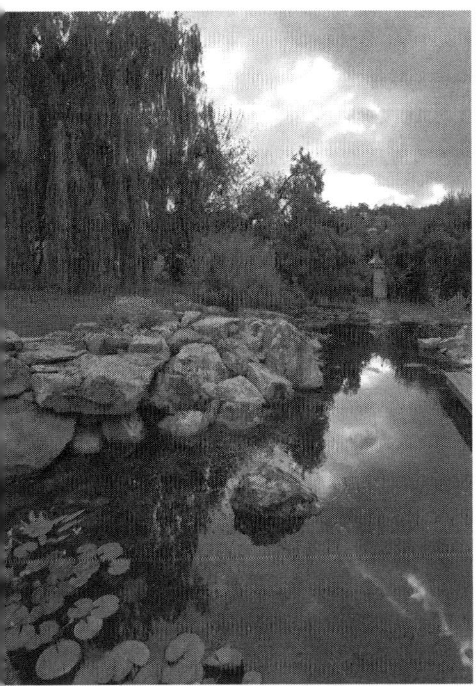

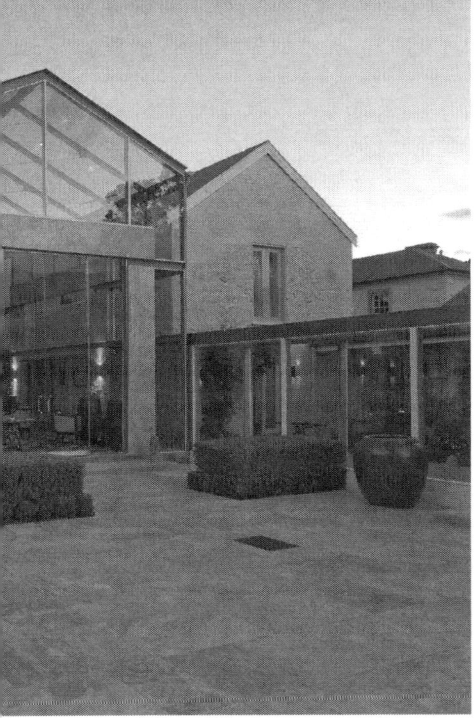

CHAPTER 6

The Islington Hotel

Something is happening to the five-star rating system traditionally used to measure the level of services and appointments of the world's great hotels—it's beginning to show signs of not keeping up with the pace. In 2007 in Milan, Italy, Townhouse Galleria declared itself to be the world's first seven-star hotel. So did Dubai's magnificent Burj Al Arab and the Emirate's Palace Hotel in Abu Dhabi, both believing they had gone beyond the boundaries of what makes a five-star hotel, unilaterally leap-frogging themselves over six-star status and creating new benchmarks for hotels everywhere. Others are about to do the same.

clockwise from top left The restrained elegance of the Islington's regency-style main entry; six rooms provide views over landscaped gardens; the conservatory; a tantalising glimpse of an Islington suite.
© Loic le Guilly

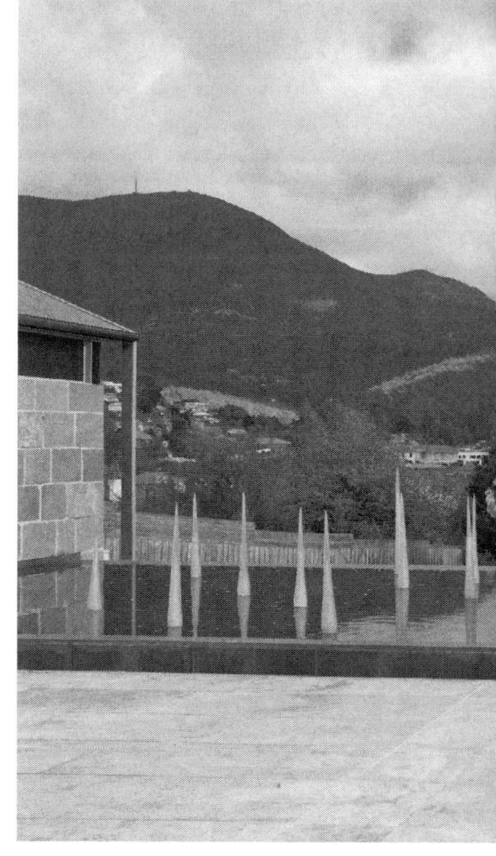

right The Islington's barbeque area and reflecting pool with Mt Wellington rising in the distance. © Loic le Guilly

Occasionally, a hotel emerges that goes beyond the boundaries of mere luxury and possesses something truly unique, something that cannot be categorised or reduced to a formula. It possesses something elusive, that can't be defined, and which has little to do with size or glitz. Well move aside Dubai, Abu Dhabi and Milan, there's a boutique hotel in, of all places, Hobart, that's knocking on your door and, though small, packs quite a punch.

You could say it's the Kostya Tszyu of world hotels. It made Condé Nast's 'Hottest 100' hotels list in 2006 and won *Gourmet Traveller*'s award for best boutique hotel in Australia in 2007 and plenty of others besides. But there's far more to this 1847 Regency-style suburban sanctuary than the sum of its significant achievements. In fact I love this hotel so much that if I could put forward one property in Australia as a candidate for inclusion in the select, beyond 'five-star' club, it would be the idyllic, historic yet ultra-contemporary Islington Hotel.

I've stayed at the Islington, my favourite 'home-away-from-home', twice, and each time felt like the whole place was mine despite it being full. Of course 'full' here means 11 rooms being occupied. What's more the entire staff departs the hotel every evening and when they go, the place is yours until the morning when they return to cook you a sumptuous breakfast. And speaking of breakfast, is there a more beautiful room anywhere in Australia in which to eat? The magnificent glass conservatory, designed by Hobart architects

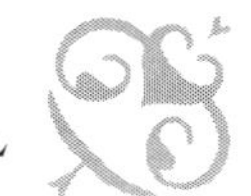

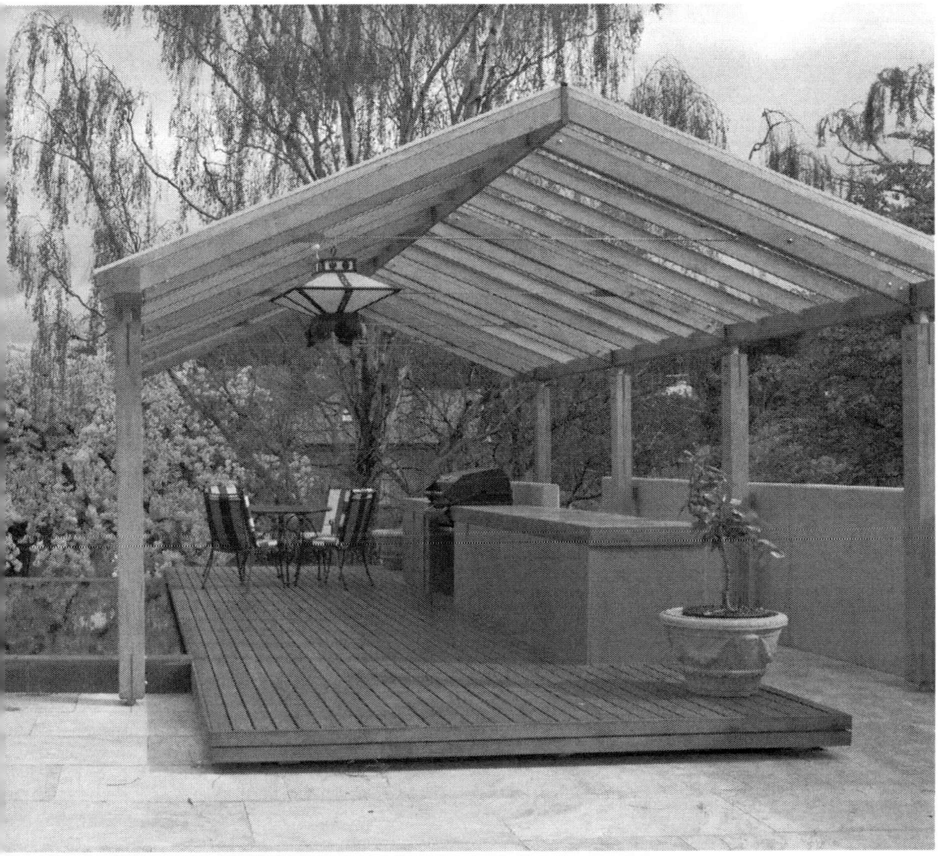

Morris Nunn and Associates and added seamlessly to the back of the house, should be the *Oxford Dictionary* definition of what makes a perfect contemporary addition to an historic property, an amalgam of old and new so right and logical that when you look at it, you just say 'yes'. Yes, this is the proper extension of the original vision, an improvement to what couldn't be done before because the designers were limited by existing technology, trapped in their 19th-century world.

Original artworks include a Picasso sketch of (what else?) a naked woman in the hallway. Australia's second-oldest tapestry hangs just across the hall in the Islington's beautifully appointed dining room, and the wine cellar is stocked with more than a thousand bottles, all of which is why the Islington has the highest insurance premiums of any guesthouse in Australia.

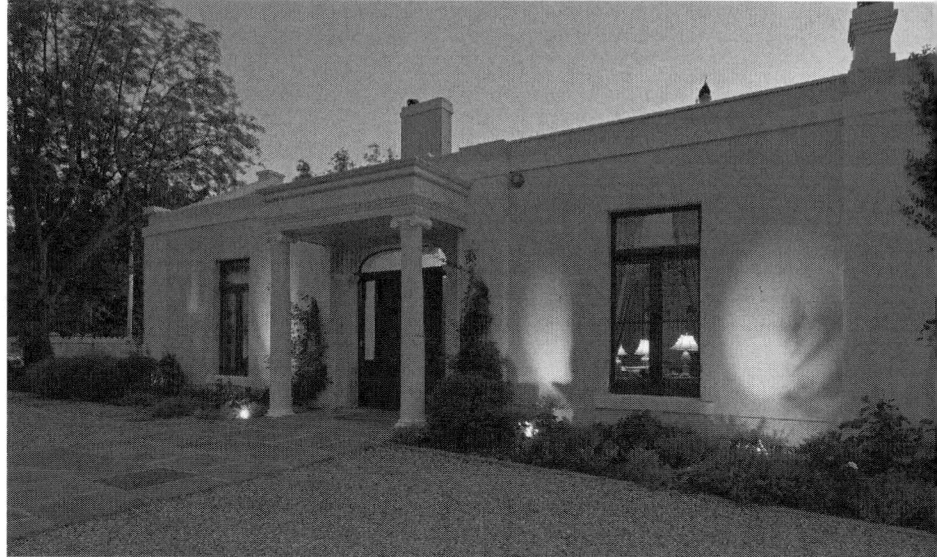

above The porticoed entry over the doorway to the author's favourite home away from home.
© Loic le Guilly

The Islington threatens to sedate you to the point of carelessness.
Butlers, chefs, housemaids and drivers are all available on request.
My first visit relaxed me so much that for the first time in my life
I managed to lock myself out of a hotel. This is no mean feat.
Achieving a state of relaxation that normally can only be gained with
the aid of a wellness centre but which at the Islington is simply a
by-product of just, well, staying there, I forgot to take my room key
with me on a pre-breakfast walk that left me on the wrong side of
a self-locking door. Stranded, if you can call it that, at 6.30 a.m. in
the Islington's garden, I decided to stroll beneath its 100-year-old
willow tree (that's heritage listed for goodness sake), then on past
its reflection pool and cherry blossom trees. It was a frosty April
morning but I had no choice other than to wait until the chef arrived
at 7 a.m. to cook me breakfast. I could think of far worse places to be
stranded. Of course, there were no other guests to be seen anywhere
because the Islington's custom-made beds don't generally encourage
those in them to wake in a hurry.

These days the Islington is home to anyone who walks through its
doors. Corporate executives and high-powered lawyers hire charter
flights to come here just so they can walk around in their bathrobes

and slippers and do, well, pretty much nothing. On my first visit I saw one guest who seemed to be dripping money. But dressed in track pants and eating a banana.

Normally, however, one of the problems with detailing the personal story of an historic building's occupants is that details are often scant. Records have usually either been lost, burned, taken by a previous owner, or for whatever reason were just never properly catalogued. So often in talking to the owners of historic properties you hear of the struggle they've had in gathering together the pieces of all those who came before them. When owners move on, so their names move on with them. The Islington, however, is different, and for this reason a rollcall of its owners over the years should be noted, if only to appreciate how historic hotels always outlive their owners. Those lucky enough to live in an historic property are really more stewards than owners, caring for it and hopefully keeping it in good repair for those that will come after them. The following list of occupants likely parallels many of the privately owned properties in this book and, in an odd sort of way, can be seen as representative of all those hotels and guesthouses whose histories are fragmentary or lost to time. So let's leave the present and begin a journey through time to the beginnings of old Hobart Town. The present will, I'm sure, be waiting for us when we're done with the past.

Thomas William Birch was ship's surgeon on the English whaler *Dubuc* when he arrived in Hobart Town in 1808. He went on to purchase several small ships that traded wheat, timber and seal skins between Tasmania's east coast and the colony in Sydney, and in the process built a beautiful home that still stands today at 151 Macquarie Street, though now sadly minus its parapet, battlements and two cannons that once kept watch over the nearby Derwent River for an enemy who never came. Birch also owned a 100-acre allotment in South Hobart, known to locals as 'Folly's Farm'. When he died in 1821 his considerable estate was valued at 40 000 pounds and a bitter fight ensured between various family members over how it was to be dispersed.

The legal tangles that followed are too numerous to recount and took many years to resolve. Birch's son-in-law, Simeon Lord, challenged the validity of Birch's will. There was one Supreme Court injunction after another. It wasn't until March 1840 that Tasmania's Chief Justice permitted the sale of the remainder of the estate.

This resulted in Thomas's wife Sarah, who had remarried in 1823, gaining Lots 25, 26, 29, 30, 31 and 32 from the subdivision of Folly's Farm, which together comprised an L-shaped block in excess of 4 acres on the corner of Anglesea and Davey Street.

The house that would one day be named Islington was constructed in 1847 and differed very little externally from what guests see today. A superb example of Regency-era architecture, the house was an unusual addition to the built environment of Hobart, accustomed as it was to its hundreds of Georgian-style residences, and remains today one of Tasmania's finest Regency buildings along with Panshanger near Longford, the Richmond Courthouse, the beautiful Lake House at Cressy, and Beaulieu and Runnymede in New Town, all of which were built prior to 1840. On 3 December 1847, shortly after its completion, Sarah's husband Edmund Hodgson advertised the house for lease in the *Colonial Times*:

FAMILY RESIDENCE TO LET
To Let, With Immediate Possession:
A Commodious and Genteel Family Residence, containing ten rooms, with kitchen and servants rooms detached; stable, coach house, and every other convenience, together with one acre of ground. The rooms are lofty, with spacious entrance hall.

By the late 1840s the elevated southern end of Davey Street, with its sweeping views of the Derwent River and the fledgling capital's waterfront, was a much sought-after address in class-conscious Hobart Town, far removed from the overcrowded and unhealthy quarter around the mouth of the Hobart Rivulet. The state's Solicitor-General lived nearby, as did the Bishop of Tasmania, the Chief Police Magistrate and the Assistant Commissioner-General.

The house had a succession of owners: Dr William Dawson and his family lived there from 1848 to 1852, and a merchantman, Thomas Hewitt from 1852 to 1858. An 1852 reference to it as a 'cottage ornee' indicates it was once thought of as rather quaint, or may have just been a reflection of its rustic exterior stonework that existed prior to the house being rendered in 1877. James Wilson, who achieved a degree of fame as a brewer at the nearby Cascade Brewery, was in residence from 1858 to 1864; and Charles Cansdell, a lawyer and barrister who arrived in Hobart Town in December 1861, moved into Islington in 1864 and later went on to become the state's Attorney-General before leaving Tasmania for New South Wales in 1869. A businessman, James Walch, whose father had run a popular bookselling and stationery business in Macquarie Street on what was known as 'Walch's Corner', occupied the house from 1869 to 1876, and Edward Manley, co-founder of the Tasmanian Club, lived there with his two sisters from 1877 until his death on 22 December 1879. His obituary in Hobart Town's *Mercury* newspaper on 24 December described Manley as 'a fine old English gentleman, distinguished alike for his genial manners and high-minded probity, yet withal modest and unassuming'.

In the 1880s the house comprised the six main downstairs rooms it has today, plus the hall, and three upstairs bedrooms. It was occupied by three sisters, Frances, Charlotte and Sophia Parsons, the daughters of Charles Parsons, an early Tasmanian pioneer who went on to purchase the property from the Hodgson family in 1882. In December 1885 the sisters moved to Blackman's Bay and let the house to an unmarried solicitor, Alexander Ritchie.

Ritchie filled the house with clutter typical of the late-Victorian period, including walnut writing and dining tables, ebony and sandalwood cabinetry, two pianos, hunting trophies and various items from China that hinted of previous travels. He purchased the property in December 1889 and added two attic bedrooms complete with dormer windows sometime during the early 1890s. Three years after Ritchie died in 1895, the house was put up for auction. The auction notice in the 27 October 1898 edition of *The Mercury* read, in part:

> Having a frontage of 2 chains (20 metres), 49 1/2 links (a link is 20 centimetres) on Holebrook Place and adjoining the property of Mrs Thomas Giblin. On this lot stands the house and convenient outbuildings. It has a depth of 4 chains 1 link on the southwest, and a depth of 3 chains 15 links on the northeast side. Terms 25%—cash at sale, and balance on completion.

The home's new owner was David Harvey, the son of a Congregational minister who grew up in London before moving to New Zealand and then to Sydney, where he amassed a small fortune working for the Tattersalls Club. He ran the first of several public sweeps on the Sydney Cup before anti-gambling legislation forced

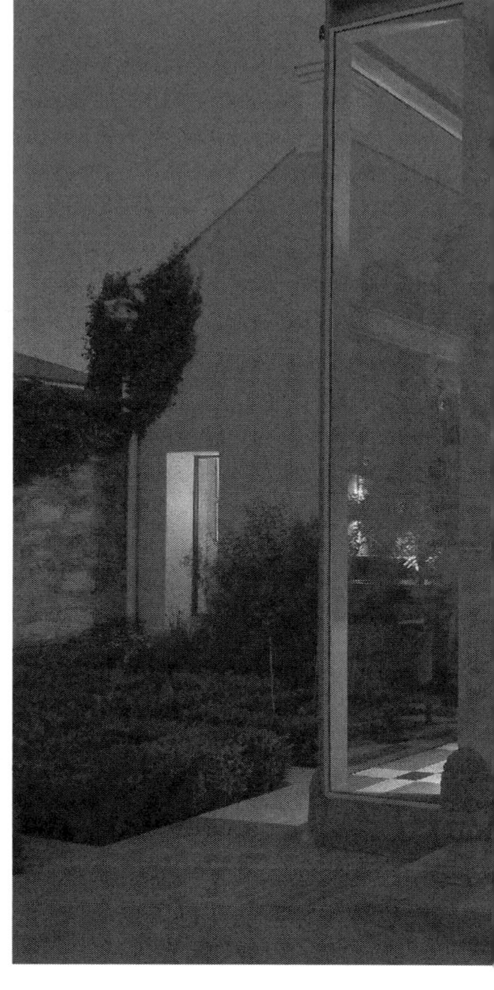

right The conservatory, designed by Hobart architects Morris Nunn & Associates and added in 2005, is a triumphant, seamless blend of old and new. © Loic le Guilly

him to sail to Tasmania in 1899. Tasmania had no law banning the delivery of letters containing sweep subscriptions and he moved into the house on Davey Street later that year, naming it 'Islington' after his birthplace in the London suburb of the same name.

Harvey gave the house to his three daughters in 1911, and they in turn sold it to Norman Walker, a schoolteacher, in 1920, who added some extensions to the first floor which involved the demolishing of a bathroom and the addition of a new bathroom on the ground floor. Walker sold the house to Howard Turner, the Manager of Perpetual Trustees, in 1929. Turner lived at Islington for the next 40 years before he sold it to Peter Stops.

Peter Stops was a lawyer and one of only two representatives at the inaugural meeting of the National Trust on 4 May 1960. Stops had a passion for the preservation of Tasmania's cultural heritage, and was responsible for salvaging the portico that once was part of 142 Macquarie Street and now presides over the Islington's north-facing entrance protecting its heavy double front doors. In the mid 1960s he also converted the original sash windows on the Davey Street side by lowering them 300 millimetres to create the sets of French doors it has today.

In 1985 Islington was again offered for sale, now with 13 rooms including a dining room, a drawing room, a library and a billiards

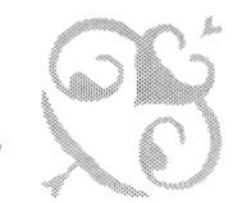

room. It was passed in at auction, but eventually sold for $350 000 to Hadyn Oxley subject to his gaining approval to operate it as a guesthouse. Islington at last made its change from private residence to hotel comprising ten suites in 1986–87, and was sold in 1992 then in 1997 and again in 2003. A lot of grand Tasmanian homes have been sold to moneyed-up 'mainlanders' in recent years, but Islington's present owner is a member of one of Tasmania's oldest families. The Islington continues to be one of Tasmania's most pedigreed— and treasured—homes, now thankfully for the rest of us, open to everyone.

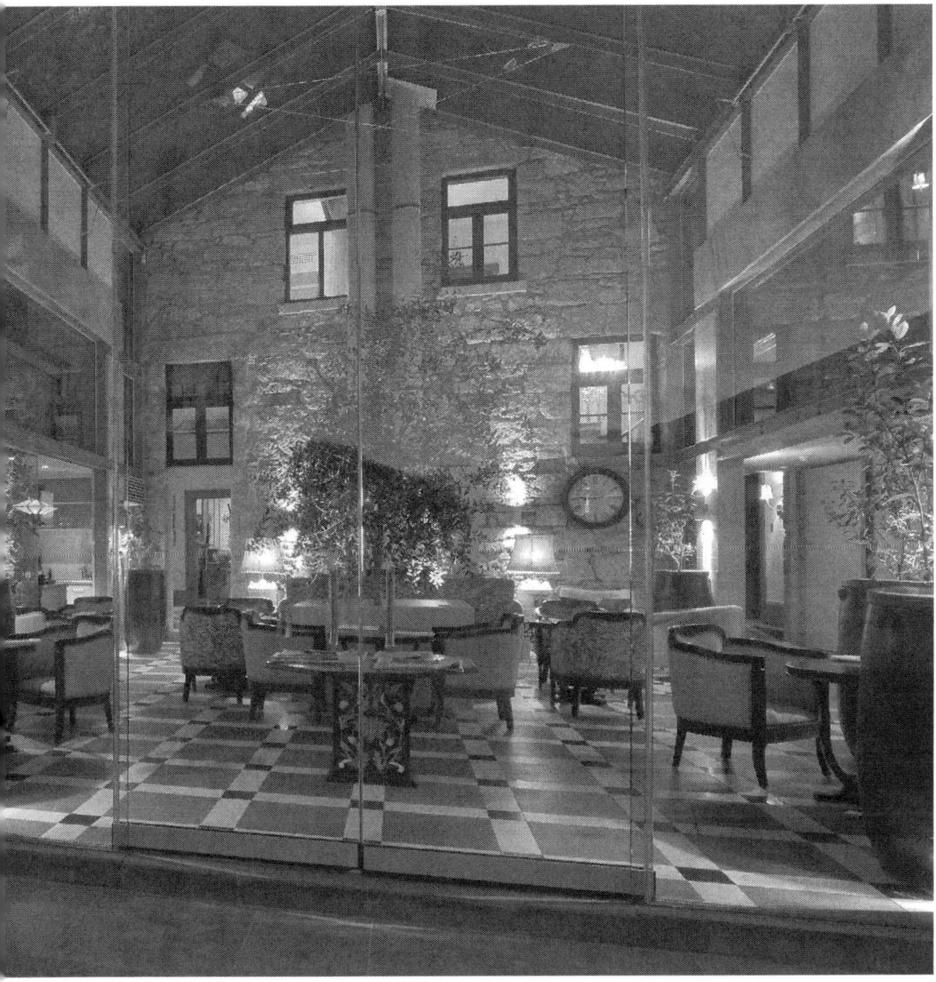

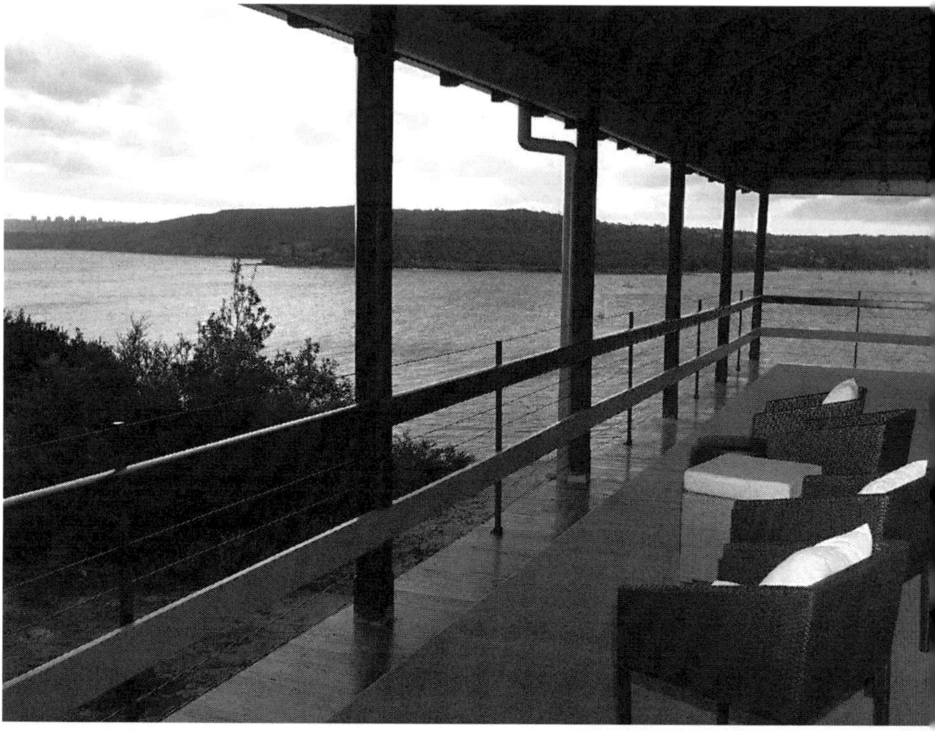

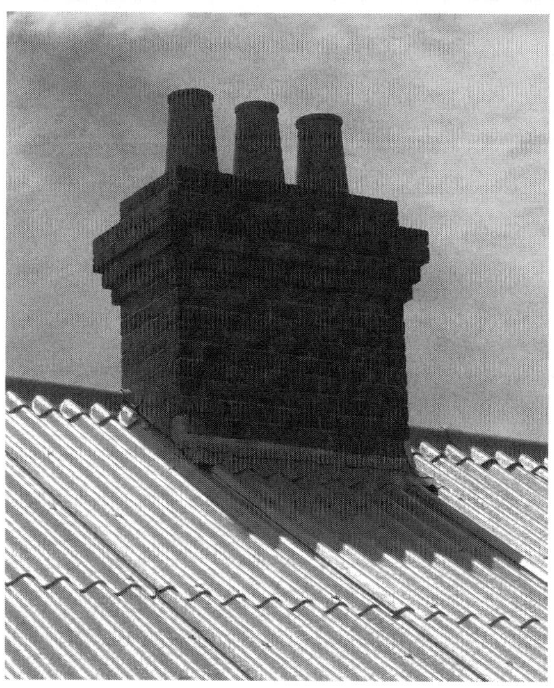

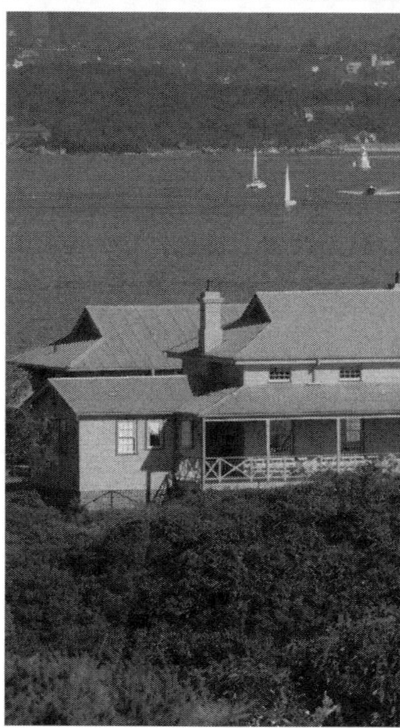

CHAPTER 7

Q Station

Of all the hotels in Australia that can boast their own personal window onto our nation's rich history of European settlement, few would be able to claim to have seen more drama, more tragedy, more despair, more stories of triumph and dreams either dashed or realised than the 65 buildings and cottages that comprise Sydney's old Quarantine Station, now Q Station, one of Australia's finest boutique hotels. It presides today over one of the nation's most diverse and significant historic sites, on a piece of once-in-a-lifetime real estate with one of the best views in the world. The site forms part of Sydney Harbour National Park.

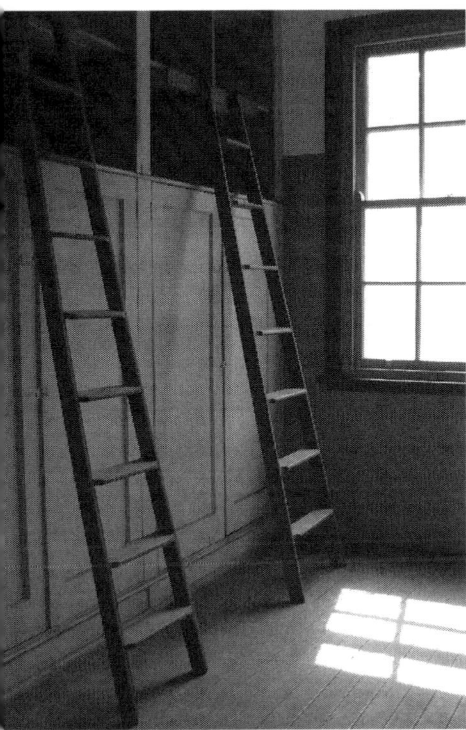

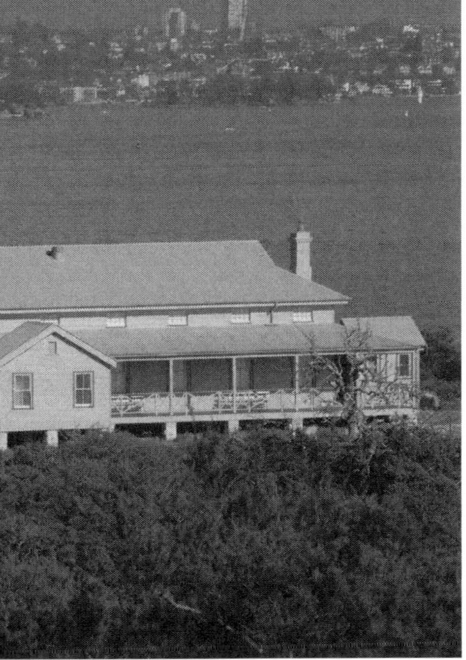

clockwise from top left Rooms open onto broad, shared balconies © Mawland Quarantine Station; a restored storage area; harbour views minus the crowds; the simplicity of terracotta, brick and iron.

For thousands of immigrants, Quarantine Beach, the harbour's first safe anchorage point after passing through Sydney Heads, was their first point of entry into Australia after months at sea. Sydney's quarantine station was not a place of internment. Passengers were, however, segregated into various 'classes' according to whether they were either First or Second Class passengers on the vessels which brought them. The First Class accommodation block had a dining room overlooking the waters of Sydney Harbour with balconies running along their harbour-facing southern side. There were certainly far worse places in the world in which one could be quarantined, a sentiment echoed by Gwen Woodward, daughter of one of the station's administrative staff when she moved into one of its three brick cottages in 1925: 'The Quarantine Station was a marvellous place to live—the views of Sydney Harbour, the free air, wide spaces.' The cottages still survive on a stretch of elevated ground with commanding views across the harbour. Capable of accommodating up to six guests each, they are a community within a community, a street in miniature.

Q Station also has one of Australia's most unique art galleries. Carved into the sandstone outcrops that line the wharf precinct at Quarantine Beach and dot the hills and coves of Sydney Harbour National Park at North Head are more than 2000 inscriptions and etchings that together represent a powerful, silent testimony of 150 years of immigration. Ranging in complexity from simple etchings to elaborate Chinese texts and artistic representations, the inscriptions are an invaluable historical record in documenting our experience of migration.

> Let weary travellers listen as we tell
> The awful treatment that to us befell
> On the 'Mariposa' many were our woes
> 'Tis a mercy we haven't turned up our toes

ROCK INSCRIPTION AT QUARANTINE STATION BY PASSENGERS OF SS MARIPOSA,

FEBRUARY 1888

Restoration work by experts from International Conservation Services have removed the accumulated dirt, sediment and plant matter from many of the worst affected inscriptions, an attention to detail that is typical of the sensitivities of the Mawland Group, the Australian-owned company that has leased the 69-acre site from the NSW National Parks and Wildlife Service. The Mawland Group specialise in environmentally sensitive development, and are dedicated to the preservation of history.

The first ship to ever be quarantined here was the *Bussorah Merchant*, for smallpox in 1828 when the quarantine station was little more than a collection of bell tents. The first buildings were erected in the late 1830s but it wasn't until 1847 that the site's first hospital was built. Five years later 150 people lived in its overcrowded dormitories and new and larger passenger steamers were bringing in people a thousand at a time. Only when the Commonwealth government took over the site in 1909 did it finally receive the funding that increased its capacity to its maximum of 1200 which, ironically, was only ever reached during the height of the worldwide 1918/19 Spanish Influenza pandemic. Since 1919 the station recorded just two deaths, and only 55 ships were placed in quarantine between 1921 and 1973. The last to be processed were a group of airline passengers who arrived in Sydney without adequate vaccination certificates in 1975.

The Commonwealth intervention saw the construction of the majority of the buildings visitors see today: dormitories, the row of freestanding brick cottages, a shower block, kitchens, the old hospital and the fumigation block, a rare example of early 20th century fumigation technology still in working order. Q Station has benefitted from a $17 million, nine-year restoration which sees 20 per cent of the hotel's revenue reinvested into ongoing site management, including the preservation of its buildings and the sensitive flora and fauna that surround them. Long-nosed bandicoots, their habitat an ever-diminishing one thanks to urban development just beyond the site's boundary, are fortunate they have the sanctuary of Q Station to retreat to.

While the exteriors of the former dormitories and other ancillary buildings look much as they would have in the early 1900s, the interiors are anything but dated. Harbour view suites have French doors that open directly onto breathtaking panoramas of Sydney Harbour, and garden view suites offer relaxing outlooks over manicured lawns. The buildings are listed on the National Estate, just one tantalising notch below World Heritage status in significance, and the place has a wonderful village feel. There is familiarity in its architecture with wide wraparound verandas and red tile roofs that take me back to the simpler days of my childhood. Its scattered buildings and interconnected pathways and roads, with staff at the wheels of electric carts servicing the needs of its guests in a neverending procession of quiet efficiency, imparts an almost nostalgic sense of community. There is nothing impersonal or superficial here. Q Station is a rare blend of high-end hospitality and everyday 'roll up your sleeves and get on with it' reality. The whole scene is strangely comforting, an almost whimsical experience in a place that, due to its presence safely ensconced within the protective embrace of a national park, can never fall victim to inappropriate development, commercialism or the common vagaries that all-too-often befall historic buildings out there in the real world.

It is, of course, possible to just hop on a ferry at Circular Quay and disembark at the Q Station wharf and experience the site as a day trip, but really there is so much to see and do here that to limit yourself to just a few hours is almost a travesty. If you can, experience it as a guest and stay at least one night. When the ferry takes the daytrippers back to civilisation at the end of each day, and Q Station settles down to the rhythm of the bush that surrounds it, you'll be glad you did. City lights illuminate the distant skyline and despite the hotel being heavily booked the night we were there, it seemed that we had the place to ourselves save for Q Station's population of ringtail and brushtail possums and bandicoots that make their home in rock crevices and hollow logs.

Dinner is down an impressive purpose-built timber stairway that provides a more direct option than the meandering but pleasant path that takes you from the dormitories down to the Wharf Precinct on Quarantine Beach. Here you can have lunch and/or dinner in the Boilerhouse Restaurant, go for a swim, or ask the Q Station staff to arrange for Manly Kayaks to bring over a kayak which you can use to explore some of the prettiest and most inaccessible beaches the harbour has to offer. Store Beach can be reached in just five minutes once you round the tiny promontory at the western end of Quarantine Beach—it's only accessible from the water, meaning there's a good chance you'll have the entire beach to yourself. Q Station can even arrange a lunchtime picnic. Just paddle back when you're ready. The waters off Quarantine Beach are also home to a resident population of 'little penguins' whose habitat includes Quarantine Beach, Little Manly Point, Spring Cove and Cannae Point. The waters off Store Beach

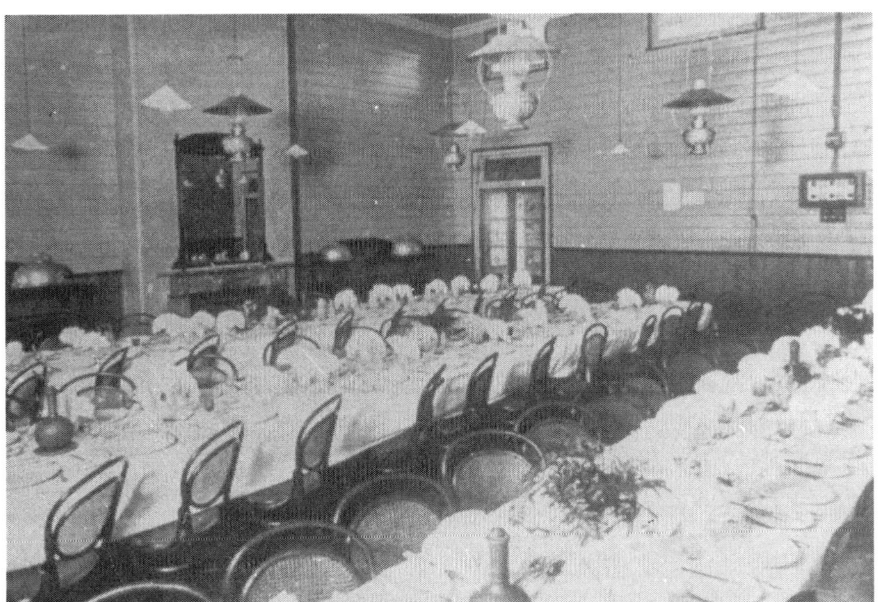

above The First Class dining room, circa 1900.
© DECCW

below The Asiatic Dormitory, circa 1919.
© DECCW

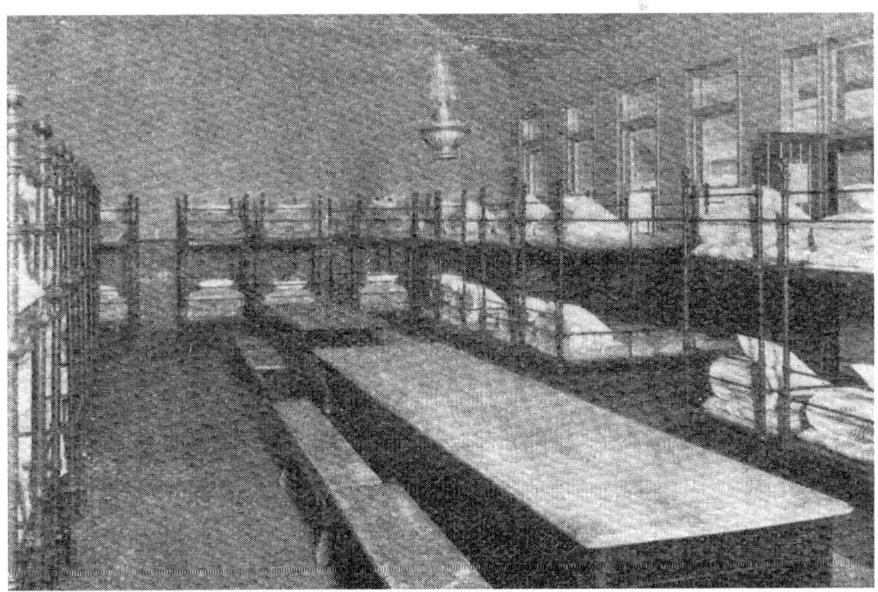

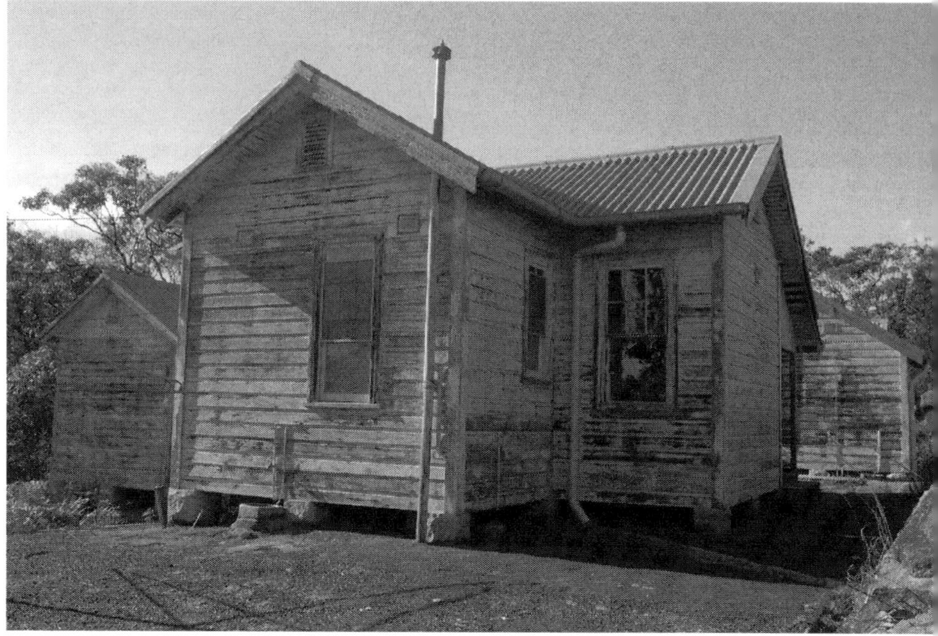

above One of Q Station's many examples of early 20th-century vernacular architecture.

and neighbouring Collins Beach also support Sydney Harbour's last remaining significant expanse of seagrass, which has been thoroughly mapped and its future distribution projected so as to reduce any unintentional damage from propeller wash and errant anchors.

There's nothing better after a day's kayaking and beachcombing than settling down to a hearty meal, and that's where Q Station's Boilerhouse Restaurant comes in. Located just metres from Quarantine Beach its interior is a great mix of past and present and the food is mouthwatering. My scotch fillet with pomme puree and caramelised eschallots in spinach and red wine sauce will live long in the memory, made all the more enjoyable from the mezzanine level high above the kitchen, amongst heritage-listed steam pipes, valves and ceiling-mounted gas heaters. The two restored boilers on the ground floor were once used to send steam through to the autoclaves and for the supply of boiling water to the station's laundries and showers. The Boilerhouse Restaurant is open for lunch and dinner seven days a week (though closes its doors at 11 p.m. to avoid distressing the nearby colony of little penguins) and for Saturday and Sunday morning breakfast.

Quite apart from great steaks and, I understand, a very good Bermagui ocean jacket, Q Station also has the reputation amongst those in the paranormal world for being the most haunted site in the country. Ghosts can be a big deal in the world of the historic hotel and nowhere in Australia will you find electromagnetic gauges going off the scale more than you will here. There are ghost tours to cater for every age, from watered-down versions for the kiddies, through to the 'Spirit Investigator' tour for the over-16s that involves a medium as well as instructions on how to operate various devices used to detect paranormal activity. For this tour you need to sign a liability waiver and you may also be asked to undergo a breathalyser test. Make no mistake, the ghosts of Q Station are seen by many as serious stuff, a long way removed from going down the end of the street to the old abandoned 'spook house' as a kid.

To spare our two children the likelihood of a fitful sleep we chose the more sedate family tour. Let me assure you though that no matter how skeptical you might be when you set out, by its conclusion two hours later, after hearing 50 or 60 emotive retellings of one unexplained event after the next, you're ready to at least accept the premise that anything is possible. There are stories of park service employees requesting transfers after arriving at Q Station just days earlier, stories of 20-tonne contamination doors closing behind tour groups after they've left the fumigation building. There are stories of pairs of feet seen 'standing' in the cubicles of the old shower block, of legs running across hilltops with no bodies attached to them, and of former patients standing in the glow of the dormitory's porch lights. My wife has an old school friend who went there once and refuses to go back. If it all seems a little scary, there are sedate, historical walking tours available too for those who are not paranormally inclined.

Whether or not you come here for the day or to stay in one of the hotel's harbour or garden view rooms or with a group of friends in one of its brick cottages, the thing to do is to come here. Q Station represents the best of what can happen when government and private enterprise combine with a common vision for restoration and preservation. It's encouraging to see that we can, just occasionally, still get it right.

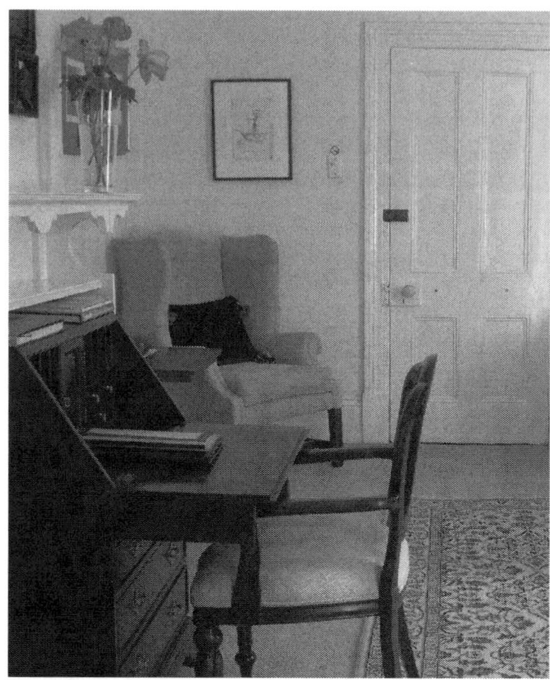
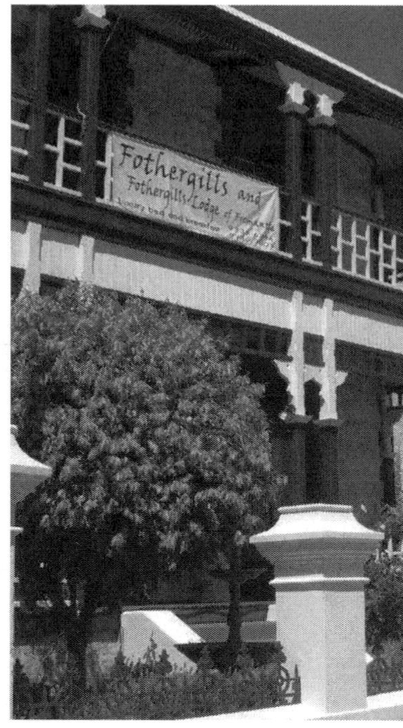

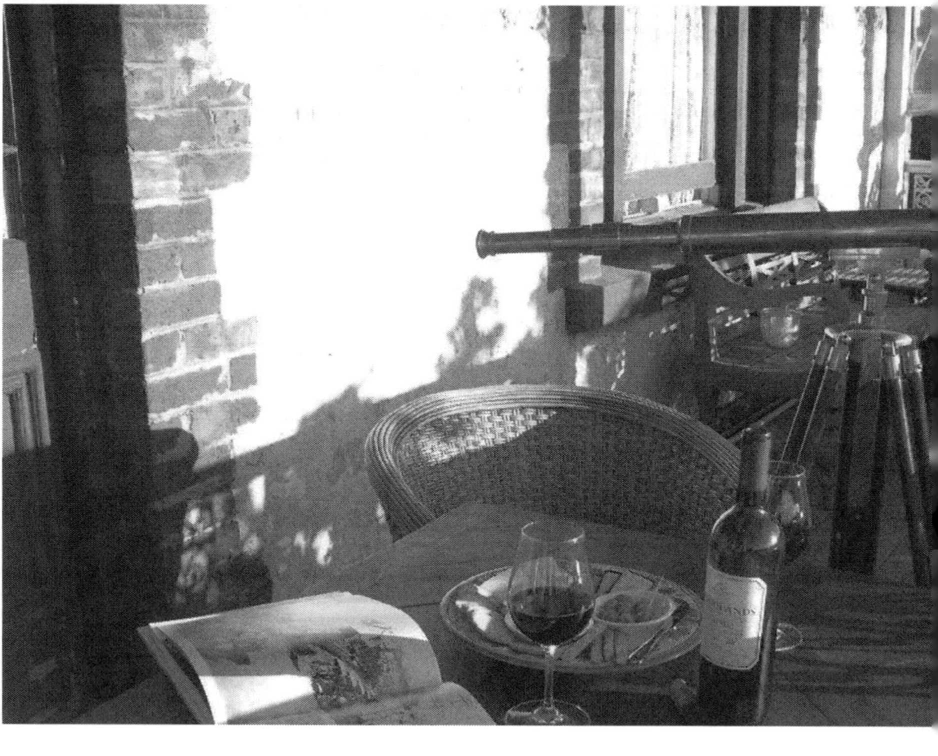

CHAPTER 8

Fothergills of Fremantle

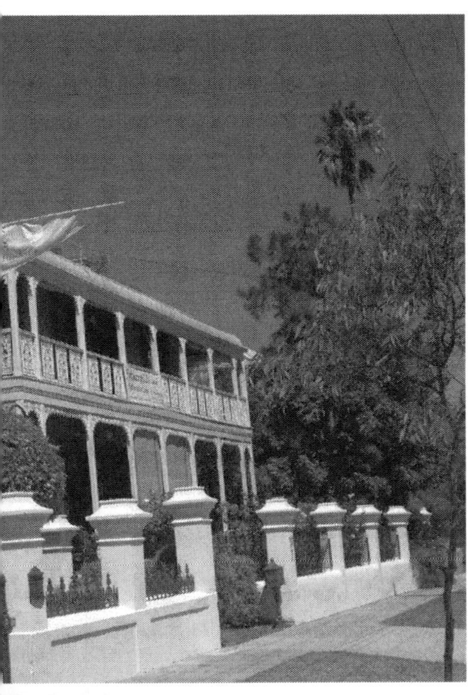

At Fothergills of Fremantle, a collection of three heritage-listed, 19th century limestone terrace houses high on Fremantle's Ord Street, I was told not to be surprised if I saw people wandering its corridors in the middle of the night like lost souls. Why? Well, it's the art. Fothergills is full of art. A deck chair with its canvas seat turned into a perfect base for a blue and yellow pastel by the Canadian pop singer k.d. lang, and works by the Melbourne-born artist Eric Smith, three-time winner of the Archibald Prize. Oddly enough, just after midnight, as I was in the breakfast room enjoying being alone with Fothergills' uplifting treasures, and becoming one of those little lost souls, a door opened, and my privileged time alone was about to end. Whoever it is, I thought, I'll just be polite, say hello, and hopefully they'll go away. Well, that didn't happen. It was Fothergills' owner.

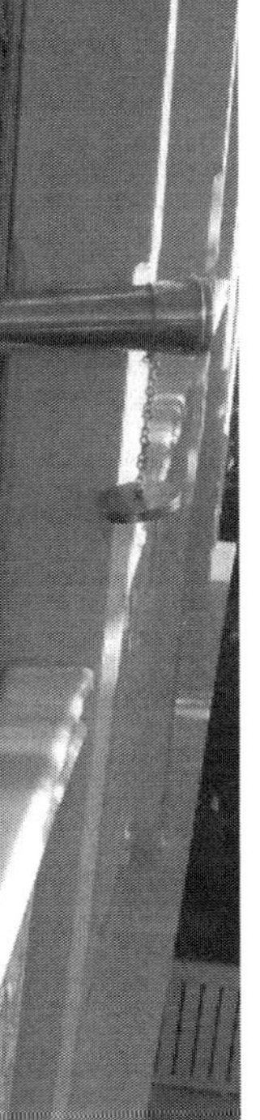

clockwise from top left
Elegant furnishings; two of the three Fothergills' buildings; views extend to the waterfront and beyond from Fothergills' elevated balconies.

The inspiration behind Fothergills of Fremantle is its owner, David. David is a general surgeon at Fremantle Hospital who loves his job and who doesn't allow the lifesaving nature of his work and the awe in which he is likely held by his patients and others to go to his head. He keeps himself grounded by referring to himself as a 'biological plumber', and muses over why society remunerates him for his abilities above other, equally necessary and honoured professions. He has a ten-year-old car and a laudable sense of civic duty. He once tried to stop a robbery by driving his car in front of some woollen-hooded burglars fleeing a local pharmacy but only succeeded in having his car trashed for his troubles. Recently he witnessed a lady being manhandled in the street and intervened again, only this time to get his wrist broken.

He doesn't go on many holidays (how can you when you work seven days a week), and when he *does* go overseas, it's to places like the Sudan where he's worked with the Red Cross to help repair the shattered bodies of the innocent victims of war. Yet despite all that he has seen he seems to be one of the happiest, most optimistic and 'together' people I've ever met and speaks to and listens to you with a quiet intent.

Wouldn't you just *love* to stay at a bed & breakfast that reflects that love and leaves its imprint on you long after you've left and returned to the real world? It isn't hyperbole—Fothergills of Fremantle does *precisely* that.

It's almost as though David can't quite make up his mind if he wants to operate an art gallery with a bed & breakfast on the side, or a bed & breakfast that doubles as an art gallery. Fothergills has all the charm of a chic, inner-city gallery, and walking through its hallways, staircases, and its many indoor and outdoor spaces, you're confronted with paintings, sculptures and eclectic works of art that fill Fothergills almost to overflowing. So if you come here please remember—take little steps. Even a short stroll here can be hijacked by Fothergills art and turned into an event, like my walk downstairs one morning for breakfast.

I left my room at 7.55 a.m., in plenty of time for breakfast at eight, and expected to make excellent time down the flight of stairs that lead to the main hallway and from there to the dining room, a lovely light-filled room added in 2005. Of course, spread over the three buildings there are seven rooms all with their own routes to the dining rooms and all with their own individual assortment of artistic 'hurdles' to conquer. But I can only speak with any authority about my own.

7.55—No sooner am I out of my door than I am confronted with two magnificent three-dimensional works of paper on canvas by Leon Pericles, a much-acclaimed artist born in Western Australia with a love of the outback and whose mediums include printmaking, sculpture and even kite painting.

7.59—In the hallway at the base of the stairs there are two panoramic photographs of Fremantle showing its development as a port and as a city over the last one hundred years. Michams Buildings and the National Hotel now stand where nondescript commercial buildings and residences once were.

8.01—Passing the staircase and about to enter the kitchen, there are four exquisitely detailed black-and-white photographs of old postcards, each with a different silhouette imposed on them—a scorpion, a raven, an ant and a small lizard.

8.03—Entering the kitchen one hardly knows where to look. Sitting atop the kitchen cupboard are three violins and two cellos, but not just any ordinary violins and cellos. One of the cellos is entirely covered with lollies: musk sticks, liquorice, hundreds and thousands, and fake teeth which had to all be lacquered to keep away the ants. It was made by children aged 12–19 of the Starlight Club at Perth's Princess Margaret Hospital. Next to it is Patchwork Cello, a cello painted in acrylics by Betsy Bush to resemble a patchwork quilt. Born in London and taught how to draw by her grandfather, Betsy, a geologist, moved to Perth in 1987 and began to paint at Fremantle's Kidogo Arthouse and has been exhibiting since 1984.

8.08—In the breakfast room at last, and here is where the most eclectic, the most imaginative treasures are displayed: seven magnificent hand-painted violins, including one by Rolf Harris, and one made entirely of string and named, appropriately, a 'stringed instrument'. It had taken me 13 minutes to walk 15 metres.

Perhaps it is through his art that David draws the nourishment he needs to be able to see the world the way he does. Certainly it seems to me that to surround yourself with beauty must have some medicinal effects. I didn't need my usual morning 'wake up coffee' that day. The art had already woke me up, had given me my 'kick',

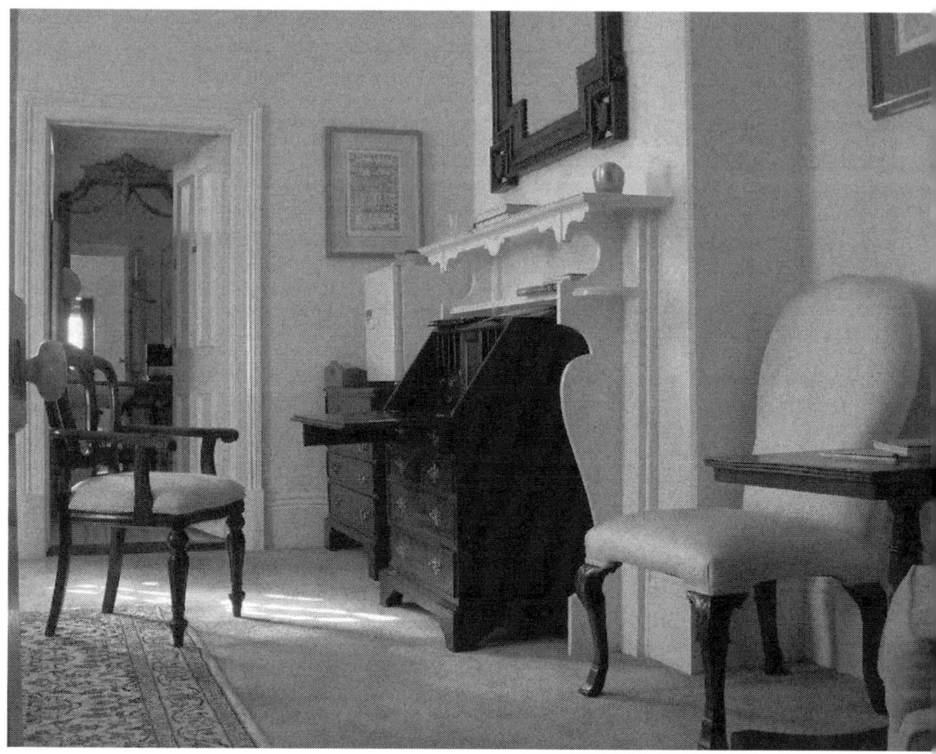

above The Endeavour Room is usually taken by the Admiral when the fleet's in town. It comes with a rear-facing balcony.

and given me the means by which I might better be able to keep the ups and downs of the day to come in better perspective.

Back to the kitchen and it's still a quarter after midnight. David, full of energy, has bounded in and tells me how he likes to assist penniless musicians to raise the necessary funds so they can travel overseas to pursue their studies and their careers. He once raised $7000 in a single night for a local opera singer who got a scholarship to London's Guild Hall, and artists sponsored by Fothergills over the years have included Just Sax, Sacha McCulloch, and Allan Meyer, the principal clarinettist with the West Australian Symphony Orchestra.

David doesn't buy art as an 'investment'—to reduce the beauty of art to a money-making exercise is, to him, 'an impertinence', among other things—he buys it because he loves it. Why else would his office look like an art gallery basement, filled with so many paintings

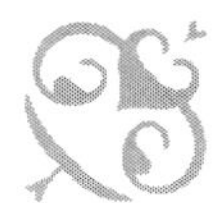

that he hasn't the available wall space left to hang them all? 'My accountant says I should stop buying art,' he admits. 'But how can I?' (He also has, squirrelled away somewhere, some antique maps and a first edition signed by the author Graham Greene, no less!)

How can he stop indeed? How can someone who still gets excited at being able to see an individual bee's 'whiskers', as he calls them, on a print in the breakfast room by the acclaimed West Australian naturalist and painter Richard Swainston, be expected to just . . . stop? So keen was he to show me one of the violins on display on top of his kitchen cupboard that he stood on an old cane chair that strained and creaked all about the place as he struggled valiantly to reach and bring it down.

The art David has surrounded himself and his fortunate guests with is, together with his skills as a surgeon, what drives him forward. The world *needs* beauty just as it does surgeons, and if you're ever in desperate need to *see* beauty and Fremantle's art galleries have closed their doors for the night, then book a room at Fothergills and spend your evening wandering its hallways and public spaces. I'm not ashamed to say it, but it was 12.55 a.m. before I extricated myself from David and returned to my room, armed with a bowl of Honeysmacks I'd snaffled from the breakfast bar! But not before he'd impulsively shown me one last, little gem.

'Orders and Ordinances For The better government of the Hofpitall of BARTHOLOMEW the leffe', was printed by James Flesher of LONDON, printer to that Honourable City, in 1652. David had recently purchased it at auction and happened to be carrying it in his pocket. It was now 12.50 in the morning but there we were, amusing ourselves reading the salaries of doctors, nurses, cleaners and administrators in 17th-century England. Not quite the thing one comes to expect from a B&B. Thankfully.

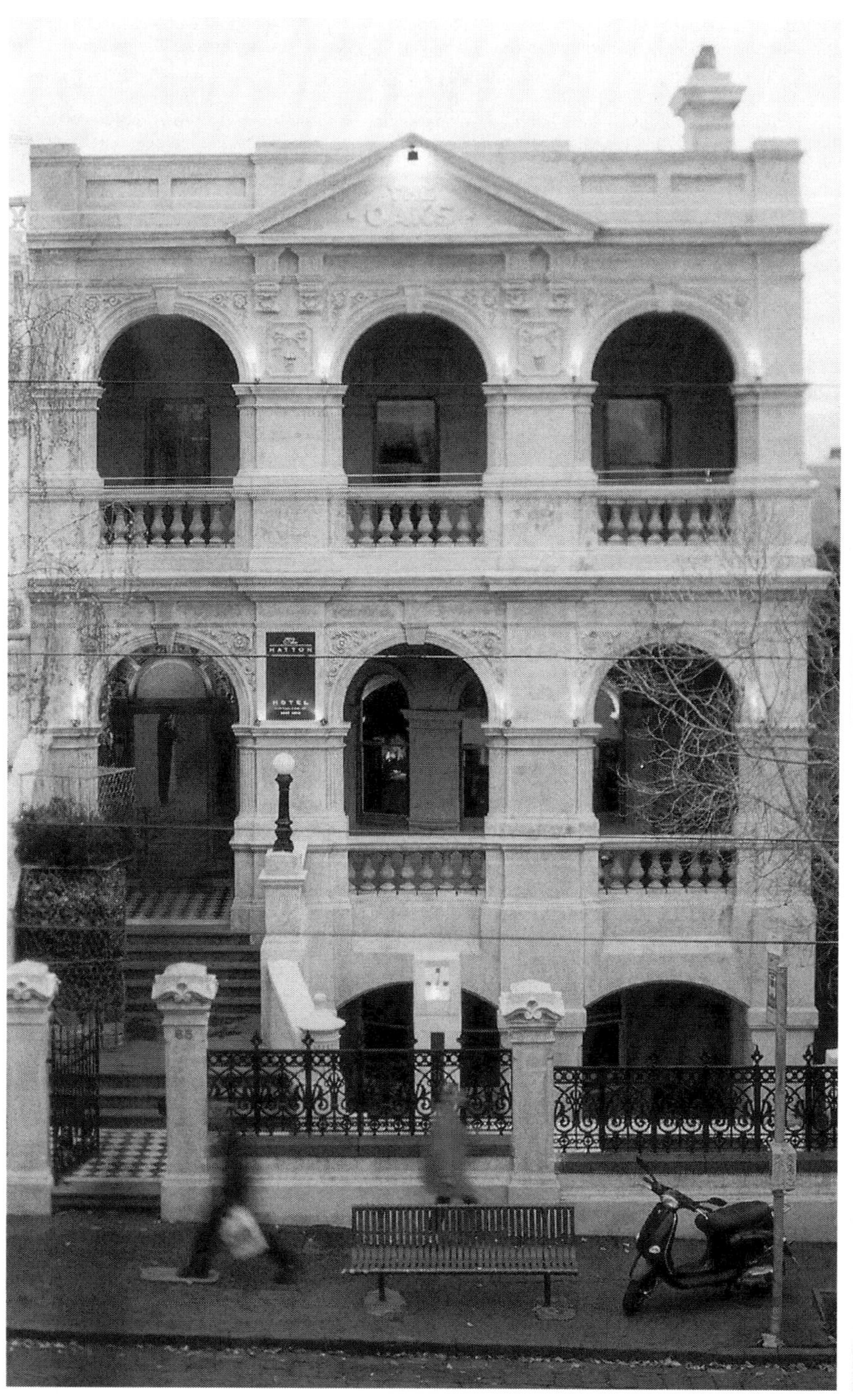

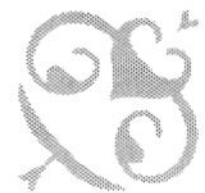

CHAPTER 9

The Hatton Hotel

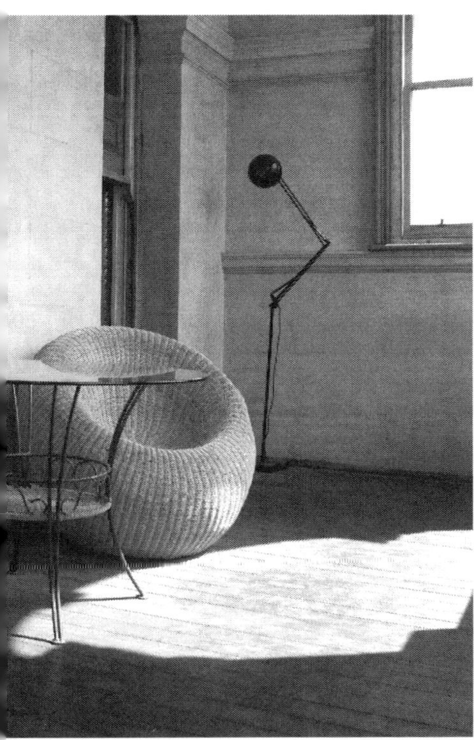

I thought I'd gotten over Melbourne, the city of my birth. After 20 years of putting down roots in my adopted Sydney, I thought time had eroded the love affair I once had, with the city's elm trees and its trams, its commonsense CBD street grid pattern, the Richmond Football Club, the Melbourne Cricket Ground, the Yarra River and Moomba and meeting friends under the Flinders Street Station clocks. But I was back. Back for one night at The Hatton Hotel in the leafy, civilised enclave of South Yarra where, suddenly those years of toil and building, convincing myself I loved Sydney's harbour and its narrow city streets and its obsession with real estate and its Danish Opera House, all went straight out The Hatton's 109-year-old sash windows.

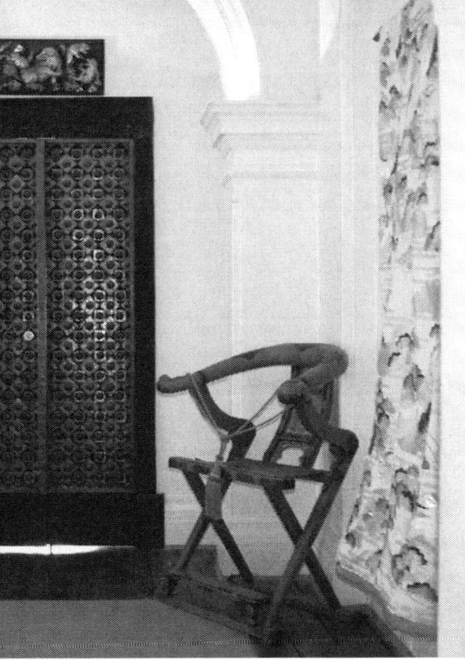

clockwise from top left The Hatton is more 'grand mansion' than hotel; one of its north-facing balconies bathed in morning sun; antiques from south-east Asia decorate the interior.

I'll talk more about my own insecurities in a moment but first I should tell you something of the hotel which I suspect may have been the catalyst of my angst, because the moment I stepped inside The Hatton Hotel it was love at first sight. Despite being purpose-built as a hotel in 1902, it somehow manages to exude the look and feel and ambience of an intimate, private home and I felt at peace with it before I even walked through the front door—No mean feat for an Italianate-style mansion that greets you with two rows of three east-facing archways and significantly columned balustrades. Inside, however, the surprises come thick and fast even if you somehow fail as I did to notice the specially commissioned *Wrap Vase* by the acclaimed Melbourne artist Emma Davies in the hall. But try as you might, you certainly won't miss the hotel's fabulous reception counter.

The 4-metre-long kauri pine countertop with decorative pressed-metal base, circa 1880, was discovered by The Hatton's owners in the showroom of a Geelong antique dealer and Andrew Hatton, son of the hotel's owner Lynette Hatton, delighted in telling me the story of its acquisition. The instant his mother saw it she simply *had* to have it. 'You can't have it,' was the reply.

'But I have to have it!'

'Will it be on public display? It must be on display,' the table's owner insisted.

After Lynette Hatton spent several frantic minutes assuring him that yes, it would indeed be on public display, the counter—which originated in an old drapery store in the tiny Western Victorian town of Jeparit, the birthplace of Sir Robert Menzies no less—at last changed hands. And just as well it did—It looks purpose-built for the space it now inhabits and is a perfect example of the care that has been taken in the placement of every last thing you see here. The place really is a wonderful synthesis of art, history, and a refreshing absence of clutter that allows your eyes to settle on and admire the things that really matter.

Every item of antique furniture and every one of The Hatton Hotel's array of eclectic artwork comes with its own individual story. The scarred workbench in the front lounge with its still-intact handmade wooden vices is courtesy of an old railway workshop in Newport. The white silk wedding kimono on display on the first floor was worn at a Hatton family wedding. The antique red lacquered

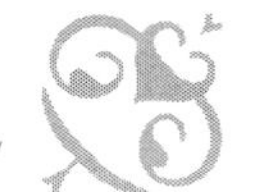

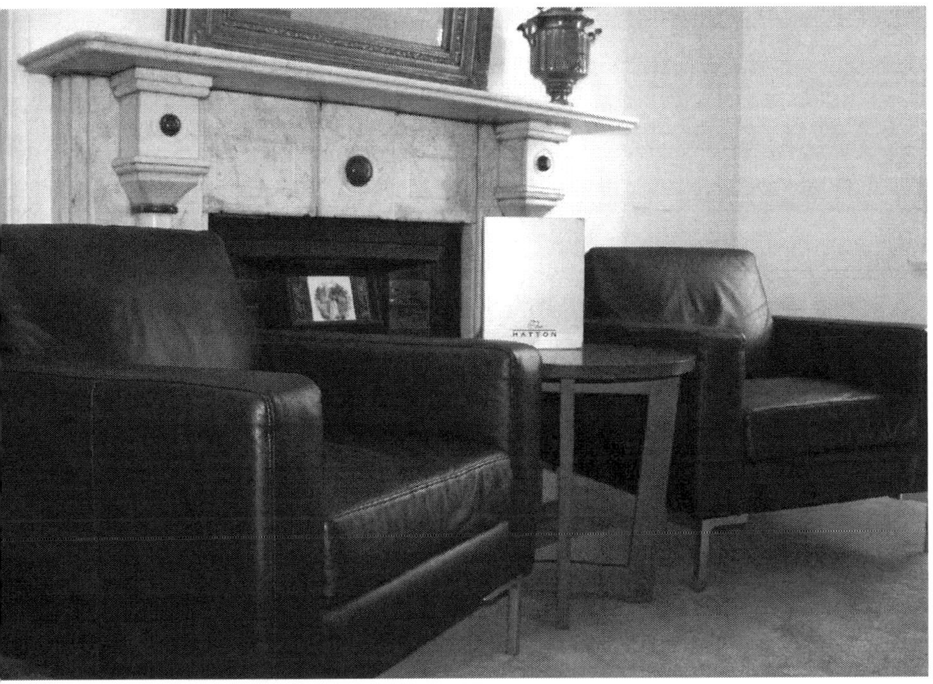

above There is nothing to distract the eye here. Interior spaces lack unnecessary clutter but are full of the things that matter: elegance, comfort and style.

folding chair beside it with its handcrafted copper joinery on the handles was once sat in by a Chinese nobleman and held aloft on bamboo poles supported on the shoulders of his servants. In the bottom hall a Baltic pine cabinet from the Barossa Valley dating to the early 1900s uses old kerosene cans as drawers and is known affectionately to the staff, predictably enough I suppose, as the 'Old Kerosene Cabinet'.

Even the brochure cabinet in the foyer is circa 1860 and came from an old miner's hut on the goldfields of Ballarat. Everywhere I looked there was one jaw-dropping piece after another, each item selected and placed with the skill and precision worthy of a museum curator. Nothing, however, was more unexpected and stunning than a series of 17th-century Ming Dynasty wooden screens that hung on the wall along the hotel's main staircase, very likely a gift to a Chinese nobleman from the Emperor or an envoy on the Emperor's behalf. Their depiction of idealised bucolic scenes alongside faded Chinese characters combined to make what should have been a pretty straightforward 30-second walk from the reception desk to my room take all of 20 minutes.

Walking down the corridor and into my room down saffron-coloured carpets and original waxed floorboards the surprises continued. Rooms here are wonderful spaces characterised by high ceilings, muted colours and minimal clutter, all highlighted by strategically placed spotlights installed by the noted Melbourne stage-lighting designer Phillip Lethlean which provide an almost theatrical look. If the inside of my head could be represented as a room, this

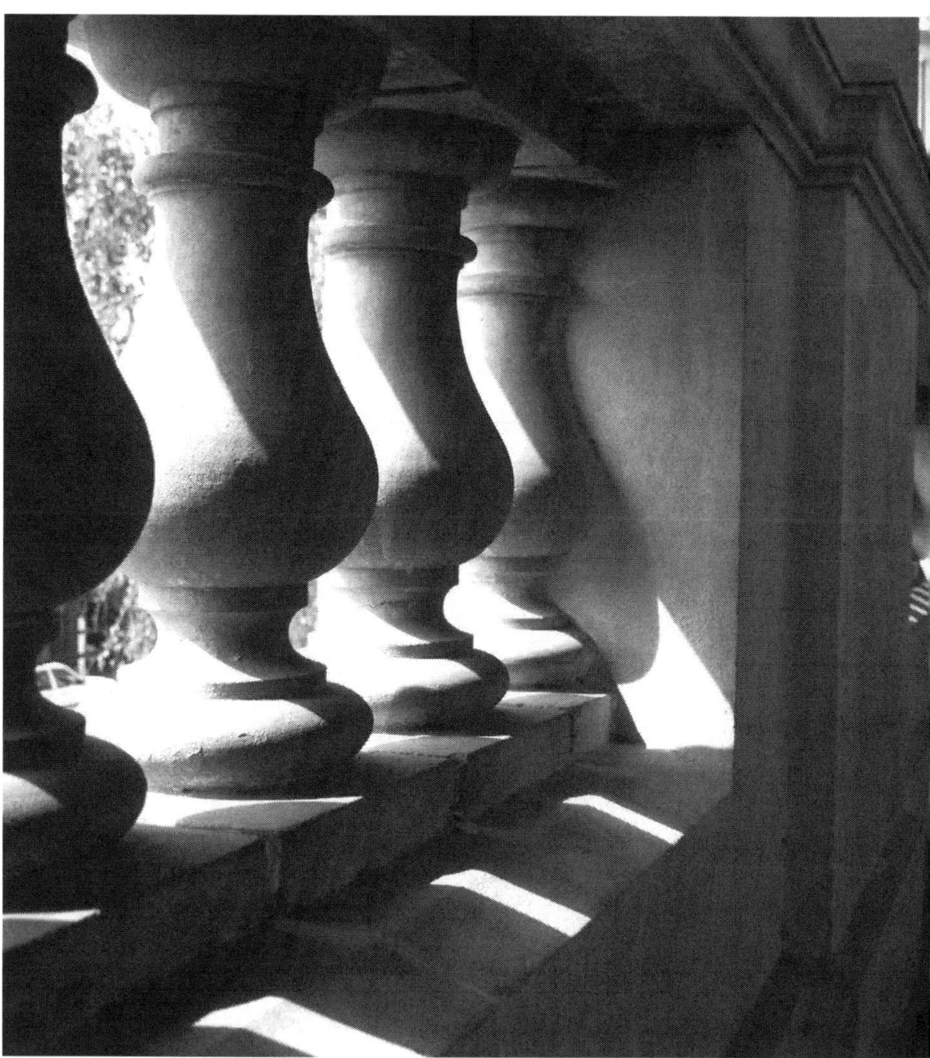

would have to be it, with all the things you need and nothing you don't. There is a microwave and small kitchenette, a large wall-mounted flat screen TV, a writing desk with two leather-bound chairs, a fabulous walk-up bathroom and a king-size bed covered in the finest linens. The hotel is a perfect blend of things historic and contemporary, with 100-year-old rosettes, cornices and balustrades blending effortlessly with 21st-century minimalism. I was in love.

Later that night after having settled into the Hatton's signature blend of past and present, I wandered barefoot outside and along Park Street to photograph some of the street's elegant Victorian homes. Walking barefoot along a city street is not normally something I'd do, but it seemed wholly appropriate. I *enjoyed* the feeling of stepping in Melbourne's puddles again, even if it meant indulging myself in an unprofitable mix of melancholy and nostalgia. Walking along the tram tracks that were warmer on my feet than the surrounding bitumen of the road, I photographed the neighbouring houses, and felt at home. I wasn't prepared for how easily I was able to slot right back into the rhythm of the city. Earlier in the evening we dined in the Colonial Tramcar Restaurant as it took us through South Melbourne and Middle Park, past not just rows but entire blocks of immaculate Federation and Victorian homes, suburbs brought back to life by

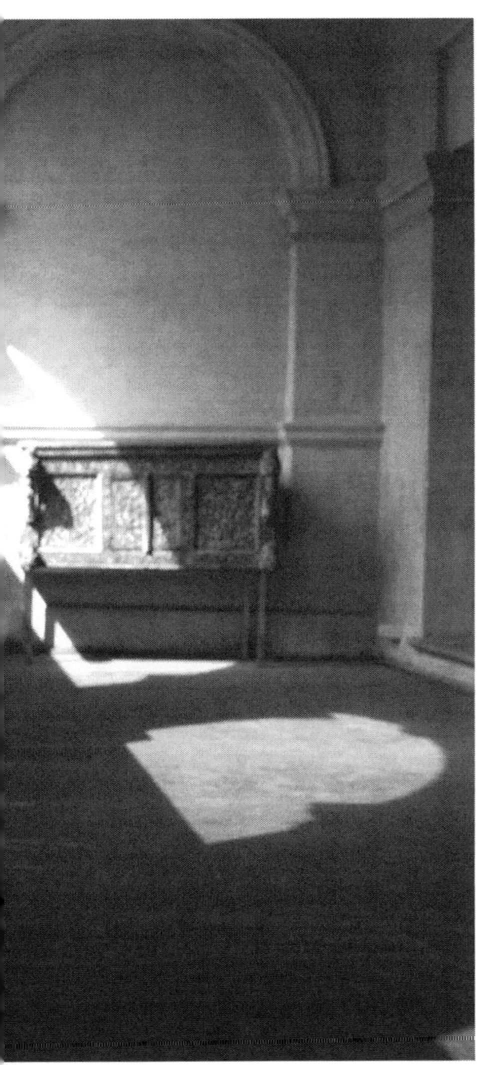

left Italian motifs can be seen everywhere, from ornate balustrades to faux arches atop ancient columns.

a new generation of families and not at all the tired, ageing suburbs I remembered them to be.

When The Hatton Hotel was completed just after the turn of the century, the cable car from the city ended at Park Street, and although it might seem on the city's doorstep now with a tramline at the hotel's front door able to whisk you to the MCG and city centre in under ten minutes, in 1902 it was thought of as an appreciable distance from the city to South Yarra and people would often make the trip here to escape the congestion of the CBD. Guests would stay not for a day or two but often for a week or more at a time.

Andrew Hatton managed the hotel along with his grandmother while he was still a student and he says the hotel catered to more of a transient boarding house crowd in those days. This was decades before the family began to renovate the hotel in 1996 in the wake of a disastrous fire in Melbourne's Kew Cottages, a residential development for intellectually handicapped men and women that killed nine people. With sprinkler systems and other safety precautions made mandatory in the city's older buildings as a result of the Kew Cottage fire, the Hattons took the opportunity to begin a significant renovation of the building, reopening it in 2000 as one of the most sought after boutique addresses in inner Melbourne. A more upmarket hotel had been created, and a more demanding clientele soon followed.

It's also a hotel on good terms with its neighbours and very much a part of the close-knit community in which it is set. Gary from the local florist shop has been walking fresh flowers down the road to decorate the hotel's reception area and foyer ever since it opened, and the local newsagency supplies it with its daily newspapers.

Today the Hatton family live on French Island in Westernport Bay southeast of Melbourne. Two-thirds of French Island is national park and home to Australia's largest community of koalas. The Hattons intend opening a cellar door restaurant in an effort to bring more visitors to the island, which only has a population of 60. In the meantime they leave the day-to-day running of the hotel in the more than capable hands of its General Manager, Taya Murphy, who loves it so much she once lived there for six years before applying to be its manager. I know how she feels.

The Hatton's warmth, its lack of pretence in the midst of a suburb that certainly wasn't lacking in it, the zen-like tranquility it exudes

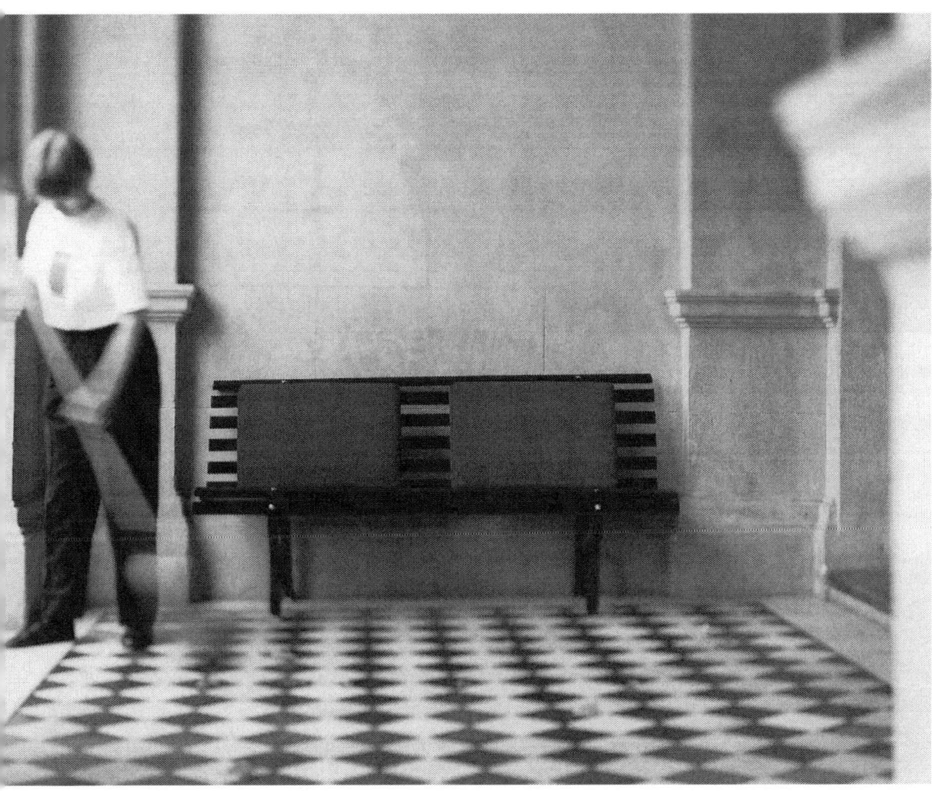

above Timeless elegance and a relaxed approach to life are characteristic of the Hatton and its staff.

and the illusion it gives you that you're the only guest in the building despite it presumably having no vacancies make it the perfect setting for indulgent self-absorption. The sound of the trams clanging by outside out-of-towners might disparage but any true Melburnian welcomes as a reassuring lullaby that whisks you off into a deep, contented sleep. How this eclectic, wonderful hotel may or may not have contributed to my sense of melancholy and wistfulness I will never really know, but I shall always remember it as the place where I realised that this city was, and always will be, my home. Go the Yellow and Black!

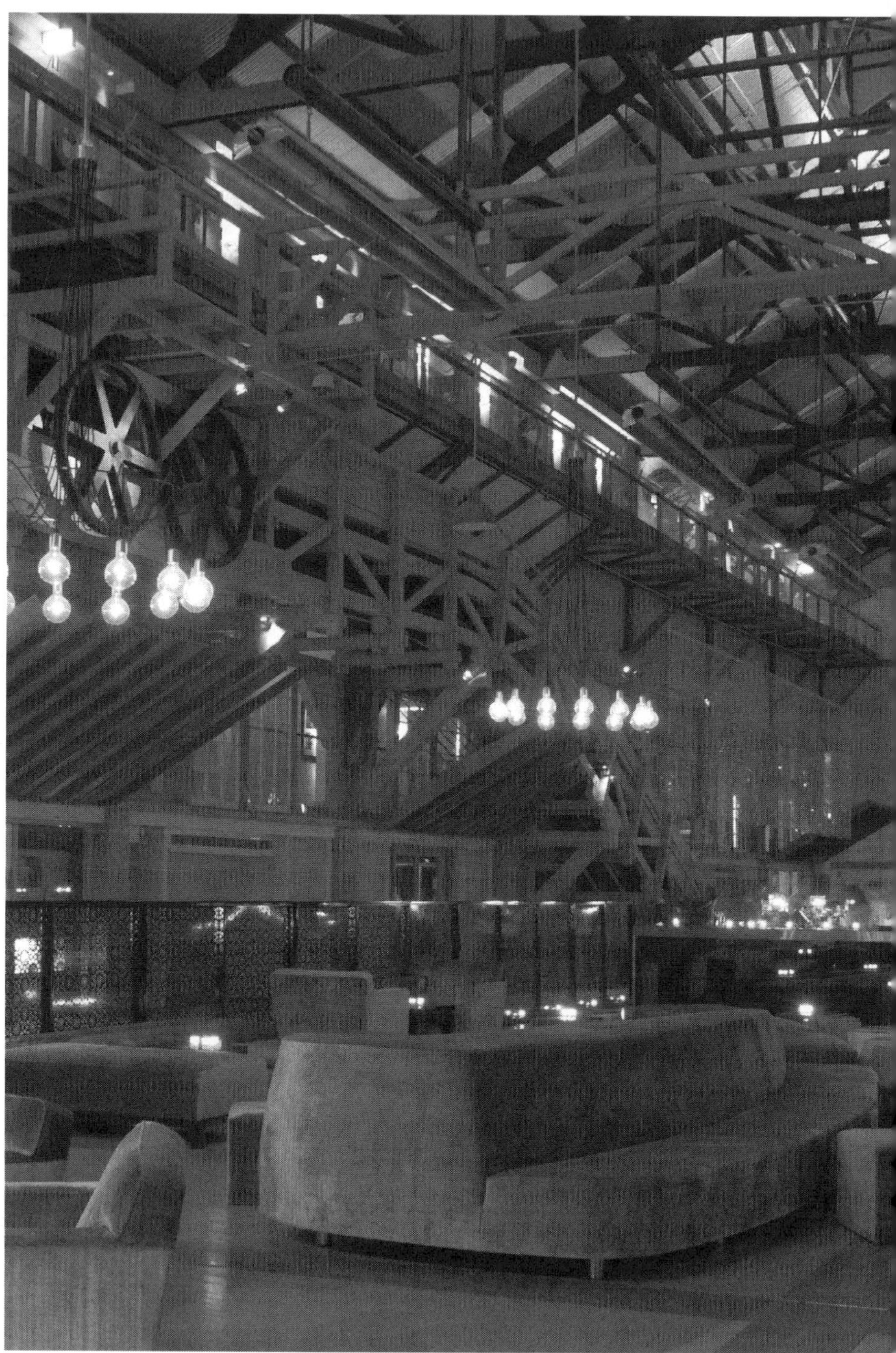

CHAPTER 10

Blue Sydney

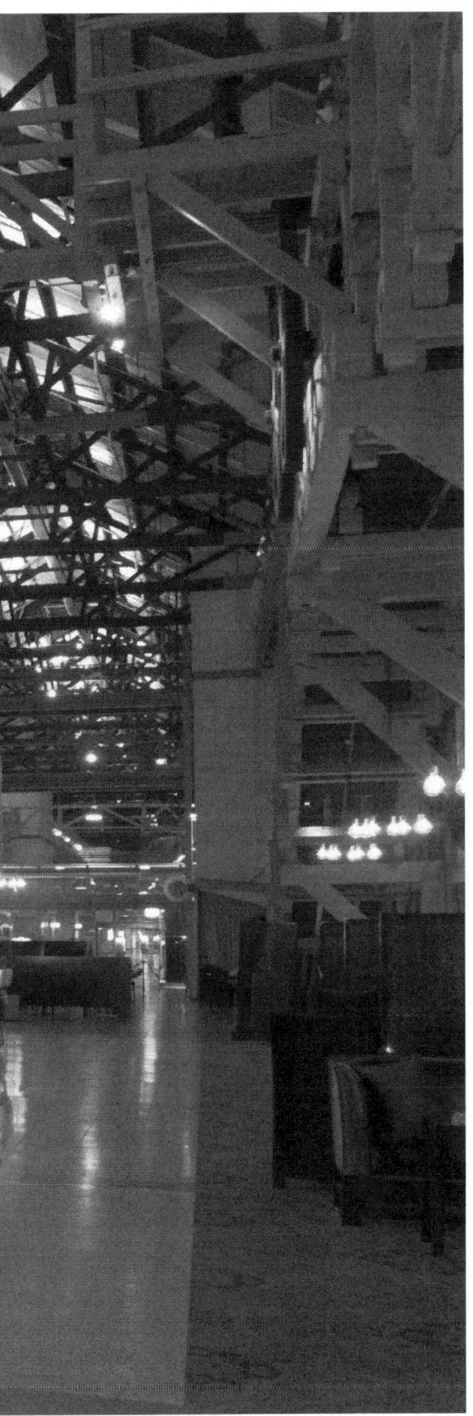

Timber pile construction, the art of sinking massive, weight-bearing timbers into either land or more commonly into the bottom of riverbeds, estuaries and such to enable a building to be constructed over a waterway, can be traced back six thousand years to Neolithic tribes in present-day Switzerland who built platforms raised above the ground on timber piles to protect themselves from wild animals. The Romans built a bridge over the Tiber River supported on timber piles in 1600 BCE, and the homes and palaces of Venice first began to be raised on piles above its tidal lagoon in 100 BCE. Timber pile construction supports bridges over the River Thames in London and the Seine in Paris and came into broad use in England in the 1830s when the first preservatives were injected into timbers to protect them against rot.

The cavernous, 410-metre long Finger Wharf was once the hub of our wool exporting industry and remains one of Sydney's largest enclosed spaces.

Thousands of timber pylons were used in extensions to New York's John F. Kennedy International Airport, and the entire city of New Orleans, which on average is 2.4 metres (8 feet) below sea-level, is built on them. Believe it or not, timber pile construction has led to the construction of some of the world's most beautiful buildings but human beings, being what they are, tend to focus on and get excited about only what they can see. Foundations, what a building actually sits on and enables it to be built in the first place, generally don't get a lot of attention which, in the case of timber pile construction at least, is a real shame.

Although the most extensive use of timber pile construction occurred in Europe and North America, destructive high tides and a scarcity of suitable timbers saw timber wharf and jetty construction there largely abandoned by 1910, meaning that today the largest timber pile building in the world isn't to be found in Europe, the United States or Great Britain, but in the Sydney suburb of Woolloomooloo on the foreshore of Sydney Harbour. Construction of the 410-metre-long, 64-metre-wide finger wharf at Woolloomooloo began on the site of Sydney's very first fish market in 1911, took four years to complete and remains today one of Australia's finest examples of Federation-era architecture. Taking advantage of Sydney Harbour's low tidal range, the wharf's existence was made possible only by the hundreds of turpentine piles that support it. Australian timbers are generally denser than their cousins in the Northern Hemisphere and the turpentine tree, *Syncarpia glomulifera*, is no exception. Soft and workable when green but extremely hard when seasoned, it has a rating of 1 on a 6-point density scale and possesses high levels of silica which make it resistant to marine borers. Australian turpentine is the timber you use if you want to build a timber-piled building that lasts.

Ships first began discharging their cargoes here in 1912 and the wharf was the only site in Sydney that engaged in 'wool dumping', the process of using hydraulic presses to compress wool bales. After the outbreak of World War I it witnessed the final goodbyes of our diggers as they boarded ships bound for Egypt and Gallipoli, many of them never to return. It was also a departure point for troops in World War II, as well as being the site where thousands of immigrants took their first steps in their adopted homeland.

The Woolloomooloo Finger Wharf is an icon of Sydney's social and economic history and remained a working wharf until the 1970s when the development of larger and more modern container ports saw it become obselete—abandoned and left derelict, an ageing dinosaur unable to reinvent itself. In 1987 the New South Wales government announced plans to demolish it. Various government members referred to it as a grey 'dunny' and an eyesore that should be 'blown to bits'. But in January of 1991 when a demolition team arrived to raze it to the ground, they were met by a determined group of local residents who resisted plans to construct a marina and resort complex on the site. The Building Workers Industrial Union then placed an interim ban on its demolition and a series of community forums resulted in a conservation plan being developed. The state government then classified it a heritage site and gave approval for its redevelopment as a hotel and residential complex.

What eventually was achieved was the retaining of the wharf and its transformation in July 2000 into a boutique hotel, first under the W Hotel brand and then, in 2006, as the Taj Hotel group's five-star blend of history and chic, 'Blue Sydney' or, as the locals call it, the Blue Hotel. Of course the advent of a hotel on the site is a comparatively recent development, and like all buildings Blue Hotel needs time to develop a history of its own, and write its own story, and this will surely happen. Blue Hotel is history 'in the making', and in the meantime has one of Sydney's most enviable addresses of any hotel, historic or otherwise.

The Finger Wharf redevelopment was never intended to be an exercise in retaining Sydney's heritage. What we have been left with is undoubtedly a compromise, with much of its interior gutted and rejigged to serve its new purpose as a very comfortable, wonderfully situated five-star hotel and apartment complex. But it should be stressed that if it hadn't come along we might well have seen the wharf lost to the city entirely. Even an imperfect, flawed outcome is preferable to watching it be bulldozed and a new structure with no connection to the community around it rising in its place. Sadly though, there is little evidence of its past use having been retained, and its overall appearance has been drastically altered. Looking at it today it is difficult to imagine what it must have been like in its prime, how its constituent parts must have appeared, how they meshed together, how it lived and breathed and flexed its powerful working-class muscles.

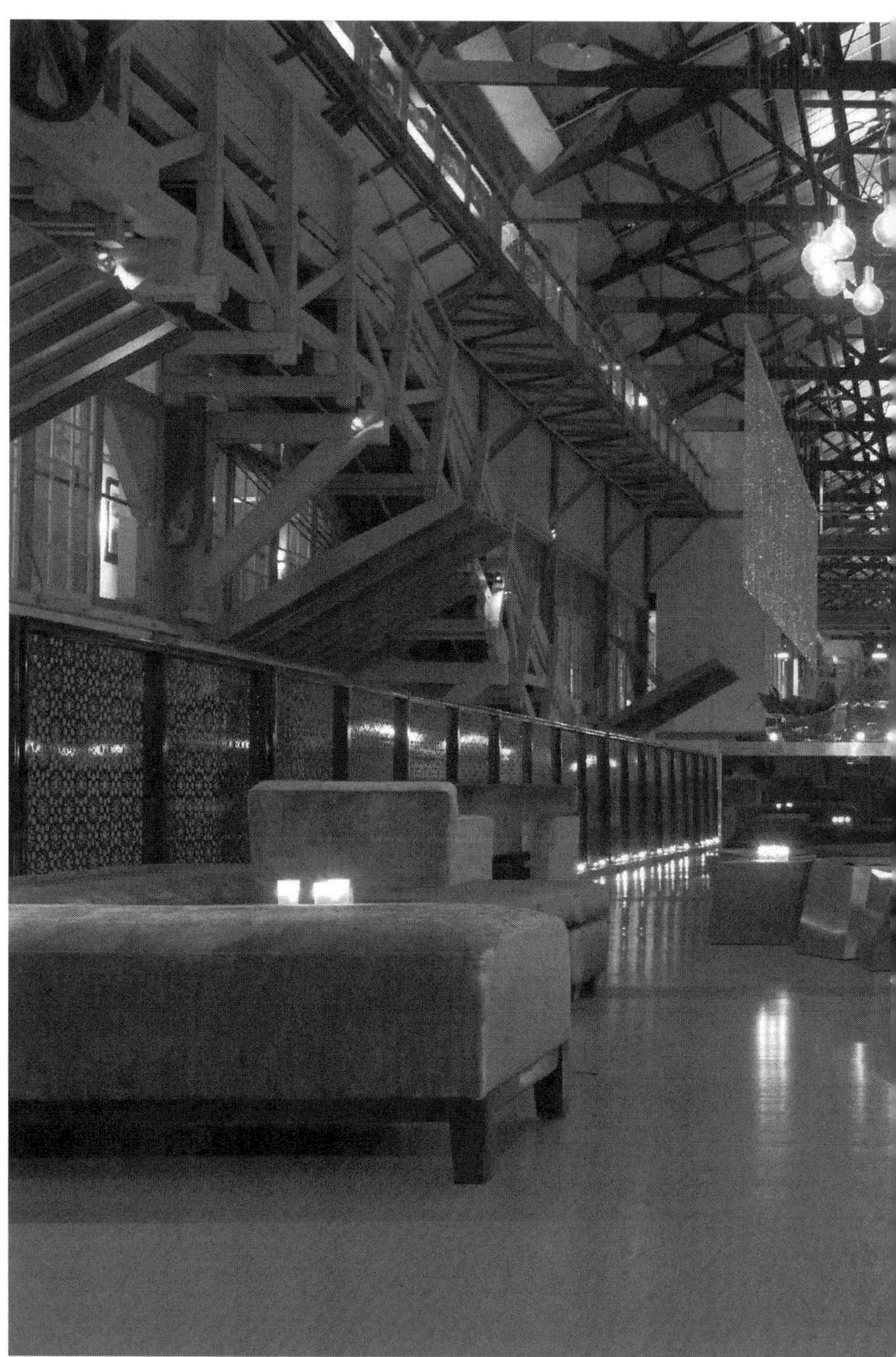

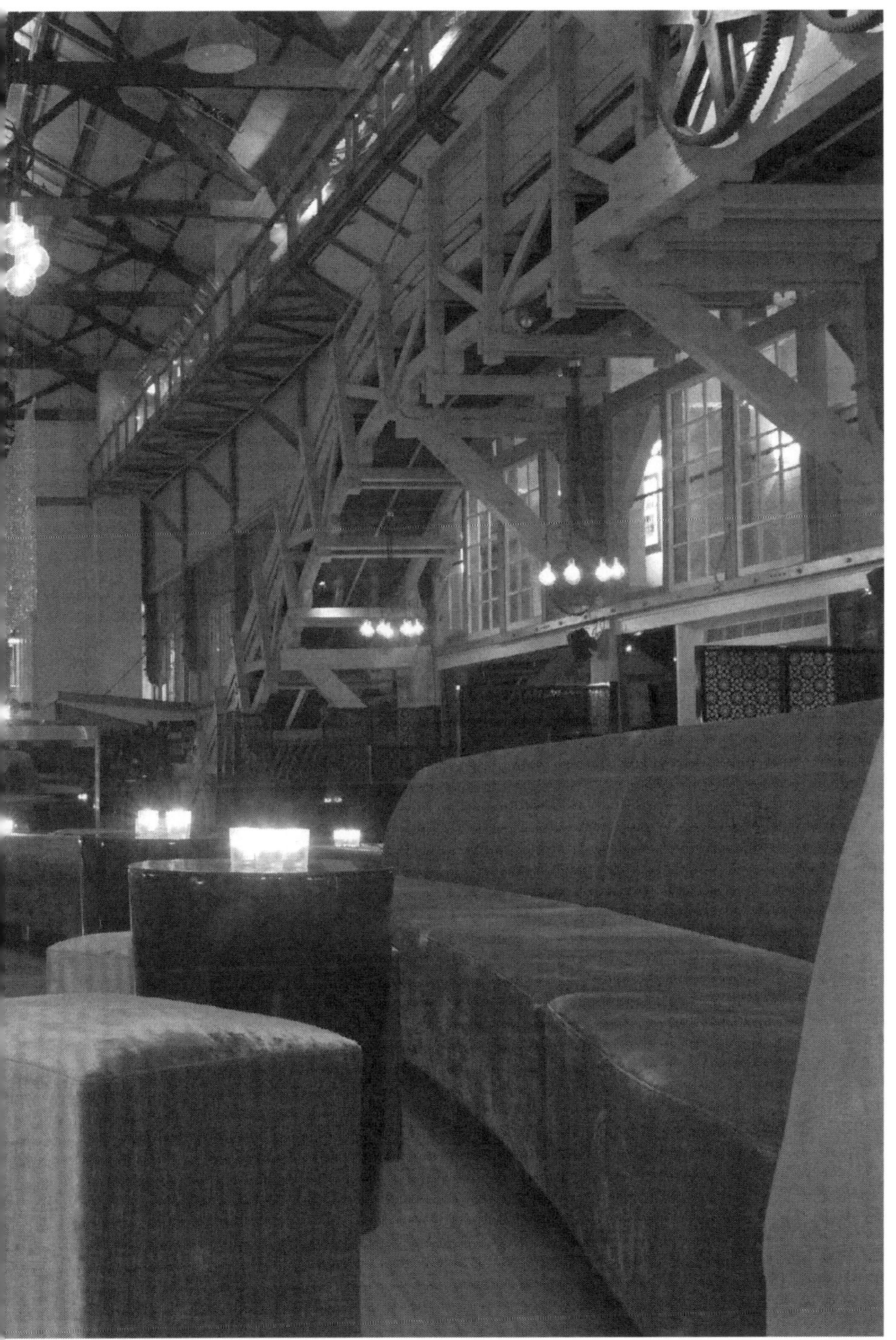

previous page The largest timber-piled building in the world is now a successful mix of heritage building, hotel, restaurants and apartments.

The wharf, however, still retains several impressive examples of industrial archaeology. The two massive conveyer belts in its cavernous interior are the only examples of electrically operated conveyors remaining in New South Wales, used to export bales of wool and other goods to markets around the world at a time when the Australian economy truly 'rode on the sheep's back'—and never fail to make an impact regardless of how often you walk by them. The wharf's interior and its majestic vaulted ceiling combine to produce one of the great enclosed spaces in the city, so long in fact you can barely see the end of it. Its sheer unbridled volume still conveys that old warehouse 'feel', right down to its dried-up pigeon droppings, the stains of which are still evident on its old crossbeams and which the heritage experts, in their tireless quest for authenticity, insist have to stay.

More than two and a half times the length of the finger wharves in nearby Walsh Bay, the wharf at Woolloomooloo is bisected by an open transcept that links its two impressive boardwalks, and its three signature pitched roofs look resplendent clad in the high grade Colourbond roofing that replaced its hundred-year old roof. It is also the only remaining Sydney wharf that has an internal roadway which the architectural firm of Clive Lucas, Stapleton & Partners adapted to serve primarily as a concourse. Also retained are three of Sydney's oldest operating electric lifts, and the wharf's original ventilation grates are still in the floor. Though mostly covered over by hotel seating, they are there if you bother to look, bringing cool air up from the harbour below just as they always were designed to do.

And, of course, there are still all those wonderful, ageing turpentine piles, hundreds of them exactly where they've always been, still supporting the building just as they always have. The developers have even instituted a 100-year management program for the precious timbers to help ensure the building will be around for another hundred years, employing sonar technology to help gauge their density and strength in addition to wrapping them in a state-of-the-art polyurethane skin, separating them from the water that would eventually degrade them.

The wharf is what is known in developer's parlance as a 'mixed use development', comprising 325 private apartments, 104 hotel rooms, function rooms, a fitness centre, car park, marina, and a string of some of the finest Sydney restaurants lining the boardwalk below. Rooms with panoramic floor-to-ceiling windows on the building's western side look straight out over the CBD, making the transition from late afternoon to evening as the city's lights come on, something to stay in your room for. Rooms on its eastern side look out over Garden Island and whatever Australian naval vessels are moored there. Now home to celebrities such as actor Russell Crowe and Sydney's former king of radio John Laws, the rejuvenated wharf is not without charm, and which, because of its scale, still manages to strike a magnificent pose.

For me the old wharf elicits the kind of emotional response I usually reserve for some of the great sights of antiquity, a modern 'wonder of the world', a towering engineering accomplishment defiantly projecting itself into the world's most beautiful harbour and able to stand shoulder-to-shoulder with the great buildings of the world. The fact something so large and so beautiful was built a hundred years ago and still stands today never ceases to impress, and despite the extensive renovations required to turn the building from a wharf into a contemporary mix of restaurants and living spaces, it remains one of Sydney's finest examples of a building still able to remind us of our social and commercial past, as well as remaining a showcase for load-bearing timbers the size and like of which will never be used again.

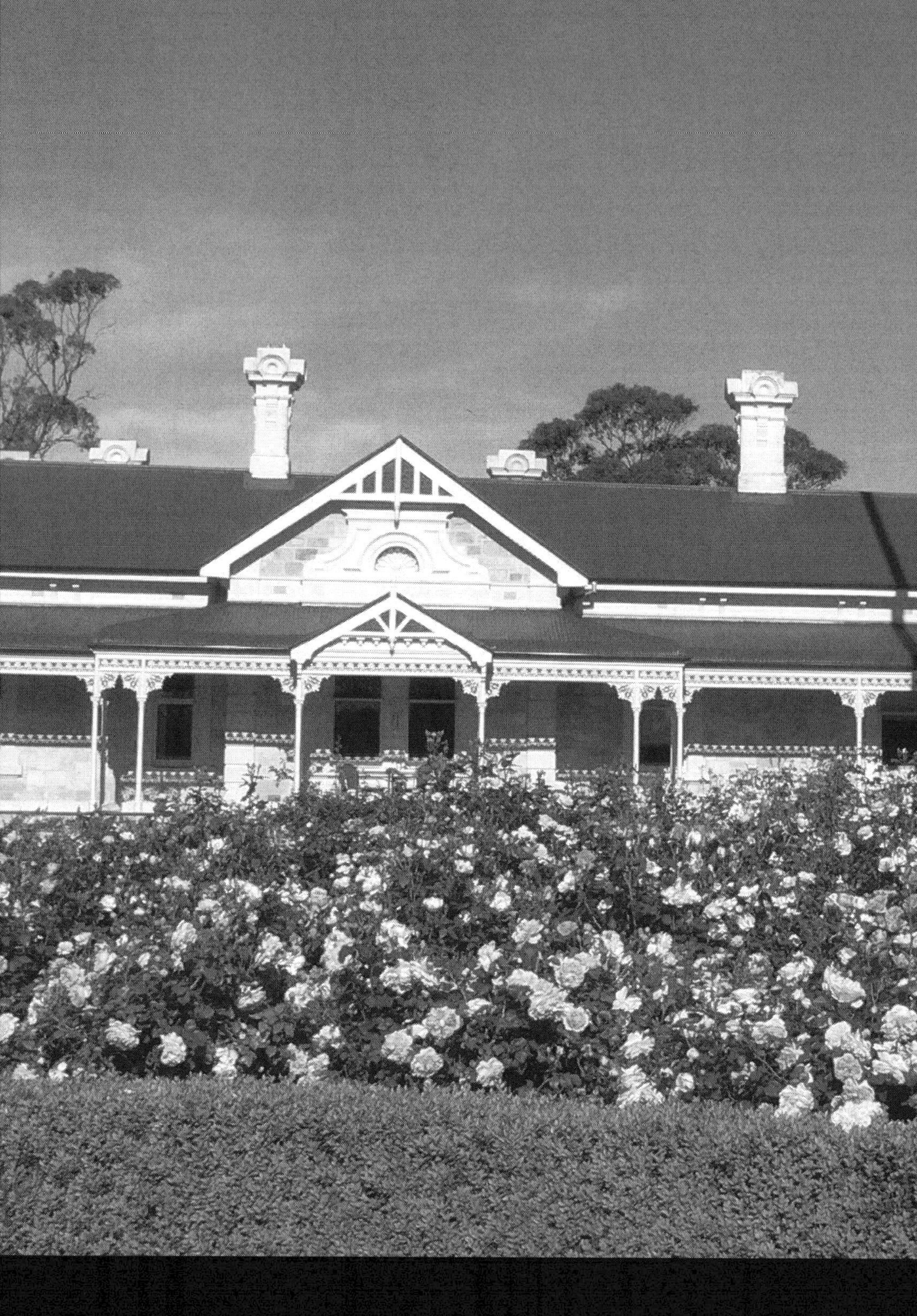

PART 3

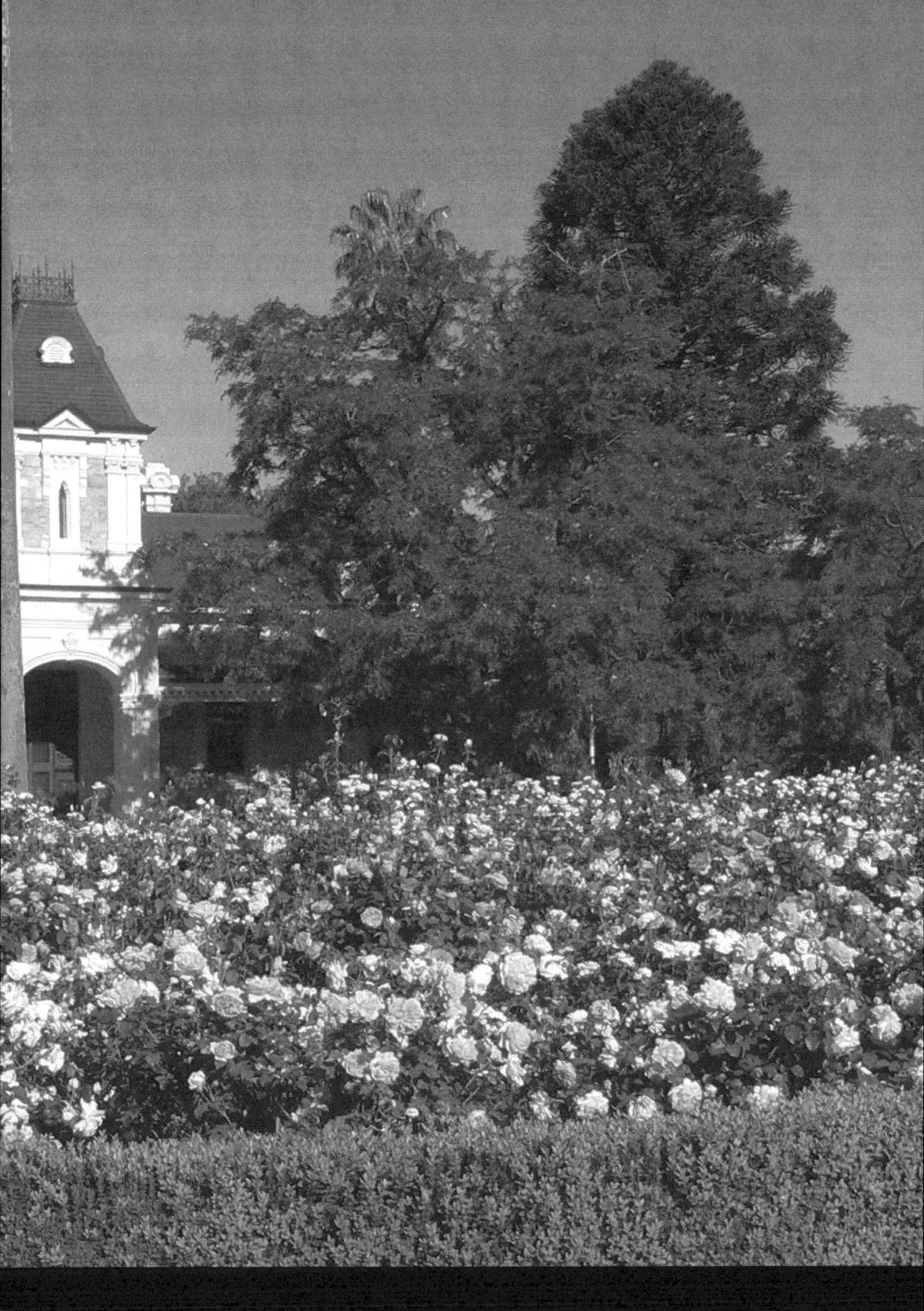

Homesteads

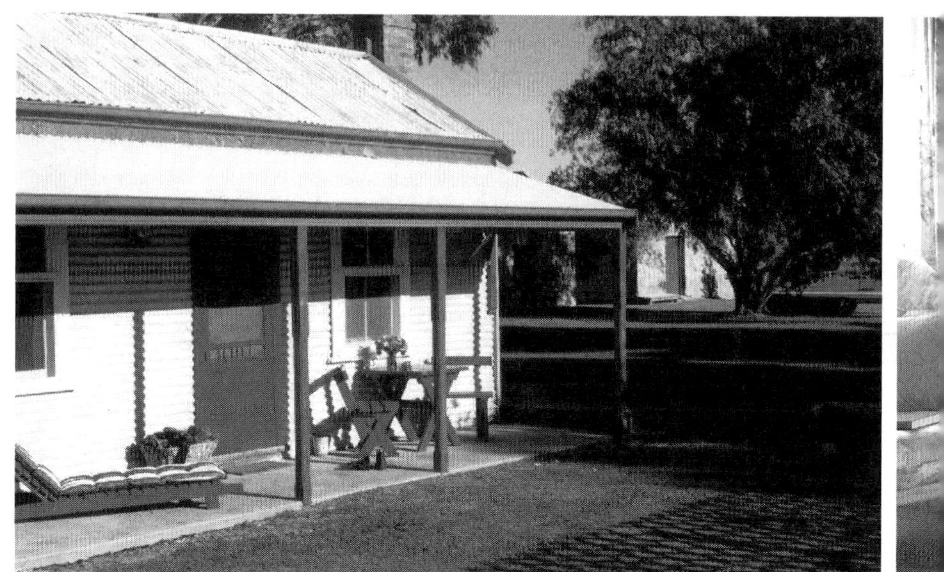

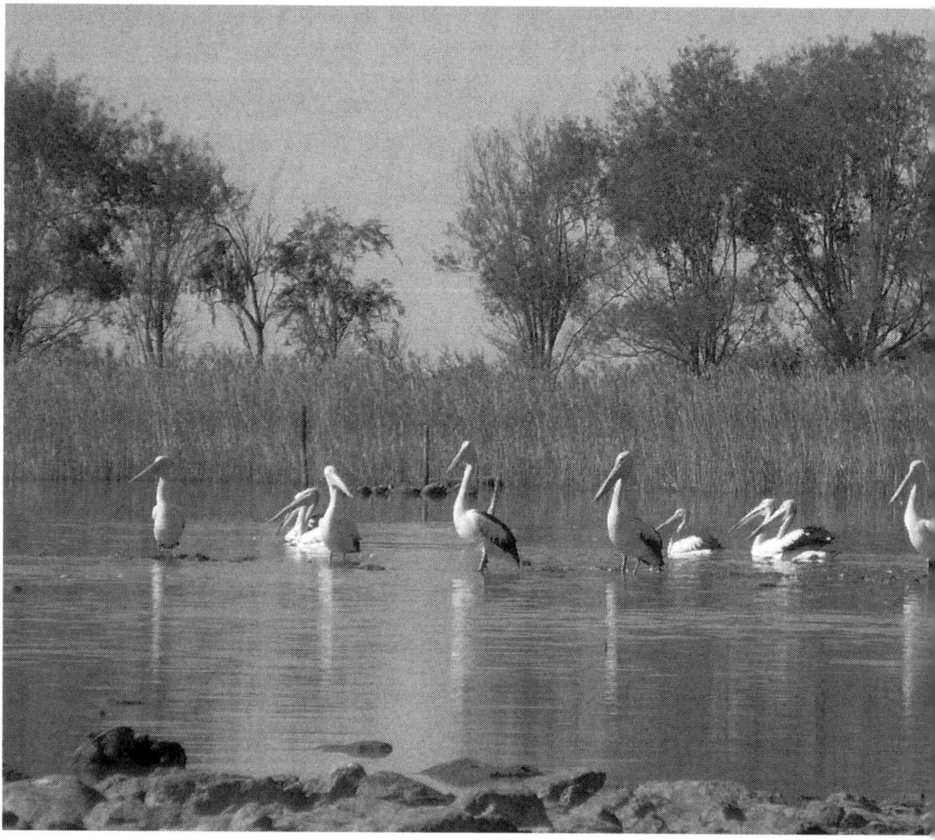

CHAPTER 11

Poltalloch Station

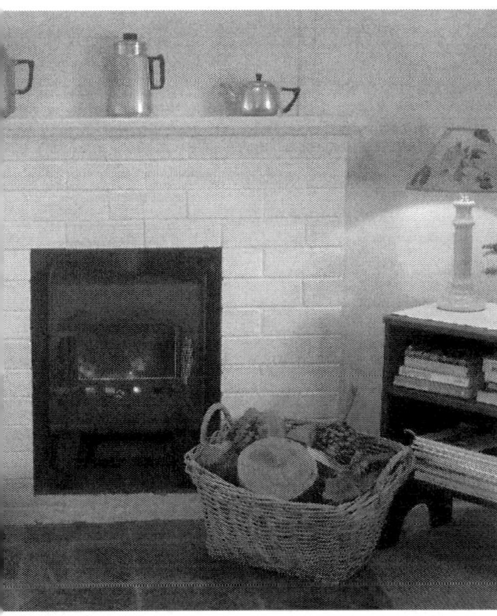

Things happen slowly at Poltalloch Station, a 5500-acre cattle station on the eastern shoreline of Lake Alexandrina in the southeast corner of South Australia. Days pass slowly, its historic buildings age slowly, and mealtimes and the spectacular sunsets that are mirrored each afternoon in the lake at the end of the day seem to linger longer than they should. Walking tours are at a leisurely pace around its plentiful collection of sheds, huts, outbuildings and worker's cottages. It might take a little time to adjust to the rhythm of the place, but a couple of days here and adjust you will, and despite its sanguine appearance you'll soon be finding plenty of things 'to write home about', like the day a black Angus cow swam across the lake.

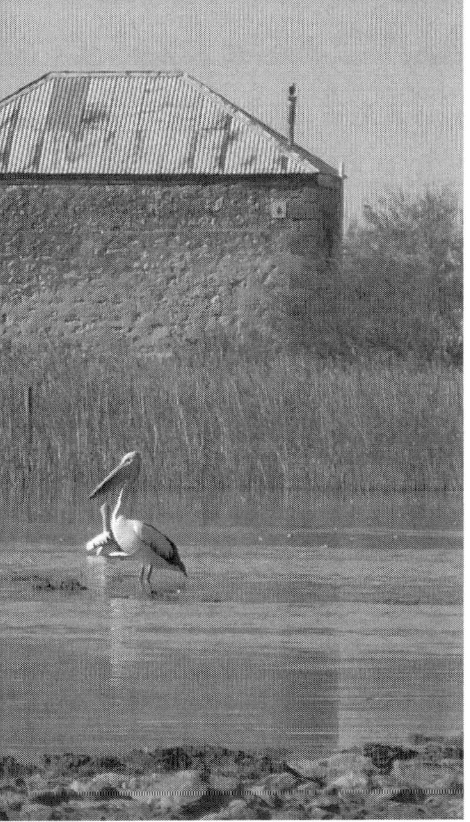

clockwise from top left Boundary Rider's Cottage accommodation; the Boundary Rider's fireplace, for that perfect night in; Lake Alexandrina and the old pumphouse.

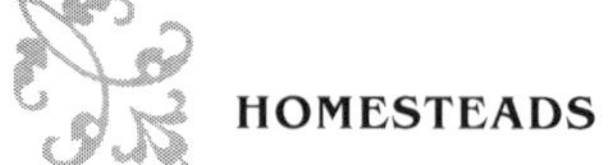

right A rewarding tour of Poltalloch Station includes a walk through its limestone stables, Blacksmith's shop, General Store and the old barn.

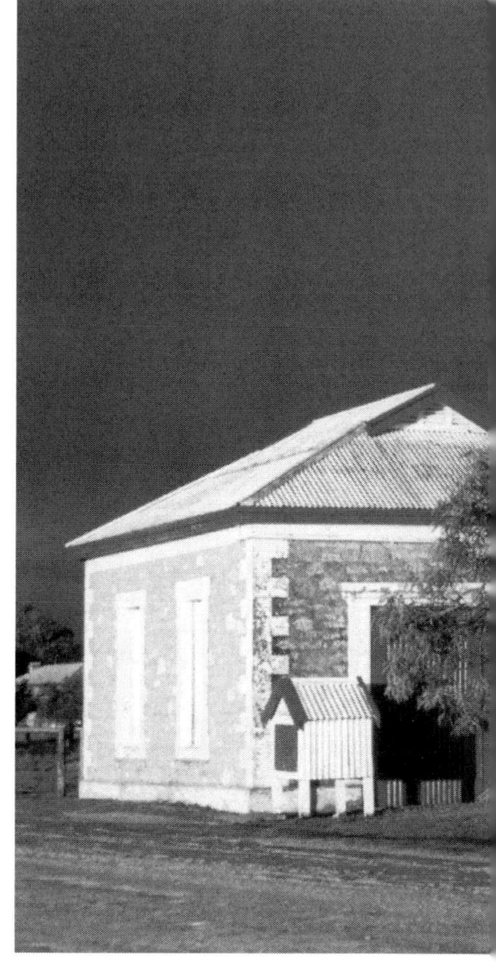

I count myself lucky I was present the day one of Poltalloch's prize black Angus cows wandered into the shallows of Lake Alexandrina, which in itself was nothing unusual as cows often wade into the shallows of the freshwater lake for a drink and to cool themselves down. Only this time the cow didn't stop till it had walked halfway across along the narrows before crossing the remainder of the lake and onto a property on the other side. The owners of Poltalloch Station, Chris and Beth Cowan, have since responded to this most unorthodox of escape attempts by fencing off all of their lakeshore paddocks. 'We'd often have a cow wander down into the lake and wade around,' Beth confided later, 'and on the odd occasion one might walk out across the narrows and we'd have to ride out and bring it in, but cows don't like to swim and to see "Arthur" swim from there across the lake was an extraordinary sight.'

Chris, Beth and Poltalloch Station are intimately connected to their environment and take their stewardship of the land seriously. Ask them about the reduced flows from the Murray River and its effect on the Coorong wetlands, and you'll be told about disappearing seagrass stocks, the demise of the pelican and of local fish populations, of the disaster that is hyper-salinity and the health of the Murray, which has

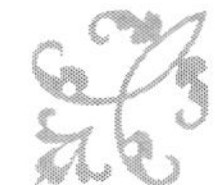

never fully recovered since its mouth closed up for the first time in 1981. At Poltalloch Station you can walk by the still waters of the lake and look back 20 metres to where its high water mark was 15 years ago. It's a sobering sight.

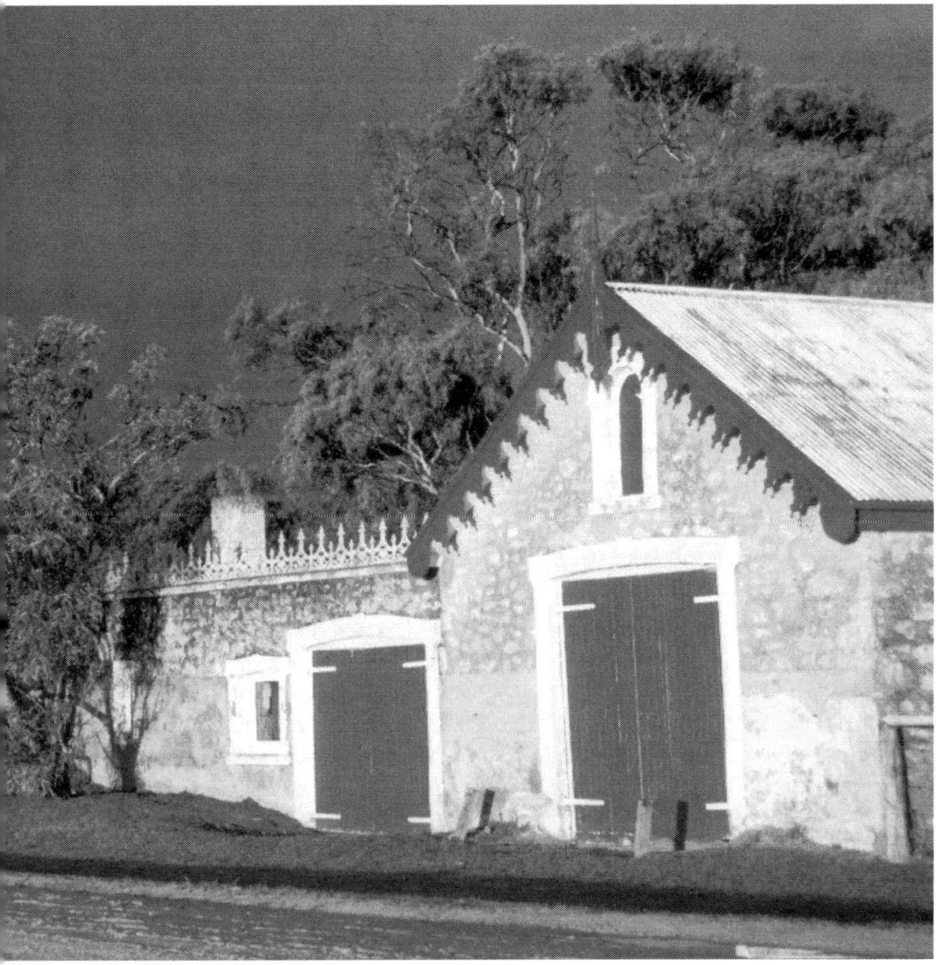

Lake Alexandrina lies between the mouth of the Murray and the Coorong, and is the veritable 'canary in the coal mine'. The Coorong's complex wetlands—a mix of freshwater lakes, saline lagoons, estuaries and ocean—sees Poltalloch Station often doubling as a repatriation centre for sick and injured birds. Cormorants, great egrets and yellow-billed spoonbills are just some of the birds that have found sanctuary in the grounds of Poltalloch over the years. An

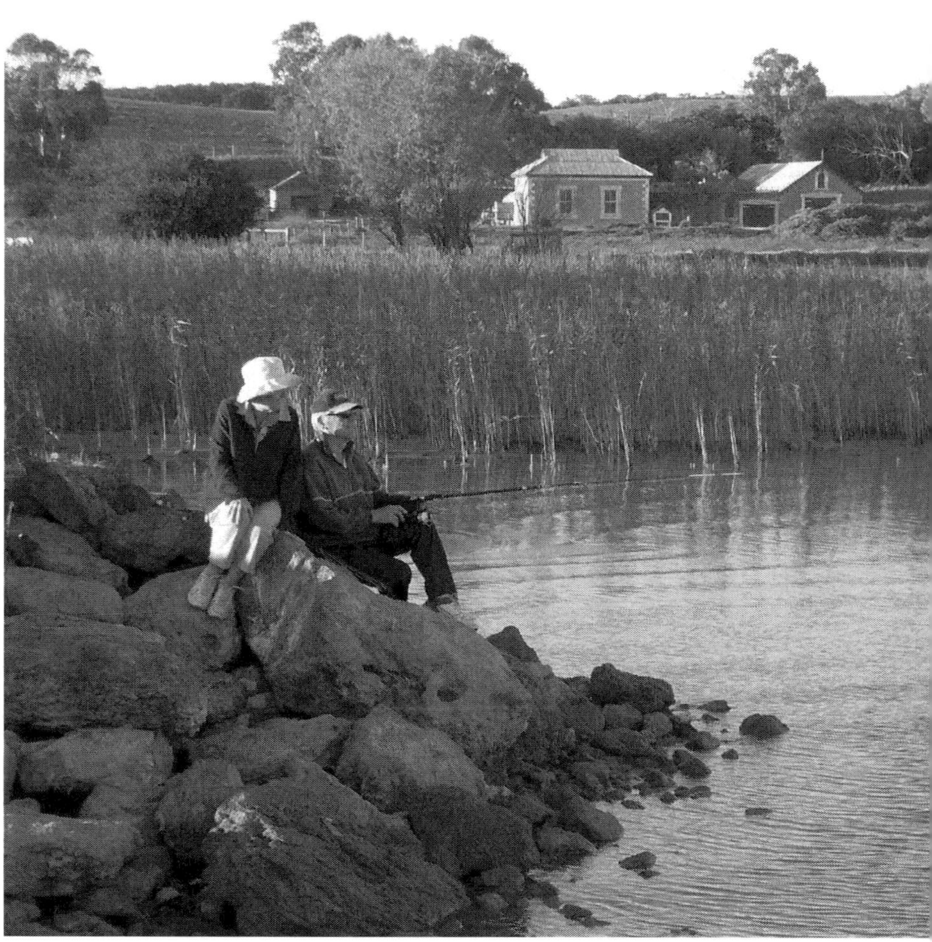

injured barn owl was recently nursed back to health in one of the station's chookyards and Beth took time out to catch field mice to feed it, storing them in one of the station's freezers. One night during an outdoor barbeque a guest was asked to bring some meat from a nearby freezer, went to the wrong one and found herself staring at a collection of frozen mice.

Scattered along the eastern shoreline of Lake Alexandrina, Poltalloch Station looks from a distance like a colonial 'village' whose

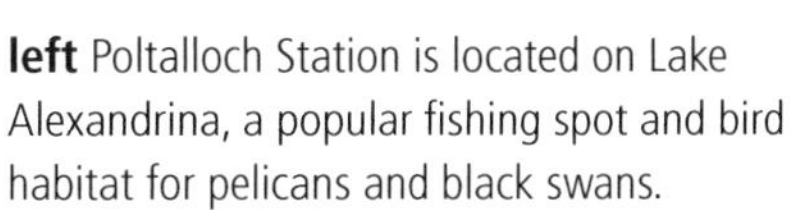

left Poltalloch Station is located on Lake Alexandrina, a popular fishing spot and bird habitat for pelicans and black swans.

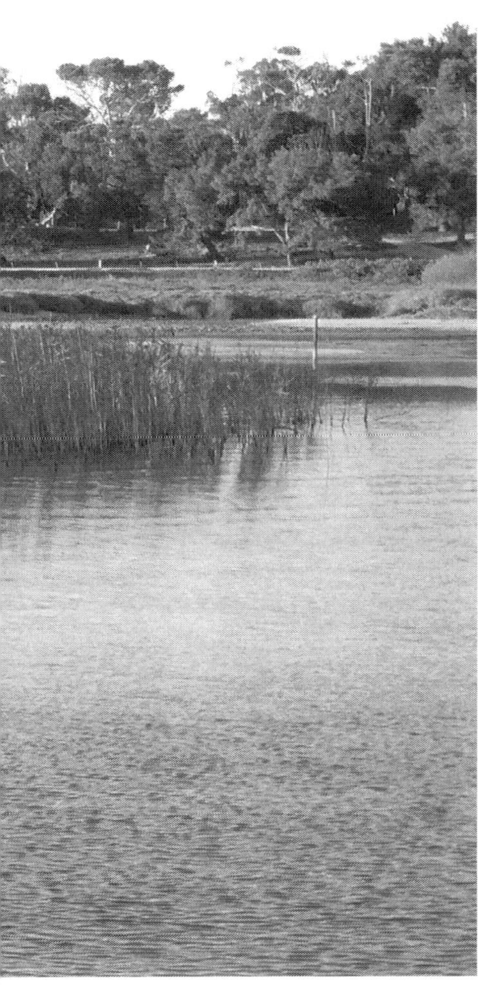

historic structures, of which there are many, are still in perfect harmony with their surroundings and with each other. Established as a cattle station in 1839 by Neill Malcolm of Poltalloch Station in Argyllshire, Scotland, it has continued as a working station ever since and now is home to one of the finest assemblages of dwellings and everyday colonial-era items to be seen anywhere in Australia. The station's oldest properties are a small lakeside hut that dates to the 1840s, and 'Old Station', the original homestead and the oldest South Australian stone home east of the Murray River. The 'Malcolm era' at Poltalloch ended with the purchase of the property by the Bowman brothers in 1873 and the buildings that survive today were all built post-1876. The Bowman's were sheep farmers and the eldest, John, began to build Poltalloch into a self-sufficient 'village' reliant upon Murray River paddlesteamers for supplies.

The Bowmans had a number of pastoral leases throughout the mid 1800s and built up their wealth when labour was often in short supply due to the ongoing Victorian goldrush. One year they even had to shear their own sheep after their shearers made for Ballarat on the strength of rumours that nuggets were literally being found on Ballarat's streets. At the turn of the century John Bowman's son Keith took over the running of Poltalloch and built it up from 26 000 to 30 000 acres. At its peak the property was running upwards of 40 000 sheep. Over the coming generations the station was divided up between various family members and the 5500 acres that comprise Poltalloch Station today includes 17 kilometres of Lake Alexandrina and Albert Channel waterfront and more than 400 acres of native bushland. The focus on livestock has reverted to cattle, notably black Angus cows that are well suited to the region's sandy soils and, as Arthur was able to demonstrate, to the lake as well.

But it is Poltalloch's impressive array of buildings and their ability to transport you back to our colonial past that is its enduring legacy. John Bowman's two-storeyed Victorian homestead cost 4000 pounds and was completed in 1883 using mostly locally quarried sandstone. The wrought iron on its verandah was used as ballast on a transport ship from England. The homestead—which has 27 rooms including a billiard room—is a private residence still in use by the family today, but Chris and Beth are happy for anyone to stroll around its landscaped grounds and enjoy the marvellous views of the lake from its elevated position.

The station's first post-1873 building was its unique, cavernous shearing shed with its double curved corrugated iron roof that was brought down river by paddlesteamer and shaped onsite. Once abuzz with 22 stands and 11 shearers to a side, shearing that once took months is now done in two days by professional shearers from the nearby town of Meningie. An old stone hut that once provided beds for itinerant shearers is now a caretaker's cottage. The shed's storage area once held more than 500 wool bales which were transported to the old jetty on railway tracks, and the shed still contains an impressive array of old wool presses. The buggy room includes a sulky that was once attached to the base of a Model T Ford and a governess cart that used to take the Bowman children on long afternoon rides. And although the windmills that were once used to pump water from the lake are long gone, the round brick pumphouse still remains.

The stone meat house still has the chopping blocks and iron hooks that were used to hang the carcasses of sheep slaughtered to provide meat for the 35 staff once employed here. There was even a general store, now stocked with thousands of items in an immaculate state of preservation including medicine bottles, matches, boxes of Bex tablets and glass balls filled with coloured powder, an early form of clay pigeon once used by Annie Oakley in her Wild West shows. The carpenter's shop includes jigs for the cutting of dovetail joints and old wooden vices. The blacksmith's shop is home to handmade nails forged on site and a groom's room for the groomsman of Keith Bowman's thoroughbred horses still contains original saddles, clippers, polo sticks and side-saddles.

There are no fragments of history here. Poltalloch Station is not a museum. It is our heritage undiluted, raw, and real.

Accommodation is provided in the Old Station Hands' cottage, the Overseer's Cottage, and a Boundary Rider's Cottage, which are not so much 'restored' as more or less unaltered with just one or two appropriate nods to 21st-century comforts. In the absence of suitable timber almost all the buildings were made of iron and stone, materials not prone to decay. A grass area in front of the Boundary Rider's Cottage resembles a kind of 'village green' ringed by the general store, the blacksmith's workshops and the old shearers' quarters. At night a well-placed spotlight bathes the green in a luminous glow. It was here that the station's workers would gather at the close of each day for meals, drinks and revelry that would go long into the night. I can think of few more tranquil settings anywhere in Australia than the view westwards from the porch of Boundary Rider's Cottage with 19th-century buildings, in the foreground, and in the west the fading light of the setting sun as it slips beneath the still waters of the lake.

For the most part, history comes down to us in fragments. Whether it's an old book, a worker's scythe, a mirror, or even a worker's stone or timber cottage. Reminders of our past are often solitary things, separated by time from the hundreds of objects that once surrounded them and imbued them with their own sense of place and purpose. It is rare to find a place where everything from a century ago is still right where it ought to be, intact and at peace, where thousands of individual items still have each other in common and combine to tell a compelling story and open a window onto our pioneering past.

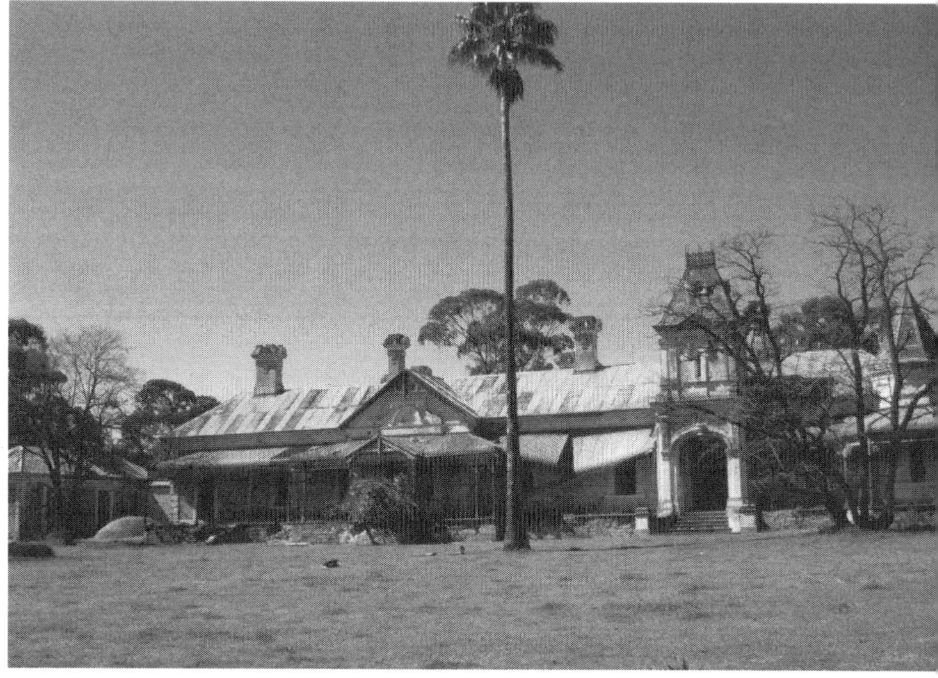

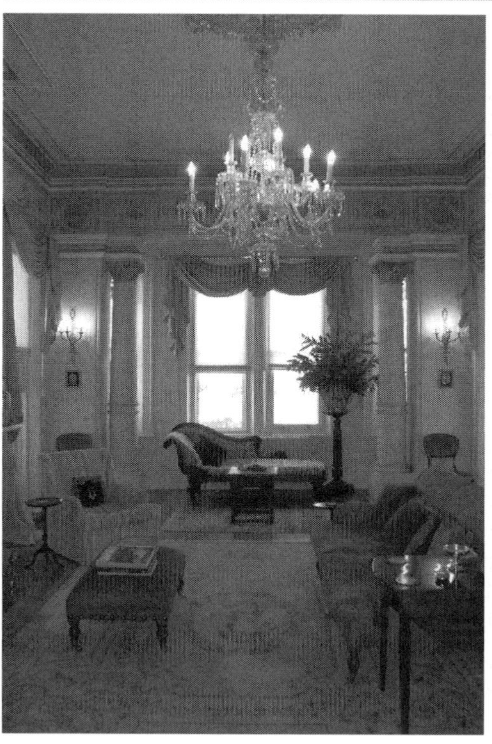

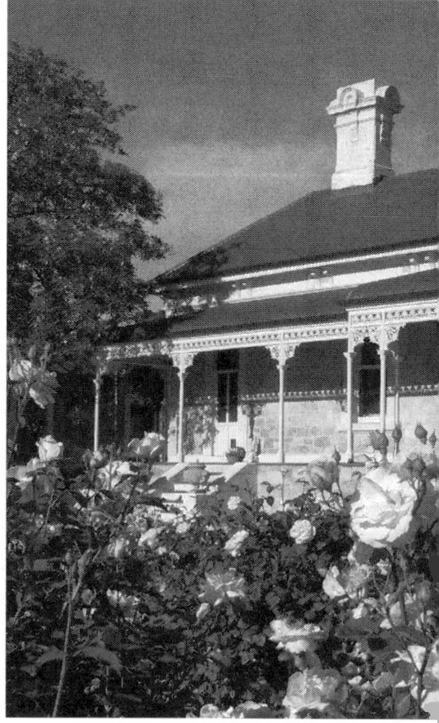

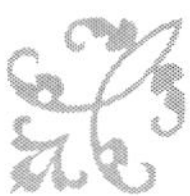

CHAPTER 12

North Bundaleer Homestead

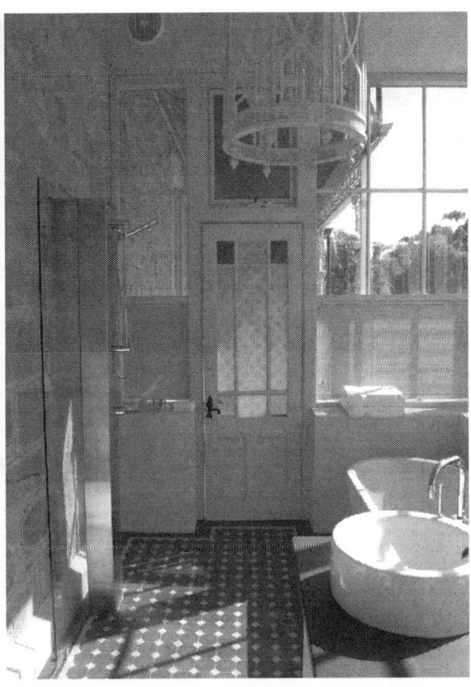

It was late in the winter of 1998 when Malcolm and Marianne Booth first saw North Bundaleer Homestead. It had been raining on and off throughout the day and the rain had captured the dust and cleared the air and you could see forever. As they approached the Edwardian homestead passing beneath an enormous rainbow and the Jamestown–Spalding road and made their way down the homestead's long driveway, the day's fading light bathed the ageing sandstone walls in rich hues of pink and red. It would be another two months before they actually made the purchase, on Malcolm's birthday in fact, but Marianne was adamant the deal had been done before they even set foot on its front porch. 'We were done like a dog's dinner,' she said.

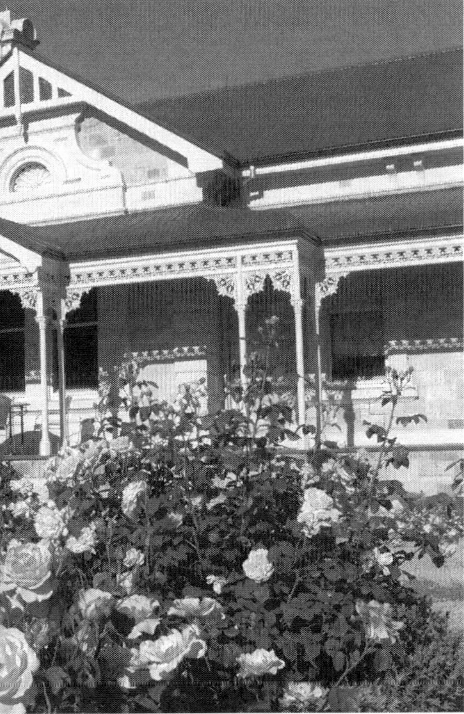

clockwise from top left A 'renovator's delight'; the Red Room's light-filled bathroom; six hundred David Austin roses say hello; the formal drawing room.

As romantic and inevitable as it seems now, looking at the perfection that surrounds me, part of me just doesn't get it. I've been sitting here in my sitting room, which runs off my gorgeous bedroom which is attached to my fabulous bathroom which occupies my positively joy-inducing east-facing conservatory, and I just don't get it. I mean, why would *anyone* want to take on the restoration of a dilapidated, sheep-infested, overgrown 1901 homestead within a hair's breadth of being demolished halfway between Adelaide and the Flinders Ranges on the fringes of the South Australian outback? What could have prompted them to go against the advice of their family, their friends, and almost all of the 1600-strong population of nearby Jamestown, none of whom wanted to touch it with a barge pole? Was it really *Mission: Impossible?*

It's fortunate that the home's previous owner (a local farmer who didn't live there but owned the land the homestead was on) decided not to bulldoze it. From all accounts it was a near thing, although the stonemason who helped in its restoration laughed when Marianne told him that razing it to the ground had once been considered. 'I'd liked to have seen them try,' he said. The house may have looked like a candidate for demolition, but it had been well built in its day, its foundations were strong, and it wouldn't have given up its position on South Australia's mid-north plains easily.

The rebuild started with the chimneys. There are nine sandstone chimneys at North Bundaleer and each one took a full week to restore. Then, attention turned to the roof, several sections of which had collapsed and taken ceiling roses, cornices and everything else with them. That might sound bad enough, but it's only when you take a look at Malcolm and Marianne's collection of 'before and after' photographs that you begin to get a sense of the herculean task that faced them.

Sections of the veranda roof on the front facade had collapsed and the verandah it was supposed to be shading had to be demolished. New concrete footings were poured and the verandah rebuilt from the ground up using a mix of new and recycled sandstone blocks from the original wall. The south-facing and east-facing verandahs were similarly brought back to life and their posts and ornate capitals cleaned and

---

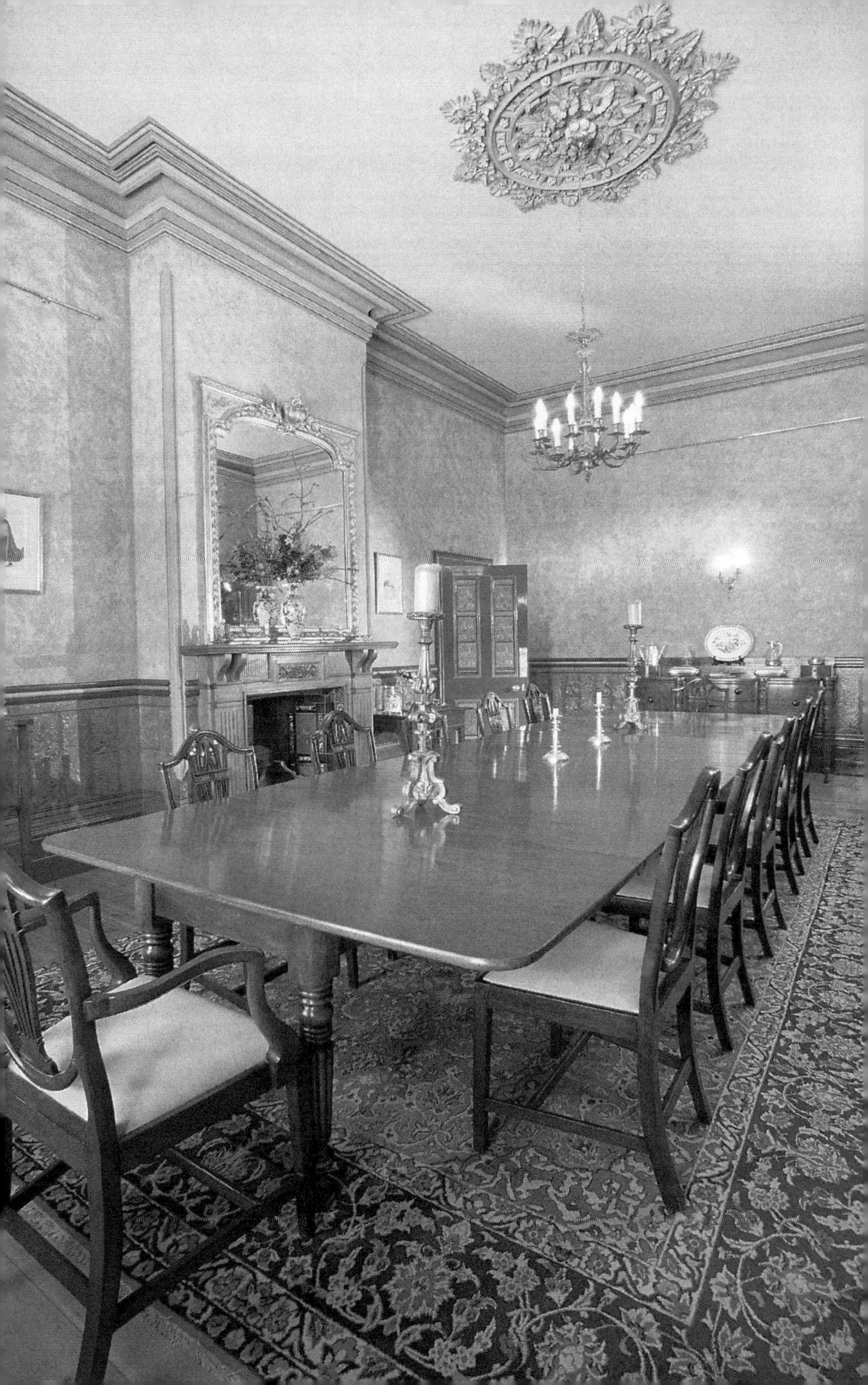

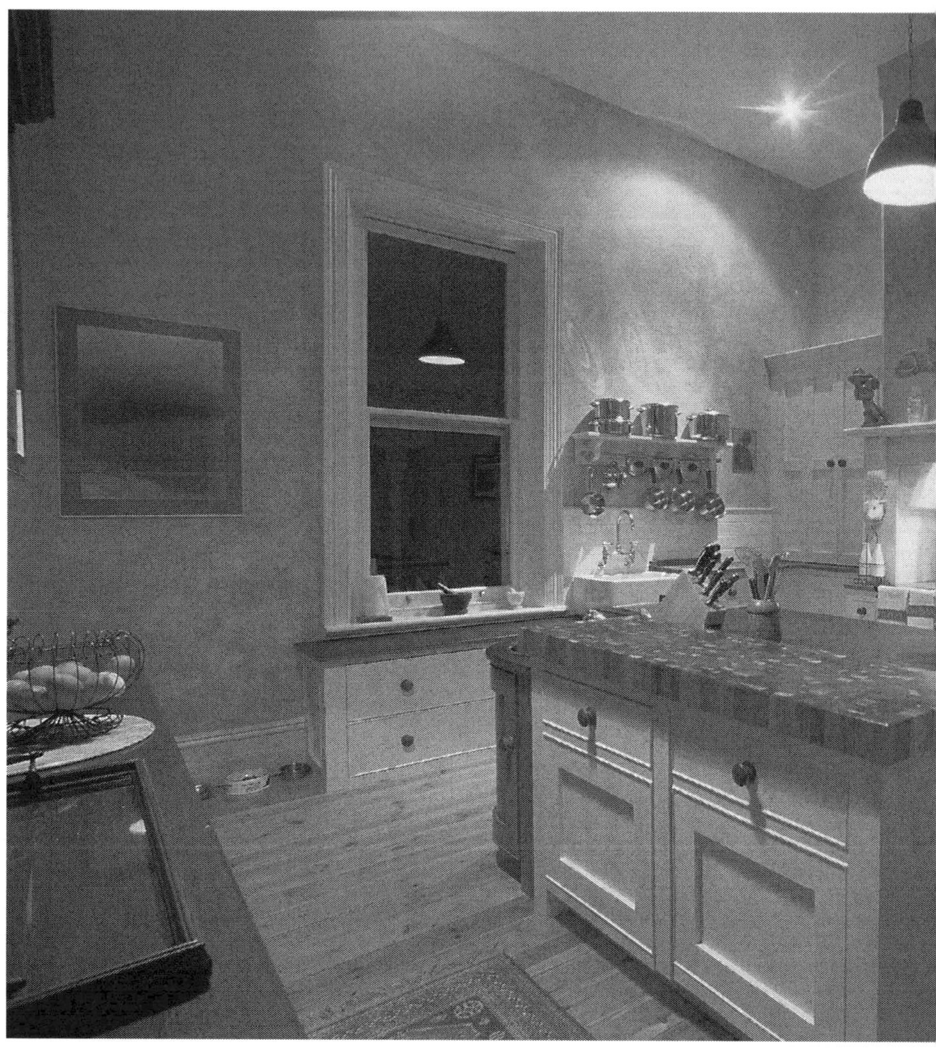

restored. The front stairs were demolished and reconstructed. The front gables were restored, the gutters replaced, and the iron lacework was stripped back and repainted. The exterior of the south-facing bay windows was cleaned and restored as were the detailed carvings above each of its windows. And that's just the exterior.

The interior will mean different things to different people, but for me it was the wallpapers that I couldn't take my eyes off. I'd never seen such extensive and intact examples of Lincrusta dados and Anaglypta, wallpapers with raised, hand-painted reliefs that gave the

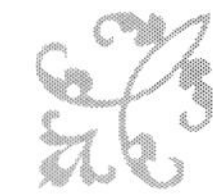

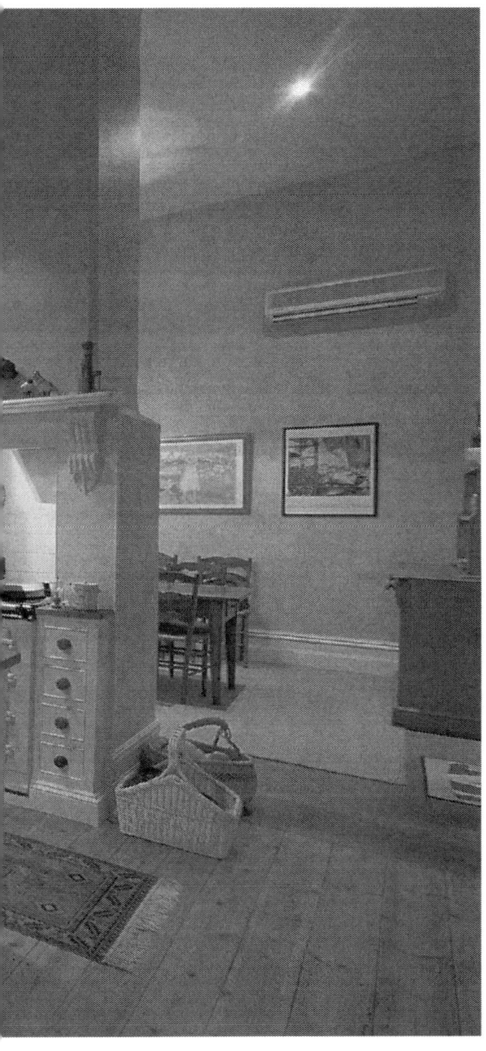

left The heart of North Bundaleer Homestead is its kitchen, with its AGA gas-fired stove and breakfast retreat at rear.

house a truly sumptuous look. And then there were the precious leadlights, hand-painted by the prominent South Australian stained-glass artist E.F. Troy and including one panel by the entry door personally signed by Troy himself. The panels had mercifully been removed from the house by the National Trust in the 1980s and kept in safe storage until the day came when someone would again take North Bundaleer under their wing. Marianne recalled the day when the windows returned and were refitted into their original frames. When the job that was thought would take a week took only a day, that became the day she felt the house had at last recovered its soul.

Tradesmen were brought up from Adelaide because there weren't enough available locally, and Malcolm and Marianne lived in a separate residence on the property during the restoration process, which took three years. The procession of tradesmen that journeyed up from Adelaide were fed and housed in some of North Bundaleer's outbuildings. Marianne cooked all their meals and also provided them with beer, wine and cheese at the end of each day so they could all stay on the property and not have to drive into nearby Jamestown. Tradesmen worked from Monday to Friday, overlapping and occasionally tripping over one another and only going home on weekends.

What they all made when the dust had settled is not just a homestead or a guesthouse, but a comfortable home, the original layout of which remains largely unaltered with bedrooms, sitting rooms, a library and dining room all coming off a stunning central ballroom.

When a hotel or guesthouse is a long way from anywhere and dining options are limited, what it can or cannot offer in regards to cuisine will often determine if a property survives or fails. Predictably, North Bundaleer manages to excel in serving its guests some mighty fine food. My dinner consisted of grilled duck breasts in a lemon and saffron-scented pilaf with fried shallots and a lemon soufflé for dessert, courtesy of North Bundaleer's own chef Leo Hollingshead and taken in the dining room around a magnificent six-leaf Georgian dining table. And like any grand home its heart is the kitchen with its centrepiece a magnificent four-oven AGA gas-fired stove, imported from England, which enables Marianne to create her own gastronomic triumphs. Just off the kitchen a butler's pantry is stocked with everything from rich Amantillado sherry to the finest of Clare Valley wines from which house guests can help themselves as often as they like. It's included in the tariff.

Getting here is an adventure. The only way you know you're closing in on it, apart from just kind of 'sensing it', is when you pass highway marker 'J15' on the road to Jamestown. Even then, when you drive through its typically rural front gate, apart from the tantalising glimpses of its chimneys rising from behind its Kurrajong trees and Aleppo pines, you can't really see it until you're almost upon it, which is precisely how its designer intended for it to be. The driveway is cleverly curved and takes you along in a gradual loop that only reveals the homestead at the point where the trees permit it to be revealed. It's quite a moment, like a curtain going up on opening night.

Then as you move closer the house reveals a series of little 'surprises'. You assume the gable ahead of you is over the entry door, but as you approach the gate that takes you into the homestead's front garden, you see that North Bundaleer is asymmetrical, with the main entry to the right of centre underneath an ornamental clock tower and a second, conical tower behind which together seem to serve no purpose other than to demonstrate the power of whimsy. Add the building's projecting south bay, corner pavilion and profusion of gables, capitals and fretwork—not to mention the 600

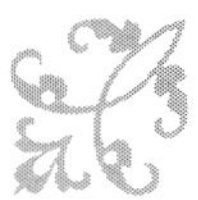

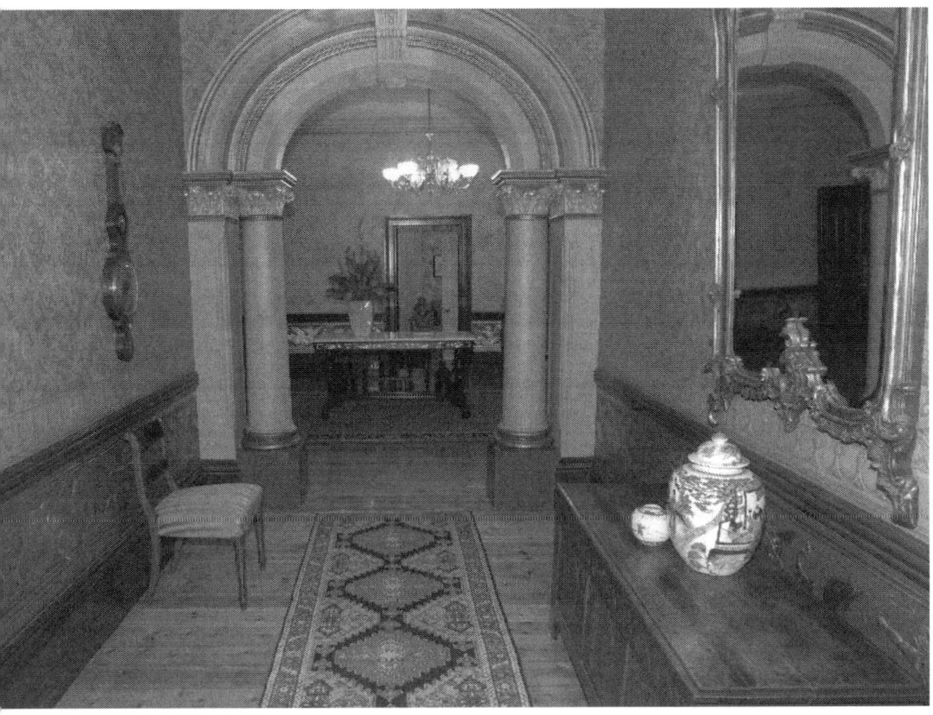

above Looking along North Bundaleer's grand entry with its hand-painted wallpapers towards the central ballroom.

David Austin roses that dominate the homestead's front garden—and you're guaranteed to fall under the spell of this beautiful home, just as its owners did before you, prior to even getting out of your car.

The region surrounding Bundaleer was first selected in 1841 by John Hughes in the wake of reports from the explorer Edward John Ayer that good pastoral land was available in the mid-north of the new colony. Once comprising more than 800 square kilometres, the property was purchased by Robert Maslin, who later divided it between his two sons. His son George Maslin became the owner of the northern portion, slightly more than 9300 hectares, which he named North Bundaleer. Sadly, though, its life as a working homestead was pitifully short. It was purchased by the South Australian government in 1911, just ten years after its completion, and was further subdivided until what was left wasn't deemed large enough to be economically viable. The house was abandoned in the early 1970s, registered on the State Heritage Register in 1983 and the

right The closer you get the more North Bundaleer chooses to reveal itself, here showing off five of its nine sandstone chimneys, each of which took a week to restore.

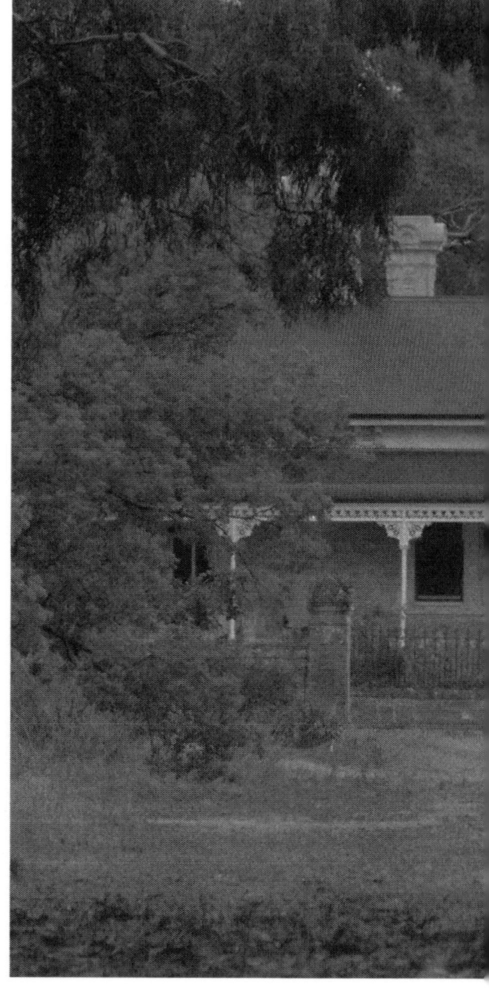

National Trust of South Australia in 1984, and had been empty for more than two decades when Malcolm and Marianne purchased it.

Then they took North Bundaleer from a building that had been abandoned for nigh-on 25 years and perilously close to falling in on itself and turned it into a five-star retreat that made Condé Nast's 2003 '80 Best New Hotels In The World' list and *Asian Geographic's* 'Ten Top Colonial Homes In The Asia-Pacific'. That's not just impressive, it's positively awe-inspiring. Along with Faversham House in York, Western Australia (see Part 5: Grand Mansions), North Bundaleer is unquestionably the 'wreck to riches' success story of this book. What was achieved in the end was and remains an unqualified triumph and the very definition of the phrase 'faithful restoration'.

Before I came to leave there was one last thing Malcolm and Marianne were determined to show me—the view from the top of their hill. North Bundaleer is the centrepiece of a 400-acre property and its setting in the landscape can only be truly appreciated from on high. The track to the hill's 'summit' is strewn with such a profusion of surface rocks that a 4WD is the only practicable way to get there, and as we bumped our way along, Malcolm reminded me that 'Bundaleer' is the Aboriginal word for 'a rocky place'.

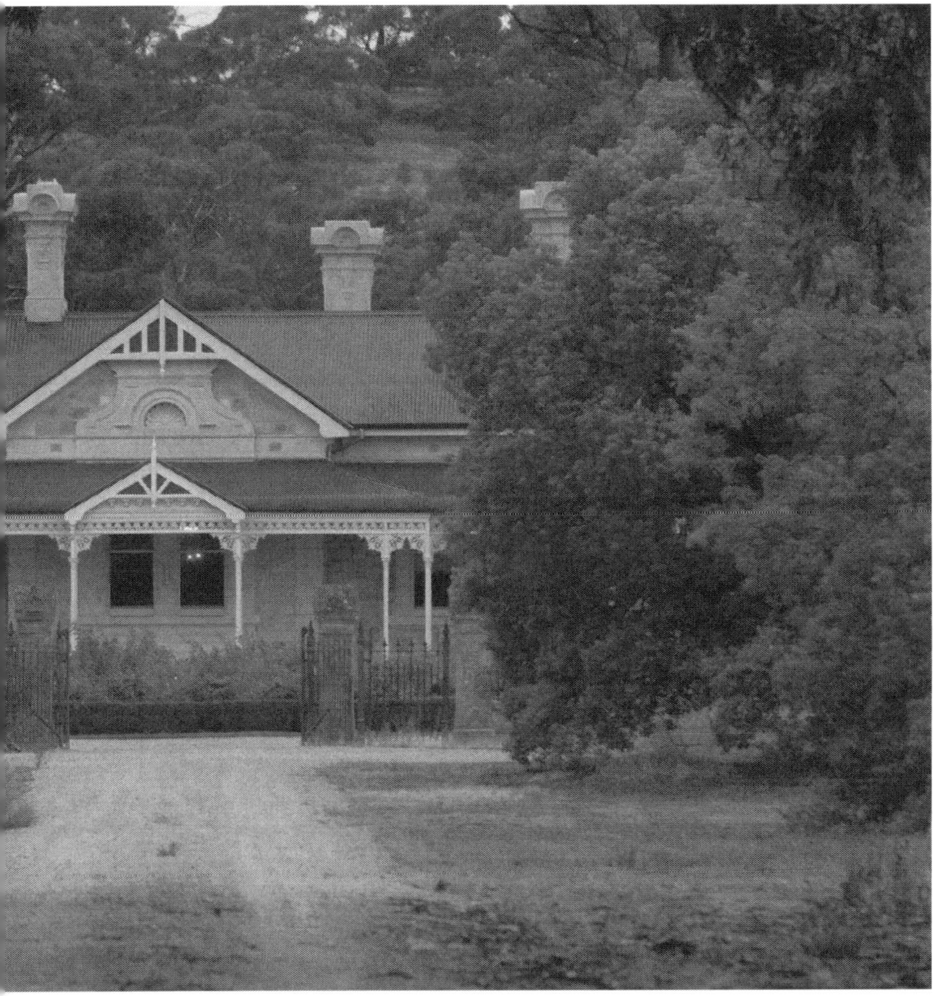

From the top you can see forever. To the north 12 kilometres away there is Jamestown. To the south are rolling hills and pastures sprinkled with cattle. To the east are the wheat fields of the adjoining property, and to the west the trees of the Bundaleer Forest. And below us amongst it all was North Bundaleer Homestead, right where it was always meant to be, ensconced in a manmade world of palms, pines and roses alongside its grove of 1000 olive trees, all planted by hand by Malcolm, a grand slice of South Australia's pastoral heritage in the midst of a Very Big Country.

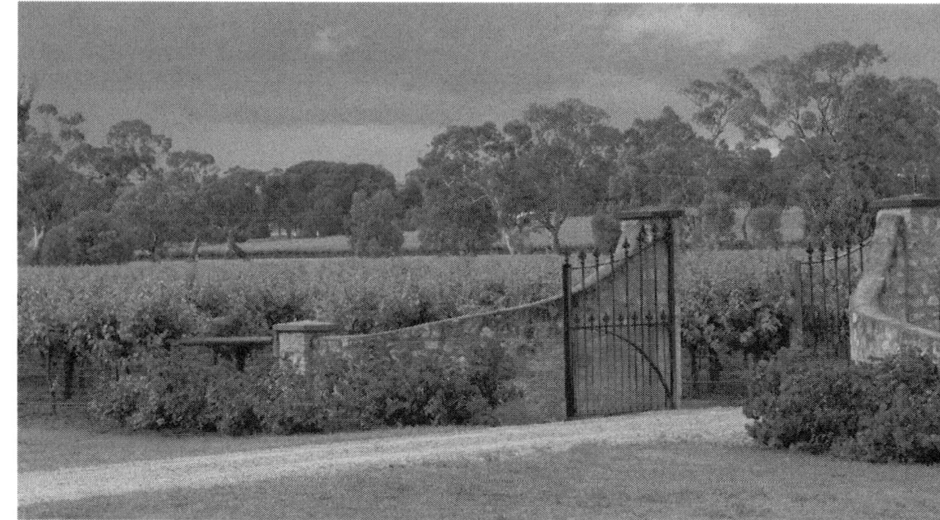

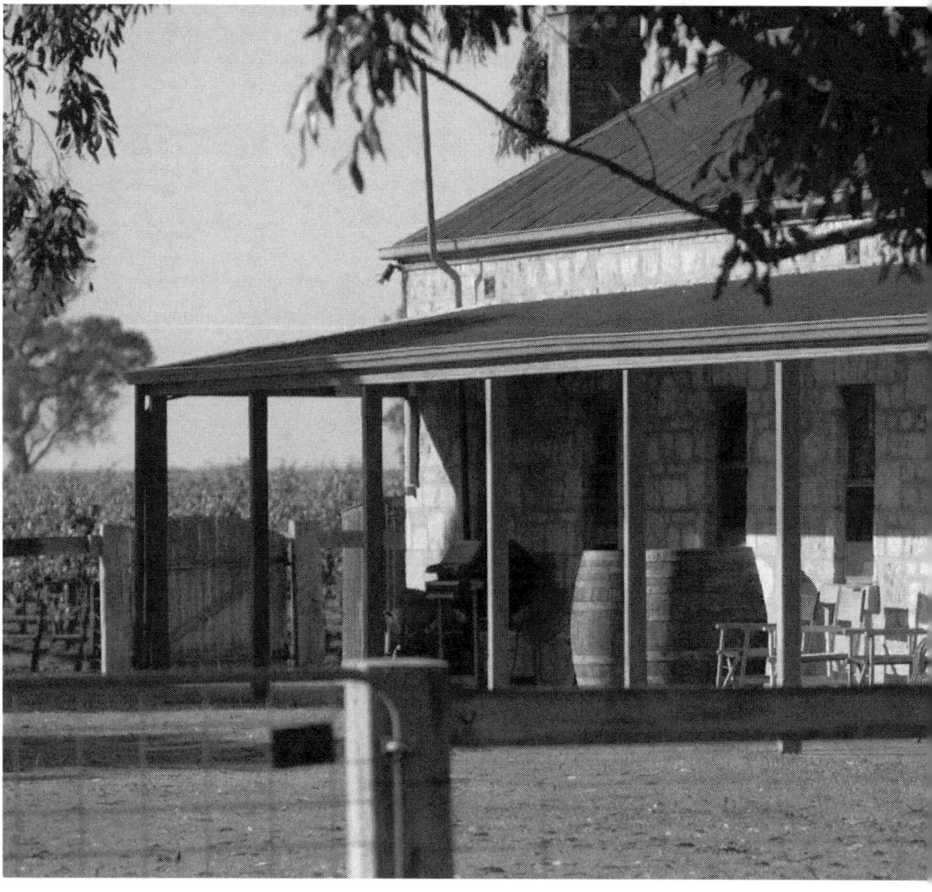

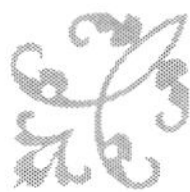

CHAPTER 13

Padthaway Homestead

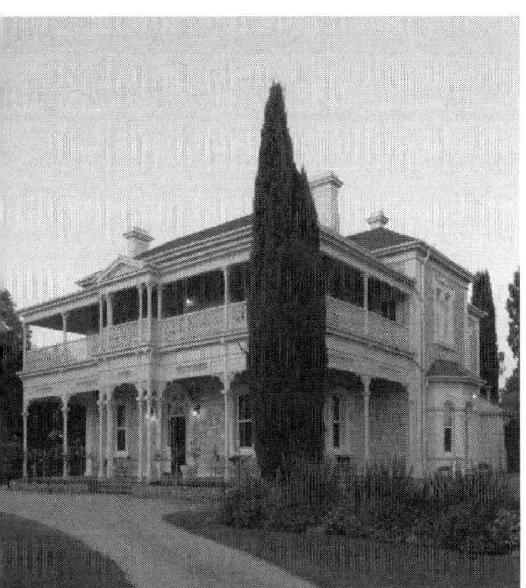

Wine tastings, or 'journeys', as my host Craig prefers to call them, are possible every day at Padthaway Homestead, an 1847 homestead surrounded by 125 acres of vines, 285 kilometres southeast of Adelaide. As an overnight guest in the house I walked from the mansion's porch to its Cellar Door with him and watched as he set up, and I looked forward to being his first customer of the day. And I would have been, too, if two middle-aged Greek couples in a 4WD hadn't muscled in and beat me to it. So I sat in the corner and decided instead I'd watch them take the journey that would, soon enough, be mine.

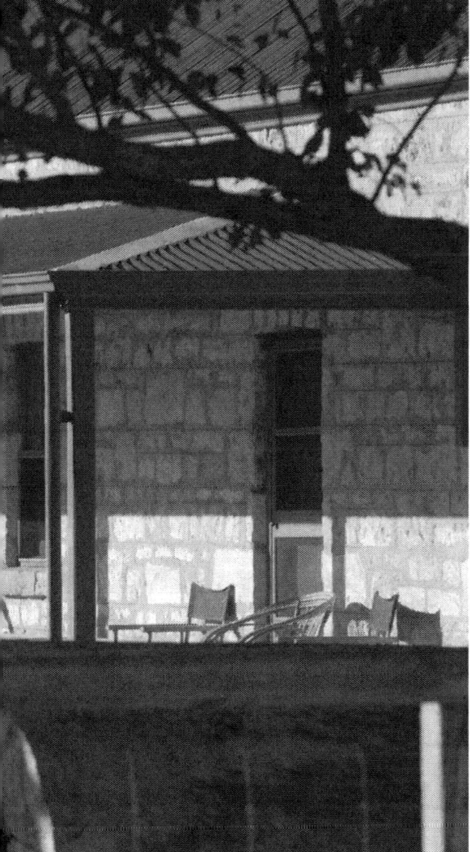

clockwise from top left Vineyards, all the way to the front gate; the 1881 homestead; the shearer's quarters, perfect for families.

107

I also determined I'd listen and learn what I could in the hope of later avoiding displaying my own gross ignorance on the subject of wine and evading the sort of embarrassing pitfalls common to anyone like myself who, sad to say, can barely tell his reds from his whites.

Greece, turns out, had been the international news story of the past two weeks with the announcement that the European Union was going to 'lend' it something like 140 billion Euros to help it avoid bankruptcy, prompting Craig to remind them that this was not, in fact, a gift and that their country would be required to pay it all back one day. From my vantage point this got the journey off to a bumpy start, though things settled down when he guaranteed his guests they wouldn't get drunk— 'You could have a sip of every one [there were 12 bottles altogether] and it won't even fill half the glass. A sip is a sip, and I'll look after you.'

Craig has a science–medical background, and as any science– medical person will tell you, they all think they can grow grapes. He started dabbling in wine in the 1970s but, like so many of us, got distracted by children, family and career, and for many years drifted away from viticultural pursuits. Only in recent years has he been able to revisit it—and his passion for the grape is infectious.

'This is a journey about fruit,' he said as he poured each of his guests a glass of Padthaway's 'ELIZA' 2004 Sparkling Chardonnay. He talked about its quality and its expression, and about the mystery of fermentation and … but the elder of the two Greek women broke in: 'We are not much for the champagne,' she said.

'WHAT?' replied Craig.

'It is nice for celebrations and things, but not for every day.'

I winced. Things were not going well. It was as if a mortal blow had been struck upon my host as he replied with feeling, 'It is nice for BREAKFAST! Oh, my heart bleeds!' and he placed his hand over his heart in lamentation. 'Do you know they refer to unwooded Chardonnay as one of the world's most boring wines because they are texturally flat?'

One of the Greek husbands interjected: 'I come from the finest wine region in the world!'

Craig took a measured breath. 'Well, ONE of them, perhaps?' he suggested graciously. It was like watching a game of chess.

The journey went on from left to right through all 12 wines that Padthaway produce, which is a lot for what is essentially a boutique brewery. Cabernet Sauvignons, a lovely Shiraz, a sparkling Shiraz

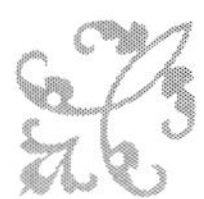

fermented in open vats, a limited release Rosé, and a superb 2006 Pinot Noir Chardonnay, and as the journey progressed we learned things. Elementary stuff, perhaps, like how Sauvignon Blanc was a 'gift' to Australia from New Zealand when, 20 years ago, our Chardonnays were too intense, too unrefined, and along came the Kiwis who said, 'Forget the Chardonnays, try our Sav Blanc'. But you need two sips here—the second sip is better than the first which was needed just to get the palate free of the previous Chardonnay they'd just finished tasting. There's more to the ritual of wine-tasting than meets the eye.

Padthaway's Sauvignon is 'acid driven'—meaning the grapes are picked younger, not 'fruit driven' which means they are more refreshing to the palate. Skins of grapes apparently contain different smelling compounds—Shiraz can have quite a peppery, spicy, cherry or plum type character for instance. One of our Greek hosts then touched a tasting bottle, and it was on again: 'don't touch the tasting bottles! After all, I don't know where your hands have been! The taste needs to remain the same for those after you.' In wine, the purity of the grape is everything.

I learned how, 25 years ago, our Rosés were far too sweet, (i.e. Mateus) but Australians, in their ignorance, thought them quite acceptable. Looking back our palates were unsophisticated. But our tastes have since matured—and our Rosés have matured, too. Instead of fruity and sweet, they are now drier and go well with Asian dishes. Pinot Noir, I also discovered, smells 'smoky' and is very light and nice to have on a hot day.

Meal times at Padthaway are a memorable experience thanks mostly to the exquisite culinary skills of Craig's wife Catherine. Even breakfast has its surprises. I had a delicious muesli which was a mix of a homemade vanilla yoghurt and a chopped up apple, left to 'age' for a few days, because, apparently, the older it gets the better it tastes—the typical sort of philosophy you'd expect, I suppose, in a kitchen surrounded by vineyards. The lamb sausages that followed were a mix of *real* meat enhanced with spinach and feta cheese and served with Swiss brown mushrooms, double-smoked bacon and vine-ripened tomatoes, and the jams at Padthaway are made with grape juice instead of sugar. How very appropriate.

Padthaway made its name as a sparkling winemaker under the Eliza brand—their top-end sparkling Pinot Chardonnay. In late 2009 their Tirage Sparkling Pinot Noir Chardonnay was runner-up for

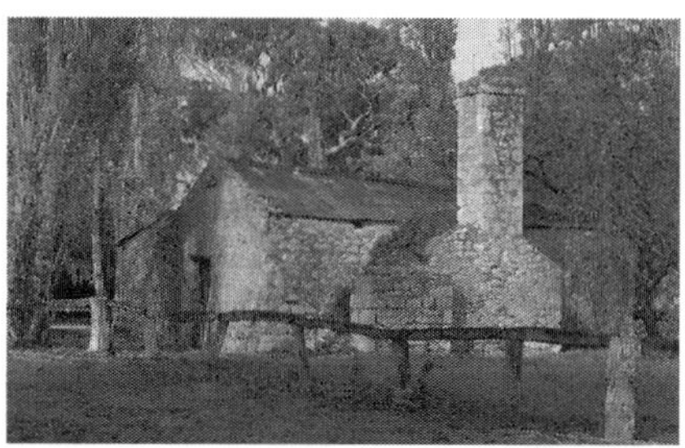

above One of Padthaway Homestead's many history-laden outbuildings.

right The symmetrical splendour of the 22-room Victorian-era mansion as seen from the front garden.

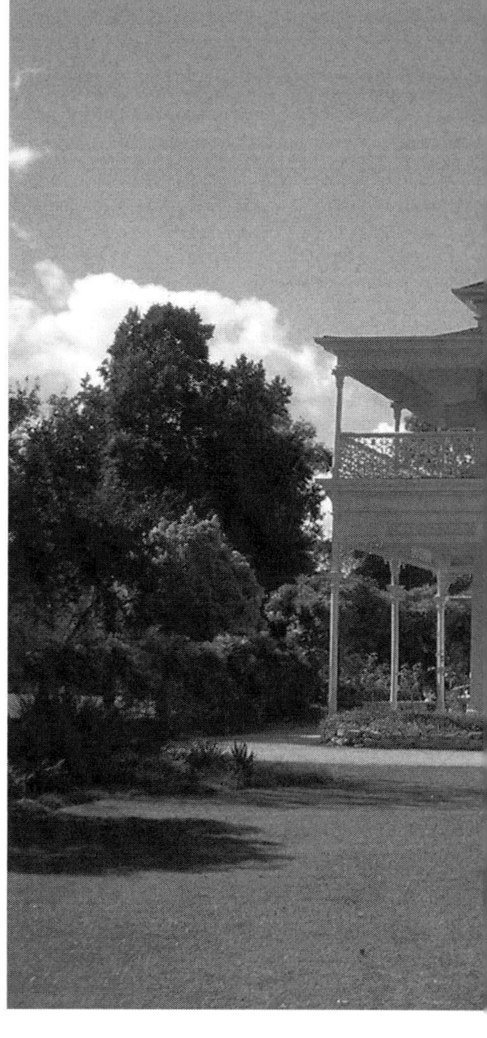

'Australasian sparkling wine of the year'. Their five champagnes are made in the 'méthode tradionnalle'—meaning you take a fermented wine, put it into a bottle and initiate a second (tirage) fermentation phase; this could take 18 months to two years. Then yeast and sugar are added, and the by-products are alcohol with a level of 12–13%, but more importantly this is when the carbon dioxide 'bubble' is formed. It's inherently bitter taste then has to be masked by adding a small amount of sugar syrup, just a few drops, to make the wine palatable. Port was added to the Shiraz I drank with dinner in order to mask the sugar, a process called 'liquering'.

Craig was 'working' his guests, giving me a wink and trying to elicit comments that would make a good story. Sadly they were in a hurry and when he said, 'I'll tell you a story' to try and keep them there, they replied, 'No stories, we don't have time!' Never hurry a wine tasting. Even *I* knew that!

'Alright, no stories,' Craig said. He finished with a Cabernet

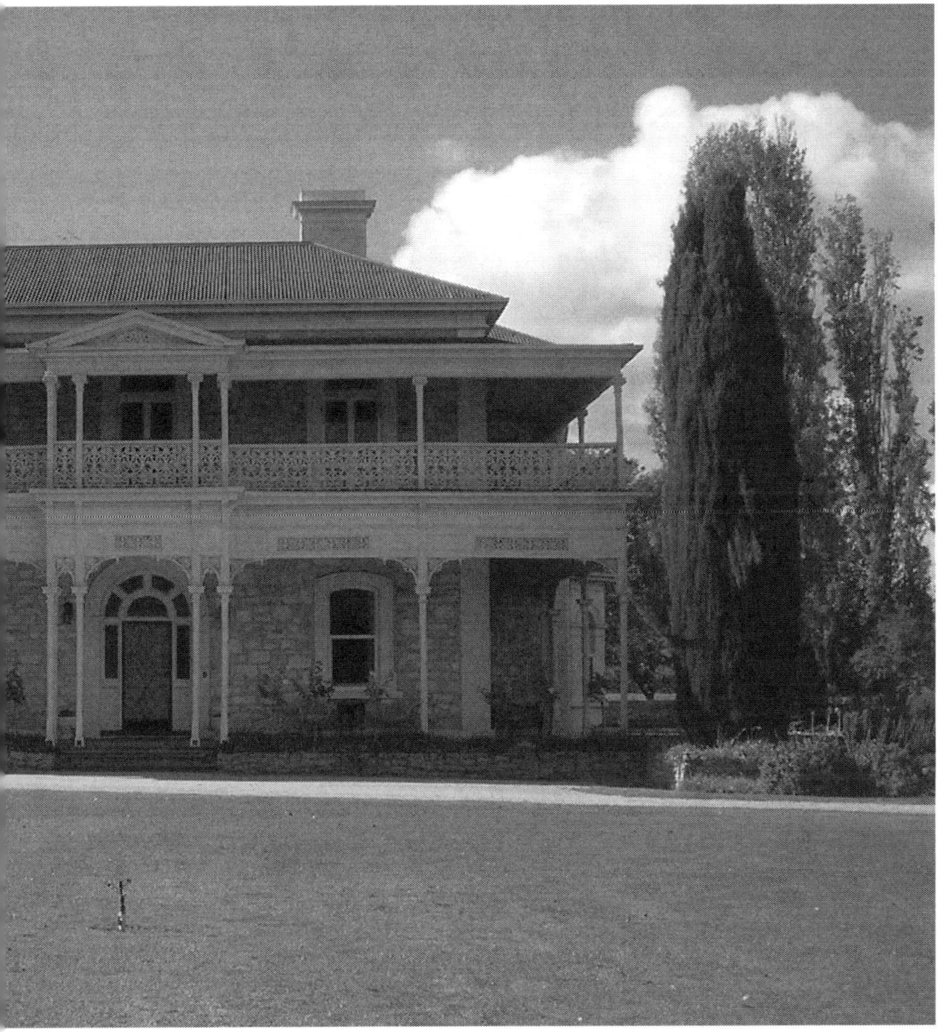

Sauvignon grown in Padthaway's own rich, red terra rosa soil, and then took a gentle swipe at those in the Coonawarra region who think they own terra rosa soil. 'But we're in a pocket of this same soil here at Padthaway—and it gives us a beautifully balanced wine, very earthy and 'mushroomy'.

At Padthaway, you can't talk about the house without talking about the wine. The house may have come first, but these days it is the wine that sustains it. Which is why, I suppose, it's doing so well. But we should really talk about the house.

Padthaway Homestead was built by a woman. Eliza Lawson was born near Edinburgh, Scotland, in 1822 and emigrated to Australia in 1848. She married a carpenter and sheep farmer, Robert Lawson, and the two of them moved to the Tatiara–Padthaway district southeast of Adelaide where they lived in the simple stone cottage you can still see near the main house today, the first stone building in the region.

Robert gained what used to be called an 'occupational run', essentially a parcel of land determined by taking a line from one perimeter tree to the next, then building a fence line from tree to tree. In the 1850s occupational runs were altered and became 'pastoral leases'. Richard took up a 50 000-acre allotment, worked the land, and he and Eliza eventually had eight children. Their second and fourth daughters died in infancy and are buried on the property. By 1860 their property had grown to encompass almost 130 square miles, and they were running more than 26 000 sheep and several hundred head of cattle.

Tragedy struck when Robert died in his sleep whilst on a business trip to Adelaide in 1876, leaving Eliza to continue on her own. However, it was in response to this that caused Eliza to at last find her own financially savvy feet. She bought out all the non-family trustees in the estate, constructed new shearers quarters and shearing sheds, and within ten years owned the freehold on the property. She oversaw an increase in her land holdings, and in 1881 commenced construction on a grand new home—a 22-room two-storey Victorian mansion in the middle of nowhere. Robert Jnr eventually took over the day-to-day running of the property. Eliza never remarried and became the archetypal family matriarch. She died in 1913 at the age of 91, the guiding force behind a truly pioneering estate in a region that didn't begin to see other homesteads constructed in the area until late into the 1930s. It's easy to see why it is only *her* initials—EL—that appear on the keystone at Padthaway's entry door and on the bottom of every cork that goes into a Padthaway bottle.

Robert and Eliza's descendants continued to live at Padthaway, with the exception of the years 1944–49 when the house was purchased by the South Australian government, until 1979 when the banks foreclosed on the Lawson family. They were permitted to stay on in the main house for a couple of years before relocating to the old stone cottage.

A consortium of buyers later purchased the property and the surrounding 125 acres and began to plan for the creation of the next

phase of the property's unfolding story, a winery they would name
Padthaway Estate. The first vineyards in the Padthaway region
were planted at Keppoch in the early 1960s by Karl Seppelt, mostly
because the land here at the time was so cheap and he couldn't afford
to buy into the Coonawarra. Hardy's soon followed and nowadays it
is a 'distinct region'—a 'GI', or Geographical Indication similar to the
appellation areas of France. Padthaway's vines were first planted by
Hardys in 1981. Up until then the land surrounding Padthaway House
was strictly pastoral. But all that was about to change.

Stories flow effortlessly at a Padthaway dinner. It had been a big
day for my hosts, Craig and Catherine. Their only daughter had flown
out from Adelaide that morning to train for two years as a sommelier
at The Gleneagles Hotel in Scotland. Their son, too, is overseas,
pursuing an education courtesy of the baseball team the 'Philadelphia
Phillies' after having played for them in the 'Single A's' league. Picked
up by the Phillies as a 17-year-old in South Australia, Angus was
taught how to bat by Craig who used to play at primary school in
Mt Gambier, represented Australia at university level for four years,
and played in the Claxton Shield series in S.A. Angus plays centre
field. Needless to say, he's got a proud dad.

There isn't a restaurant within 50 kilometres of Padthaway, so if
you stay here be prepared to eat here. I could think of worse fates.
Its elegant dining room provides a perfect stage for the strutting of
its food and wines. Craig sees his role as encouraging people to have
fun with wine, and Catherine never tires of providing the perfect
meal. When you come here and combine it all, the wine, the food,
the house, the conversation, its collection of historic outbuildings and
the purity of its vines, well, what more could you possibly ask for?

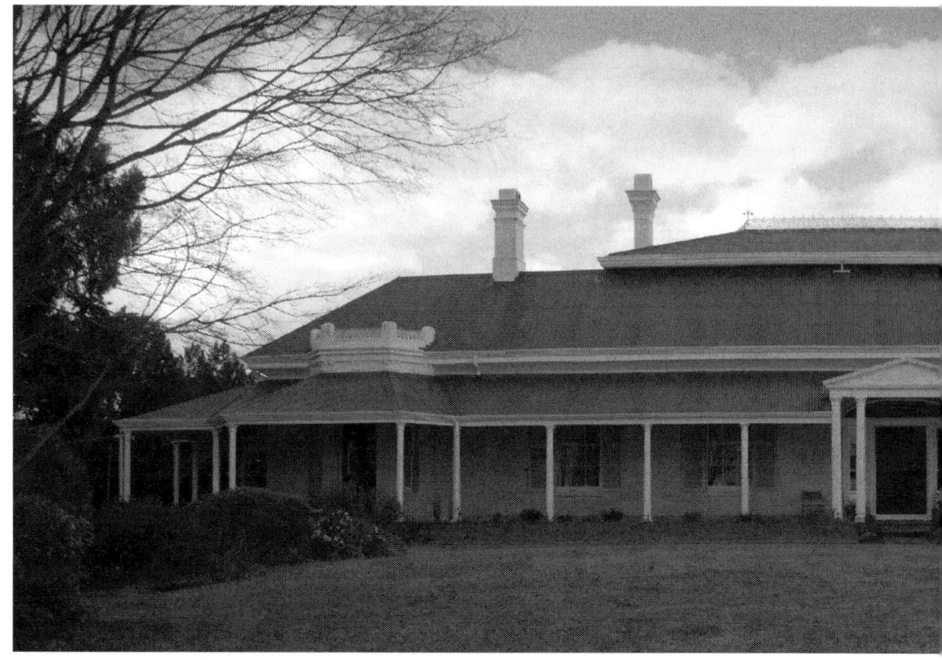

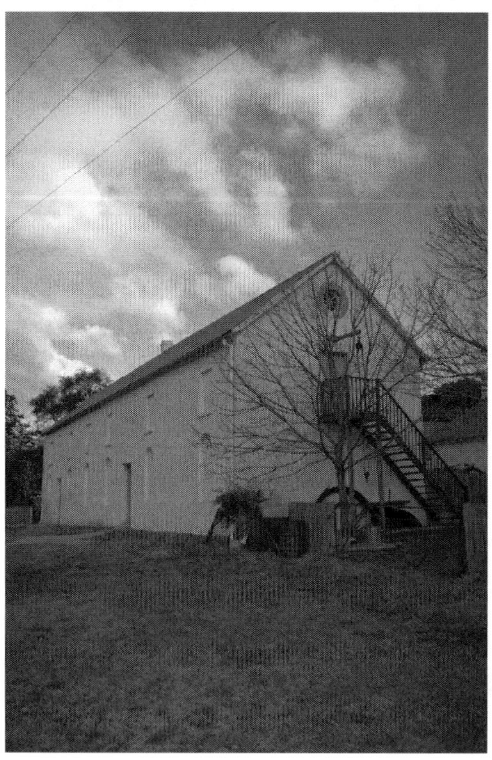

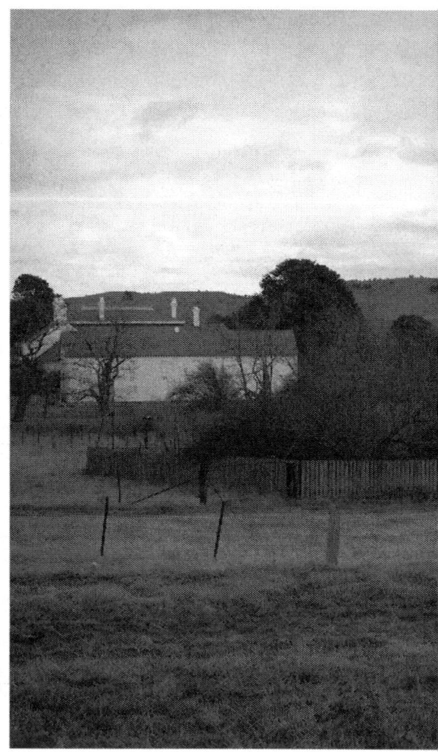

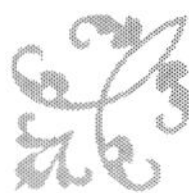

Bedervale Homestead

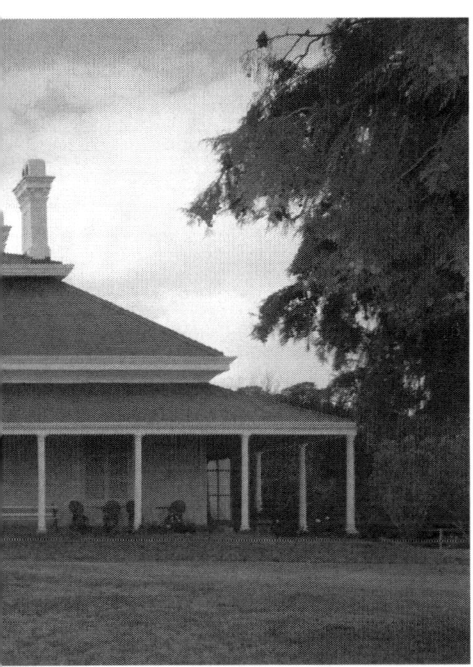

When I began to write this book, people warned me that I'd be encountering my fair share of ghost stories. Ghosts seem to be an unofficial 'must have' in the world of the historic hotel, a sort of 'spiritual status symbol', and proprietors and managers often talk in casual, off-hand manners about what they like to call their 'permanent residents'. Most were unashamedly 'manufactured'; they were told with too broad an accompanying smirk. Most ghost stories are simply that—stories. Guests, for the most part, enjoy hearing tales about things that go bump in the night, and there's certainly no shortage of people who like to tell them.

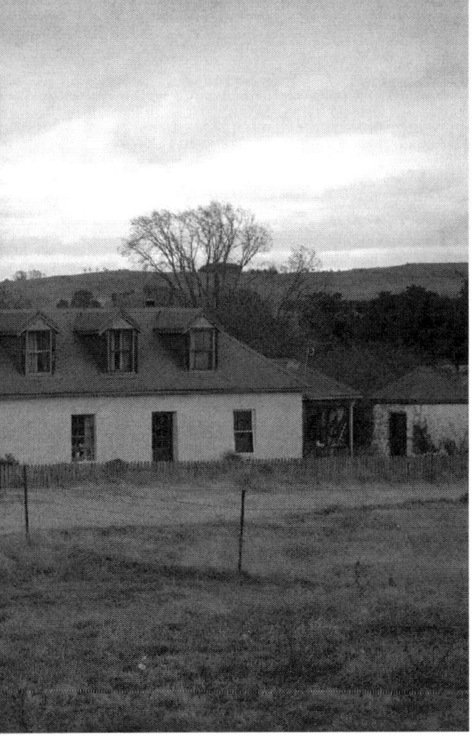

clockwise from top left Bedervale's contents were purchased en masse by the National Trust; Gardener's Cottage; the homestead's immaculate two-storey Georgian stables.

For the sake of the book's integrity I didn't want to be led down every spooky path offered me and so I promised myself I'd take any and all ghost stories with a grain of salt, and mostly I did. There were a couple of exceptions, though. Q Station at North Head is known to be one of the most haunted sites in the country; and there was one proprietor in Tasmania with a very specific story to tell who then immediately asked me not to refer to it—it's cost them enough business already. Then late one Saturday afternoon I arrived at Bedervale Homestead, outside Braidwood in southern New South Wales, and although I didn't know it at the time, was about to be offered up a ghost story I simply couldn't refuse.

I was sitting with the homestead's owner Margaret and her daughter Victoria over a cup of coffee in the 'new' dining room, an addition Margaret's late husband Roger added at the southern end of the verandah simply because the rooms in the original house were too cluttered with national treasures to ever be turned into effective living spaces. Victoria, a sculptor and artist who was once chased out of Pakistan's Hunza Valley after being mistaken for a foreign spy, returned to Australia and lived for a time in Queensland before moving back to Bedervale after her father passed away, to help Margaret with the hundred-and-one things a property like this needs done every day. Victoria began her public life with exhibitions at Sydney's Holdsworth Gallery in 1975, and several fine examples of her work can be seen today scattered throughout Bedervale's extensive gardens.

Margaret and Roger purchased the house in 1973 and one of the first stories they heard after moving in was of the lady in the gatehouse a century or so ago whose job it was to open and shut the estate's iron gates whenever a horse and carriage passed through. One rainy night, however, she was absent for reasons unknown, forcing Bedervale's then owner, Mr Maddrell, to alight from his carriage and open the gate himself. Her absence so incensed him that he terminated her employment the very next morning. The woman, whose name is lost to history, responded to the termination of her employment by placing a curse on the house.

A lot of odd things began to happen at Bedervale soon after Margaret and Roger moved in. The windmill blew down and the roof on the gatehouse mysteriously caught fire. The water tank then collapsed, the dog died, and so did a horse. Then Margaret began

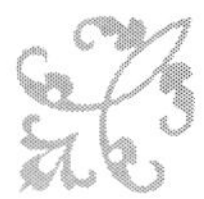

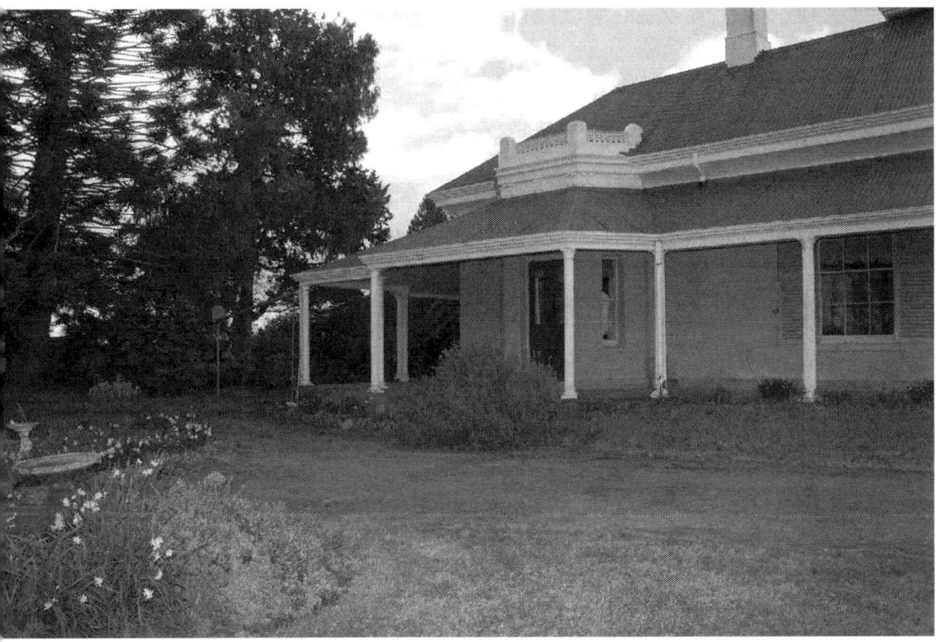

above An Edwardian-style dining room was added by Roger and Margaret Royds in the 1980s to provide some practical living space in a household overflowing with historically significant furniture.

hearing screams in the middle of the night. She'd get up to see what it was but there was no electricity in the house in 1973, only oil lamps, the flames from which cast unnerving reflections on the home's many items of period furniture, mirrors and old paintings. Although there seemed to be no one there, this went on for quite some time.

Margaret, who is every bit as conservative as I am, that I wouldn't be at all surprised if, like me, she voted to retain the monarchy, the yardstick of any true conservative, then told me she'd feel breaths of air going past her in Bedervale's hallways. There was also an occasional knocking on the floor by her bed. She'd go round the house to see if the children were awake, perhaps playing a prank. But they were always asleep. Then one night she found a small door hidden in one of the homestead's staircases, one that used to lead up to an old nursery that was once located outside the house before a later extension brought it inside. Margaret opened the door to the staircase and pointed her torchlight inside. And shone it straight onto Emma's face.

Emma Coghill was the daughter of John Coghill, a landowner with extensive sheep and cattle interests in the Macarthur district

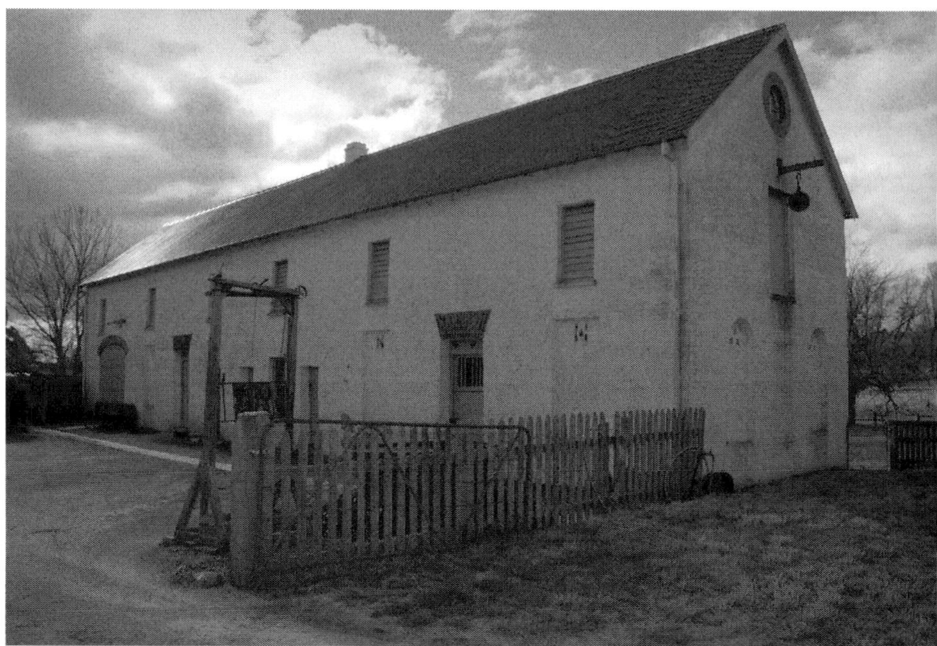

above Bedervale's stables are set across the driveway from the main house and remain one of the country's most intact examples of Georgian architecture.

south of Sydney and the man who commissioned the construction of Bedervale in 1836. There was another painting under the stairs as well, that of Elizabeth, Emma's elder sister. When John Coghill died in 1853, Elizabeth, being the elder of the two girls, inherited Bedervale, something Emma was never able to come to terms with.

Margaret got both paintings out from under the stairs, cleaned them, and hung them on the wall in the dining room. After that things seemed to settle down.

Years later Margaret attended a National Trust event at Sydney University and by chance met a chap from the Trust who had some correspondence relating to Bedervale and told Margaret: 'Ohhh, I'm so pleased to have found you! I have a letter that has been in my father's letters from Emma Coghill, complaining at how she hadn't received her share of the estate when her father died.' Emma Coghill's husband had written a letter to this man's father saying how she hadn't received her share.

Margaret, having been made aware of the feud between the sisters, immediately thought, 'Ohhh, no, I've put them in the same room!'

When she returned to Bedervale strange things began to happen with water stains around Emma's portrait. During a heavy downpour, water seeped through the wall above Emma—but everywhere else in the house remained dry and the source of the leak was never found. A few Christmases ago a couple with their young daughter came to stay at Bedervale. They'd never been there before and Margaret related how she was walking with the family past Emma's portrait when the little girl stopped in front of it, looked up and said, 'There are things all around her'. Nobody else saw anything out of the ordinary but the girl insisted she could see things swirling about Emma's face. That was enough. Margaret decided it was time she called in the artillery. Anglican artillery.

Geoffrey is a retired Anglican minister who now lives a quiet life somewhere in Canberra. I telephoned him that night, actually, and asked if he wouldn't mind talking to me about the experiences he had at Bedervale in the wake of Margaret's phone call so that, if nothing else, they might act as a brake on my own by now rampaging imagination. Well, he had no problem with talking about it, but said he'd prefer to wait until after my deadline for this book had passed, after which I was welcome to come down 'for coffee and biscuits'. He explained, 'I made several visits there. When you come here I'll tell you about the events in the rectory and the church'.

'Oh,' I said, 'there were incidents in Braidwood as well?'

'Oh yes'. But it would all have to wait. 'Where do you live?'

'Picton,' I said, which is two hours from Canberra, to which he replied with the sort of statement only a retiree with plenty of time would say:

'Oh, you're only down the road! You must come down for a chat!' Which made me think there must be rather a lot to say. I can hardly wait.

Bedervale Homestead is, of course, infinitely more than just the backdrop for a few ghostly tales. John Verge, the architect responsible for Sydney's colonial treasures Elizabeth Bay House and Camden Park in Menangle, New South Wales, charged Bedervale's owner Captain John Coghill the sum of 16 pounds to design his new classically Georgian homestead. Construction began in 1836 and the house was completed in 1842. It was designed to face south, not for any aesthetic reasons but to make the house as 'cool' as possible because, as the owner of any historic property will tell you, it's a lot easier to heat a cold house than it is to cool a hot one. The hardwood floors, elaborate cedar interiors and the black ash columns that line its south-facing verandah were all locally cut. Its sandstone came from Bundanoon in the Southern Highlands and every brick you see was made onsite. Six successive generations of Coghills lived there for almost 130 years and its contents reflect the changing tastes and styles of a nation from the Victorian through the Edwardian periods, to 1973 when Margaret and Roger purchased it. Keeping the house in the one family also explains how virtually all the original furniture and other objects in the house were able to avoid being dissected, preserving them exactly as if the Coghills had only just left. All the furniture and contents remain in their original setting, and the homestead, with its two flanking wings and its magnificent two-storey barn all set around a central courtyard represents one of the most intact assemblages of rural colonial-era buildings remaining in New South Wales.

At slightly more than an hour's drive southeast of Canberra Bedervale might be a tad isolated, but when you have the quality of early Australian furniture and antiques that Margaret and Victoria have under their roof, people in the know tend to find you. People like Gordon Brown, one of the hosts of the ABC's popular television show *The Collectors*. Brown and his crew spent two days at Bedervale filming a segment for the show that aired on 13 November 2009. And when he arrived and saw what they had in the homestead's entry hall, he almost—in Gordon Brown-style—fell over with excitement.

Few objects are more prized in Australia today than good examples of early colonial furniture made from Australian cedar, *Toona australis*. The main reason for this is that there just isn't a lot of it around anymore. Cedar exports began in 1795 and 'cedar-getters' plundered the forests of eastern Australia, cutting down everything from 100-year-old giants to saplings, and by 1850 even the great cedar stands of Moreton Bay and those along the banks of the Clarence River were gone. Now all we have left is the furniture, *rare* furniture that also happens to age particularly well and, under the right circumstances, can look every bit as good today as it did in 1850. Cedar was made to be aged. It is the Bordeaux of the timber world.

In Bedervale's entry hall Gordon found them: a matching pair of Sydney-made cedar card tables, circa 1840, two of the earliest pieces that had been made for the original homestead. Under normal circumstances just to have one such table would be considered fortunate, but to have two which have not only survived in excellent condition but also managed to remain together in the one household for 170 years is nothing short of extraordinary. Gordon described the tables as being of 'national significance', with an estimated value between $150 000 and $200 000. And if you're like the rest of us and love happy endings and worry what might happen to them if Bedervale were to be sold, fear not.

Everything at Bedervale, from its sumptuous pair of 1840s bookcases all the way down to its cutlery and the paintings and sketches on its walls, are owned by the National Trust, who purchased it all in 1975, ensuring that the collection will never be broken up, including the 150 pieces of Rockingham porcelain to be found in Bedervale's dining room. The Rockingham Pottery Company supplied British royalty with its rococo-styled porcelain for decades and pieces were being commissioned for British and European aristocratic families right up until the company closed in 1842.

It should come as no surprise that the ABC had Bedervale in its sights. The homestead is accustomed to film crews who search it out whenever they need a period home with sweeping views and, just as importantly, no out-of-place reminders of the 20th century on its far horizons to ruin the shot. In 1970 *Ned Kelly* saw its star Mick Jagger walking Bedervale's broad verandahs. *The Year My Voice Broke*, starring Noah Taylor, Ben Mendelsohn and Graeme Blundell, was filmed here in 1987; and Margaret still has the hole in her cast iron stove inadvertently drilled by one of the film crew after they'd borrowed it to use in a scene. Leo McKern, Geoffrey Rush and Dame Joan Sutherland came to Bedervale in 1995 to film *Dad & Dave: On Our Selection*. Margaret fondly recalled the sight of our nation's Grande Dame of opera playfully hiding from the film crew in the woodshed out back and poking her head out through the shed's timber-shuttered windows. It is a priceless memory. How many hotels/guest houses can boast they once had Dame Joan Sutherland delighting in a game of hide-and-seek in their own backyard?

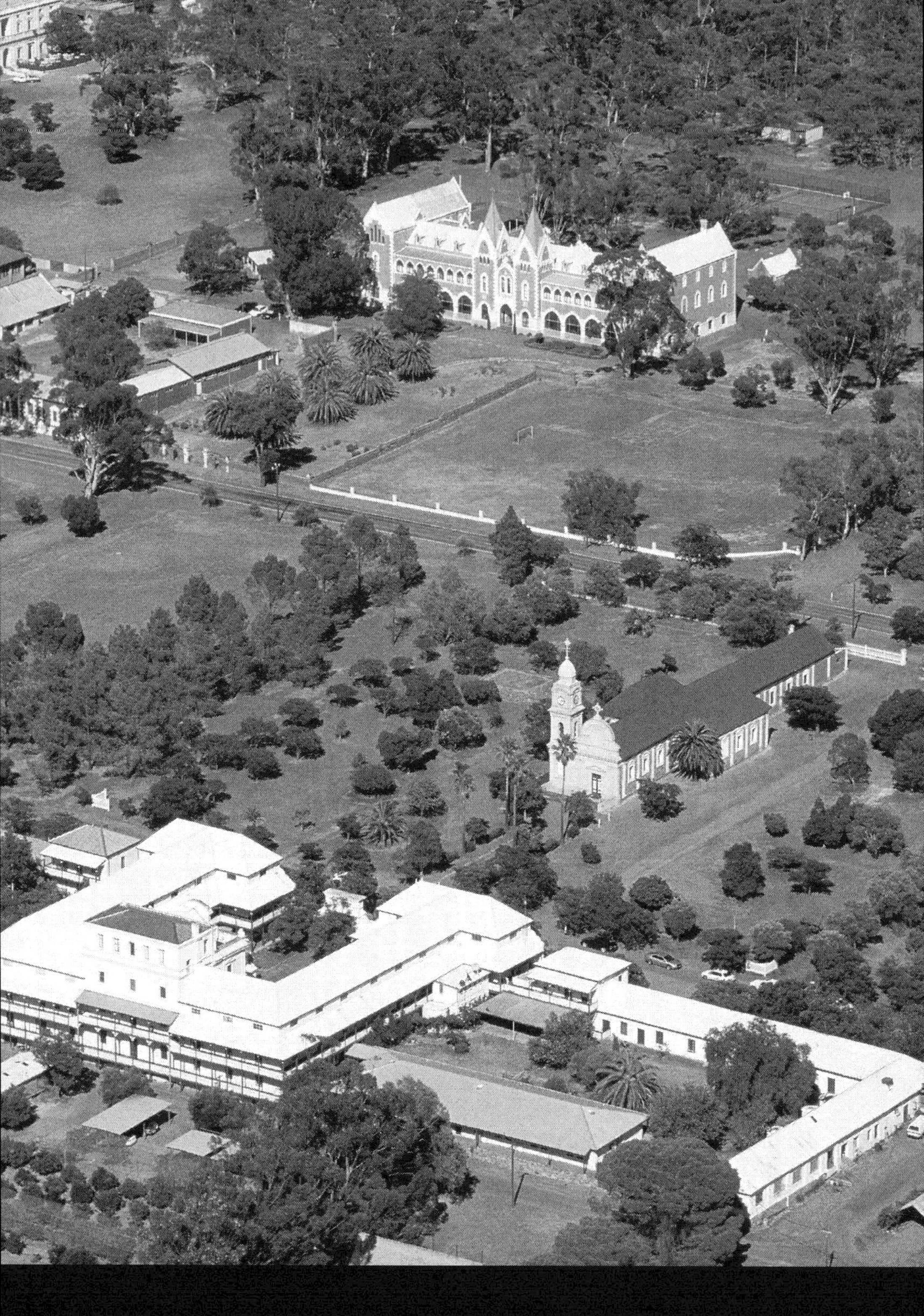

PART 4

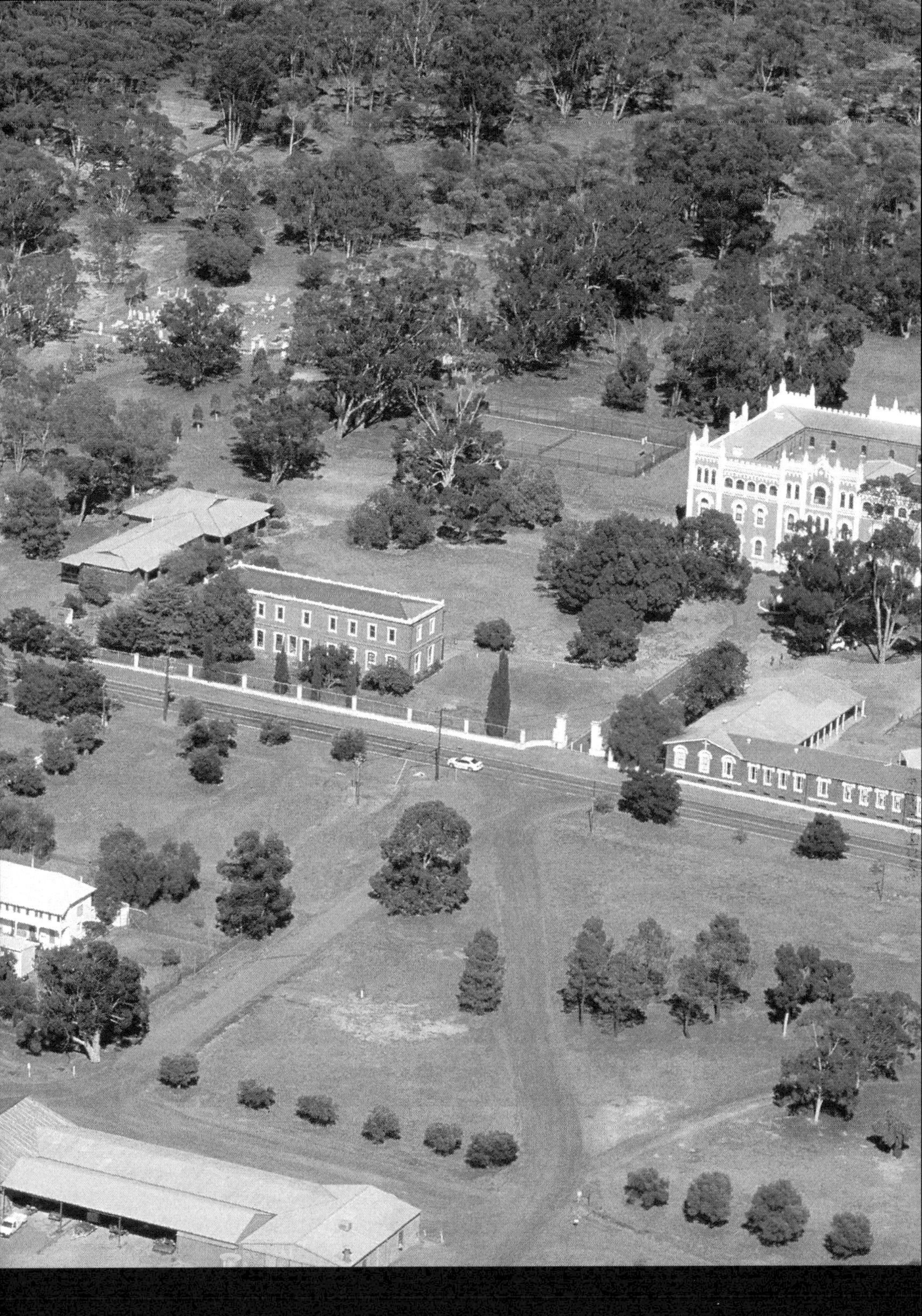

Country Towns

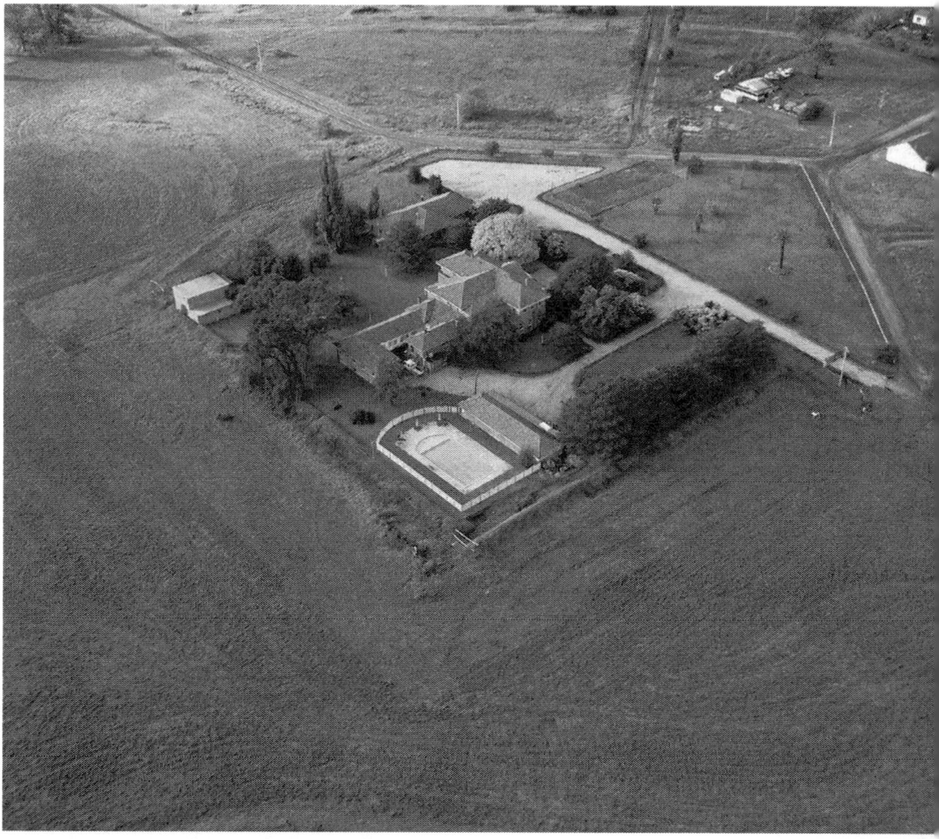

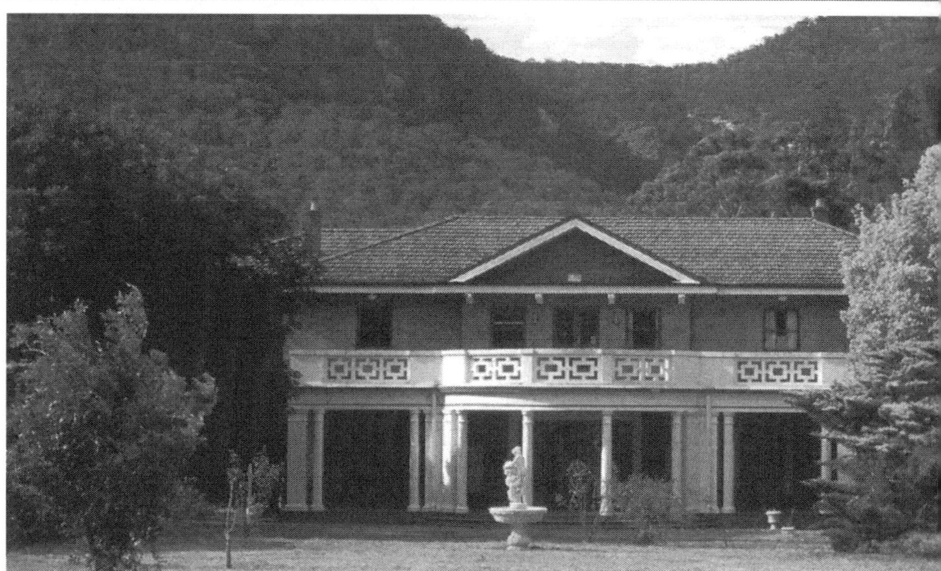

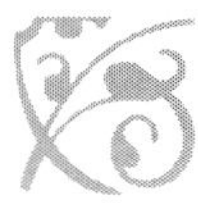

CHAPTER 15

The Glen Davis Boutique Hotel

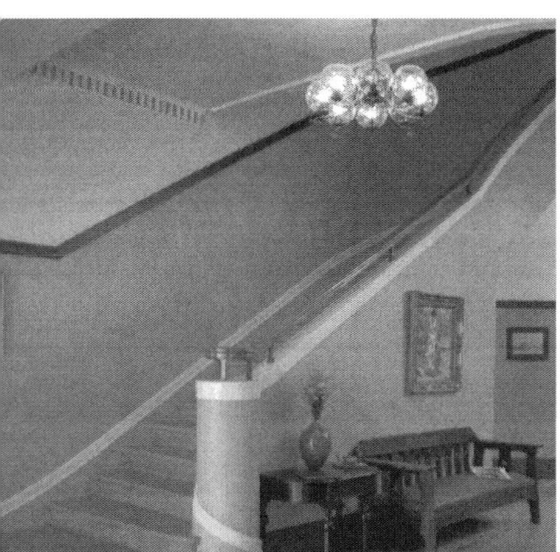

Alongside the front door of the Glen Davis Boutique Hotel deep in New South Wales's Capertee Valley, about four hours northwest of Sydney, there should be an elegant brass name plaque and two Greco-Roman statues to welcome you. Sadly, they were pilfered long ago along with many other original items during the hotel's ten years of abandonment prior to its current owners, Adam Botham and Alison Barnes, purchasing the classic Art Deco building in 2003.

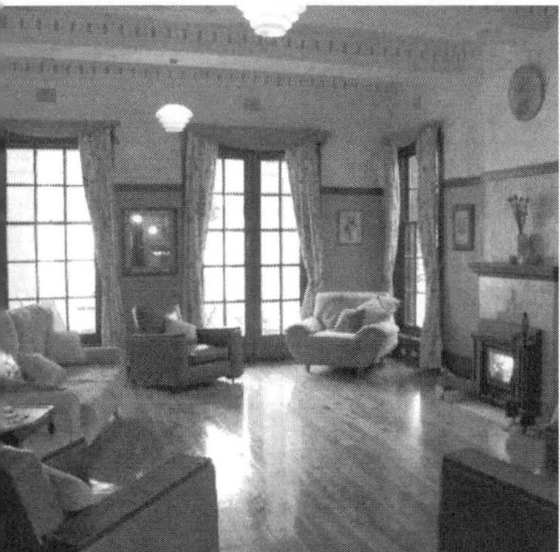

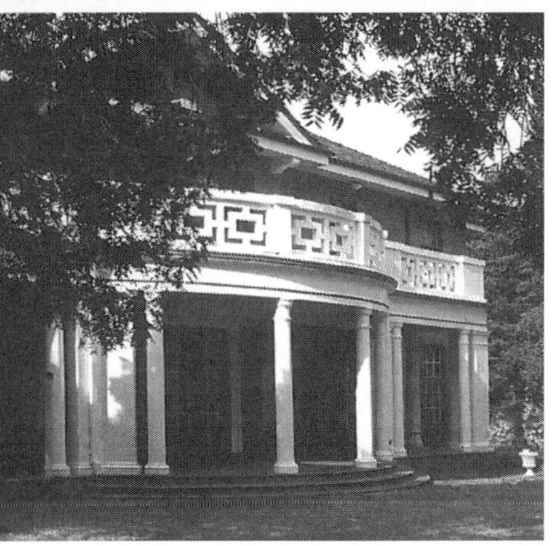

clockwise from top left A Canberra-like symmetry can be seen in Walter Burley Griffin's design for the town of Glen Davis; the hotel's Art Deco staircase and lounge room; its unique white columned portico is a triumph from any angle

'I'm not sure about the statues, but I'm pretty sure I know who has the name plaque,' Adam told me as we stood beneath the hotel's signature white portico. 'It's still in the local area, it's just a matter of getting it back. And don't worry, I'll get it,' he adds with a determined smile.

Determination is something Adam and Alison possess in abundance, which is just as well, as they continue to restore this unique hotel, one piece at a time. Despite having renovated several properties over the years and sharing a deep love of history and architecture, this would prove to be a project that would test their endurance and dedication like no other. The hotel, once touted as 'the finest hotel west of the Blue Mountains' at the time of its construction in 1939, was in a state of complete neglect by the time they, and their five children, moved to the valley in 2003. The drive to restore it was a shared dream, but nonetheless a dream that would never have been realised had Adam's mother Gay not stumbled upon it during a trip through the Capertee Valley in 2002, and then all but dragged her son out there to have a look at it. To Adam it seemed as though the hotel had fallen from the sky and landed with a thud in one of the most beautiful valleys he had ever seen. The first page of the Glen Davis Hotel's long road to restoration had begun to be written.

Preferring not to apply for heritage funding despite qualifying for assistance, they chose instead to restore the building as they saw fit, without the sort of bureaucratic interference that so bedevils many an historic restoration. A refusal to plunge themselves into debt means work may have at times been slow and tedious, but at least it was progressing on their own terms. From 2003 to 2007, working from old photographs and numerous personal accounts, Adam reglazed more than a hundred windows and sanded more than a thousand square meters of cypress flooring. As the saga of the name plaque suggests, he is also part detective, and in late 2009 managed to track down and repurchase some of the hotel's original doors. He also resealed and brought back to life the hotel's 20-metre saltwater swimming pool. Alison packed more than 80 kilos of plaster back into the walls and columns of the dining room, and in the process covered over the names of dozens of past squatters. She also spent countless hours stripping paint and removing wallpaper, had the mammoth task of sewing new curtains for all the hotel's windows, and even had to use acid to remove the carpet that a previous owner had, for some

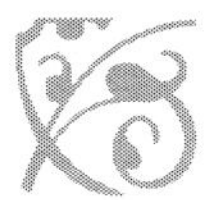

unfathomable reason, glued onto the beautiful terrazzo staircase in the hotel's lobby. Everywhere you look here you see history uncovered, like the hotel's 70-year-old driveways and many of its paths that were buried under accumulated layers of dirt and rubbish which, once removed, exposed the still-intact brick edging. Alison and Adam's pride in bringing the hotel back to life is self-evident, and in the process they have provided their children with a never-to-be forgotten example of how hard work and dedication can overcome even the most insurmountable of obstacles.

The hotel received its first guests in 2007, and Adam and Alison have already begun to accumulate the sort of personal anecdotes that easily convince you that what they have managed here is far more than just the successful renovation of an old building. Like the time the CEO of an unnamed bank came to stay and was so distraught when it was time to leave that he was seen crying. He left an embarrassingly huge tip and confided to the staff how he was dreading emerging from the valley, which has no mobile reception, back into a world where his phone would begin to ring and the respite from society afforded him by the valley's 600-metre-high escarpments would come to an abrupt end. On another occasion two elderly former residents of Glen Davis flew over from Perth for a two-night stay after seeing the hotel profiled on television.

In the hotel's lobby an aerial photograph of Glen Davis dated 1941 shows the hotel standing triumphantly at the very centre of town, the design of which bears a more-than-passing resemblance to the structured symmetry of Canberra. When I remarked that the fledgling town's paths and roads extended outwards from the hotel in a very purposeful, Canberra-like way, Alison confirmed that Glen Davis had in fact been designed by Walter Burley Griffin, the designer of our nation's capital, who decided that the Glen Davis Hotel should be to Glen Davis what old Parliament House was to Canberra. Before the foundations were even laid, this was always going to be far more than just another country hotel. It would be the town's focal point, its heartbeat.

> Then slowly we crawled by the trees that kept tally
> of miles that were passed on the long journey down.
> We saw the wild beauty of Capertee Valley,
> as slowly we rounded the base of the Crown.
>
> HENRY LAWSON, *SONG OF THE OLD BULLOCK-DRIVER*, 1891

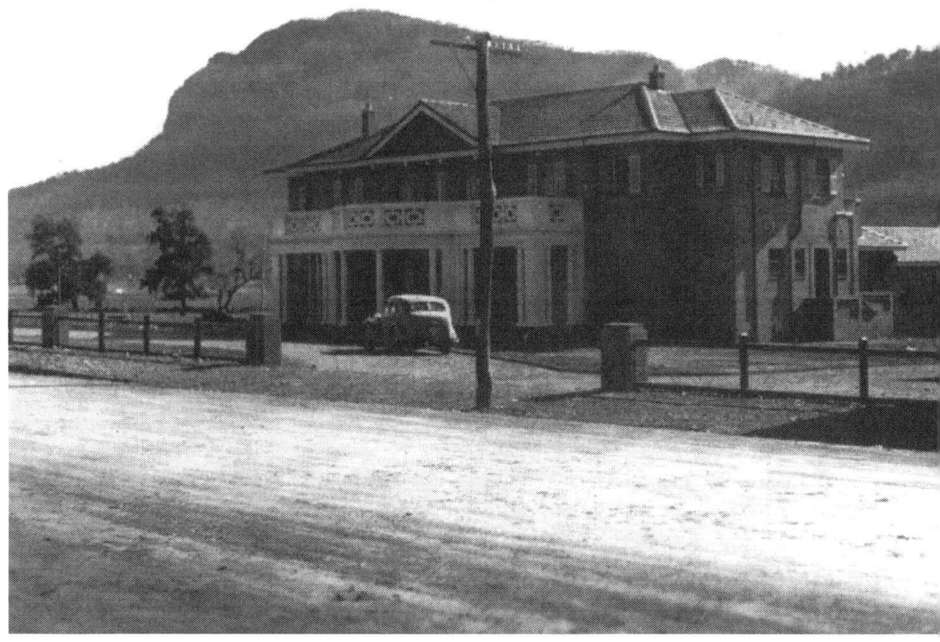

above The pioneering credentials of the Glen Davis Hotel can be seen captured in this photograph, circa 1939.

Henry Lawson was the first Australian to put into words the rugged beauty of the Capertee Valley, though it's fair to wonder how many more verses he may have devoted to it had he known he was looking at the western extremities of the world's second largest enclosed canyon. The Capertee Valley is longer than America's Grand Canyon by almost a kilometre and its sandstone escarpments soar to more than 600 metres in height, encircling the valley from a bottleneck 20 kilometres west of Glen Davis before expanding eastwards, broadening out to be more than 30 kilometres wide at their widest point. Amongst the first Europeans to see the Capertee Valley was the explorer James Blackman, who passed by it on his way to Mudgee in 1821.

The valley first came to national prominence in the 1930s not for the landforms that rose from its valley floor, but for the vast geological deposits that lay beneath. The Capertee Valley, it turned out, was

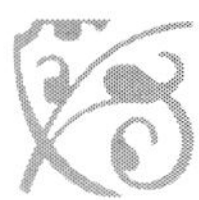

far more than just escarpments, slot canyons and rugged, towering monoliths. It was also home to one of the planet's largest reserves of high-grade oil shale.

The mining of oil shale first began in New South Wales in the 1860s with the opening of the Pioneer Kerosene Works at American Creek near Port Kembla, a relatively small-scale operation that produced paraffin and kerosene for use in oil lamps. The Capertee Valley deposits, however, soon saw mines established at Airly Village and Torbane; and by the turn of the century, mines throughout the valley had extracted more than 135 000 tonnes of shale. In 1937, rising tensions in Europe prompted the Australian government to establish the National Oil Proprietary Limited (NOL), a joint partnership between government and private enterprise to help develop and sustain the nation's self-sufficiency in oil supplies. This led to NOL dismantling the nearby oil shale site at Newnes that had been closed since 1934, and transporting its plant and equipment 11 kilometres from its site in the Wolgan Valley to an old tunnel first cut in 1881 on the eastern rim of neighbouring Capertee Valley, on the back of government promises of tariff protection and various rail concessions from the New South Wales government.

Government estimates indicated 1 tonne of Capertee shale could yield anywhere between 200 and 500 litres of crude oil, and the new, purpose-built mining town of Glen Davis was envisioned as having a population of between 2000 and 3000 people. The future was looking bright and construction soon began on a school, a post office, shops, and a cinema. And one very grand hotel.

Designed by the Sydney architectural firm of Spencer & Spencer for its owner W.J. Lees the Glen Davis Hotel cost 15 000 pounds to build, an unheard-of sum for a Central West hotel. Its entry was graced by an ornate columned portico, which alone made the statement that here was a hotel that would do more than simply service the needs of its community. It would be a symbol of the town's coming wealth. The stunning Art Deco-inspired staircase led upstairs to 25 rooms, all of which enjoyed magnificent views of the surrounding escarpments, and it had a sumptuous lounge and formal dining room.

The Glen Davis Hotel was the only hotel in New South Wales that had its main bar separate to the main building, an unambiguous statement that Australia was far from immune to the class-ridden influences inherited from England. The hotel even had upstairs and downstairs cleaners. When a nondescript motorcyclist rode into town in the early 1950s with plans to start an open-air cinema, the then-manager of the hotel refused to put him up.

The bar was once the largest in terms of surface area in New South Wales, and the hotel was a proud and confident expression of elegance and prosperity at a time when the future of Glen Davis, with the government underwriting its growth and endless deposits of shale beneath it, seemed guaranteed, and over the years the hotel hosted visiting dignitaries and government officials. But the good times would not last.

By 1941 more than 4.2 million gallons of oil a year was being extracted and within six years the town's population swelled to more than 2500. Supplies of shale, however, consistently fell below expectations, and the mine rarely operated at full capacity. Technical and financial difficulties became almost endemic, and when combined with increasing imports of oil from the Middle East, both the mine and the hotel closed in 1952. The mine's plant and machinery were disassembled and taken away, and the hotel was purchased by the Catholic Church, who converted it into a Marist Brothers retreat house, and the bar became a chapel. But even the Marists found the isolation of Glen Davis, by then largely abandoned, too much to bear and it was sold to a local man who used it as a farmhouse.

The last chapter in the restoration process will be the workers' bar. Adam and Alison have already begun uncovering the original tiled floor, which played host to a peculiarly Glen Davis form of two-up where you not only relied on the luck of the toss but also that the coins landed within the tile's grout lines. Illegal gambling was a routine event in the workers' pub, which witnessed several police raids by Sydney's '21 Squad' and was the focal point for many a fight between locals and the resident Asian population who were working the mines in the hope of eventually being granted citizenship. The bar area, which is taking a necessary back seat to the main building, will eventually be transformed into a function centre with a commercial kitchen, selling locally brewed boutique beers and wines from the Mudgee–Rylstone region. There are plans afoot to re-create a replica of the original bar, though on a somewhat smaller and less 'troublesome' scale.

Glen Davis is a half-hour drive east of the town of Capertee and is located in the midst of some of the most spectacular escarpments to be found anywhere in Australia. Whilst there, you can climb Pantoney's Crown, now the centrepiece of Pantoney's Crown Nature Reserve; and staff at the Glen Davis Hotel can arrange tours of the ruins of the old oil shale works, which are now on private land, including the impressive retort building where the oil and shale were heated and separated. If time and stamina permit, you can even hike along the 20-kilometre Pipeline Pass that follows the route of an abandoned railway line to the site of the old Newnes mine.

These days Glen Davis almost qualifies as a ghost town with a population of just 20, give or take, and the Australian bush is gradually reclaiming the buildings and scattered remains of its shale works. But the Glen Davis Hotel, empty for so long it came with a reputation of being haunted itself, triumphantly survives as testament to the vision, dedication and tenacity of its owners.

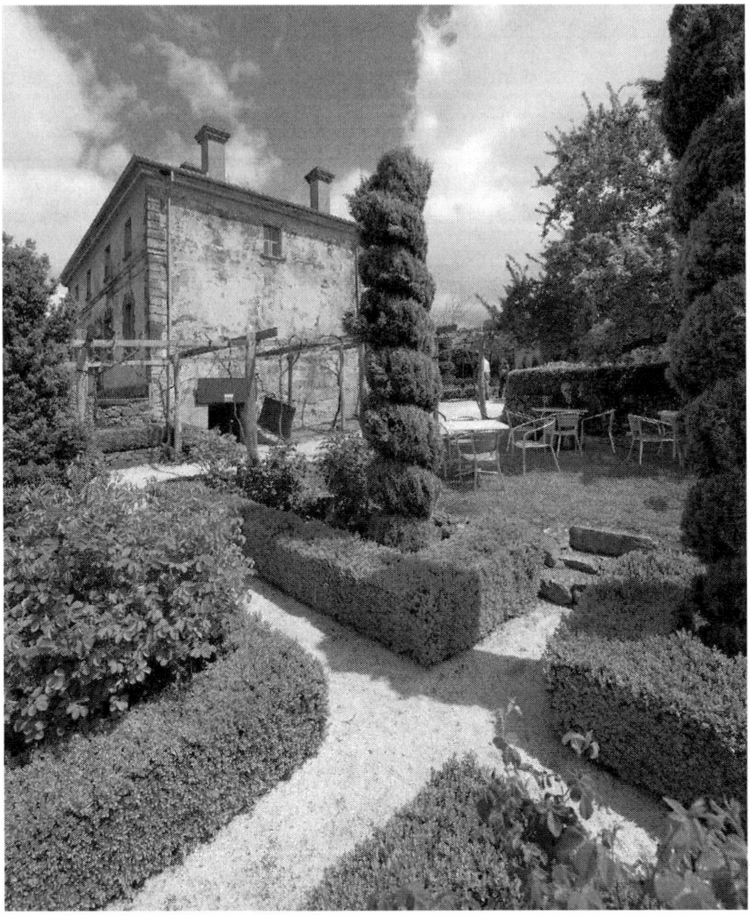

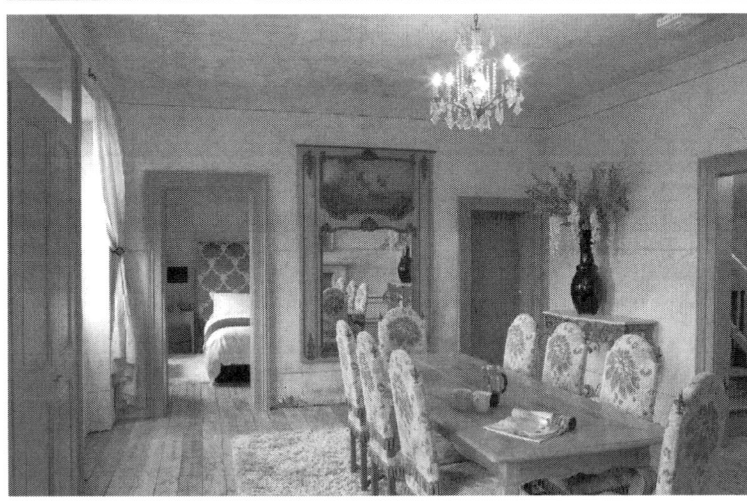

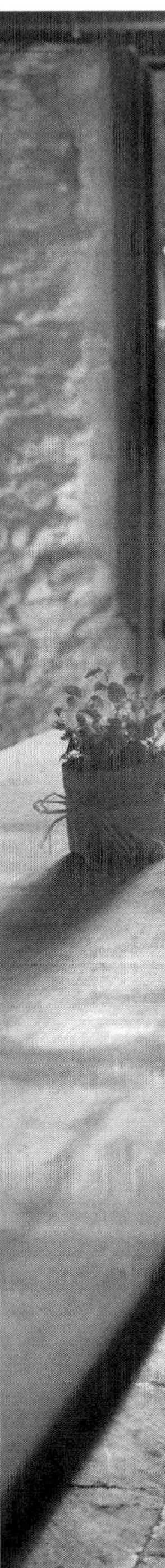

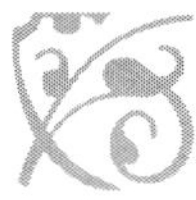

Peppers Springs Retreat & Spa

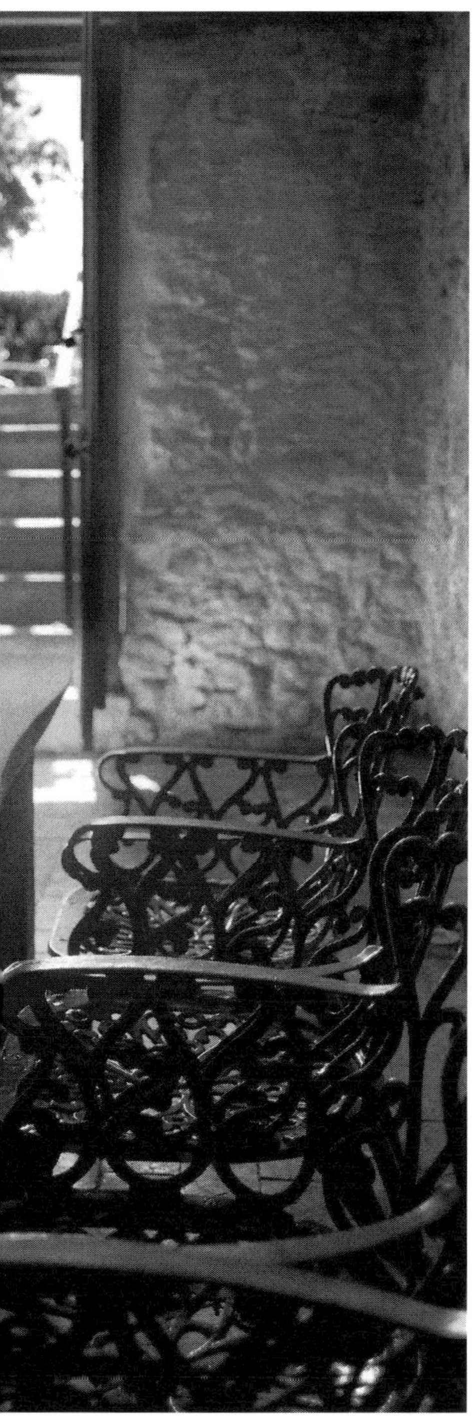

Fabrizzio Crippa arrived in Australia from Lombardy, Italy in 1855, one of many Swiss and Italian immigrants who settled in and pioneered the development of the region popularly known today as 'Spa Country', the collection of mineral springs that course through the hills surrounding the Central Victorian town of Daylesford. In 1861 Crippa was one of three native Italians elected to the Yandoit and Franklin Road Board, a far-sighted authority for its time which set aside and protected the Hepburn Mineral Springs in the face of encroaching goldmines in the wake of the discovery of the precious metal in 1851.

clockwise from top left Villa Parma and its European-inspired gardens; Villa Parma's cellar; the dining room in Villa Parma.

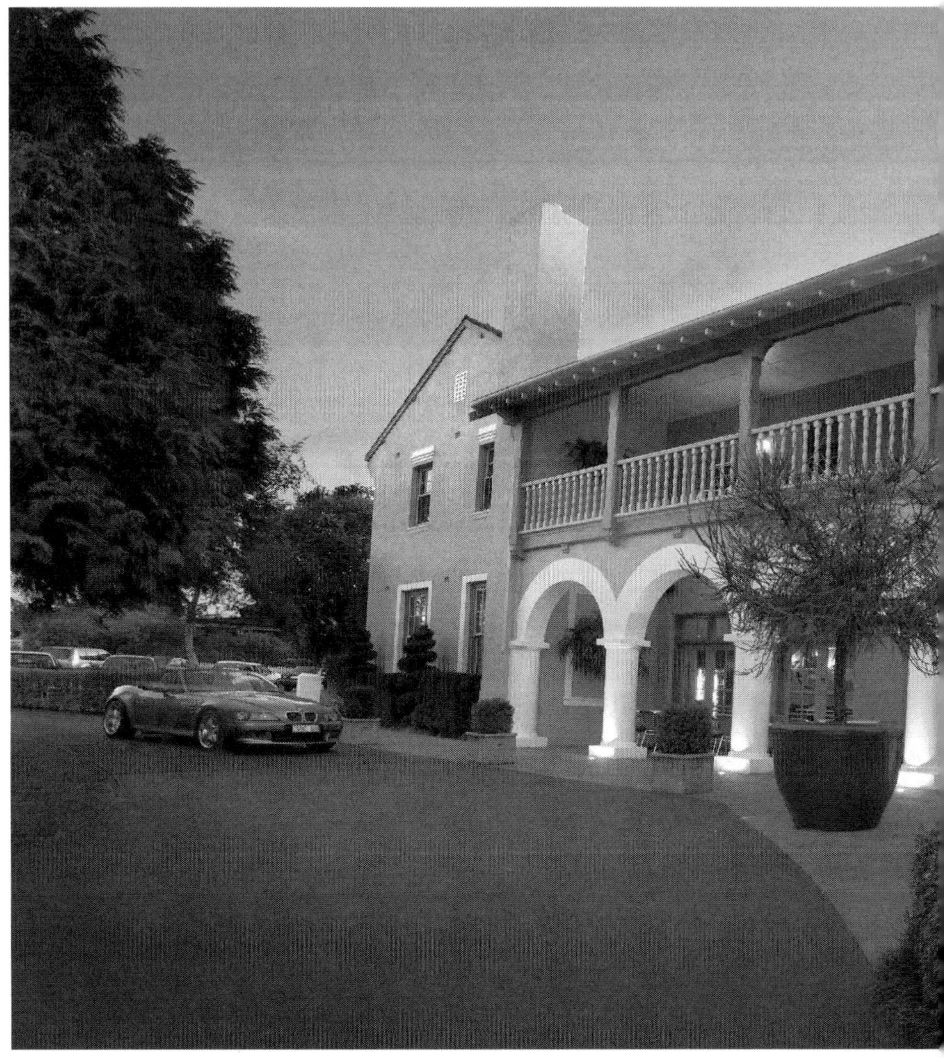

Europeans came here in their hundreds, drawn by its curative waters and the sense of nostalgia for the baths and springs of their homelands which the region engendered. Instead of tailings and pollutants, the hills around Daylesford remained dotted with chestnut and mulberry trees, grapevines and European-styled formal gardens. By the mid-1860s Crippa had in excess of 15 000 vines in his orchard. Crippa went on to become an acknowledged expert in viticulture. The vines are all gone now, although the chestnut trees are still here, but by far the most enduring legacy Fabrizzio Crippa

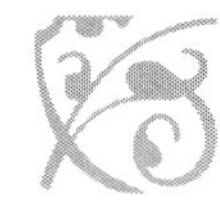

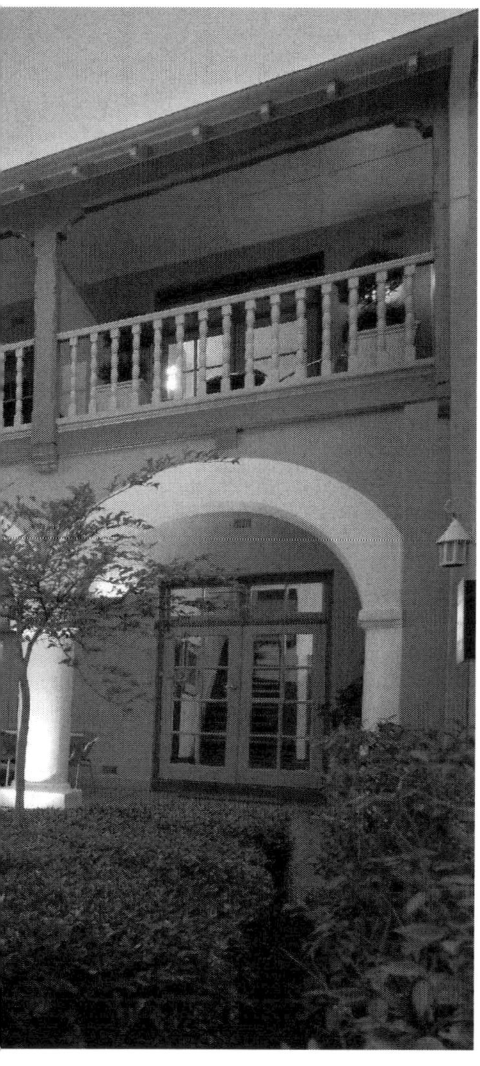

left The main guesthouse at Peppers Springs Retreat & Spa. Opinion is divided as to the precise year of its construction. Dates vary from the mid 1920s through to the early 1930s.

left to us, and dare I say to the nation, was his house.

In the late 1850s Crippa purchased a parcel of land from a local man, William Pratt Snr, that ran north along the boundary of what is now 10th Street, from Doctor's Gully to the Main Road, and began construction of Parma House, a rendered, classically styled two-storey villa every bit as Italian as anything in Italy. He sold Parma House in the late 1880s and moved to Melbourne, where he died in 1892.

Parma House was one of the few houses to survive the horrendous bushfires that swept through the town in 1906 but had less luck surviving the ravages of time. By the mid 1970s the house had succumbed to neglect and was known to locals as the 'ghost house'. A demolition order was being considered by the Victorian government and a fire in 1984, the cause of which is still debated, extensively damaged the roof and ceiling. The following year the rapidly ageing property was purchased by Richard Rigby and Franchek Kasek who renamed it Villa Parma and began an extensive period of restoration.

Paint was stripped to reveal the home's original colouring, its roof was replaced, a garden was planted, and the basis was laid for this gorgeous old building to be transformed into the Villa Parma we see today and which, in the opinion of this humble writer, is one of Australia's most beautifully proportioned and aesthetically pleasing residences. It remains so authentic, in fact, that television advertisements featuring Italian-themed products have been filmed here because it's a whole lot cheaper than flying a film crew to Rome. It is impossible to look at Villa Parma and not imagine for a moment that you are in the hills of Umbria.

Designed and built in the style of an Italian Renaissance palazzo, Villa Parma originally had three upstairs and three downstairs bedrooms, with its external walls a mix of handmade bricks and bluestone. Edgings are sandstone with dark stone quoining surrounding the front downstairs windows, sidewalls and front entry door which opens into the dining room rather than the more common hallway, a rare but wholly appropriate departure from tradition. Casement windows, louvred window shutters, a hip roof and four beautifully rendered chimneys help to complete the picture. If you can't afford to take the family to Italy, you could always bring them here. All that's missing are the Vespers. And you mustn't leave without visiting the purpose-built cellar and water well that was once home to Fabrizzio Crippa's award-winning 'Parma House Red'.

Adjacent to Villa Parma is the main hotel, Peppers Hepburn Springs, the third building on the site. The original guesthouse was built in 1864 and was either demolished in 1900 or lost to a bushfire in 1906, depending on what account you listen to. Opinion at first seemed to me to be split as to precisely when the present hotel was built, with dates ranging from the mid 1920s through to the early 1930s. Nobody seems to be able to locate any title deeds, and to confound me further, council records of building approvals weren't even required here until 1975! There is a liquor license somewhere in the Public Record Office, but nobody was able to find it.

One elderly resident, Maurice, claimed he remembers watching builders excavating the hotel's cellar as he rode by on his bike on the way to school in 1935. Or was it 1936? The daughter of the hotel's builder Graham Carrick remembers she was ten years old when a photo was taken of her mother laying the hotel's very first brick, which would place the year as 1932. The final piece in the puzzle was at last supplied by a local historian, Jon Stephens, who located an advertisement in the local *Advocate* newspaper dated 14 September 1935 that read:

NEW HOTEL OPEN. LARGE CROWD AT WEEKEND.
The new Mineral Springs Hotel was opened for the first time on
Saturday. Satisfactory bookings were received for the weekend
and rooms in the old premises and Parma House were
occupied.

An advertisement in Melbourne's *The Age* newspaper provided
additional tantalising details:

New Mineral Springs Hotel—Now Open For Guests. Excellent
Accommodation.
Hot & Cold Water In Rooms. First Class Cuisine. Garaging For
20 Cars, two asphalt tennis courts. Sewered—tariff from
3 Pound 10 Shillings to 4 Guineas.

The new hotel could accommodate 27 people in the bedrooms
on its second floor, and the ground floor dining room had a staff of
17 and could seat 100 diners. The private dining room was once a
card room, and off that was a claustrophobic space lined with writing
desks that used to have a radiola. The 'radio room' was a magnet
to Saturday night crowds who'd travelled for up to three days from
Melbourne and where the average stay was in excess of a week, an
intolerably long time to be cut off from the news of the day. Despite
its isolation, however, the reputation of the spring's restorative powers
saw more than 100 000 people annually make their way to the
Daylesford and Hepburn Springs region.

In 1963 the Mineral Springs Hotel went into voluntary liquidation
and the building, minus Villa Parma, was sold to a Mr Brown; and
then, in the mid 60s, to the monkey-loving Captain Dyson, whose pet
monkey would eventually bring the hotel into serious disrepute. Early
one winter's morning the cooks arrived to prepare breakfast which
involved lighting the stove and closing the stove door to allow it to
warm up. When the cooks returned to the kitchen after collecting
firewood, they smelled something akin to singed fur. They opened
the stove door and out leapt one very distressed monkey, which was
unfortunately seen by guests, fleeing the kitchen at a cracking pace.
The infamous 'monkey in the oven' story was born. Patrons began
finding alternate establishments in which to eat and hence to stay,
and the hotel entered a prolonged period of decline.

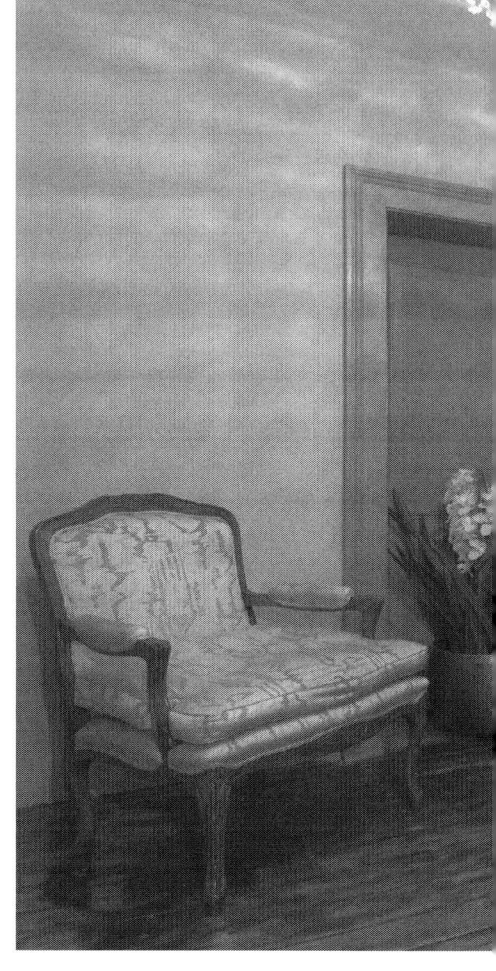

right A Villa Parma suite.

The hotel was again purchased in 2000, and Villa Parma in 2006, by Wayne Cross and Chris Malden of Malcross Investments Pty Ltd and detailed refurbishments were commenced. The hotel's restaurant, DECO, was opened in 2003 and in 2004 the hotel's purpose-built Mineral Spa opened in the grounds of the Springs Retreat. The hotel became a member of the Peppers brand in 2005, and in 2007 the now heritage-listed Villa Parma opened its doors to guests for the first time on 15 August, by the Victorian Minister for Tourism, Tim Holding. Wayne and Chris had, in the meantime, turned their attention to creating a very European kind of garden.

For anyone who has ever spent any time in the great gardens of Europe, a walk through the formal gardens to the rear of Villa Parma delivers an overwhelming sense of deja vu. Just months before my visit to Villa Parma I'd been strolling the 25 acres of gardens that surround the 16th-century former royal residence Villa d'Este, now one of the world's most luxurious hotels on the shores of Lake Como in northern Italy. Though no comparison in terms of scale, I couldn't help but be reminded of that sun-drenched afternoon in Italy as I walked through the gardens of Villa Parma.

The proportions, the geometric principles, the choice of plants, the statuary—it was all here but on a refreshingly human scale. The garden is a testament of the dedication to authenticity, not to mention an all-too-rare eye for detail, on the part of Villa Parma's new owners

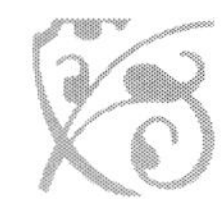

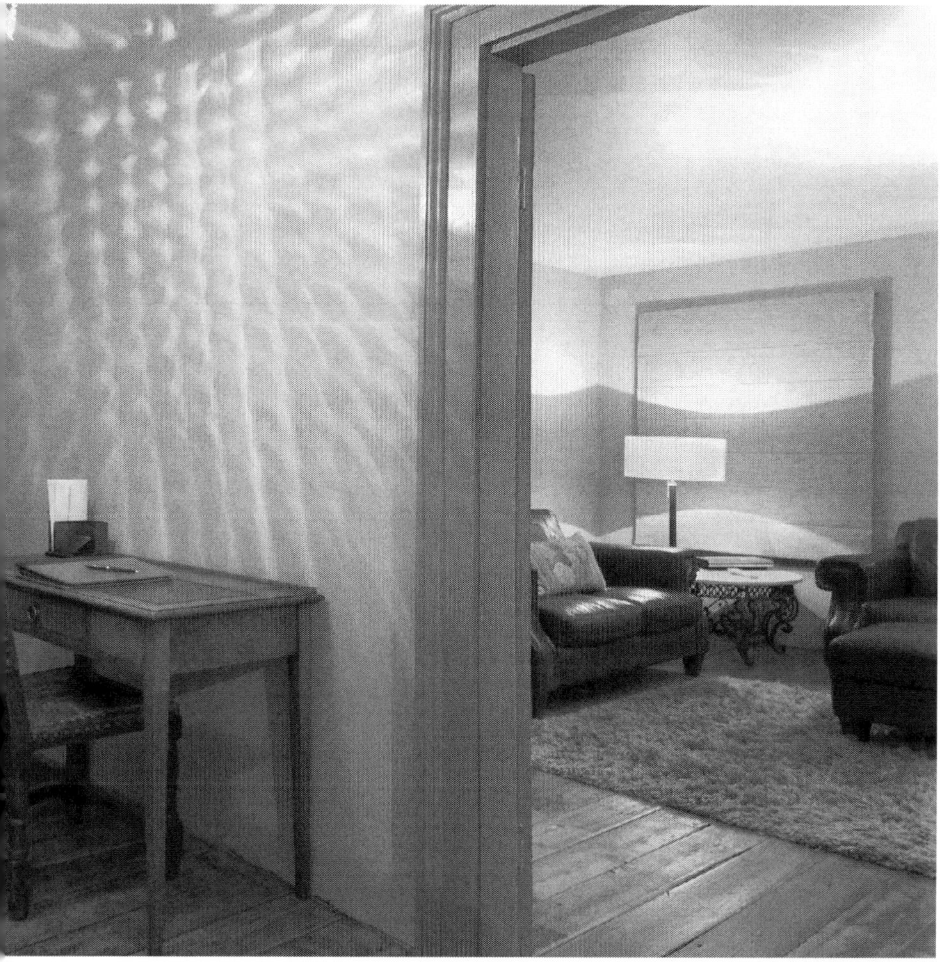

who brought it to life following the principles of the original garden
plan first laid down by Fabrizzio Crippa almost 150 years before.
At Villa Parma you'll still find grapevines interspersed with citrus
trees and plantings of vegetables and tobacco along with mulberry,
chestnut and pear trees, herb gardens, and a magical 'secret garden',
a lovely rectangular space surrounded by a hedge of scented bay
trees that provide absolute privacy and which can only be accessed
through an old wrought iron gate that looks as though it may have
been lifted off its hinges and brought here from the gardens of Villa
d'Este itself.

Magnifico!

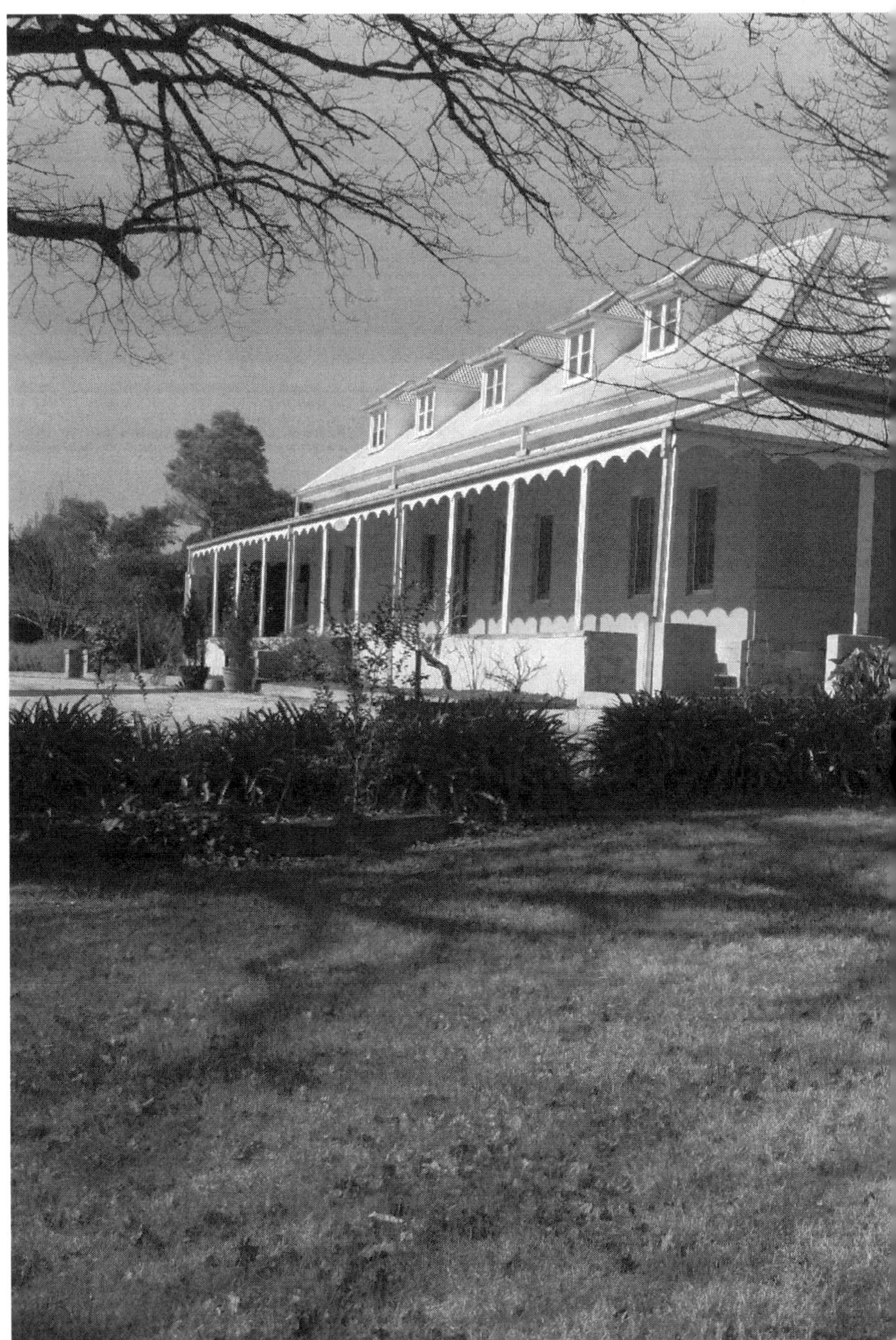

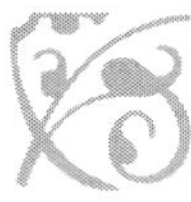

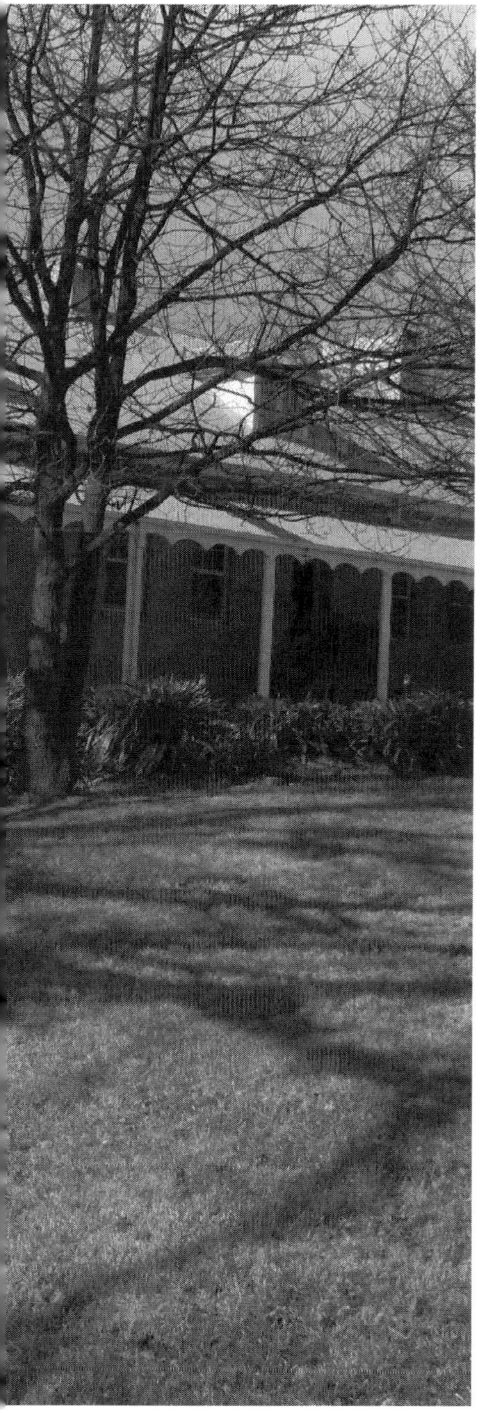

CHAPTER 17

Fitzroy Inn

Visitor's books can provide interesting glimpses into the past life of an historic property and can reveal all sorts of insights into a community's social norms. The two ageing visitor's books in the guest lounge at the Fitzroy Inn, a superbly restored 1836 Georgian with ten rooms in the foothills of New South Wales's Southern Highlands, are no exception. The first thing you notice as you begin to turn their pages is the penmanship, with comments written in beautiful cursive scripts, their letters ending in swoops and whirls and ornate flourishes indicative of a middle-class or privileged clientele. The guests of Oaklands, as it was once known, came mostly from the wealthier suburbs of Sydney— places like Strathfield, Ashfield, Mosman and Woollahra. People who could afford to travel to the 'country' for their holidays.

left First opened in 1836 and known as the 'Traveller's Inn', the Fitzroy Inn has been accommodating guests for over 170 years.

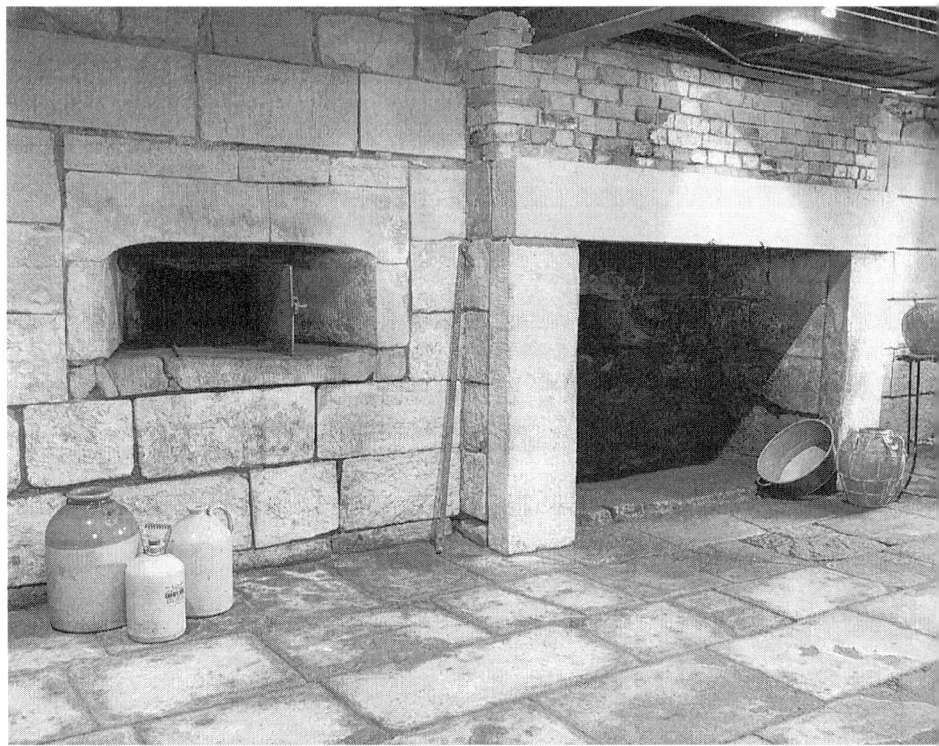

above Beneath the floorboards of the inn can be found one of the best-preserved colonial kitchens remaining in Australia.

What is also apparent are the number of comments indicating many guests had either visited the old inn many times before and were now back for their third, fourth or even fifth visits, or had never been here before and were so impressed by what they found that they fully intended to come again. Often several pairs of surnames would appear bracketed together, indicating they arrived as a group. Poetry was also a recurring form of expression, all the way from one or two verses to entire journeys.

The first and oldest entry was written by a Marjorie Kershaw from Ashfield in Sydney who must have come to the inn for her Christmas holidays. She arrived on 24 December 1923 and her summing up of her experience is succinct and to the point. 'Very jolly,' she wrote. Mr and Mrs Lawrence of Punchbowl wrote in April 1938, 'In life's ups and downs, all the "downs" are "ups" at The Oaklands.' And in May 1943 an R.B. Rule of Mosman thought everything here was just, well, 'nice'—'Oaklands is a very nice place, very nice people and very nice meals served by a very nice waitress.'

These days Oaklands is, of course, the Fitzroy Inn. Unlike some historic hotels, however, the Fitzroy Inn was built to *be* an inn and has been offering weary travellers rest, on and off, for almost 175 years. And it is, I can assure you, still a *very* 'nice' place to stay.

Paul Lovell, together with his brother-in-law and business partner Cosmo, first visited the house in the late 1980s. Although it was being lived in at the time, it was also in a period of slow decay. They immediately saw its potential and before the day was over had made an offer to purchase it. The property was eventually purchased by the two families in 1987 and it was used as a weekender until the decision was made to return the building to its original status as one of the finest accommodation houses in the Southern Highlands.

The building was gutted, its doors, windows and all its plumbing were removed and replaced. The convict-era cellar and the old kitchen—tucked away in its own subterranean world below the floorboards of the inn and one of the most intact examples of a true Georgian kitchen remaining in Australia—was revived by stonemasons who worked for five back-breaking months removing, cleaning and then replacing every one of the floor's pieces of sandstone flagging. There is also an extremely rare example of a convict-era water well, right in the middle of the kitchen floor, hand-cut through the shale that runs deep below the buildings foundations. There is even a convict cell here, complete with an original set of iron shackles and hand-turned bars that once combined to secure prisoners overnight on their way from Sydney to Berrima Jail.

Renovations proceeded at a frantic pace over a six-month period to get the inn's doors open as soon as possible. The vision was to open it before the 'new millennium', and this was achieved, with a month to spare, on 1 December 1999. The revitalised Fitzroy Inn was once again open to the public.

The 5 acres on which the inn sits today were purchased at auction by a James Foster in 1835 with the proviso that he must construct a dwelling on the site within two years. This he did, and the first recorded licensee of the inn was George Cutler in 1836, who named the impressive Georgian building the Kangaroo Inn. Unfortunately George was a nefarious chap and was shipped off to Van Diemen's Land because a large portion of the sandstone that he had been contracted to supply for the new jail at nearby Berrima somehow managed to end up in the walls of the inn. The building was renamed the Fitz Roy Inn in 1850, and in 1875 became a rather exclusive boy's prep-school until its headmaster more or less abandoned his post and decided to go off in search of diamonds. Before he left, however, he installed Australia's very first lawn tennis court right where the current one now stands.

Usually I'm wary of 'this was the first' claims made by managers and owners of historic hotels, but Paul's appears to be legitimate. The Sydney Lawn Tennis Club was formed in 1880 and the Lawn Tennis Association of Victoria in 1892, and the court at Fitzroy Inn was said to have been laid during the time the inn operated as a dormitory, which would place it sometime soon after 1875. 'We haven't had anyone refute our claim at this stage—in fact a lady recently wrote a letter to me and said she was related to the very person who brought the racquets and balls out to Australia from England.'

There are some lovely spaces in this old inn, but nowhere did I feel my pulse race quite as much as it did when I stepped inside the old Smoker's Room, a fabulous room that, although a part of the original house was, at some point between the years 1910 and 1920, completely redecorated in the Arts and Crafts style of the time. Everywhere I looked in this room I was seduced by the grace and craftsmanship of the movement that was begun by the English writer and artist William Morris who, together with the architect Phillip Webb, rejected both the opulence and the mass-produced interiors of the Victorian era and initiated a return to the more traditional art of individual craftsmanship.

Paul told me the door to the Smoker's Room was what was known as a 'faux oak' finish, over Australian cedar. Excuse me, over Australian cedar? How could anyone could think they'd improve the look and feel of cedar by applying a fake English Oak wood grain? Once inside the room, however, my misgivings evaporated.

Oak panelling 2 metres high sheathed its four walls and was capped with a small running bookshelf held in place by a series of beautifully crafted supports. The ceiling is coffered, of course, and in the corner was a fabulous American burl drinks cabinet from the 1930s which Paul is fortunate to still have in his possession. When the inn was being used as a weekender in the early 1990s, it was left empty during the week and was difficult to secure. Sure enough

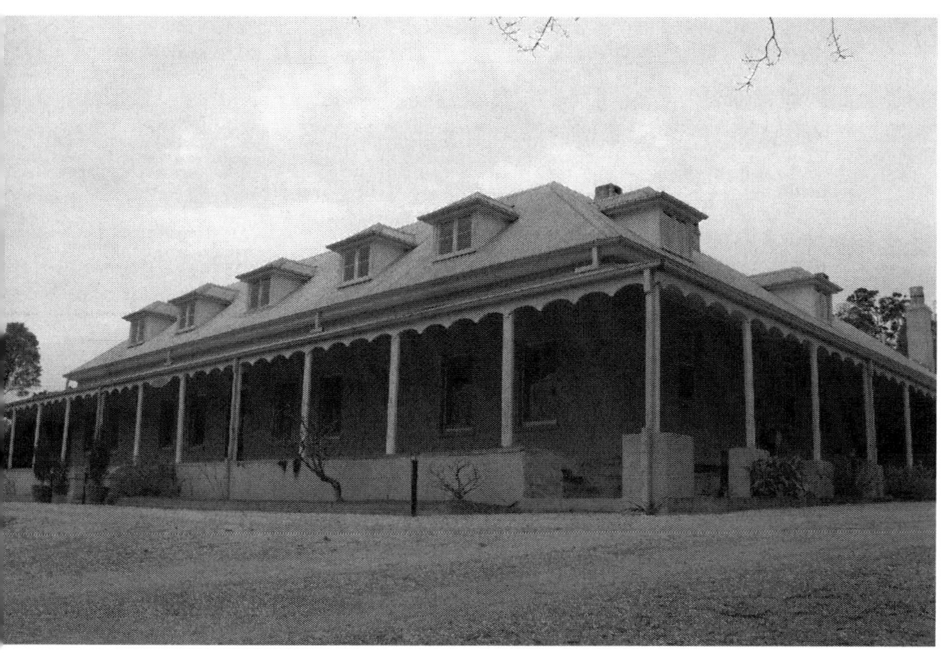

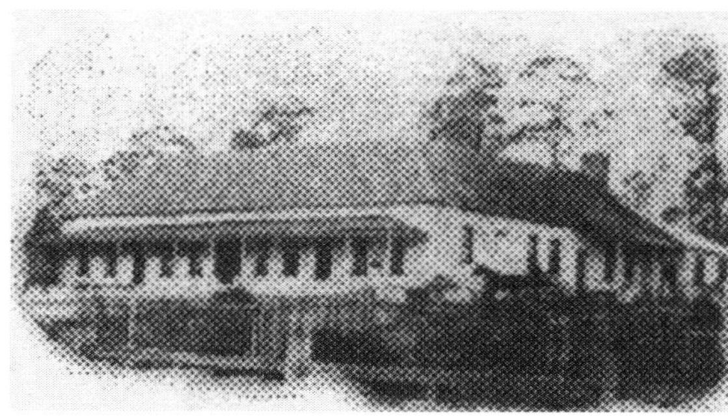

above The Fitzroy Inn in the Southern Highlands of New South Wales has been welcoming travellers for over 170 years.

left A grainy photograph of the 'Old Fitz Roy Inn', circa 1860.

one weekend Paul came down only to find someone had forced their way into the inn, found their way to the Smoker's Room and damaged the area around the cabinet's keyhole. 'It cost me more to restore it than it did to buy it,' he says. Another treasure is a four-door leadlight cabinet recessed into one of the walls that actually used to be a doorway that led through to the dining room next door. The door in the dining room is now permanently closed, and the timber panelling in the Smoker's Room artfully disguises the old door frame. Its window sills are so deep you could serve dinner on them, and its fireplace, faced with Edwardian-style bricks, is one of five working

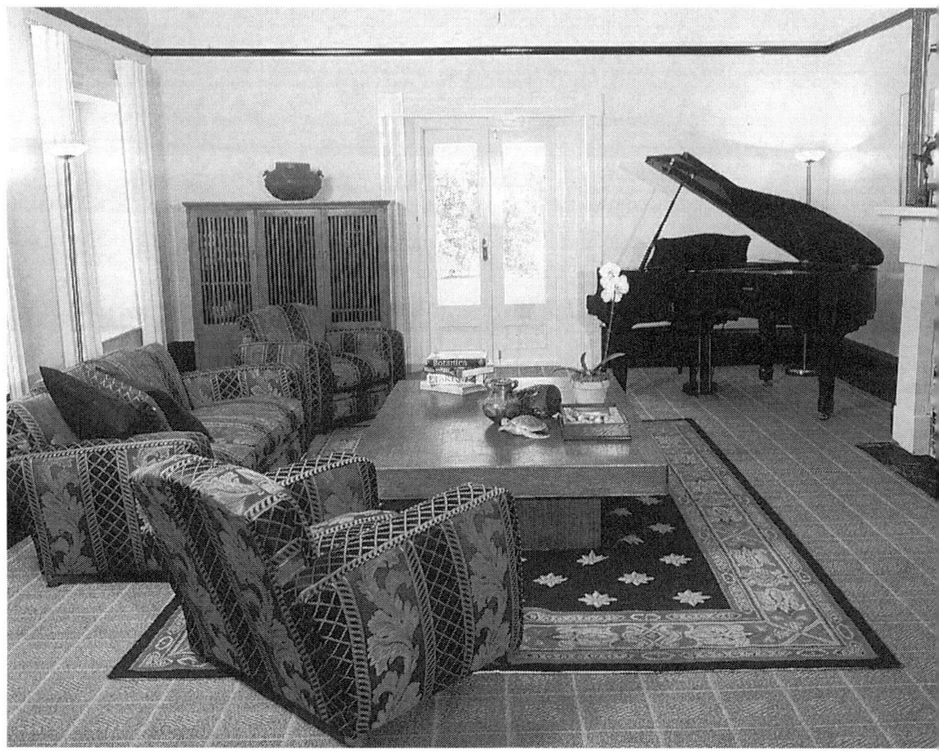

above The Fitzroy Inn's light-filled main lounge is a welcoming mix of history and creature comforts.

fireplaces found throughout the inn. It's enough to make Mittagong's 'Sturt School', which in the 1950s did much to initiate an Australian revival in the Arts and Craft tradition, very proud.

Of all the hotels and guesthouses in this book, the Fitzroy Inn is the closest to my home—a mere 30-minute drive away, and proximity certainly has its advantages. I can't wait for winter to set in so I can come here with a bottle of port, bring my favourite book, and spend a night rugged up on its Chesterfield lounge.

Like most people who own an historic property and run it as a hotel or guesthouse, Paul is committed to it seven days a week. The Fitzroy Inn is his life. Which, of course, isn't to say there aren't other things he wouldn't like to do if he had the time. He's been to Europe and would love to return there one day, and is one of those fortunate enough to have been to a concert in the magnificent Manaus Opera House deep in Brazil's Amazon jungle. He's even been to the remains of the astonishing city of 'Fordlandia', the short-lived, prefabricated city built in the Amazon rainforest in 1928 by the American industrialist Henry Ford. But what he'd most like to do is return to France, seek out an archetypal French farm and 'just lay down in its loft'. He'd stay a few weeks, become part of the ebb and flow of daily village life and leave sightseeing to the tourists. He'd get to know the local chefs, the village baker, visit its cellar doors, taste the local food and let its wines linger on the palate, go to sleep under a plane tree and wake to play petanque and watch the sun set.

Sounds awesome, Paul. Let's go.

THE OAKLANDS
Oaklands is a cosy place
The best for young and old
Swimming, tennis for the young
In weather hot or cold

The food, we think, is excellent
The waitresses the same
Especially our Doris
To please us is her aim

The folk around the fire-side
Who chatter all the day
Find the life at Oaklands
Plentiful and gay

When you find you're leaving
Do not shed a tear
For it may be possible
To come again next year

A POEM BY 'THE THREE HOLIDAY-MAKERS', DOROTHY WOODHOUSE,
MYRNA MACDONALD AND GREGORY CHESTER, GUESTS OF THE FITZROY INN,
FORMERLY OAKLANDS, 20 MAY 1942

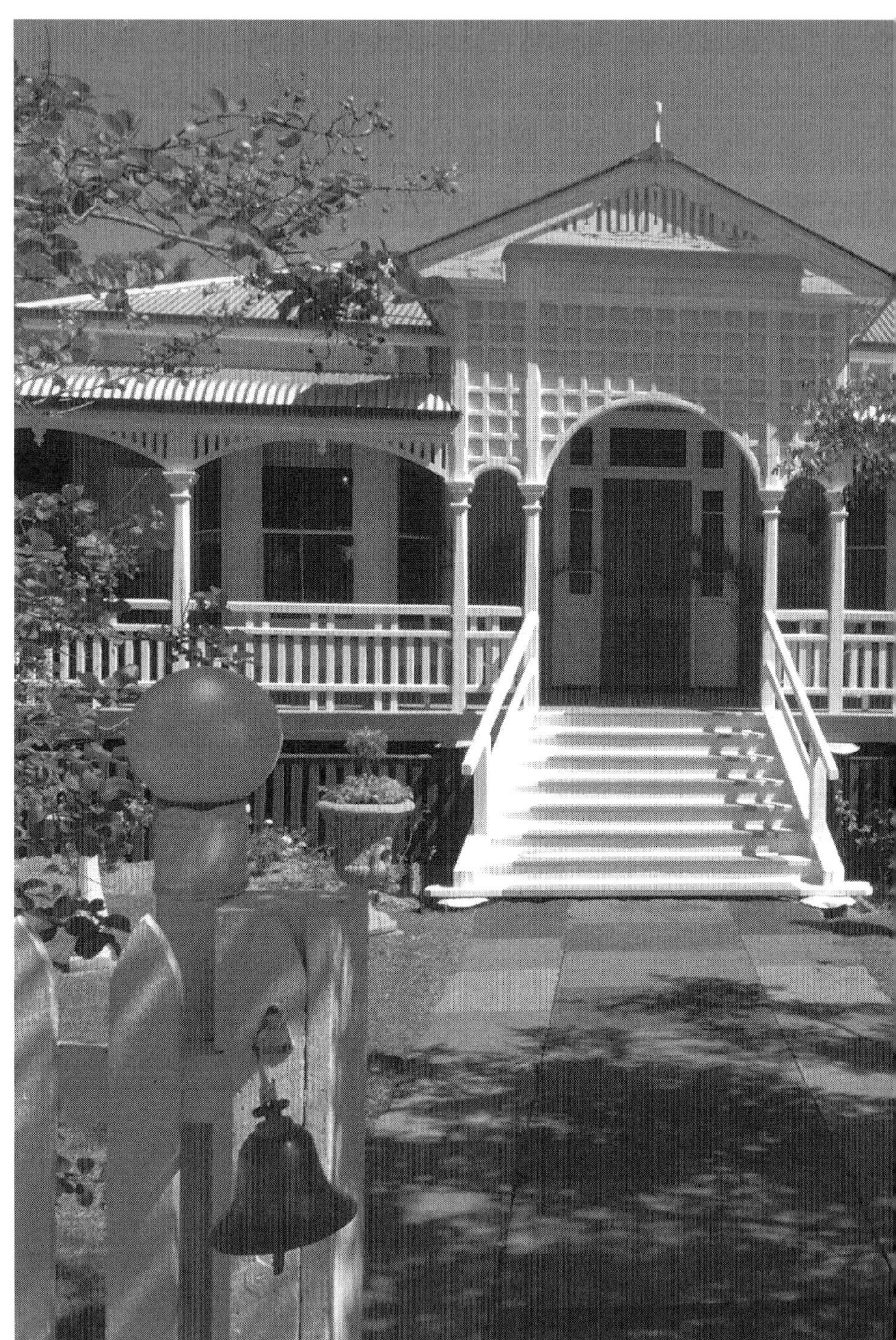

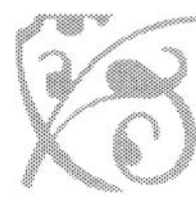

The Wiss House

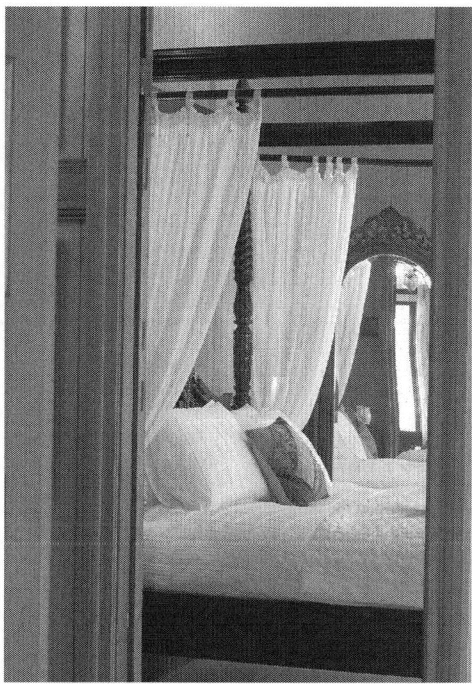

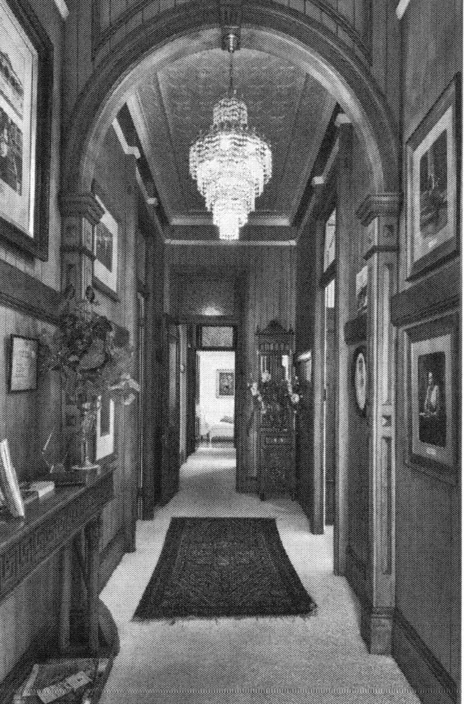

Historic hotels and guesthouses can often find themselves embroiled in the unseemliest of fights: over preservation, refurbishment, restoration and renovation. There have been countless fights between owners, heritage committees and local citizens, not to mention the ongoing battle between the past and the present, about how much to preserve and how much to compromise in a building in order to accommodate 21st-century needs and wants. But never in the world of the historic hotel has there been a fight like the one that began in 1992 in the tiny southeast Queensland town of Kalbar, population 700, a fight that made headlines across the country and was debated on talkback radio from Perth to Brisbane.

clockwise from top left The Wiss House is a symphony in wood; four-poster beds and full-length mirrors add to the charm; the timber-panelled main hallway with pressed metal ceiling.

In a very real sense, the tiny Federation-style Wiss House, at 7 Ann Street, Kalbar, went into battle not just for itself but on behalf of historic houses, guesthouses and residences alike, everywhere. And won. But to appreciate the significance of the building and just why so many people, from concerned citizens to the Heritage Council and Queensland's State Government, were prepared to fight for it, you need to know a little of its history.

Kalbar first appeared on the Queensland map as Engelsburg (The Town of the Angels) in the 1870s when an influx of immigrant German farmers settled the region the English thought of as 'rubbish country' and refused to farm. To look at Kalbar's rich, black volcanic soil today, you'd be tempted to wonder what the English possibly could have been thinking. By the turn of the century Engelsburg had became the centre of a small, closeknit rural community in what was called the Fassifern Scrub District. By 1900 the town had two hotels, three blacksmith shops, two storekeepers, two cabinetmakers, an auctioneer, a fruiterer and a carpenter, and was growing in importance as a centre for dairying and cattle.

Lionel Wiss was a German immigrant. He married Maria Wiuff in 1890 and, along with the Bickerton family, owned many of the town's commercial properties and became its principal storekeeper. The Wiss Brothers General Store was known as 'one of the best country stores in Queensland'. Due to anti-German sentiments during WWI, however, the name of the town was changed in 1916 from Engelsburg to Kalbar. The family was well-respected and during the Great Depression local farmers were kept solvent through the issuing of credit facilities by the Wiss and Bickerton families.

Lionel built Wiss House in 1900 on a residential subdivision that created most of the eastern half of the town. All of its four guest bedrooms, its hallway, front sitting room and dining room have floor-to-ceiling timber-panelled walls. The ceilings in its hallway and two front bedrooms are pressed metal and hoop pine and fine examples of cedar joinery are everywhere.

Wiss died on 11 January 1932 at the Oakland Private Hospital in Ipswich. He was 66 years old. After his death his widow Maria appointed her daughter, Adeline, to run the estate's business affairs until the business was sold in 1947. Maria died in 1957 but Adeline and her sister Phyllis remained in the house until the 1970s.

In November 1991 Robert and Judy McVicker purchased the Wiss

House for $160 000, and then shocked the residents of Kalbar by announcing their intention to move the house closer to Brisbane to the town of Mount Warren Park, 100 kilometres to the east, after receiving legal advice that an error in the conveyancing relating to their purchase of the house meant they would be able to move it despite it having been listed on the Heritage register. Their intentions didn't sit well with many Kalbar residents who had grown up around the Wiss House and considered it to be an intrinsic part of their community. In an attempt to prevent its relocation, the public petitioned Boonah Shire Council to Heritage List the property, which it was given in August 1992.

Despite having been listed, on Saturday 10 April 1993 residents of Ann Street stood aghast as a demolition/removal team arrived without warning and began removing trees and the Wiss House's front fence. The following day, 11 April, its new owners ordered workers to begin its relocation in defiance of the heritage listing, and workers started to remove its roof. A telephone call from Joy Dwyer, a counsellor from nearby Boonah Shire, to the Queensland Heritage Minister Molly Robson led to the minister issuing a 60-day stop-work order, which was delivered to Robert McVicker at 7.00 p.m. that evening. Breaching the order could have resulted in the McVickers incurring fines in excess of a million dollars.

And so the battle over the fate of the Wiss House, and potentially any other historic property in the country, hotel or otherwise, was joined with the McVickers claiming they had no idea the property had been a candidate for heritage listing at the time of purchase. In the days following the issuing of the stop-work order the McVickers camped on the verandah of their new house, still minus its roof, to guard against vandalism and theft, and at one point threatened to leave it exactly as it was if they were prevented from moving it, and the residents of Kalbar could, if they wished, sit by and watch it slowly rot.

Robert and Joy McVickers cannot in a sense be blamed for believing they had a right to relocate a house of which they were the legal owners. But their purchase was just one in a nationwide trend of historic properties being purchased and relocated. Australia's built heritage was being shuffled around like houses on a monopoly board, and the time had come to draw a line in the sand. The Wiss House would be that line.

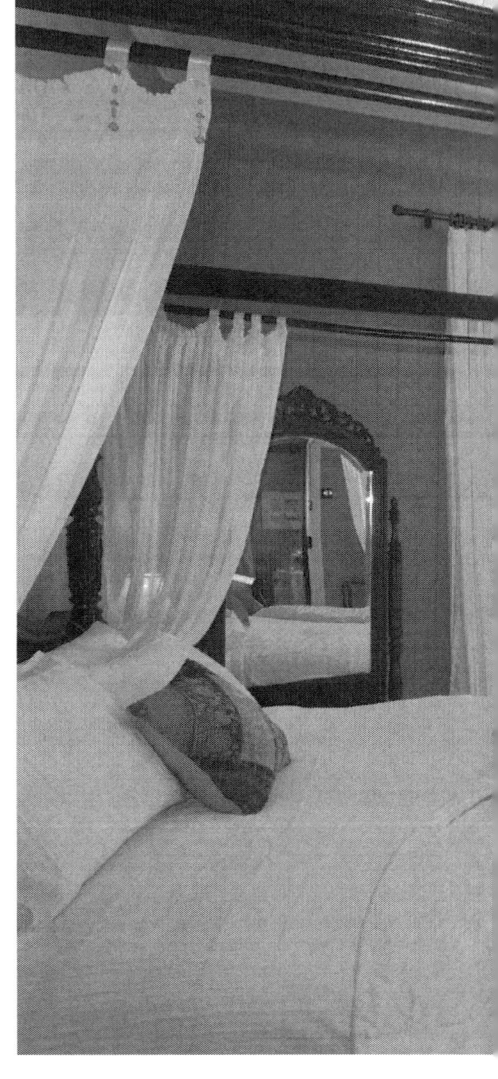

right There are four bedrooms in The Wiss House, each one individually designed and decorated. Note the timber panelled ceiling.

The fight would be a nasty one, with emotive headlines such as 'Heritage House Tug-O-War' (*The Queensland Times*, 12 April 1993), 'Family Takes On Town Over Home' (*Gold Coast Bulletin*, 13 April 1993) and 'Heritage Clamp On House Moving Plan' (*The Australian*, 19 April 1993.) And it would eventually exact a heavy toll on the McVickers, who were outraged that at a time when the state government was ignoring Heritage Council objections to turning the old Treasury Building in Brisbane into a casino, they were being victimised because they were two 'little people' wanting to move one small, residential building intact from one location to another.

Kalbar's residents were split over the issue. While many were distressed at the prospect of a piece of their history being taken from them (a petition was signed by 150 Kalbar residents in June 1992 who wanted to see the house preserved as a piece of the town's heritage), the majority sympathised with the McVickers, particularly as the house wasn't officially listed on the Heritage Register in November 1991 when they purchased it. Talkback radio stations across the country took up the cause with callers debating the merits of its possible relocation, with some defending the rights of an owner to do what he or she wanted with their own property on the one hand, and the opposing point of view that 'community' is sometimes more than just people, that buildings themselves can be a part of a community and should be left where they are. Should historic properties be simply ripped from their environment? How far do owner's rights extend over buildings that helped define the very towns in which they are set?

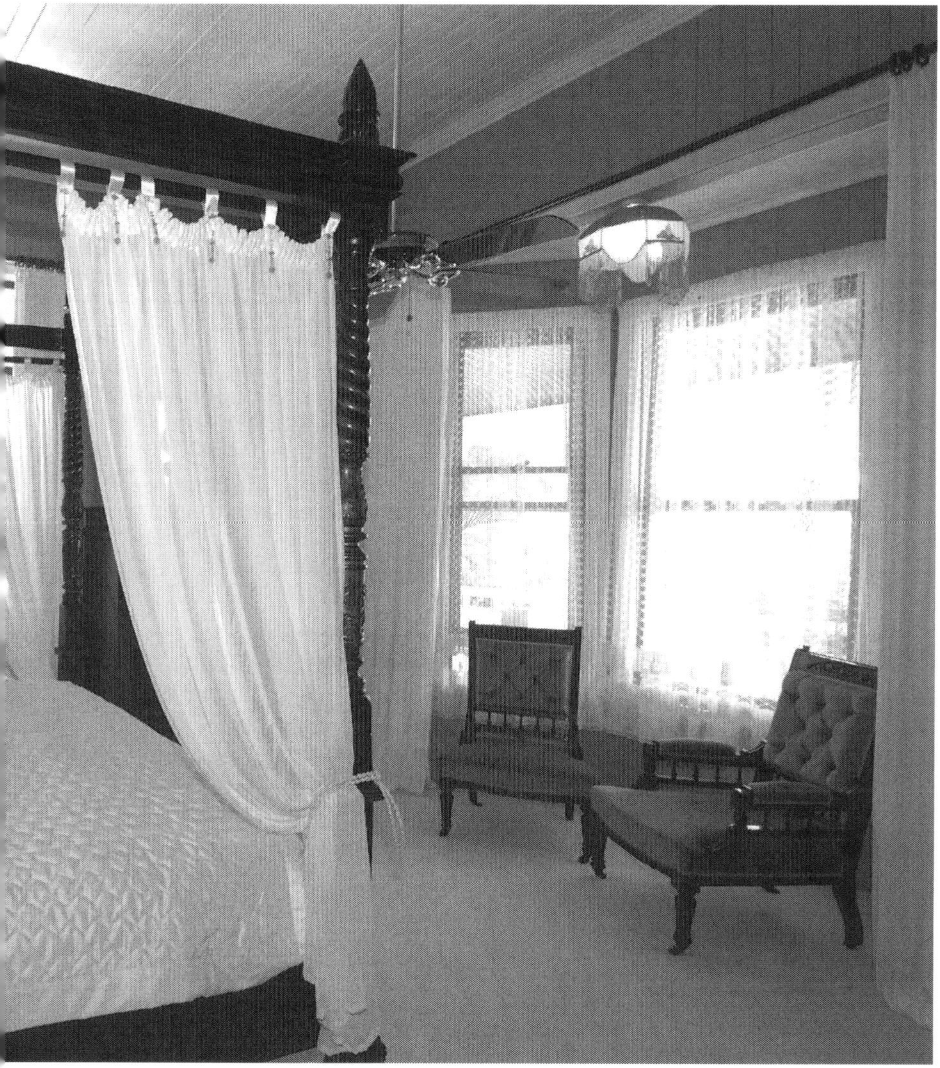

The fight went to the Planning and Environment Court. Jan McVicker likened the experience to a child custody battle. The Heritage Council argued that the house was an intrinsic part of the town, was now listed, and should not be moved and that the McVickers were aware of the Shire's objection to its removal before the Heritage Act became law in August 1992. As far as the Heritage Council was concerned, the house belonged to the community.

The Heritage Council spent 3 million dollars, employed three Queen's Councils and fought the battle for some nine months. In August 1993 the dispute was resolved out of court when the National Trust of Queensland, the Boonah Shire Council and the Department of Environment and Heritage jointly purchased the house from the McVickers for $160 000, the price they themselves had paid in November 1991, plus $35 000 to cover their expenses. Within a year councils across Australia all had in place Heritage Laws designed to keep Australia's history exactly where it was built, and whenever a challenge arose in the future, the Wiss House was used as the precedent to keep our built heritage precisely where their original owners always intended it to be.

In 1995 the house was later sold to historic-home enthusiast Douglas Panton who grew up in Maryborough, Queensland's 'heritage city', and whose father was involved in the preservation of Claremont House. Panton put the house on the market on 11 January 1997 but it lay empty until purchased by Sara Watson in October 2003, and who remains its proud owner to this day.

Sara Watson's background is in interior design. She owned the Boathouse Cafe in Daylesford, once written up as 'The Gates To Paradise' in Melbourne's *Herald Sun* newspaper before leaving Victoria and moving to Kirra Beach on the Gold Coast where she opened a cafe. She then moved to Boonah near Kalbar in search of a house she could run as a B&B. The Wiss House was for sale. She drove there, met its owner Douglas Panton at the front door, immediately fell in love with the house, and within half an hour had signed a deal. Sara transformed the Wiss House into the B&B it is today, installing a commercial kitchen, living quarters out back, and a swimming pool.

The amount of timber in this house is astonishing. Hoop pine three-quarters of an inch thick (2 centimetres) at $38 per lineal metre (that was 2003 prices) comes to more than $100 per length. I'm on the couch in the sitting room and have just counted 50 lengths of it on one wall alone—that's $5000. Multiply that by the walls in four additional bedrooms, two hallways and a dining room, then add all

the timber in its ceilings and the wraparound verandah, fretwork
trims, bay windows and multiple sets of French doors, and it's easy to
see how the value of its timbers was calculated by Sara's accountant
in 2003 as approaching $800 000.

Elsewhere in Kalbar there is the Wiss Cottage, built in 1890, where
Lionel and Maria lived before moving to their larger house in Ann
Street, and beside that is the Wiss Emporium, built in 1909. Here you
can find traditional clothing, jewellery, paintings by local artists and
handmade quilts by a local quilter, Margaret Mauchlan, and you won't
believe her prices. Quilts that would cost $200-plus in Sydney can
be purchased for around $60. Marjorie quilts for the love of it, and is
happy to sell them for a price that barely makes up for the material,
not to mention the hours spent sewing. My suitcase was fairly bulging
with them.

The French–Australian co-production *The Tree*, about a 10-year-
old girl who, together with her mother, believes the spirit of her dead
father lived on amongst the high branches of their tree, had some
exteriors filmed on the outskirts of Kalbar. The actress Charlotte
Gainsbourg, who starred in the film, lived in the Wiss House for three
months during the filming of scenes in the Kalbar area. Before she
left she gave Sara a copy of the script plus numerous stills from the
movie, which makes interesting reading while sitting on one of the
many wicker chairs that line the verandahs of this peaceful little place,
a peace that gives no hint of the battles it once fought on behalf of
vulnerable historic buildings everywhere.

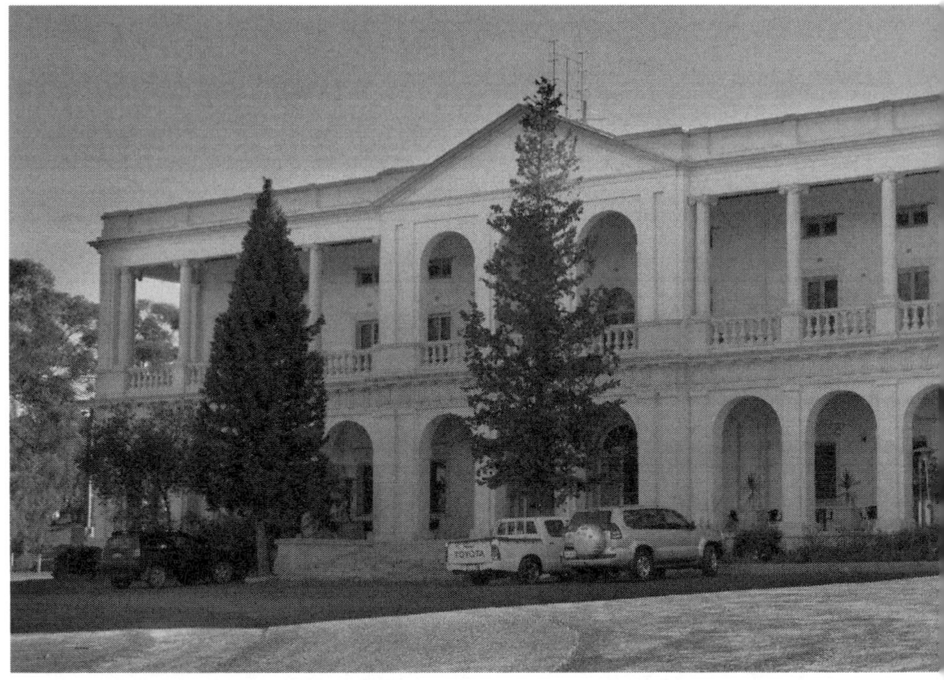

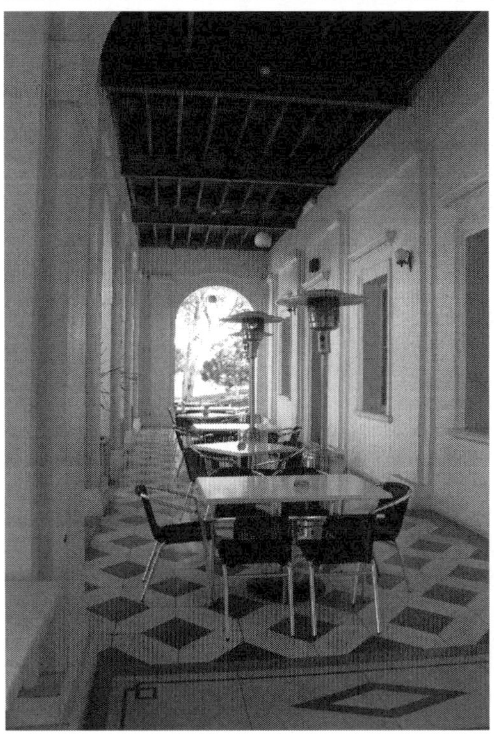

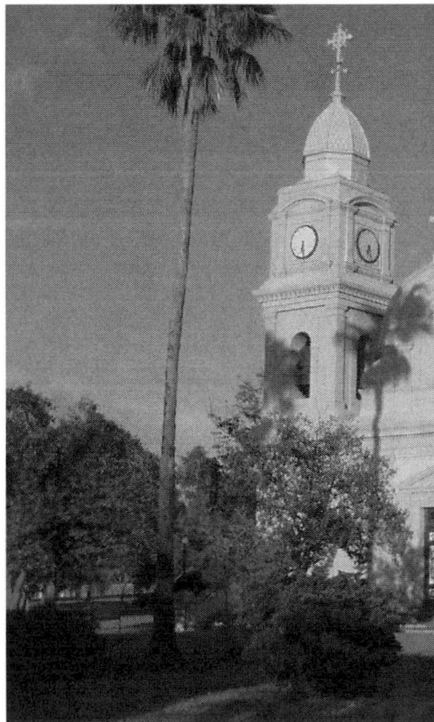

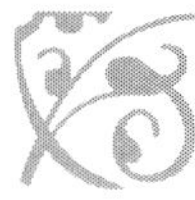

CHAPTER 19

New Norcia Hotel

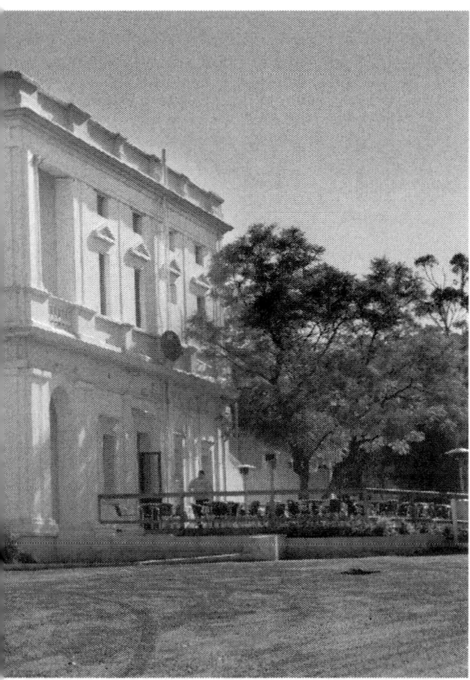

The early decades of the 19th century weren't easy ones for the Spanish Catholic Church. Beginning in 1812 Spain's conqueror Napoleon Bonaparte confiscated the church's property, although this was only a temporary inconvenience and the rights of the church were re-established by King Ferdinand in 1814 after the Spanish War of Independence. In 1835 it happened again with a pronouncement by Spain's Minister of Finance, Juan de Mendizabal, confiscating the church's possessions and suppressing its monastic communities. For two zealous, young Spanish Benedictine monks desperate to express their faith, enough was enough. It was time to leave.

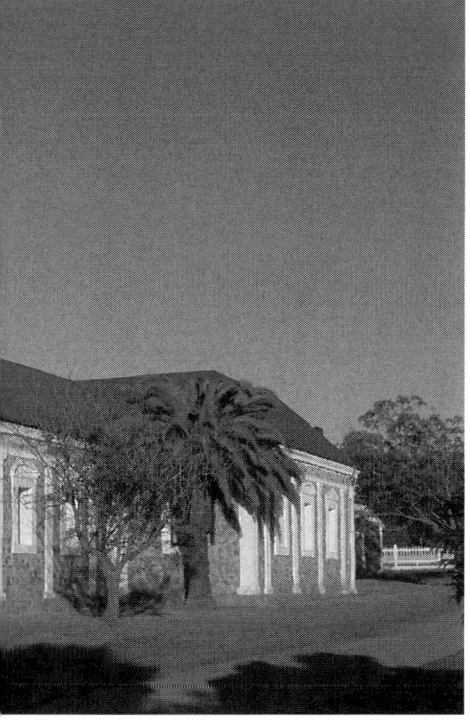

clockwise from top The New Norcia Hotel was originally a hostel built by Benedictine monks in 1927; the Abbey church is the oldest Catholic Church still in use in Western Australia; the hotel's ground floor balcony.

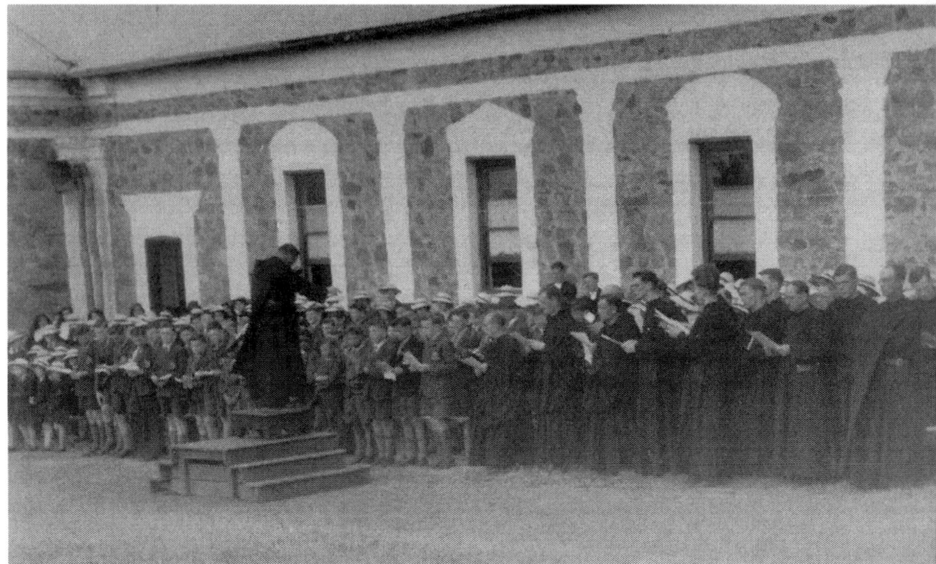

above By the 1920s New Norcia had been transformed by the monks from an inland mission for Indigenous children into a centre of education for all.

Dom Jose Benito Serra fled to Rome in 1835 and from there to the Abbey of the Most Holy Trinity near Salerno. Dom Rosendo Salvado followed Dom Serra to Salerno in 1838. Then in 1844 the two men petitioned the church hierarchy in Rome to send them overseas as missionaries so they could work together and continue their missionary calling, and it was decided they would be sent to Western Australia with the newly appointed Bishop of Perth, the Right Reverend John Brady. Serra and Salvado would at last be able to work together towards their shared, cherished ideal—to create a solid monastic family in Australia which, through hard work and faith, would become manifest to the Indigenous population and be a mission through which Indigenous people would gain an education and, in the process, come to know God.

They arrived in Fremantle in January 1846, a time when nothing was known about what lay beyond the limits of the district of Perth. Dom Salvado, together with Serra, two other monks, a catechist, a bullock wagon full of provisions, and a cash reserve of 3 pounds given him by the Diocese of Perth, set out in the direction of New Norcia. After a week the party set up camp on the bank of a small spring 5 kilometres (3 miles) north of where New Norcia lies today.

On 1 March 1846, in the presence of a small group of curious Aborigines, they presided over their first Mass, and took their first steps in establishing a mission. There were setbacks, of course. Their Irish catechist, John Gorman, died, and a novice became ill and had to return to Perth. Dom Salvado wrote in a letter to the diocese in Perth, 'I can say that I have watered the Australian soil with the sweat of my brow and with the blood of my lacerated feet.'

By April 1847 a small stone house, measuring 12 metres by 5 metres that would be both chapel and dwelling for the two determined monks, was built on the banks of the Moore River. Further setbacks were to come, however. Dom Serra was ordered to return to Rome in 1848, and the following year Dom Salvado, too, was returned to Italy to raise funds and recruit more missionaries: he wouldn't return to New Norcia until 1853, when he arrived with 43 Benedictine postulants and 7000 pounds.

In 1859 a decree from Rome separated the New Norcia mission from the Diocese of Perth. This was the mission's great turning point. New houses and orphanages were built for the Indigenous communities, classrooms were built for the children, a flour mill was established, new roads were constructed, storehouses and workshops sprung up throughout the community, and more than a hundred stone wells were sunk into the surrounding bush to provide water for increasingly large flocks of sheep. Soon Australia had its first, and to this day its only, monastic town.

After his death in 1900 Dom Salvado's successor, Bishop Fulgentius Torres, realised New Norcia could not continue indefinitely as a mission and began to transform it into a centre of learning. Many of the grand public buildings you see here today, the former St Ildephonsus' College building for boys and St Gertrude's for girls, were built under Torres's rule. New Norcia had its own olive press, flour mills and post office. It had a police station, machinery sheds and a blacksmith's shop. And it had a hostel, built by the monks in 1927 so parents could make extended visits to see their children who were boarding in the monastery's schools. When more educational institutions began to open in the region in the 1940s and early 1950s, and New Norcia's student numbers began to dwindle, the hostel was converted into a hotel in 1955 and has been the New Norcia Hotel ever since.

I arrived at 2.30 in the afternoon and received my first sense of being somewhere with a little more soul than most when I stepped out onto my balcony, a giant 40 metre by 4 metre verandah that I found myself sharing with everyone else who happened to have an east-facing room. It was tempting to linger. It seemed everyone was enjoying a glass of New Norcia's Abbey Ale, a delightful blend of pale malted barley and Belgian candy sugar brewed with imported hops and fermented with a Belgian Ale yeast and available on tap, in six packs or cartons from the New Norcia Hotel bar.

But be prepared. Rooms at The New Norcia Hotel don't have televisions, data ports or mobile phone reception and none of the rooms, so far as I could tell, had bathrooms. Instead there are shared bathrooms at the end of the corridor. But what is wrong with that? I, for one, found it refreshing to have an absence of the things that can prevent you from reading a good book or having an early night or enjoying a walk along a shared balcony and making new friends. The New Norcia Hotel achieves without even trying what most hotels don't even attempt—it creates a sense of being 'in community' with others, including whatever it was that was crawling around in my roof, and under normal circumstances I would have loved nothing more than to linger and chat the night away about the pros and cons of the Reformation or the Doctrine of Transubstantiation or laughing over *The DaVinci Code* ... but I'd become a little lost on a gravel road on the two-hour drive north from Perth, and was late for a meeting with a *very* important archivist.

Peter Hocking lives and works at New Norcia as its resident archivist. He began his working life as a Latin and Greek classicist but soon realised that career prospects for a Latin and Greek classicist were poor at best and instead became a rare books cataloguer at Cambridge University in England. He went on to establish a library service for a college in Sweden before coming to Australia to teach librarianship at Perth's Curtin University. Peter had a brief association with New Norcia in the 1990s when he became involved in the relocation of the library's most precious documents and books from the southern wing of the monastery to their new home in a safe, purpose-built library, which meant he could get a good night's sleep again and not worry about it all going up in a fire. He now works at New Norcia from Mondays to Thursdays and continues to lecture on librarianship at Curtin every Friday and, by his own account, has a wonderful life. An archivist by day,

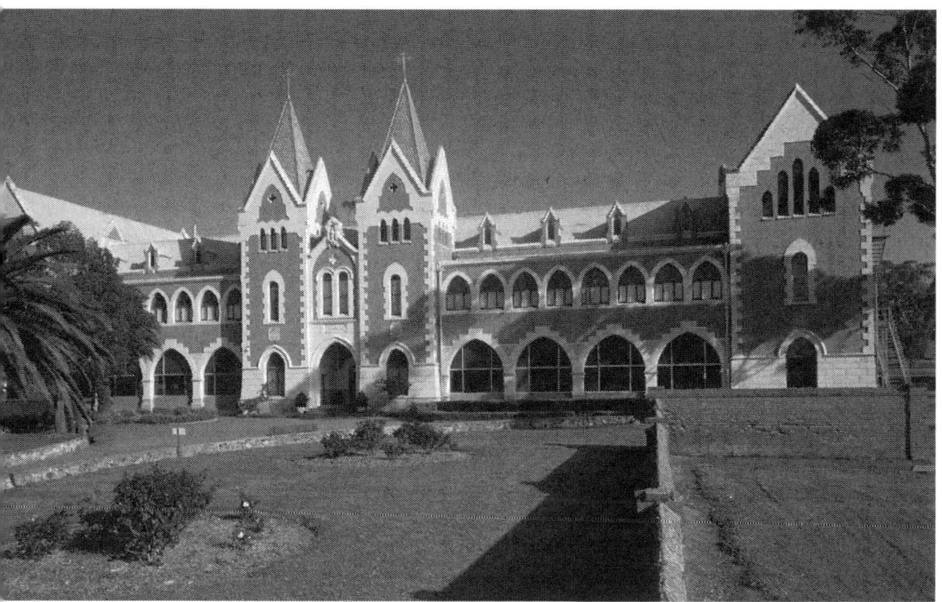

above St Gertrude's College for Girls, completed in 1908, is one of two colleges constructed at New Norcia under the reign of Bishop Fulgentius Torres.

he spends his evenings either preparing for his Friday lecture or playing his Casio keyboard with headphones well and truly on so as not to intrude upon the monastery's Grand Silence, which kicks in every evening at 8.30. We met in his archives office, and decided to go for a walk.

Walking around a monastic community can be a tricky affair. There are, of course, many places you are allowed and most welcomed to go, but there are also a few places you might want to think twice about going, and then there are areas that you just, well, that you probably just shouldn't go. Monasteries are not churches, they are not just religious institutions. They are people's homes. The getting of keys and the acquiring of permission from the right people to access certain areas that might involve the crossing of courtyards and in order to *get* to those areas can often require a lot of etiquette and a keen awareness of the sensitivities of the monks. But Peter had decided we had to brave a crossing of the monastic courtyard, because he wanted to show me one very special library. So we ventured out onto and across the courtyard, feeling like we were 'creeping around', seeking the optimum route through the garden, tiptoeing and holding our breath. But we made it, and went inside. I'm so glad that we did.

New Norcia's original library was designed and built by the gifted Spanish craftsman Juan Casellas. It has a beautifully decorated pressed metal ceiling and elaborately carved timbers and hundreds upon hundreds of individually hand-hewn notches along the supports of all the library's shelves, allowing every last shelf to be adjusted by height to accommodate whatever sized books are placed in them. Most of the books, letters and documents that were once here are now in the new library across the road, including the monastery's oldest book, a 1508 encyclopedia entitled *Margareta Philosophica*, and a personal letter to the monks at New Norcia written by Queen Isabella II of Spain.

The library at New Norcia currently has more than 80 000 books, about 2000 of which have a publication date prior to 1801, which is a rather significant date for the publishing industry in Australia—1801 is the year Australia published its first book, which of course means anything published prior to 1801 was, of necessity, imported. The new library is closed on Mondays and I wasn't able to see inside, but there was still *one* collection here in the old library that hadn't been moved, and Peter was rather anxious for me to see it.

In the 1860s a French theologian and author by the name of Jacques-Paul Migne (1800–75) decided it was time someone brought together into a single collection of volumes every Greek as well as medieval and classical Latin manuscript known to exist at the time. It was an unheard-of undertaking, and yet here I was looking at the results of Migne's herculean task—approximately 500 volumes covering an entire wall of an anteroom just off the main library. The volumes were packed so tightly together that from a distance they resembled some kind of three-dimensional wallpaper in varying shades of faded brown and tan. Surprisingly the collection is not considered valuable in monetary terms, but what it lacks in dollar value it more than makes up for by the fact that this is a *complete* collection. Not a single one of the 500-odd volumes is missing. If you ever come to New Norcia, you'll have to grit your teeth and ask to see it, because neither Migne's collection nor the old library are on any of its organised tours.

Leaving the library we made our way to the cemetery. All the monks who have served at New Norcia and passed on are buried here and the entire cemetery with its 200 plots is about to be 're-mapped' by another archivist and a new database established. Every plot was recently photographed by Peter from a cherry-picker, no less, and each will be located by GPS so the expansion of the cemetery over the last 150 years can be assessed.

Perhaps it was the visit to the cemetery where we lingered over the grave of the last Spanish monk, Dom Paulino Gutierrez, who died only last January at the age of 99, just five months short of his 100th birthday, or the eerie stillness of the afternoon's fading light—whatever it was it was a sombre reflection of Peter's that this community, once alive with two vibrant and boisterous school communities (both have now closed), seems at times more like a ghost town. Where once there used to be rugby clubs, rifle clubs, a radio club, hockey, football and sports carnivals, and hundreds of students is now home to a museum, an art gallery, a roadhouse, a gift shop, and, of course, the New Norcia Hotel. In July 2010 there were only nine monks in residence, although this, I was told, represents an 'upward' trend. Everybody certainly seems busy enough. There isn't enough time for Peter to do all the cataloguing and other tasks that are required of him. New archival material still arrives, he says, 'by the truckload' as numbers of monks and nuns in other monasteries dwindle and the decision is made to close them down and send their material to New Norcia for safekeeping.

For the visitor to this remarkable community, particularly for anyone possessing a Christian faith, there's no end of worthwhile pursuits. Why not start your day with a Vigil at 5.15 a.m., or if you sleep in and miss that there are Morning Prayers which are then followed by Mass in the Abbey Church and more prayers at midday. After lunch Afternoon Prayers are available from Mondays through Fridays with late afternoon Vespers before dinner, and if you missed all that because you decided instead to take the New Norcia River Walk through the community's farm paddocks and spend a leisurely hour or two strolling along the Moore River, there's always the evening Compline (traditionally Prayers at the End of the Day). Or why not arrange to have a chat with one of the monks on any day but Sunday in the Monastery Parlour and ask them the question that everyone has always wanted to ask of a monk: 'So just what is it you *do* all day, anyway?'

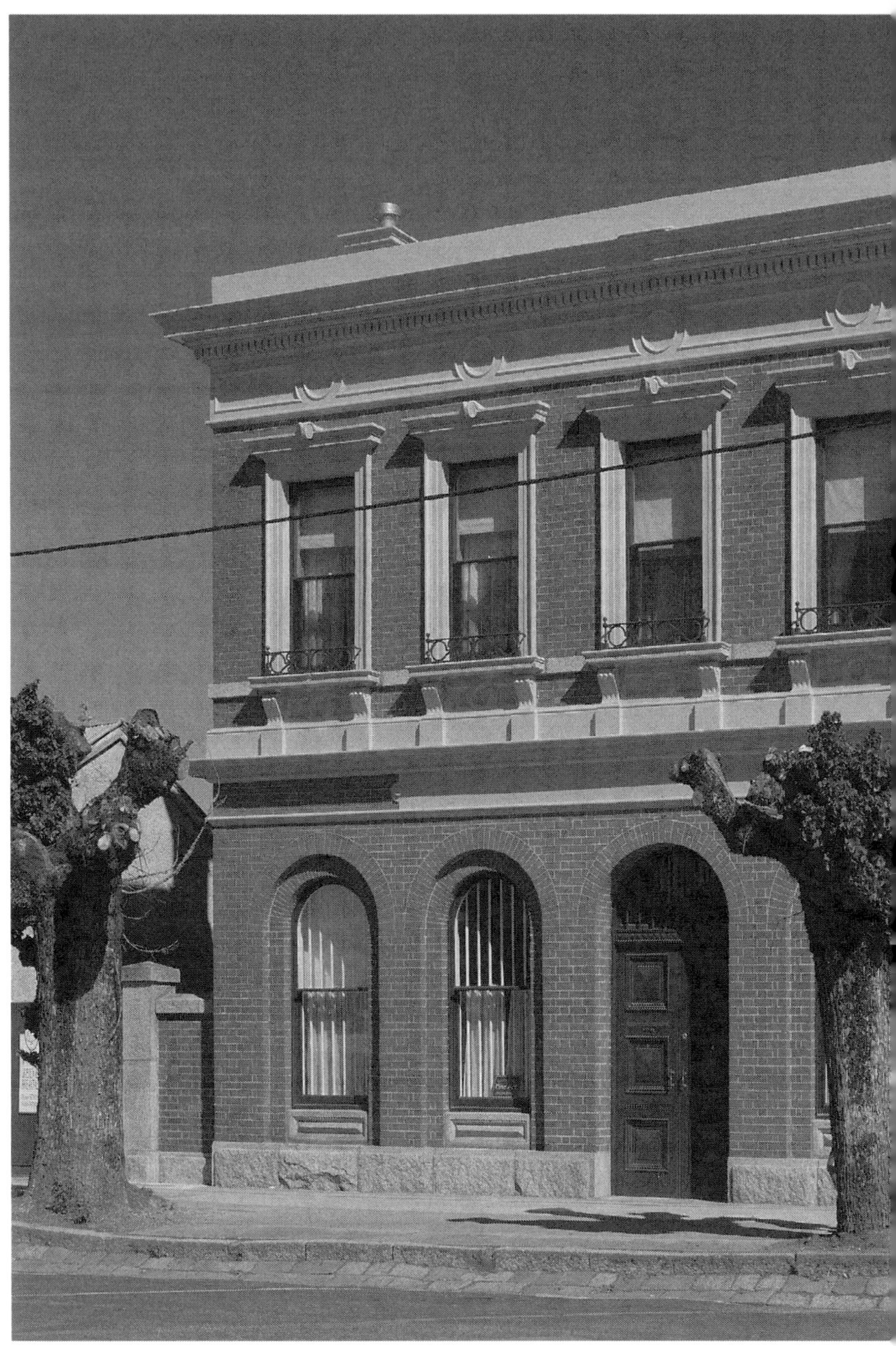

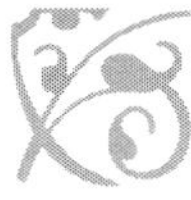

CHAPTER 20

Freeman on Ford

Freeman on Ford's napkins are embroidered lace work and its mirrors are sterling silver. So are the hair brushes you find on your mantlepiece that sits over your period fireplace and the teaspoons with crystal droplets used for afternoon tea which, by the way, is complimentary. Local jams, berries and breads from the town bakery accompany scrumptious morning and afternoon snacks, and the lemons in its cakes are picked from the lemon tree out back.

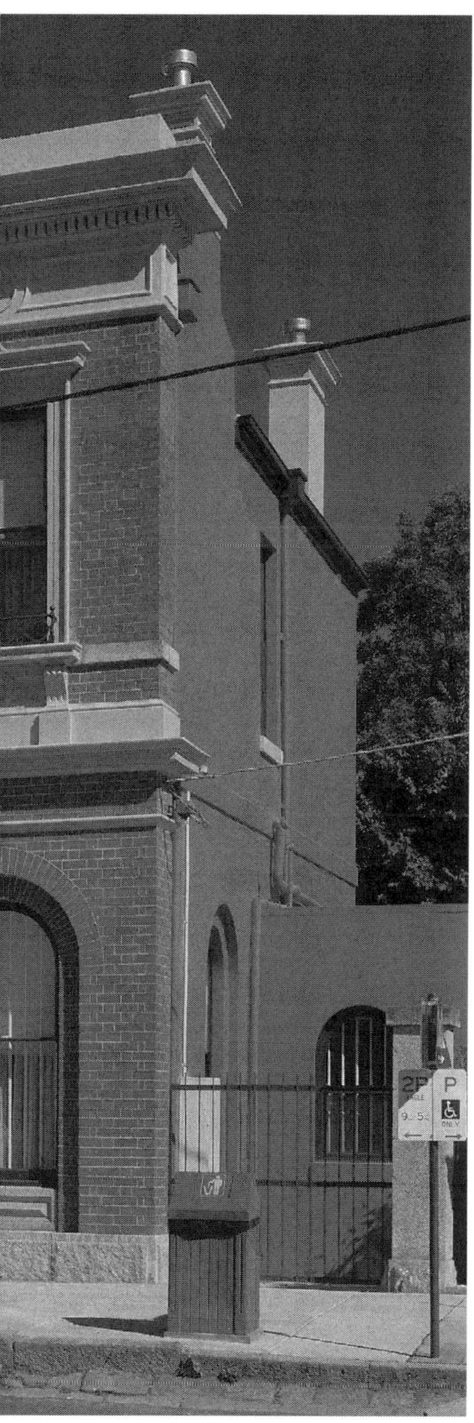

left Commercial architecture was never so elegant. Built as the Oriental Bank in 1876, Freeman on Ford became a convent for Brigidine nuns in 1886. From 1906 it was reborn as a branch of the State Savings Bank of Victoria, which it remained until 1988.

Its owner, Heidi Freeman, described people who have cried when it's come time to leave. For Heidi and her partner Jim Didlios, who owns The Confectionary House in the Melbourne suburb of Thomastown and whose scorched almonds, fruit choc drops and original homestyle choc honeycomb have occasionally found their way into the pockets of grateful guests, it's not just about the welcome when you come and stay at the only five-star accommodation in Beechworth, Victoria's prettiest town. It's about making their home your home. Heidi thinks nothing of taking 20 minutes to tell you of her trip to Albury to search for light fittings or fabrics for the new extension at the rear of the property.

Heidi and Jim have turned their dream of owning the perfect B&B into reality. The two-storey brick building on Beechworth's Ford Street, designed by architect Leonard Terry in 1876, was the Oriental Bank until 1884, built to service the financial needs of the area's 5000-strong community of Chinese goldminers. In 1886 it was purchased by the Reverend Dean Tierney on behalf of St Joseph's Catholic Church for 1000 pounds and turned into a convent and school under the auspices of the church's Brigidine nuns, becoming only the second Brigidine convent to be established in Australia. When a new, larger convent was constructed in nearby Priory Lane in 1906, the building again reverted to a bank, this time the State Savings Bank of Victoria which it remained until sold as a private residence in 1988. Heidi and Jim purchased the building in 2002 and have been renovating it on and off ever since.

Heidi loves to talk about the little things she's done here. Things like the childproof gate at the top of the stairs installed by a State Bank manager who lived upstairs with his young family that she insists on leaving intact, not because it serves any useful purpose or possesses any historical significance but simply because it tells a story. Or the tiny little elf-like door that looks to have been taken right out of a Roald Dahl book that she fastened to the trunk of the elm tree out front, just to bring a little magic to the streetscape and to delight the young and the young at heart as they walk by. In a world where little time and attention are applied to things that don't add something to the bottom line, it's refreshing to see someone who adds things to the world just for the sake of whimsy. Not all their ideas were greeted warmly, however. Heidi and Jim's decision to paint over the building's rather awful pink exterior that

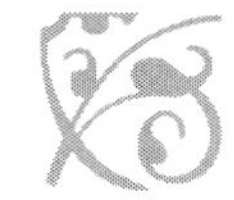

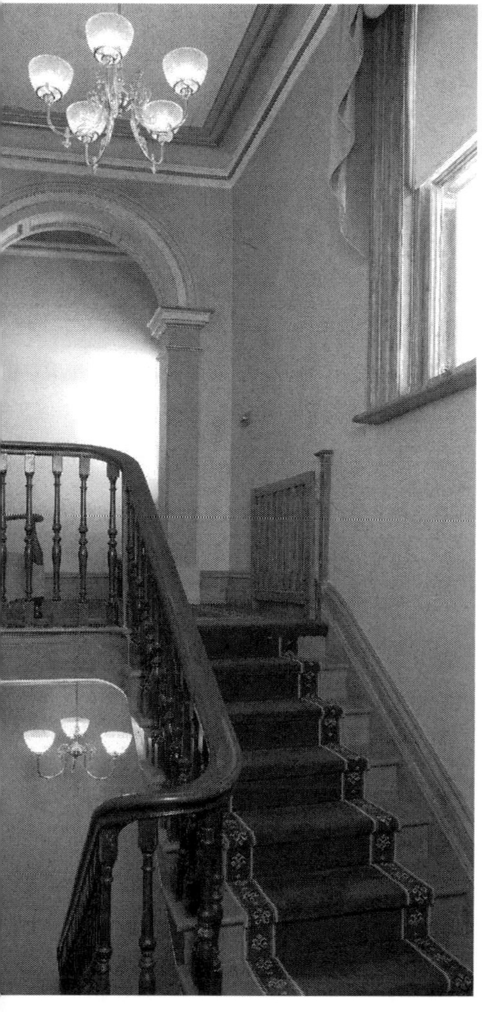

left Freeman on Ford's main staircase. Note the child-proof gate at the top of the stairs, a reminder that even as a bank, the building was still a family residence.

most Beechworth residents had grown up with, and return it to its original terracotta, generated much community ire.

Sigrid Thornton, John Jarrod, Jennifer Hawkins, Bruce Beresford and the Premier of Victoria John Brumby have all stayed here, as has Australian artist Ken Done who told Heidi over breakfast one morning how much he loved the palette of colours she'd chosen in his room and that he couldn't have done better himself. Attention to detail is her passion. So is being the perfect host. Like one cold night in the midst of winter when an elderly Russian man who couldn't speak a word of English turned up on the doorstep looking for a room. She took him in, sat him in a chair, tucked him up in a blanket, and made him a cup of tea. The old man kissed her hand in gratitude.

The former bank has to rate as one of the state's most beautiful commercial buildings. Small though it may be, its proportions are perfect and its meticulous, ongoing restoration has seen nothing overlooked. Compromise just isn't in Heidi's vocabulary.

The bank closed in 1988 and was used as a private residence from 1991 to 2002 when Heidi and Jim purchased it from its then-owner Mary in the face of buyer interest from as far afield as Southeast Asia. Heidi and Jim immediately fell in love with it and were thrilled that its owner chose them to be its new stewards. 'Mary, why are you

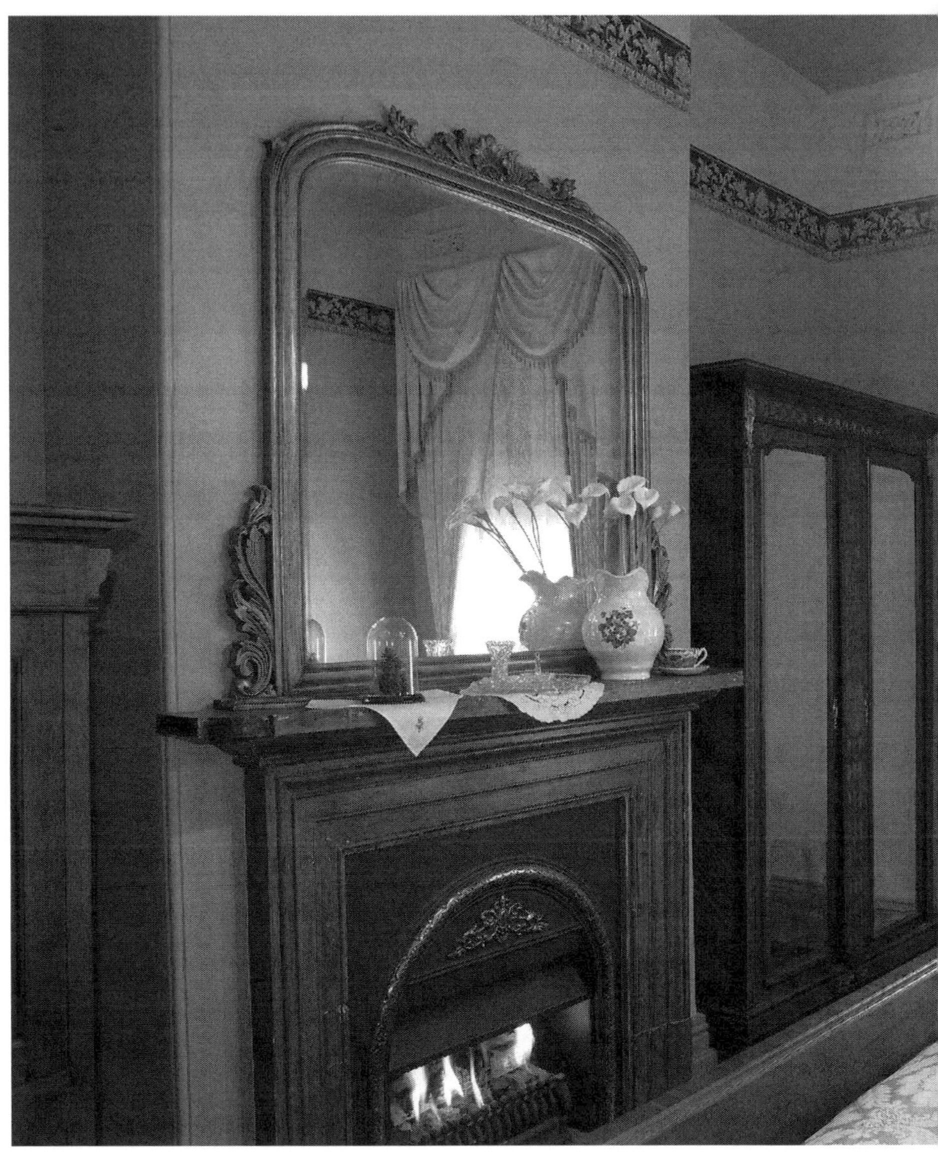

offering it to me?' Heidi recalled asking her.

'Because I know you're not going to 'gut it' and also because I know you'll make a success of it,' came the reply.

This was no random purchase. Heidi told me she felt she had been almost destined to buy it as a way of honouring her late father, Michael Isaac Freeman, who ran a number of drapery stores

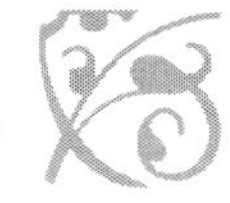

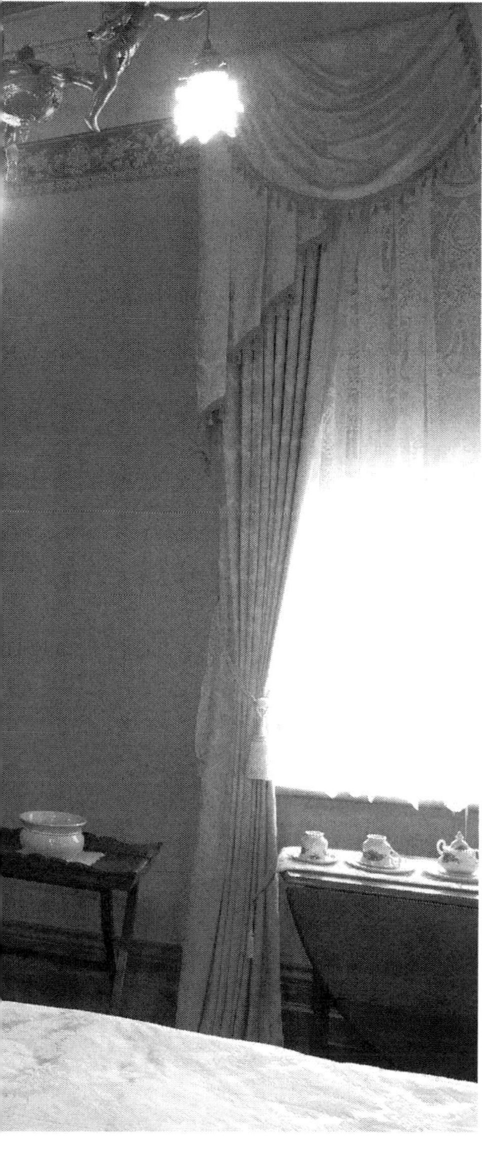

left A gas fireplace, lace doilies, flowers and fine china—more like Grandma's place than Beechworth's only five-star accommodation.

throughout country Victoria and purchased his Beechworth store, 'Freeman, The Bargain Draper', in 1952. It was the largest shop in town, boasting four separate departments and selling everything from women's and baby wear, and men's and boy's clothes to furniture, carpets, suitcases, bedding and kitchenware. Michael Freeman arrived in Australia from Poland in 1928 and was at times a teacher, philanthropist and soldier; he could speak six languages including Arabic; and was one of the first men in Beechworth to enlist when World War II began in September of 1939, serving in the Intelligence Corps and being wounded whilst on active duty in Libya. He and his wife Herta became parents to four children: Michael, Graeme, Helen and Heidi. Heidi is no 'city slicker' who came to Beechworth with a need for a 'tree change'. Far from just another urban transplant, Heidi and Jim are as much a part of Beechworth as the vineyards on its hillsides and the granite in its buildings.

Always looking at how Freeman on Ford can integrate itself into the community that surrounds it, the removal of a large pair of timber gates, that for years had kept hidden a quite beautiful hand-built sandstone wall of considerable age, suddenly opened up the garden and, in so doing, gave it back to the town. Its removal also created a quaint little courtyard that encourages passers-by to come in off the street and experience its stillness. With the help of a few family members Heidi then purchased a 2.4-metre high bronze and copper statue of Ned Kelly and is a popular spot for the hundreds of people each day who use it as a backdrop for family photos.

The old bank's original front door has a welcoming timber exterior but its internal face is no-nonsense steel, complete with all the hardware and sliding iron bars befitting a bank in a goldrush town that saw in excess of 4 million ounces of gold (115 tonnes) taken out of the ground in the 14 years since gold was first discovered here in 1852. Fifteen hundred kilometres (900 miles) of water races were cut through its hills, more than in any other Victorian goldrush town. Rivers and streams had their courses altered, and it's been said, though never proven, that a miner once rode his horse down Ford Street with the horse wearing horseshoes made of solid gold.

Freeman on Ford's stunning bank vault, with its curved brick ceiling reminiscent of an 11th-century Norman arch and whitewashed granite walls, will one day become a massage room and the old banking chambers now serve as the reception area. Floorboards have been polished and three stunning Victorian-era chandeliers now shed ample light on the room's intricate cornices that seem to be a mile away on impossibly high ceilings. New ceiling roses have been added and specialised plasterers have been employed to restore some missing florets by creating fresh moulds then piecing them together like three-dimensional jigsaws.

In the 1860s the allotment ran all the way from the bank's rear wall down to Loch Street but was later partitioned to make way for the 'Cassidy House', a typical early 20th-century cottage that was home to the Cassidys and their nine children. Full of period character with ornate plasterwork, highly decorative windows and an old woodstove in the kitchen, the children sold it to Heidi upon the death of their mother with the promise it would be retained and run as a self-contained cottage. The house now represents yet another stage in Heidi's unfolding passion for restoration and will be linked to the main building via a new swimming pool and landscaped gardens. Two new family suites have also been added to the rear of the old bank, each with views to the rear of the Cassidy House through a series of floor-to-ceiling bifolding timber doors.

Sentimental reminders that hark back to her father's old drapery stores include mannequins in period Victorian dress and old fabrics turned into cushions. Monopoly, chess, Scrabble, Trivial Pursuit and books, from a guidebook to Buckingham Palace to Henrietta Leyser's *Medieval Woman: A Social History of Women in England 450–1500* are in the intimate downstairs sitting room to relax you, an effortless task thanks to Heidi's innate ability to create spaces that are welcoming, that lack any attempt at pretence, that encourage you to walk down from your room or when you return from dinner and behave as you would in your own home.

Heidi and Jim will sometimes even take guests in their own car to old goldmining sites, to Woolshed Falls to look for kangaroos and to Opera in the Alps, an annual outdoor concert that brings opera from the concert halls to the people, held each year at Beechworth's Mayday Hills Oval. Organised by Australian Music Events, previous singers have included Marina Prior and David Hobson with support from the Opera in the Alps choir and the Melbourne Youth Orchestra.

When Freeman on Ford at last becomes the perfect haven it is destined to become, it will be the turn of The Star Hotel just up the street to benefit from the Heidi and Jim treatment. Recently purchased by the crusading couple, the Star's Casino Room boasts one of the best examples of a pressed metal ceiling remaining in Victoria and, on a more grisly note, once bore witness to a goldfever-inspired murder. I've a feeling that in just a few years from now, Freeman on Ford could have some very serious competition.

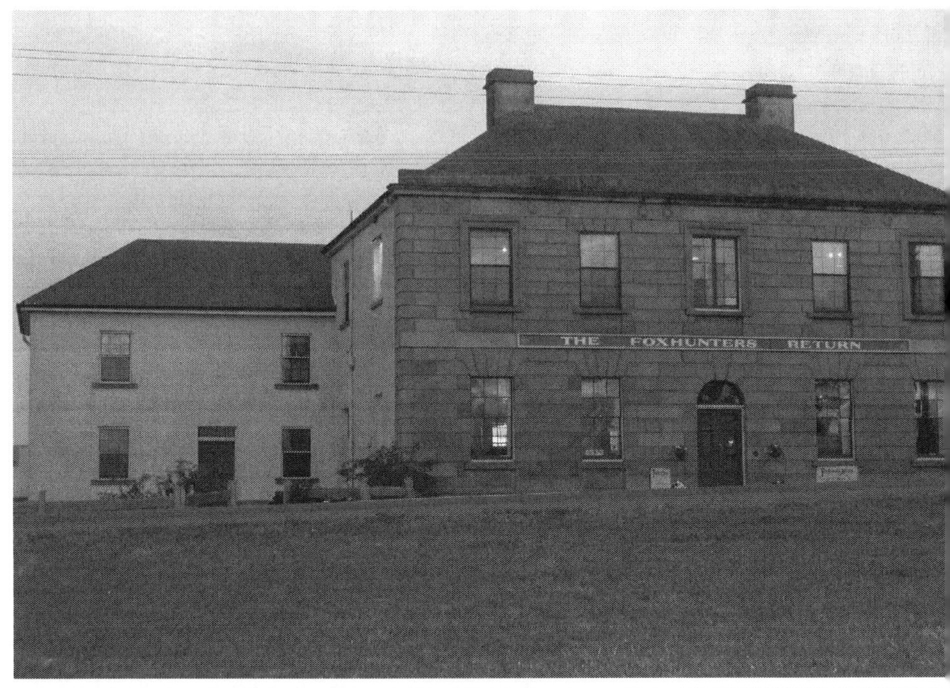

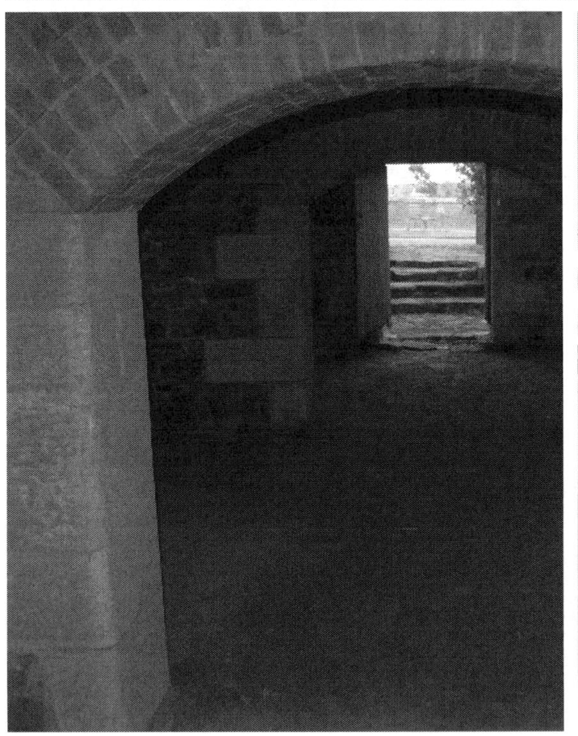

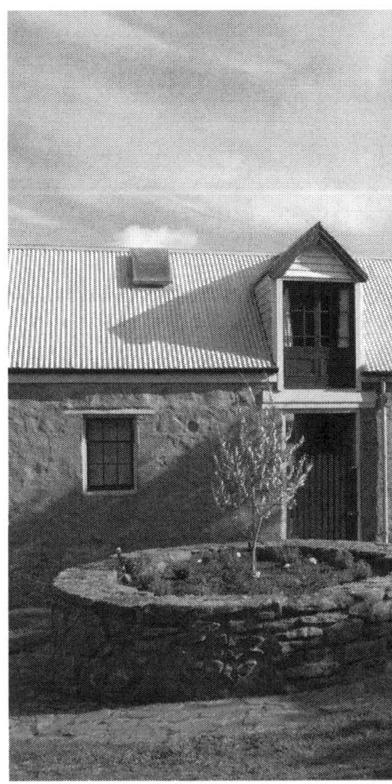

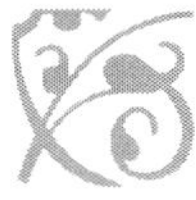

CHAPTER 21

Foxhunter's Return

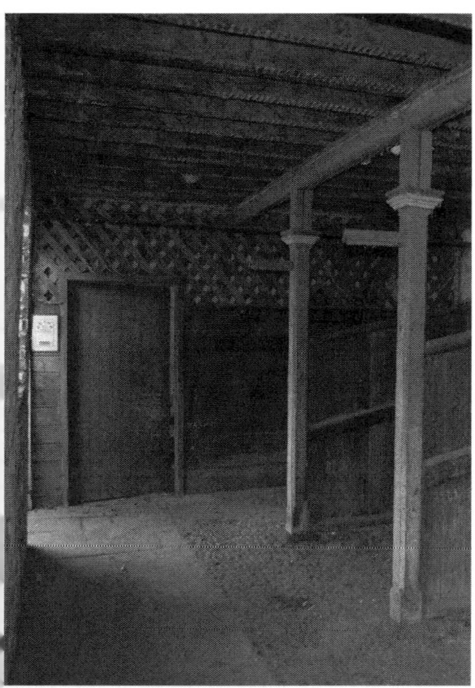

Ian Boersma is the Heritage Works Manager at Heritage Tasmania and loves to talk about Foxhunter's Return. Especially its outdoor toilet. Unlike similar properties in Melbourne and Sydney that have tended to have their ancillary structures and outbuildings lost or eroded over time, very little has been altered at Foxhunter's, a time capsule in the Tasmanian midlands. Here you can imagine the daily life of an old inn happening all around you, and with the addition of a few horses and people in period dress you'd have the perfect 19th-century movie set. But it is the fabulously preserved colonial timber 'dunny' out back, with not just one seat but two situated side-by-side, that gets Ian's pulse racing.

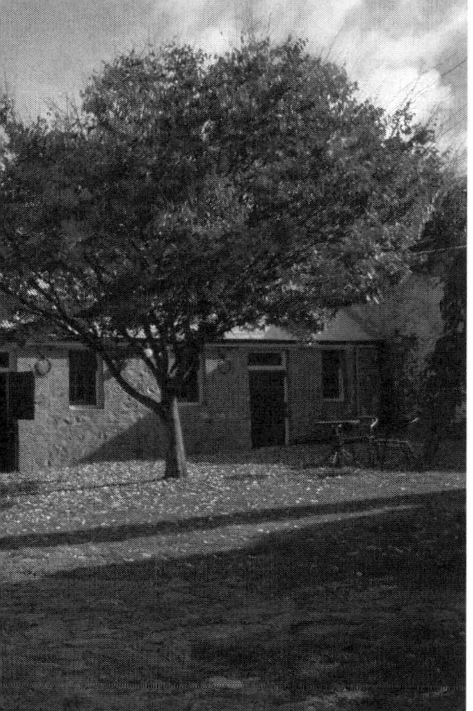

clockwise from top left From a distance Foxhunter's Return looks much as it did in the 1840s; the old stables; Foxhunter's courtyard; the cellar.

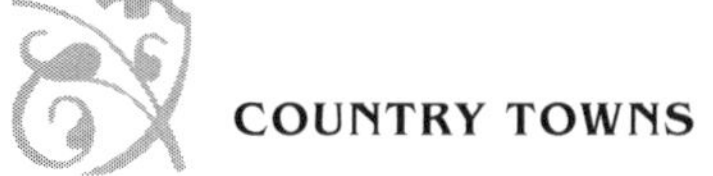

right The view of the back of the inn from the stables showing the hand-dug well topped with bricks from Campbell Town's own clay pit.

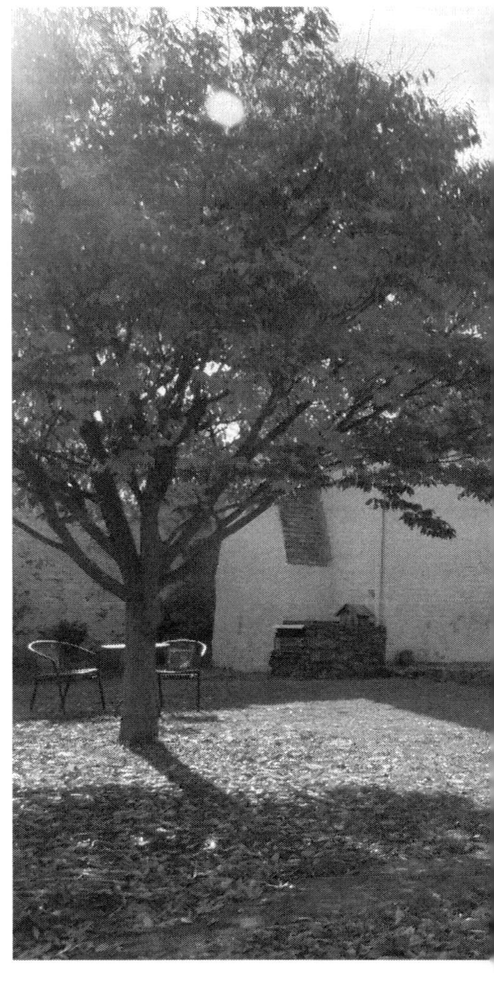

When small timber structures like this became irrelevant 50–75 years or so ago, when people began to realise it made more sense to place a bathroom inside the house, most outdoor toilets were either knocked down or converted into storage areas. For there to be such an intact example of a 'redundant structure' (that's 'heritage-speak') like this is quite an extraordinary find and Tasmania's heritage people lost no time in encouraging Foxhunter's new owners to retain it.

Nowhere in Australia is there to be seen such an intact and sumptuous example of a 19th century coaching inn, complete with its yard stables and appertances. It is essential to Australia that this building be preserved.

FISHER LUCAS ARCHITECTS, SYDNEY, 1975

Foxhunter's Return, an old coaching inn on the banks of the Elizabeth River in the central Tasmanian town of Campbell Town is an odd name for a property in a state that isn't supposed to have foxes, though that's not to say there haven't been plenty of sightings over the years. A fox was brought from the mainland for a foxhunt near Oatlands in 1864 but later killed, and in 1890 two turned up in Hobart and were also destroyed, as was a young female that appeared on the outskirts of Launceston in 1972. In 1998 a European

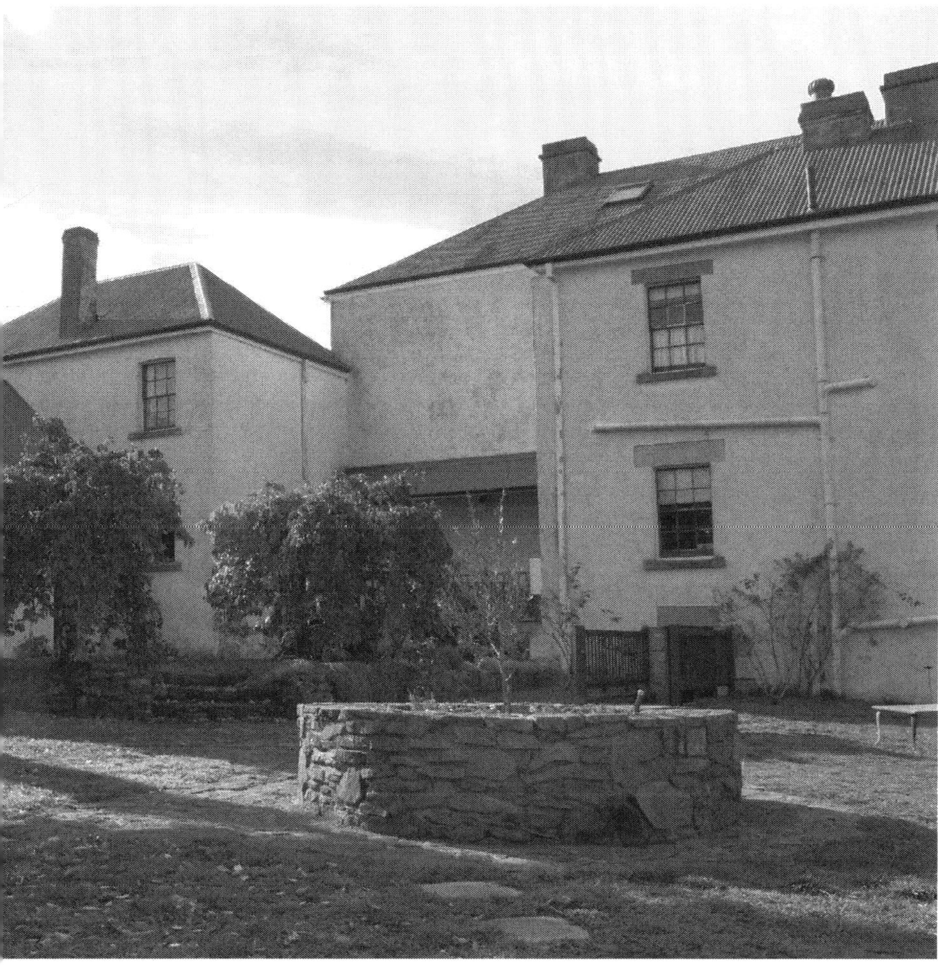

red fox escaped from a ship moored in Burnie harbour and despite a widespread search has never been found, and in 2001 two foxes were shot near Longford. Foxes have been largely responsible for Australia's appalling record of mammal extinction on the mainland and Tasmania's reputation as an international fauna haven is due in no small part to the absence of the fox.

Which all just adds to the peculiarity of the inn's name, and I've been more than a little frustrated in my attempts to get to the bottom of it. Most likely it was named at a time when the English aristocracy in Tasmania may have either had plans to establish the sport of fox hunting in the colony, or perhaps were just plain homesick? In 1927 the Mercer family purchased Foxhunter's Return and had a pet stag which they used as a de-facto fox on the old Midland Hunt Club that met outside the Melton Mowbray Hotel. But a stag is a long way from a fox. Perhaps it was just an expression of nostalgia? Or perhaps I should accept that there are some things in this world that occasionally just become lost to history.

Foxhunter's Return is a real heavyweight in the world of the historic Australian hotel. Designed and built by the Irish master stonemason Hugh Kean, construction began in 1833 and took seven years to complete, using convict labour and even employing a Mr Martin Cash, who would later go on to become one of Tasmania's most notorious bushrangers. Foxhunter's Return has been classified by the National Trust who call it 'the finest and most substantial hotel building of the late colonial period in Australia', and it's difficult to know just where to start in detailing its wealth of antiques and architectural features.

The striking east-facing facade is in the Regency style and made entirely from dressed sandstone, with the remainder of the building composed mainly of freestone and locally quarried bluestone. Its foundation is hand-hewn sandstone, and its bricks are from Campbell Town's very own clay pit.

What strikes you the moment you walk in through the front door and into the hallway is the inn's magnificent, gravity-defying sandstone staircase, cantilevered on three sides and laced with a beautiful wrought-iron balustrade which takes you to the first floor. The staircase is a masterful piece of engineering, particularly when you consider the weight that must be in it, not to mention the fact the whole thing is cut from a single piece of stone. One of the first things Michael did after moving in was to strip the white enamel paint off the sides and top of the staircase that someone long ago thought might be an effective way to seal it against moisture, in order to expose the original sandstone.

On the ground floor there is a dining room, lounge, kitchen and a guest bedroom. The first floor is mostly for private use, but in the upper level, reached via an old cedar staircase, are the attic rooms that have been converted into two bedrooms and an ensuite. There are eight rooms in total including the Stable Master's Room in the original 1833 stable block with gorgeous views across Foxhunter's courtyard. The cobblestones that make up the floor of the stables out back are from the Elizabeth River.

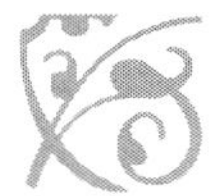

But of all the 'rooms' at Foxhunter's, it is the partitioned rooms in the cellar beneath the house that get Michael really excited. He calls them his 'Harry Potter rooms', and they truly are worthy of the subterranean world of secret passageways that lie beneath Hogwarts School of Witchcraft and Wizardry. More an extensive network of rooms than a cellar, an old kitchen with its baking oven remains set within one of its walls, and iron bars are still in place in other rooms that were once holding cells for the many convicts who were used to build it. Michael first thought his underground world would be an ideal space to one day host conference dinners, but that plan had to be shelved when Kath decided to turn it into a bookshop.

Shire Publications is a UK publisher with a unique reputation for filling in the 'gaps' in the publishing world by producing small, affordable non-fiction paperbacks on the often-neglected little things in our lives, things such as old buttons, the development of thimbles, or the crafting of corn dollies, through to the history of the London bus, medieval masons and World War I British postcards. Kath, who lived in the UK for several years, has a fabulous little bookshop at Foxhunter's and stocks almost the entire range of Shire publications, currently in excess of 1000 titles and all written by experts in each individual field. In fact the collection is so agreeable and so affordable that I defy anyone to spend an evening at Foxhunter's and *not* buy one. Not content with Shire's titles Kath is also thinking about starting her own series, an Australian range that might include such things as old shearing sheds, Victa lawnmowers, windmills and so on. When they were shown through Foxhunter's for the first time and Kath saw the convict-era sandstone holding cells, they both fell in love with it, and Kath knew she'd found her bookshop. All that remained was to put their signatures on all the right places and buy the 177-year-old coaching inn that stood above it. Oddly enough, Heritage Tasmania have no issue with them knocking a doorway through one of the cellar walls to join two rooms together should the bookstore grow over time and require more space.

Foxhunter's Return lies roughly halfway between Hobart and Launceston, a strategically ideal location in a state where you can't find a petrol station open after 9.00 p.m. and travellers who didn't possess the foresight to fill up their petrol tanks for that early evening drive to Hobart or vice-versa usually find themselves spending the night in Campbell Town, which is hardly an imposition. Established

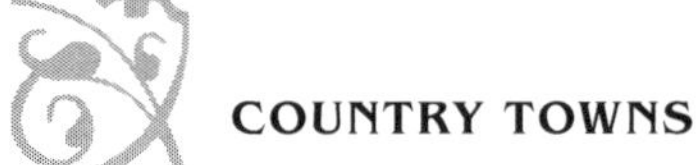

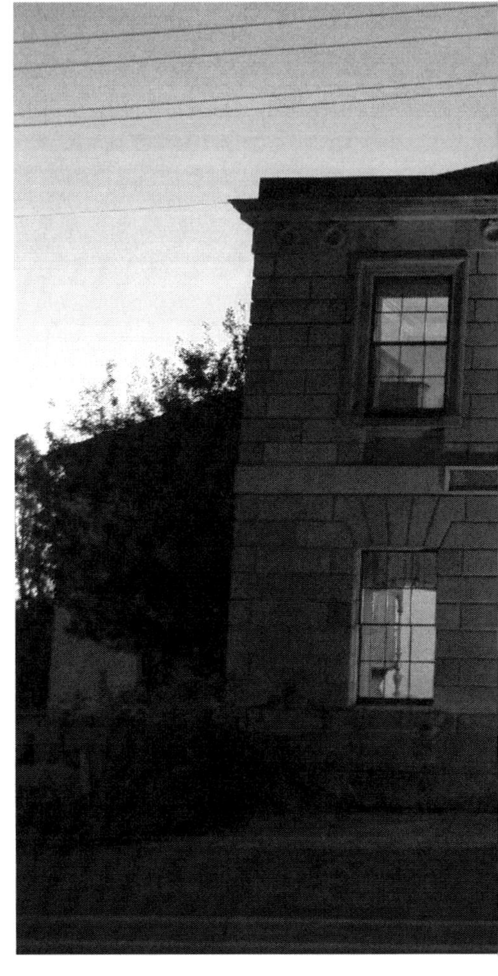

right The National Trust describes Foxhunter's Return as 'the finest and most substantial hotel building of the late colonial period in Australia'.

in 1821 as a garrison town by Governor Macquarie who named it after his wife Elizabeth Campbell, it is the centre of an important wool-growing district with the Campbell Town Agricultural Show Australia's oldest show, established in 1838. As far as heritage is concerned, Foxhunter's is in good company here with the town home to more than 100 buildings that are a century or more old, 35 of which are listed on the National Estate.

And speaking of national treasures, we cannot forget Foxhunter's bridge. Well, technically not *its* bridge, but it's so close to the inn it might as well be. Tasmania is justly proud of its bridges and why shouldn't it be? It has the three most beautiful in Australia—Richmond Bridge (1825) over the Coal River in Richmond just north of Hobart, Ross Bridge (1836) on the Macquarie River in the midlands town of Ross, and Campbell Town's own Red Bridge (1838), spanning the Elizabeth River right across the road from Foxhunter's Return. Red Bridge replaced the town's original bridge at the base of the aptly named Tragedy Hill, which was constantly being inundated after every heavy rain. The foundation stone of Red Bridge was laid under the direction of Captain Frederick Forth of the 21st Royal North British Fusiliers on 21 October 1836 and the bridge was completed in 1838, at its peak employing more than 220 convict labourers working for 6 pence a day. The magnificent triple-

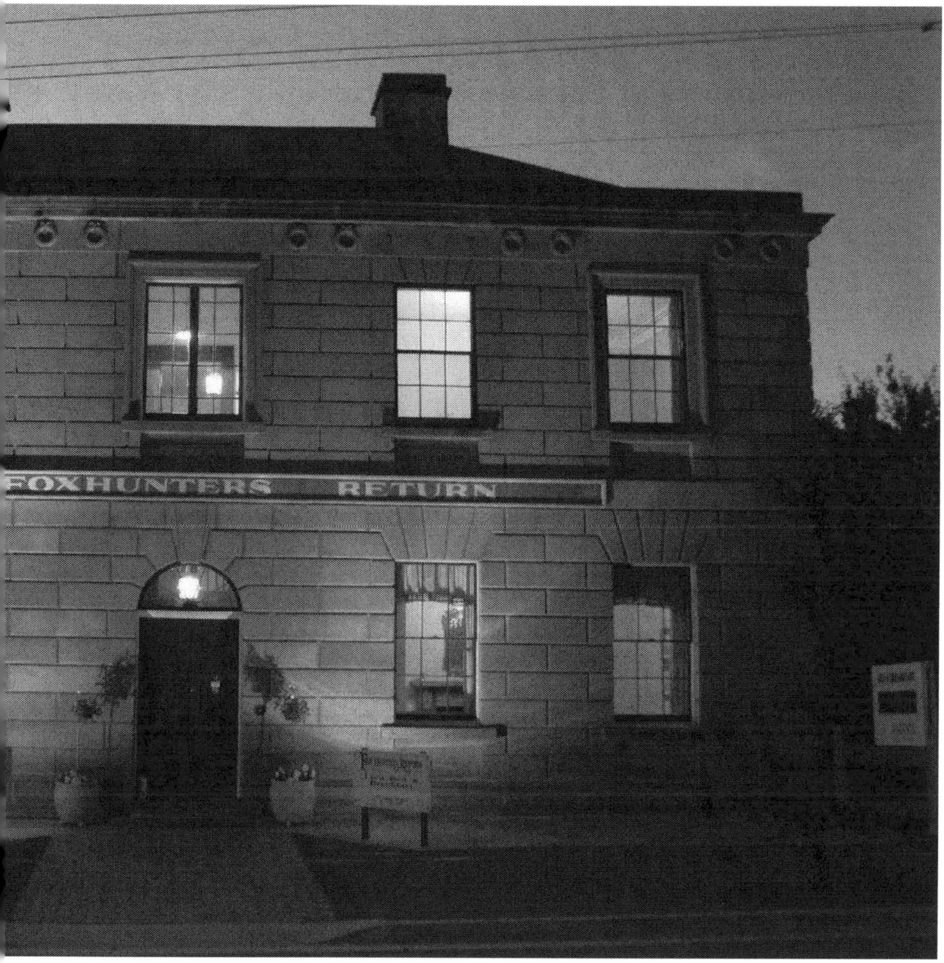

arched bridge, the oldest surviving arched brick bridge in Australia,
was designed by James Blackburn, an English civil engineer, architect
and former convict who was sent to Tasmania in 1833 for forging a
cheque for 600 pounds. Red Bridge contains almost one and a quarter
million handmade bricks, and when it was finished the Elizabeth
River was diverted to flow beneath its three 7.6-metre arches. Despite
being built for the horse and carriage, today the graceful arches
of Red Bridge are crossed by more than two million cars that pass
through Campbell Town along the Midlands Highway between
Hobart and Launceston each year.

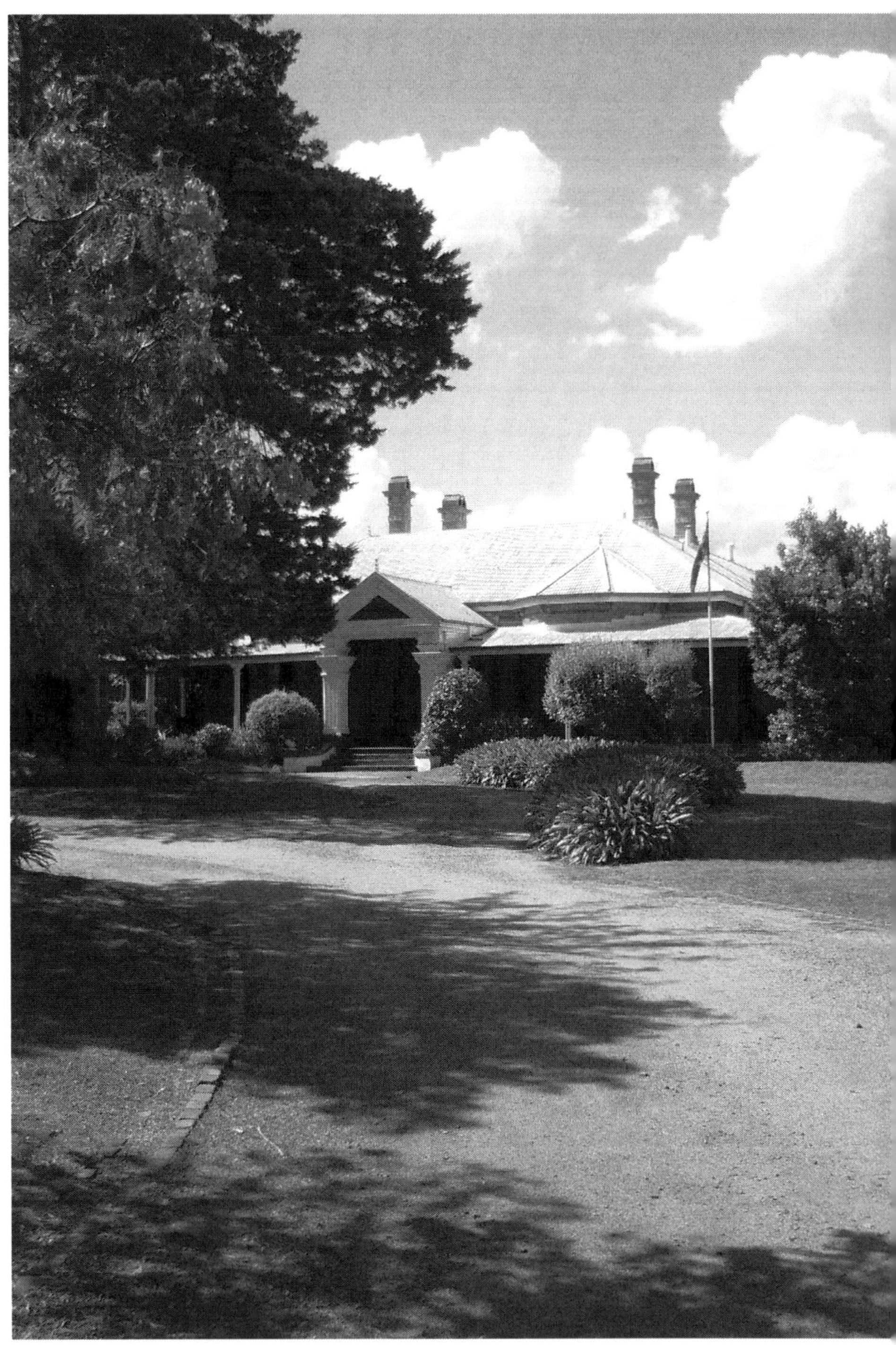

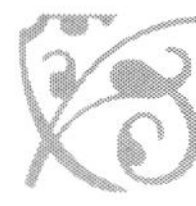

Vacy Hall

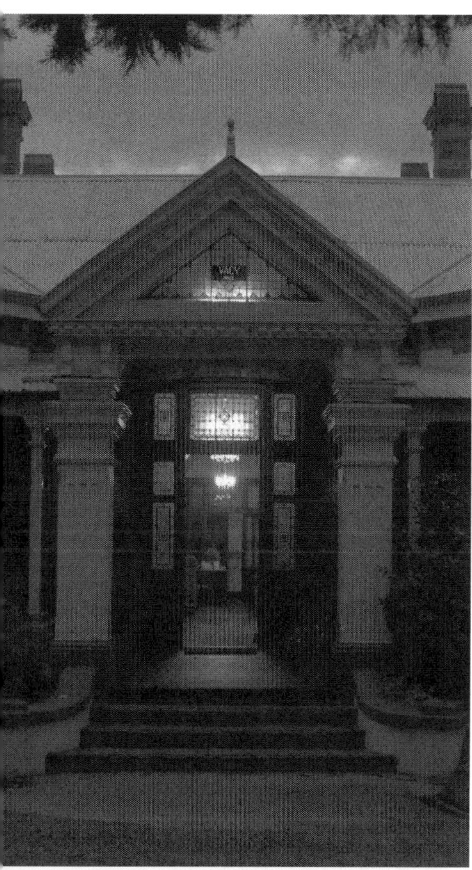

I'd just finished talking to Graham Higgins, the 'current steward', as he likes to put it, of Vacy Hall, and was walking back along the wraparound verandah towards the front entry door, when a group of new arrivals piled out of a Mercedes sedan and made their way up the front steps. Somebody said, 'Good afternoon,' and I replied, 'Hello everyone—welcome to Vacy Hall! I'm the owner!'

'Where's your identification?' someone asked. Well, my cover was blown, and I was forced to admit that I, too, was a mere guest. But for a few moments I was, to someone in this world at least, the owner of Toowoomba's Vacy Hall. And it felt *good*.

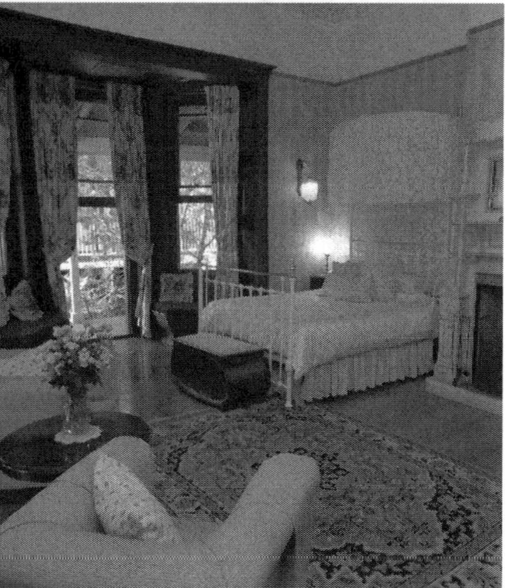

clockwise from left Vacy Hall intrigues with its interplay of skillion roofs, chimneys, verandahs, projecting bays and twin-hipped corrugated roof; the gable pediment over the south entrance; the James Marks Suite.

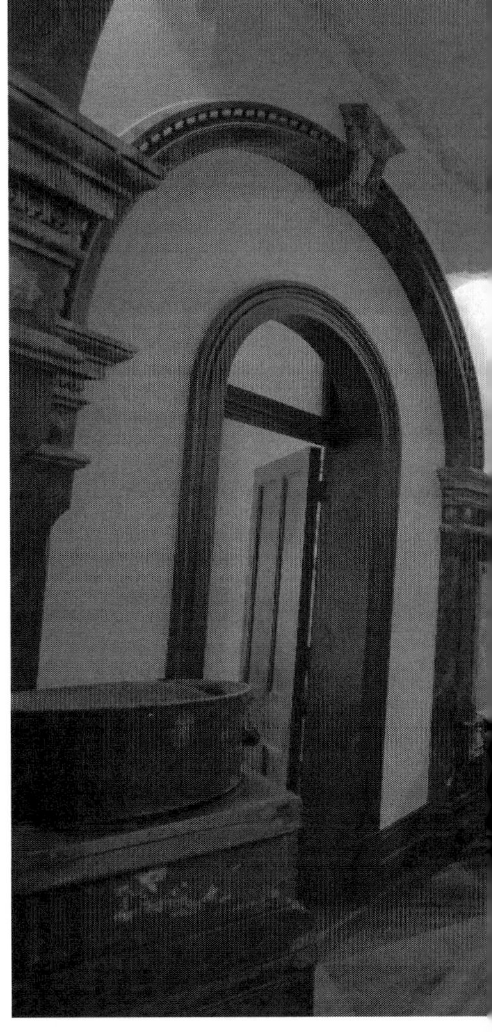

right When you enter Vacy Hall, the magnificent octagonal entry and main hallway with timber mouldings and faux marble columns will stop you in your tracks.

The 'old' Vacy Hall was a timber residence built in 1873 by James Taylor, an early Queensland pastoralist and Member for the Western Downs in Queensland's first Legislative Assembly who later gained a seat in the Legislative Council which he retained until 1893. He had it built as a wedding present for his daughter Ann Sophy to Gilbert Cory, who was the young manager of Taylor's Cecil Plains Station. When the first Vacy Hall burned down in 1898, three years after James Taylor's death, it was decided by Ann and Gilbert and the trustees of Taylor's estate to rebuild the home on the same site and with a vow that the new home would never burn down again. The prolific Toowoomba-based architect James Marks was approached to design the new house and was told, simply, 'Build a house that won't burn down'.

Vacy Hall was built in brick with every fourth row laid on their ends in a typical English garden bond pattern which creates internal air pockets that significantly improves the insulative quality of its walls but which also takes a lot longer to lay. The bricks for the new home were brought up on trains from Brisbane's Redbank brickworks and added to the significance of Vacy Hall, a lone brick building in a sea of Toowoomba timber. Each room is an individual fire 'cell' with concrete ceilings. The building's foundations were dug by a team of

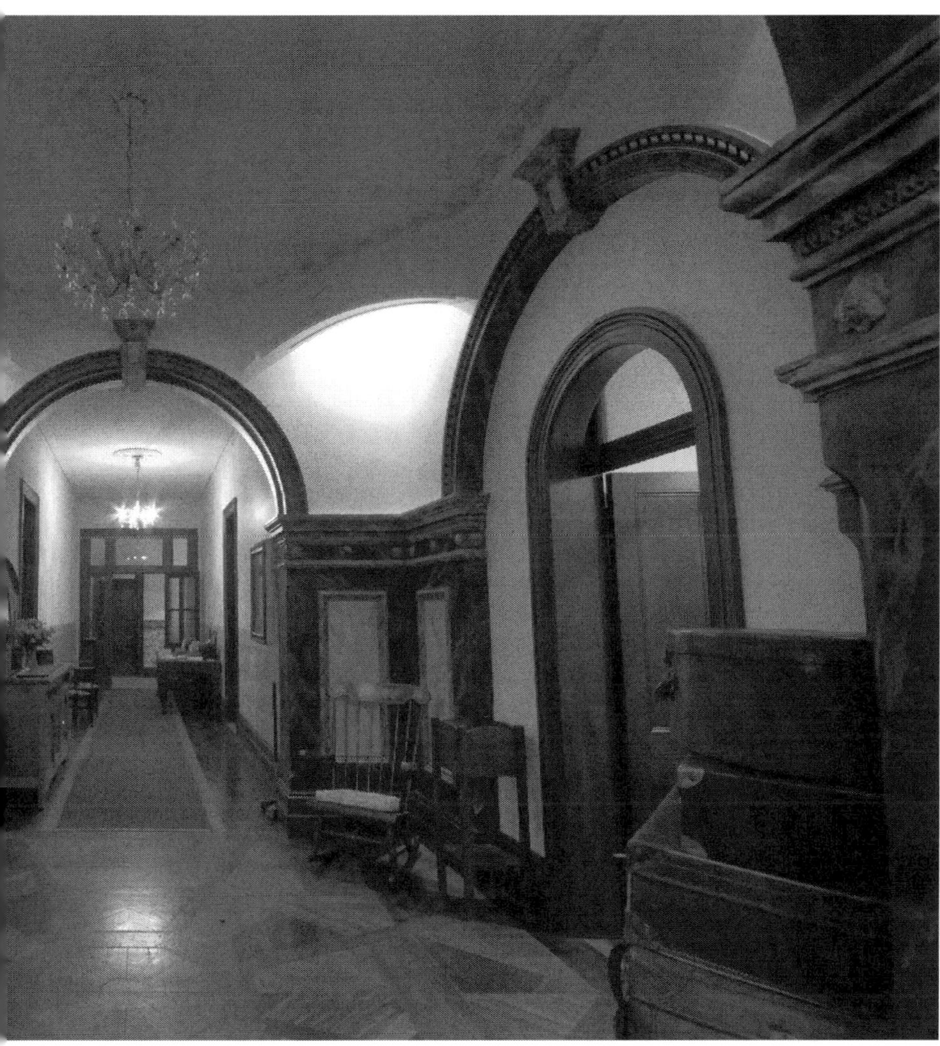

'navvies', that resulted in trenches 4 metres deep to accommodate the bluestone foundations that the new building was to sit on. With the external brick walls themselves reaching a height of 4 metres this of course means that, wherever you stand in Vacy Hall's park-like gardens and look at this stunning home, there's almost as much of it lying hidden beneath the surface as there is above.

Vacy Hall is an L-shaped, single-storey building with a double-hipped corrugated iron roof with hipped projecting window bays. A beautifully preserved verandah—with no discernible evidence it

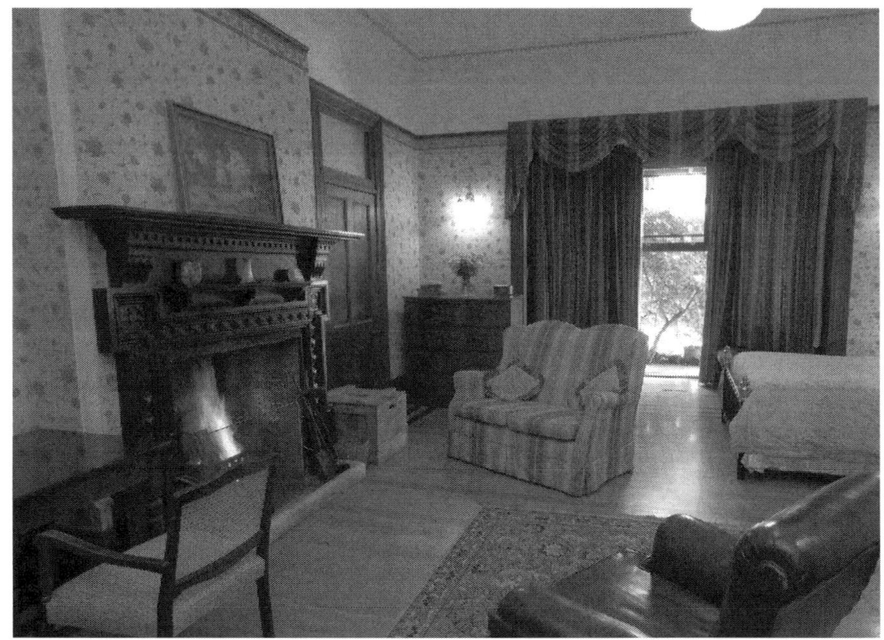

above The Gilbert Cory Suite has an ensuite complete with cast-iron claw-foot tub and walk-through sash windows that give access to the verandah.

has ever needed restoration of its hardwood boards—surrounds it, and the whole thing is topped with a low skillion roof supported by squared verandah posts. It's also a good 2 metres in width, making it an eminently practical outdoor space. In the centre of the entrance pediment, the words 'Vacy Hall' are inscribed amongst a sea of surrounding leadlight, and the entry door has a fanlight above and leadlight sidelights. Once you step inside, however, nothing prepares you for the grandeur of its hallway. Graham told me the first word that invariably comes from people's mouths is 'Wow' as the sheer scale and opulence of the house begins to sink in. There's the octagonal-shaped central hall with faux-marble finish to its arches and columns, done by a local Toowoomba craftsman just a few years ago and which, from a distance, would fool all but the keenest of eyes.

Graham Higgins is a straight-talking guy who loves his new home of six years and is passionate about its proud heritage. We found a nice spot in the sun on the verandah to chat and, strengthened by a pot of freshly brewed coffee, he told me a little of his own story. His professional background was as a radio journalist in Queensland

and South Australia and he worked for Macquarie Radio when it was
owned by the Fairfax group. He then went to work as a political
staffer for John Moore, the President of the Queensland Liberal Party
and the coiner of the phrase 'the white shoe brigade' (a pejorative
term then used to describe Gold Coast land developers who had
the ear of the state government in the 1980s). Post-politics Graham
enjoyed a 16-year career in the recruitment consulting industry and
developed a key economic indicator for labour demand that was
recognised by the Commonwealth Treasury as being one of the most
reliable predictors for employment growth in the Australian economy.

In 2003 he was living in Brisbane and feeling in need of a change.
One morning he saw a tiny ad in the classifieds—a *real* 'tiny ad'—so
tiny in fact that Graham held the thumb and index finger of his right
hand horizontal to the ground and just a half inch apart in front of
me to emphasise just how close he was to never knowing Vacy Hall
existed. So he decided to drive the hour and a half to Toowoomba,
fell in love with it, or, as he preferred to say, fell into a 'delusional
kind of romance', and promptly bought it.

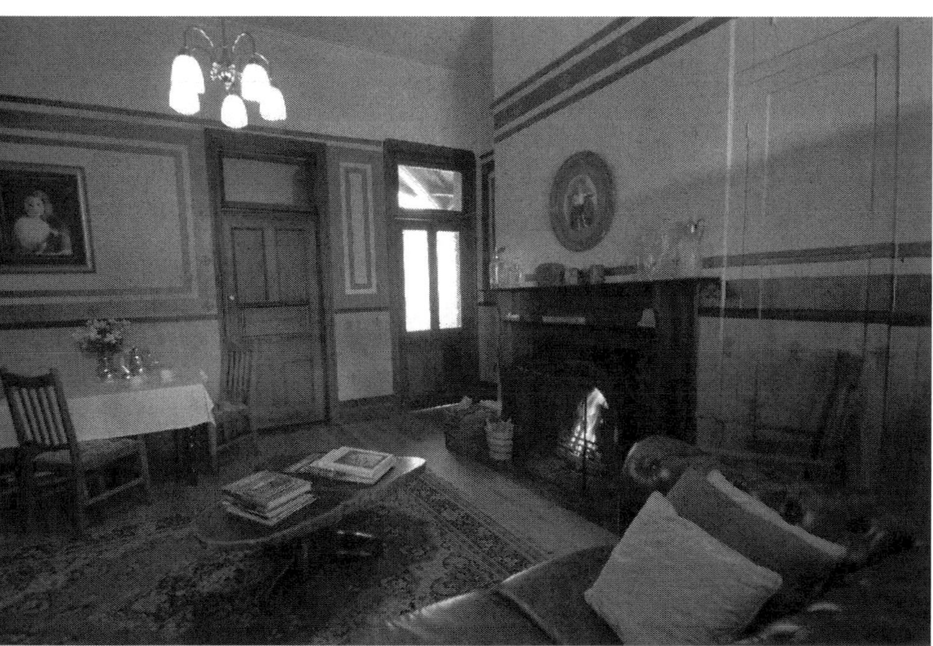

above The sitting room is the perfect place to relax and enjoy a refreshing morning or
afternoon tea.

Vacy Hall is practically unique. I mean, where else can you get a
95-square colonial mansion on more than an acre of land on the edge
of a CBD? Restaurants, cinemas and shops are all close by, which
is why Vacy Hall doesn't do dinners. There's just no need with the
wealth of dining options that exist just two-minutes drive away.

Graham lives on the property in a small cottage in the garden. He
loves Vacy Hall but works it, like all owners of historic properties do,
seven days a week. On those occasions when he needs a break or
merely a change of scenery, he might go into Brisbane or Stanthorpe
to visit friends and go on some wine trails, but by and large he enjoys
the proximity to the house and is always on call to come to the aid
of a guest. Does he ever get away? Yes, of course, or you'd slowly
go mad. 'Cabin fever' can strike you in a heritage B&B on the quiet,
residential edge of a CBD just as easily as in the woods, and it's
good to be able to escape, not to do anything in particular, but just
to regain some 'balance'. As a guest it's easy to arrive at a successful
B&B on a nice sunny day and, if it's quiet, be lulled into thinking that
hosting one might be quite a lovely thing to do. You might, though,
want to dwell on that, and do the math.

Mention any suppressed desire to run a B&B to Graham and
you not only get a story like the one above, or as many more as
you've got time for, but you also get a cautionary reminder about
the numbers. 'Well, let's see—an average five rooms rented per
night multiplied by 365 days times six years? That's 20 000 people
or, if you prefer, 20 000 breakfasts, or 10 000 rooms to clean, 10 000
bookings to take from 15 different independent travel websites. And
then there's the paperwork. Truckloads of it.' Sure, they're the sort of
numbers faced by anyone in the industry, really. But they give you
pause for thought nonetheless.

For the most part this has not been a book about how many
rooms a property has or the amenities they offer or how big they are.
But I think it's time I made an exception. My room is big, maybe
9 metres by 7. It has 4-metre-high ceilings with intricate plaster
cornices and two stunning bay windows framed in solid timber
surrounds, each with their own central sash windows that open out
onto the wraparound verandah outside. There are two brass beds,
a double bed with a canopy and a single in the other corner, an
armoire, two comfortable armchairs around a small coffee table,
original timber floors and a working fireplace fully stocked with wood

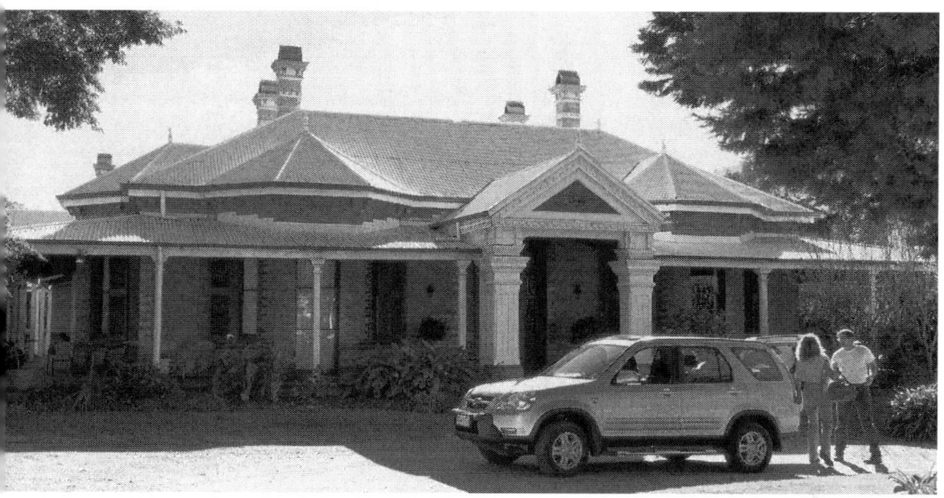

above Vacy Hall is just two minute's drive from the restaurants, shops and cinemas of the Toowoomba CBD.

and a box of matches on the mantelpiece. There's just nothing sadder than an old, disabled fireplace that does little more than add a touch of ornamentation to a room, but at Vacy Hall you can light it, should the mood overtake you, its chimneys still 'breathe'.

Vacy Hall is on every heritage list that matters. It is listed with the Australian Heritage Commission, the Queensland Heritage Council and the National Trust of Australia, and its inclusion as Lonely Planet's preferred place to stay while visiting Toowoomba should allay the concerns of 21st-century travellers.

As a father of two what I liked most was the presence of a fully functioning Hills play gym on the side lawn for the kids. You see, at Vacy Hall you can look as hard as you like and I guarantee you, you won't find so much as a hint of pretentiousness in a place that, it could be argued, has plenty to be pretentious about. So come here and let your kids knock themselves out on the play gym that says, 'Sure, we're an antique-filled B&B, but we actually *welcome* children'. Feel free to open those sash windows in your room and step straight onto the verandah. And yes, by all means, light that lovely fireplace.

What a refreshingly rare trifecta.

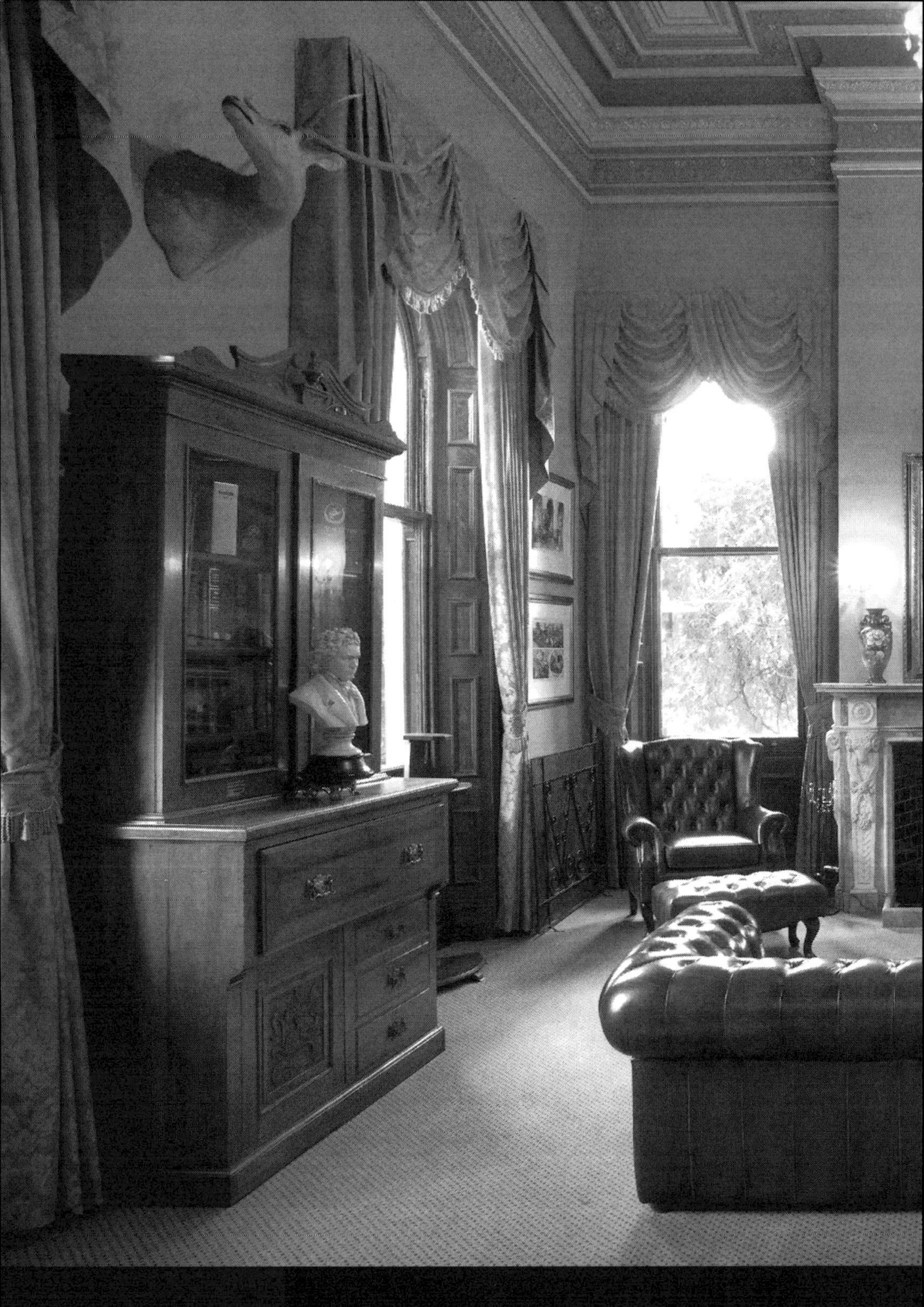

PART 5

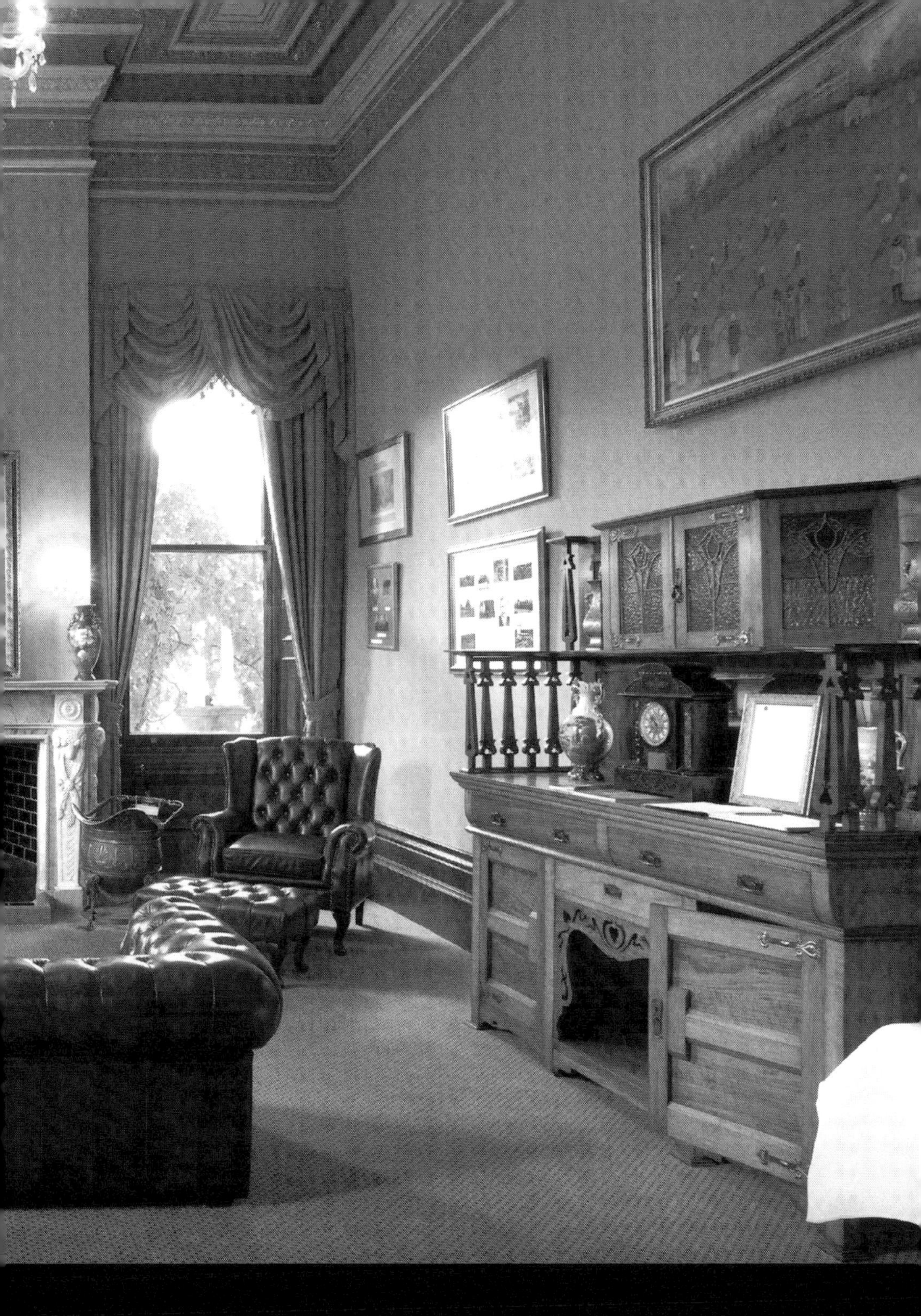

Grand Mansions

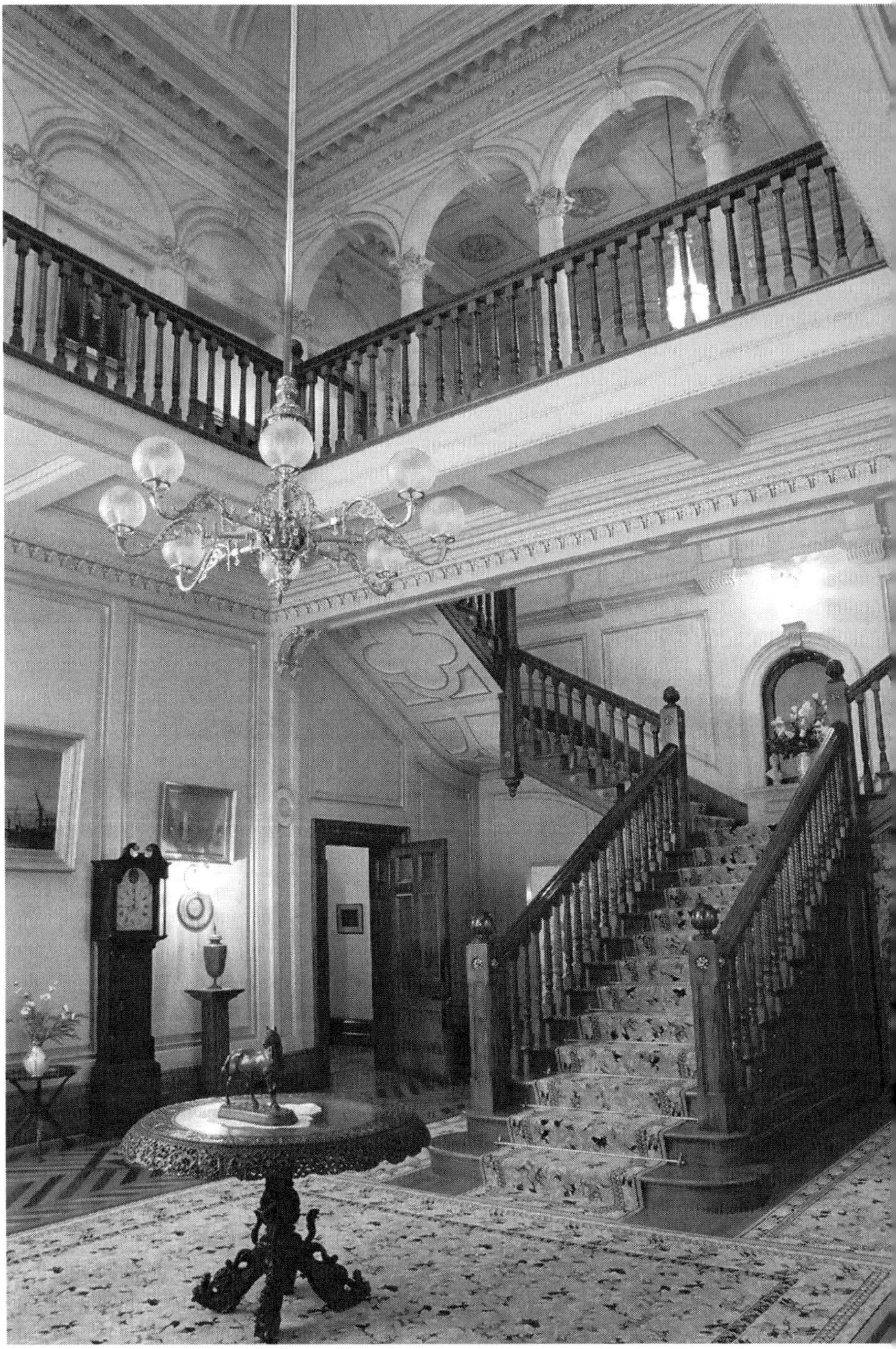

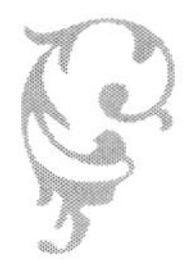

CHAPTER 23

Martindale Hall

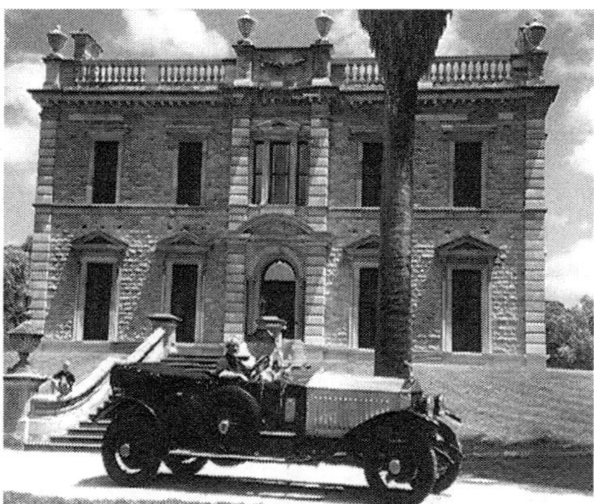

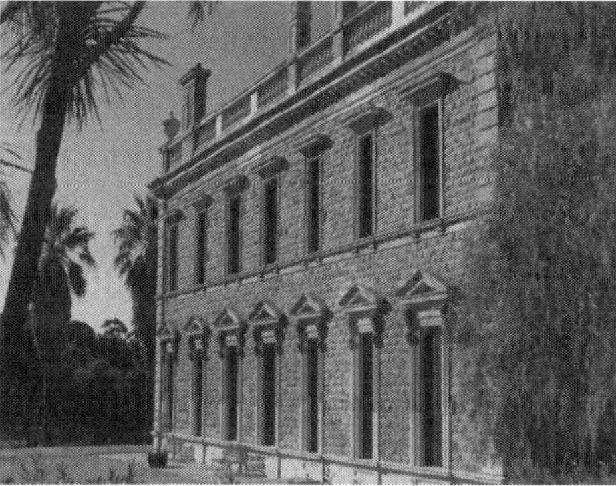

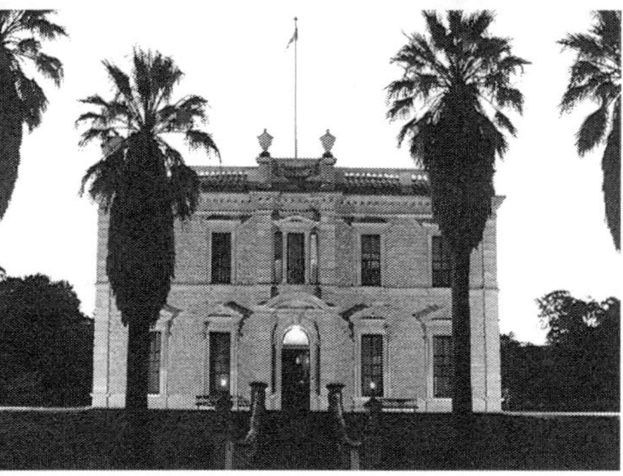

If you're contemplating flying to Adelaide, and you would like to stay at Martindale Hall, an 1879 Georgian mansion that looks like it was picked up from a wooded hillside in Hertfordshire or Kent and dropped intact into South Australia's Clare Valley, then take my advice and get a morning flight. Not because it's a long way—it isn't—but an afternoon flight might mean you don't arrive till evening. And once here you're very likely to want to spend two or three hours in its library. In Martindale Hall's library, time has no meaning. Ten minutes becomes an hour. One hour morphs into two. I went to bed some time after midnight, woke at eight the following morning, missed out on my six o'clock walk, and was ten minutes late for breakfast! But oh, it was worth it.

clockwise from left Martindale Hall's foyer, with its T-shaped staircase and overhanging galleries; top to bottom Georgian symmetry at its boldest.

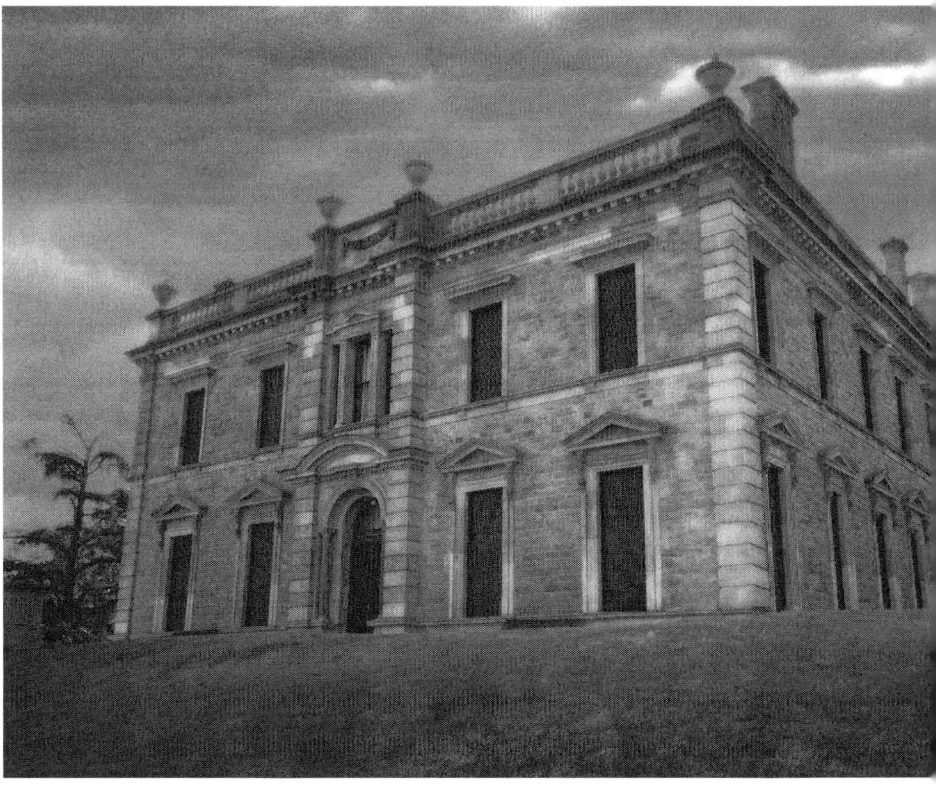

above The two windows at the front, upper right, are the windows to Miranda's bedroom from the classic Australian film *Picnic at Hanging Rock*. © Vanessa Size

It's extraordinary what you can learn during the course of an evening spent in Martindale Hall's library. For instance, did you know that in 1876 Philadelphia was spread over 82 700 acres and was, in terms of area, the largest city on earth? And Philadelphians apparently loved their homes: the city had 151 153 dwellings, a larger proportion of homes to population than any other city on the planet, with the total value of its residential and commercial property estimated at a tick over $585 million dollars. Its streets were illuminated by 605 miles of gas pipes, 658 miles of water pipes that brought the city its water from the nearby Schuylkill River, and to cap it all off this proud city was about to be host to the '1876 Centennial Exhibition', a year-long celebration of art, industry and agriculture in honour of the signing of the Declaration of Independence in 1776, an event the like of which the United States had never seen before.

To help people navigate their way around the exhibition, the Centennial Board of Finance produced a guidebook, *Visitor's Guide To The Centennial Exhibition And Philadelphia 1876*, approved by the Director-General and the only guide book authorised to be sold on the exhibition grounds. I don't know how many copies of this guide still exist. Probably, I'd venture to say, not too many. But there *is* a copy in the library of Martindale Hall, all the books of which were once a part of the private collection of John Mortlock, Martindale's former owner. In addition to being a guesthouse Martindale Hall is also a museum, open Mondays to Fridays from 11.00 a.m. and from noon to 4 p.m, on weekends (Admission: Adults $10, Children $2.50, Pensioner and Student concessions $7.50). There are, however, refreshingly few roped-off areas, and guests are encouraged to relax and treat it like a home. You dine on the original dining table, you can play billiards on the original table in the library and you can even read the books!

In the library of Martindale Hall there's an 1888 copy of *Life of Ralph Waldo Emerson* and *The Truth About Hell: A Defence Of The Hell Of The Bible* by C.C. Walker dated 1931. There are travelogues such as *In Seven Lands* published in London in 1916 by Ernest Alfred Vizetelly; *My Life With The Eskimos* (1927) by Vilhjalmur Stefansson; and *Quito To Bogota* (1911) by A.C. Veatch—men who laid the foundations for future generations of travel writers like Paul Theroux and Bill Bryson, pioneers who risked their lives travelling beyond the boundaries of empire. There's a copy of *The Fair Maid of Earth* by Sir Walter Scott, published in Edinburgh by Adam & Charles Black in 1863; *Astronomy* by J. Norman Lockyer, MacMillan, 1890; and an 1878 copy of *An Introduction To The Study Of Heat* by J. Hamblin Smith. The library was built around a glorious 1878 Stevens & Sons, London, snooker table that still has its original felt and was placed here where it still sits today in 1879 before the library's outer wall was completed. The collection is of national significance and is something that all Australians should be grateful has been preserved. It belongs to us all.

Martindale Hall is quintessentially English, a mix of Georgian and Italianate influences and bears a striking resemblance in miniature to Cliveden in Berkshire, England, the former home of America's first multimillionaire John Jacob Astor. Martindale Hall was built for Edward Bowman Jnr, whose family first settled in Tasmania in 1829 but whose father, Edmund Bowman Snr, moved to South Australia in

1836 and in 1855 purchased the land on which Martindale Hall now stands. English tradesmen were brought from England to construct it and returned there again when the job was done. Its walls are a metre thick and it and the nearby coach house are both built of local Manoora sandstone.

Martindale Hall remains in a remarkable state of preservation, so much so that when Peter Weir needed an appropriately grand backdrop for his classic 1975 film *Picnic at Hanging Rock* he came here, despite the rock itself and the story around which it was set being 670 kilometres away near Mt Macedon in central Victoria. The dry air of the Clare Valley and a degree of relative isolation have combined to produce a natural environment for preservation, and nowhere is this seen to better effect than on Martindale's internal walls. In the world of the heritage hotel one of the first things to succumb to the ravages of time is wallpaper. But at Martindale instead of little more than fragments of 19th-century wallpaper surviving under glass in picture frames so guests can have a glimpse into the mind of the 19th-century interior designer—*entire rooms* here still have their original wallpaper triumphantly intact, and not only intact but in a remarkable state of preservation. The wallpaper in the library, for instance, was hand-block-printed in the library itself.

The White Room and the Blue Room are Martindale's master bedrooms, so-called because they are the only two that come with ensuites—not modern ensuites shoe-horned into some tiny space that was once something else, but 120-year-old ensuites with timber baths and fragile porcelain tap ware. The White Room into which I retreated and set up a temporary 'work station' was the room Peter Weir chose to be Miranda's bedroom in *Picnic at Hanging Rock* and was left just as it had been in 1975 and no doubt significantly prior to that. Even the dressing table was still to the right of the front-facing window where Miranda and her friends endlessly brushed their hair before setting out on their fateful picnic. The Blue Room was the bedroom of Martindale's owners: Edmund Bowman Jnr from 1880 to 1891, William Mortlock and his bride Rose from 1891 to 1913, and the home's final owner, John Mortlock, from 1913 to 1950. Its blue wallpaper dates from the early 20th-century.

There are ten bedrooms at Martindale today including two in the back two corners of the mansion that were used by the cook and housekeeper. Interestingly, they are on the same level as the two master bedrooms, an uncommon egalitarian touch despite there being a series of 'servant's stairs' at the back of the house that enabled the staff to move up and down throughout Martindale's various levels without having to disturb those in the 'front' of the house.

Downstairs by the old kitchen a series of 'speaking tubes' were installed by the Bowmans in the 1880s that would carry a whistle to rooms throughout the house to attract the attention of staff. The Mortlocks later installed a 32-volt generator and a series of 'bells' that were activated by push buttons installed in each room. A number would drop down into a series of tiny windows to indicate which room the call had come from: No. 1 was the front door, No. 4 was the dining room, No. 5 was the Gun Room, etc. Down the hall the Butler's Servery acted as a transition point between the kitchen and cellar to the dining room and it's worth stepping inside just to see the marvellous lead sheet surrounding the sink designed to prevent water getting onto the cupboards below. The dining room is, like everything else here, original with its magnificent 1891 mahogany dining table still used to entertain Martindale guests.

Touring English cricket teams used to play games of cricket on Martindale's lawns. There was a polo field, a racecourse and even a small lake for boating. As you walk in through Martindale's front doors and across the black-and-white marble floor of its entry, what strikes you first is its glorious handcarved Tasmanian blackwood staircase. You begin to notice the 'little things': oil paintings by Will Longstaff, other paintings from the Turner School, an alabaster Taj Mahal night light, a hand-carved Padouk table from India, and finally the beautiful Huon pine inlaid floor on which it all sits. As Martindale's only guest that night after its manager said goodnight and left, it was like being inside a museum after closing time.

Of course there's more to Martindale Hall than just a grand residence. The coach house is reached via a 300-metre path from the main house and has a grandness all its own. Inside there's room for a half dozen carriages, and stables at the back with floors of wooden blocks bevelled to look like cobblestones but providing a soft surface for horses' hooves. In the centre of the coach house is a rectangular concrete floor with a fall towards its centre where a grate would take away the water used to wash down its carriages and horses. Its interior brick walls are finished in a limewash and the original A-framed trusses above support a new slate shingle roof that was

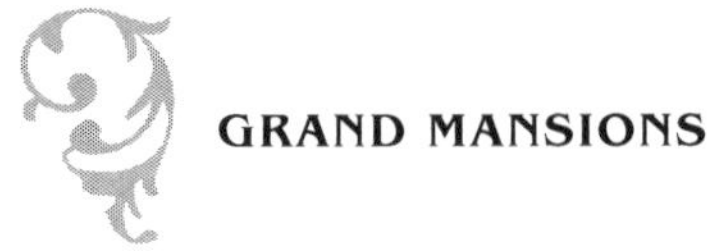

right Replete with arches, columns, Corinthian capitals and rare portraiture, Martindale Hall is a beguiling mix of historic hotel and renaissance gallery. © Vanessa Size

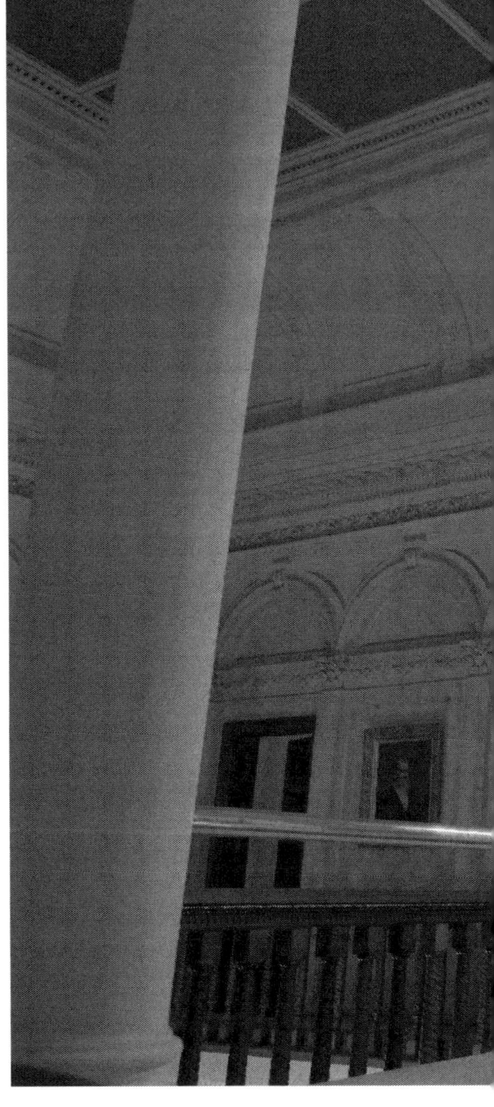

installed in early 2010 and cost 500 000 dollars. There are two front offices with wooden floors and timber-panelled walls each with their own fireplace, and two additional fireplaces in the corner of each of the two carriage parking bays.

In Martindale Hall there is history in every room. The Smoking Room has a very rare Japanese ceremonial samurai suit of armour and a Chinese swivel chair made of cherrywood in an odd mix of English Chippendale and traditional Chinese design. Rifles on display include an 1853 Enfield musket and an 1890 Soper hunting rifle, and the skull of a dugong that was harpooned in 1937 by John Mortlock's chauffeur, Jeff Thrum.

As I sat in Miranda's bedroom the next morning putting the finishing touches to this piece I began to hear voices. The museum has opened for the day and the house is full again. I consider myself fortunate to have seen it empty in the dead of night as Martindale's sole occupant, walking from room to room as I journeyed around the house, and then to witness it come to life again as visitors from Adelaide and who-knows-where walked its rooms and passageways, adding to the ebb and flow of one of Australia's truly great houses. I've been up on its roof (courtesy of two electricians who came to do some repair work),

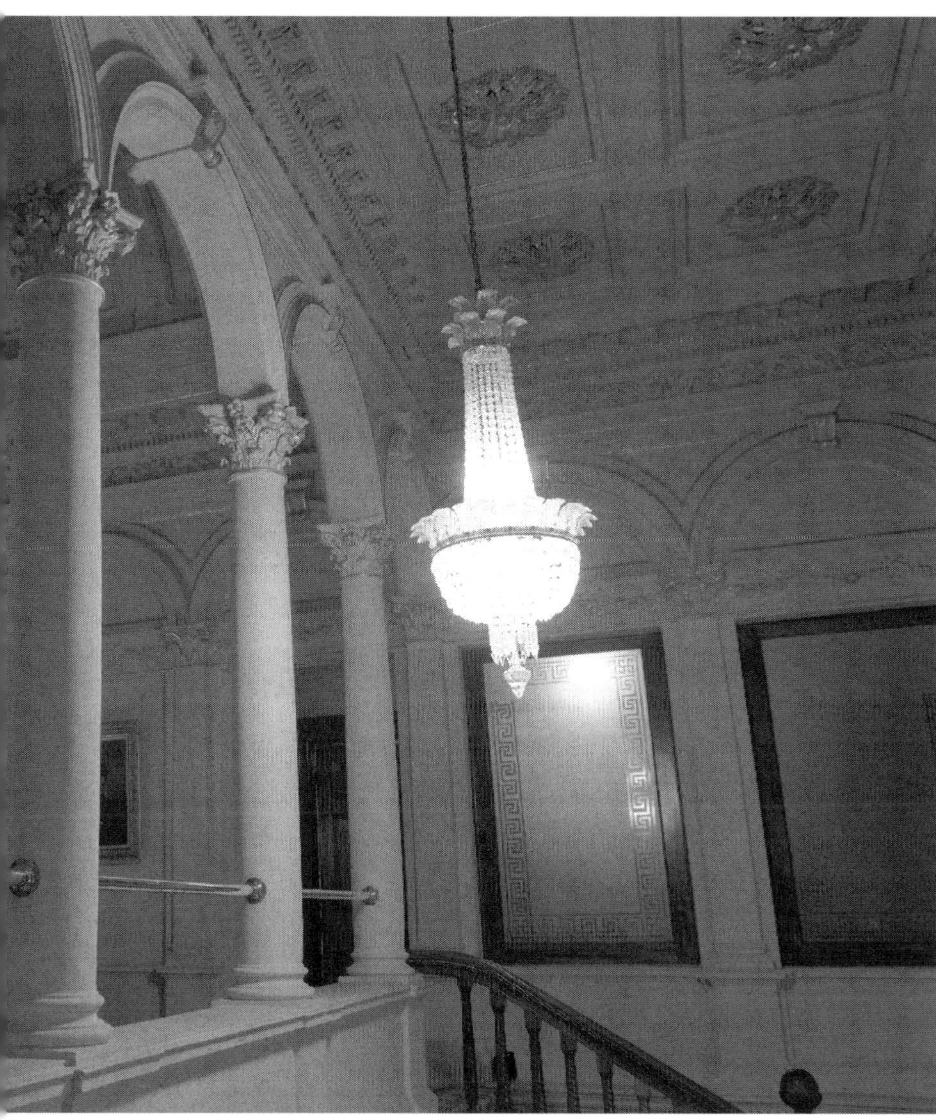

which once was used by the women of Martindale to watch their men play polo, and I've descended into its cellar and seen a little of the labyrinth of passageways that tunnel their way beneath its floors. I feel I know this place, and it's comforting to think that however long it might be until I visit again, Martindale Hall will still be here, looking just as it does now, waiting patiently to welcome me anew.

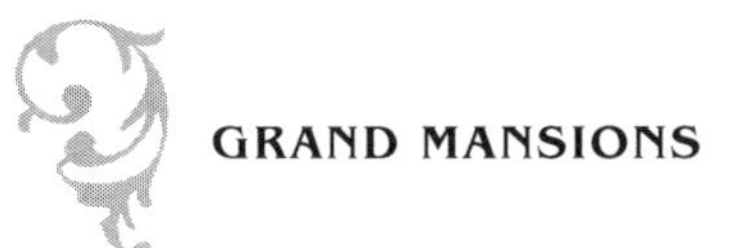

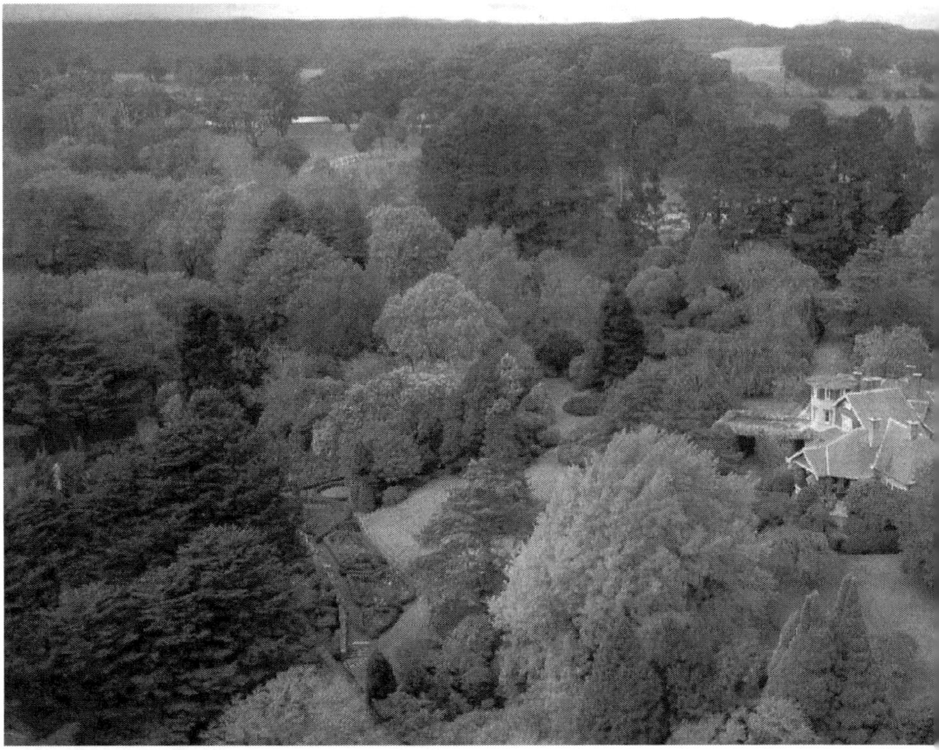

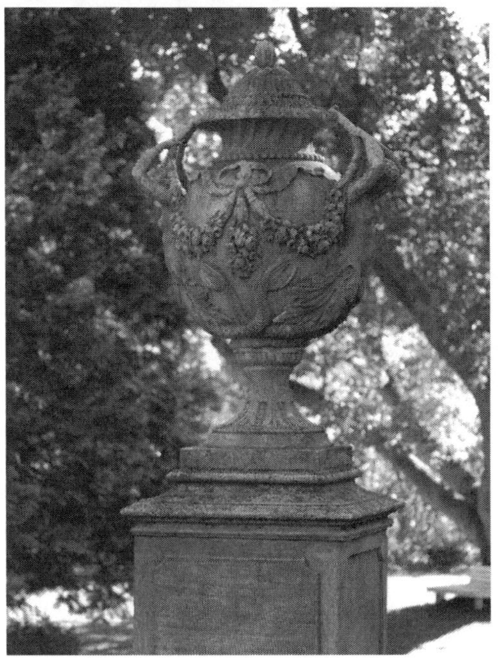

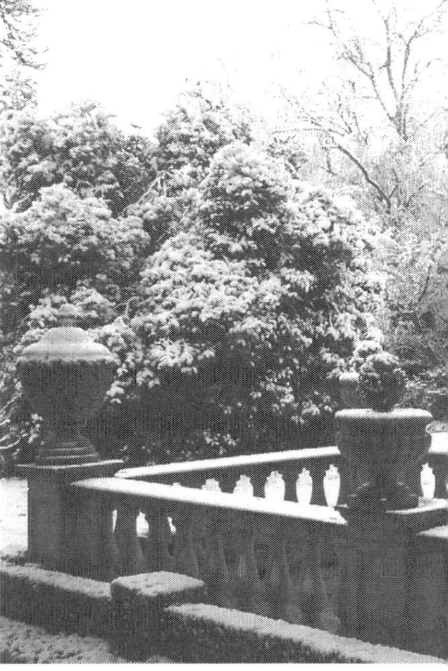

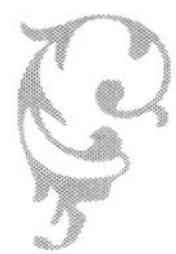

CHAPTER 24

Milton Park Country House Hotel

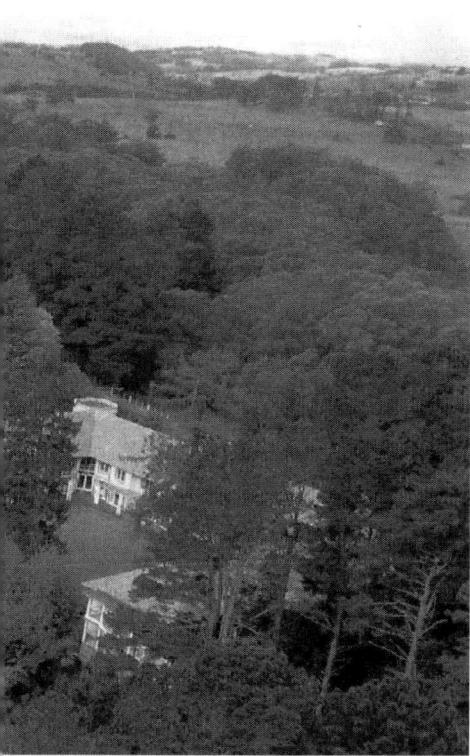

I've lived in the Wollondilly Shire south of Sydney now for seven years. Long enough, you'd think, to have become aware of all of the truly significant historic properties in my own backyard. Like Milton Park, just outside the Southern Highlands town of Bowral. As I walked through its world-class gardens, past the old coach house and its Fairy Walk and its 90-year-old elm trees and the two weeping beeches that are supposedly the oldest of their kind in Australia, I couldn't believe Milton Park had almost escaped inclusion in this book, when what *should* have happened was me thinking— 'A book on historic hotels? Sure, I'll write it. Hmmm, better call Milton Park.' Obviously my research skills need refining. This place is a cracker.

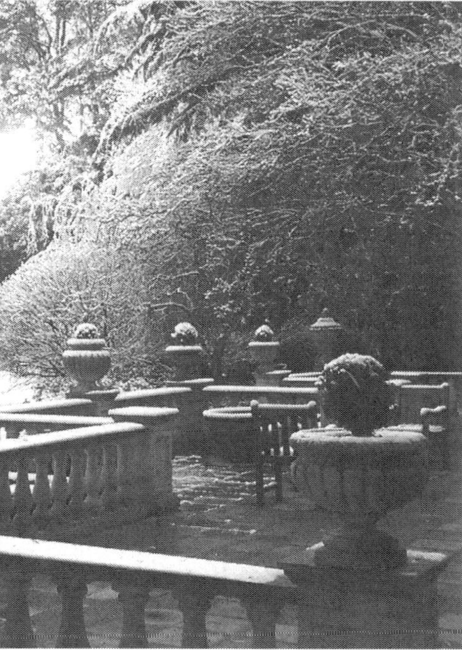

clockwise from top From the air Milton Park seems more Botanic Garden than country retreat; two views of what has been rated the world's eleventh best private garden.

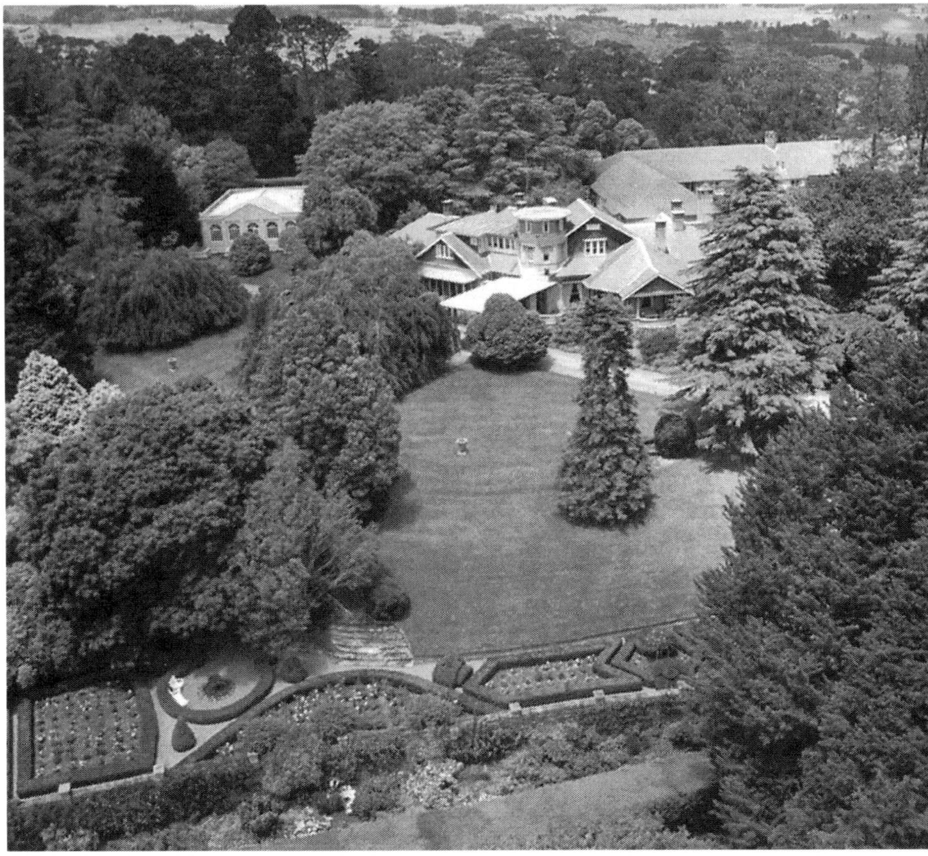

above The gardens are a delightful mix of geometric Edwardian lines and rambling woods.

Milton Park is a secluded, manmade world of landscaped gardens, old growth hemlock trees, elms and English oaks, which became all the more extraordinary to me after I was shown a photograph of the house in its early stages of construction. At the turn of the century there was nothing here. I mean *nothing*. No trees, no terraces, no shrubs, not even any flowers as best as I could make out from the grainy sepia images I was shown—just a bare hill and the beginnings of a mansion. I wish I could convey how extraordinary the transformation is—from nothing to a verdant, world-renowned oasis with a reputation in the botanic world such that whenever its chief gardener, David Smith, advertises a gardening position, they have to field applications from Sydney's Royal Botanic Gardens. Anyone but anyone who is a gardener wants to work here. And why wouldn't

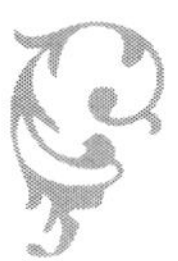

you? The gardens here at Milton Park have been rated as the 11th best privately owned gardens in the world. In the *world!*

In 1910 Tony (Anthony III) Hordern purchased Mansfield Farm, then 1200 acres, and contracted the Hordern family's preferred architects, Morrow and Du Putron of Sydney, to build him a mansion—a mixture of Federation and Arts & Crafts style with touches of American bungalow and Art Nouveau influences, with Welsh Penrhyn slate shingles, the finest in the world on its roof and portions of its external walls. Fortunately, for this grand old home, the Dobler Family, Milton Park's present owners, have proven to be masters at preserving the property's built history, and when replacement shingles were recently required, they weren't content with replacing the 100-year old shingles with 'look-a-likes'—they imported Welsh slate from the Penrhyn Slate Quarry in Wales, the very same quarry out of which the original shingles came.

These days Milton Park hosts car launches for Rolls Royce, Bentley and Aston Martin, and their ballroom, with its reinforced, purpose-built floor, is where the cars are displayed. 'Just last Friday we had 18 Rolls Royce Phantoms and Bentley GT's including their new "Continental GTC Speed" parked in here and outside,' explained Mark Dobler as he took me on a tour of the property. They also cater for between 46 and 50 weddings each year and have numerous fundraising nights (recently the Australian Chamber Orchestra performed here and tickets were $500 each and $100 000 was raised for charity). Last week Mark and his wife had their second child and it was only then that Mark realised Bowral Hospital had a 'Milton Park Wing', the result of some of the charitable dollars the hotel has given back to its community. I quickened my pace to keep up with Mark on what was a 'whirlwind' tour. That evening a Macquarie Bank conference had booked out the entire property. Milton Park is a busy place.

Although quick, my tour turned out to be the longest of any property in this book. And we *still* missed things. Mark apologised for it, too, referring to it as the 'shortened version', though still full of its historical tangents and personal memories as Mark's fingers pointed this way and that, revealing the property's past and making it come alive, the big things and the small. Like the photo he has somewhere and is still to find for me of a little boy swinging on the old iron lace gates we just walked through. 'That little boy was Kerry

Packer—chubby little thing he was. I'll try and find the photo.' When two small stone obelisks were unearthed in Milton Park's Bluebell Wood it was decided to mount them on a couple of gate posts, just to provide some ornamentation. (The Bluebell Wood consists of in excess of 500 000 bluebells that grow alongside daffodils, tulips, snowdrops and jonquils under a grove of birch trees and is possibly the most serene 100 square metres in New South Wales.) One day an old Bowral resident who used to work at the house saw the obelisks and told Mark that he remembered them and that they'd in fact once been gravestones for the Hordern's two great danes, 'Prince' and 'Duke', both of whom were descended from the same line as the great danes that belonged to the former British Prime Minister, Sir Winston Churchill.

Under the Horderns' guidance Milton Park became known throughout Australia for its stud Guernsey, Hereford and shorthorn cattle as well as Clydesdales, mountain ponies, and birds. The floor over the old carriage house used to be a temperature-controlled pigeon loft that would send and receive pigeons from the Horderns' retail stores in Sydney. In the coach house we walked through the seven guest rooms all linked to a common living area that the Packers and the Murdochs occsionally rent out. Every one of the stable doors is original, as is much of the area around the stables on the ground floor. Externally the building looks much as it did in photos from the 1920s. An old story, let's hope its apocryphal, goes that when Anthony Hordern was in his twilight years he spent a lot of time in the coach house's loft doing 'experiments' on his birds in the hope of creating new budgie colours. According to the talk, he tried to breed canaries with budgies in an attempt to create budgies with new colour variations.

Just beyond the coach house are some of Milton Park's Scottish Highland cattle—great long-horned, 700 kilo beasts with their two-layered coats, one an under-down and the other a coarser, outer layer that protects them from the fierce Scottish (and Bowral) winds. They didn't come this time when Mark gave the call, but they're always down there in the south paddock somewhere, and are quite domesticated.

Milton Park's isolation also lends itself to being a preferred getaway for celebrities and superstars, who come here more often than you'd think. 'We had Enya stay here a few weeks ago for two

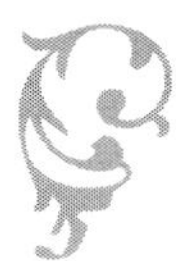

weeks, she stayed in this room, actually. Had a driver on call 24/7 at the front gate in case she wanted to go anywhere but to the best of my knowledge she didn't even leave the hotel. She's a very private person. Just last week Sir Anthony Hopkins was here, he stayed in this room too, as a matter of fact. He's a lovely chap, a great gentleman.' Milton Park gets a massive amount of repeat business and more than 85 per cent of its guests come from Sydney. It's very 'clubby', which perhaps might explain why I missed it for so long. John Olsen, often acknowledged as Australia's greatest living artist, often stays here.

There's a helipad here, too. Pilots love it because, and this has to be confirmed, apparently it's likely that Milton Park is situated on the highest point of land anywhere between Sydney and the Snowy Mountains—850 metres above Fort Denison according to Mark—and the land drops away in every direction the moment you lift off and pilots love to fly off down into the surrounding valleys.

We made our way to the new spa and gymnasium complex—it's relatively new, cost $4 million, and was awarded 3rd Best Spa in Australia recently by American Express. Normally I don't talk much on spas because I'm not a spa person, but something Mark said at the door to the steam room as my glasses were fogging up still sticks with me. 'My wife and I travelled to spas all over the world before we built this, and everywhere I went the steam rooms had flat ceilings and water would condense and fall, drip, drip, drip, onto my head. I didn't like that. So we designed our steam rooms with a raked ceiling to take the water away and to the sides. As far as I know it's the only one like it anywhere.' No drips in a steam room. That's impressive, and typifies the sort of care and attention to detail that Milton Park is all about.

Walking back towards the house we make another stop. Three years after Anthony Hordern's first wife Viola died in 1929, he married Ursula Mary Bullmore, and it is largely due to Mary's vision (with some help from the English School of Landscape Design who came out from England specifically to help the Horderns in the task) that the garden changed from the formal, rigid Edwardian lines laid out by Anthony to the series of gentle terraces culminating in the garden's magnificent rose garden that we see today. Mary also loved swimming, and today you can still see it—Australia's very first filtered swimming pool—which began as an inground pool but was raised to

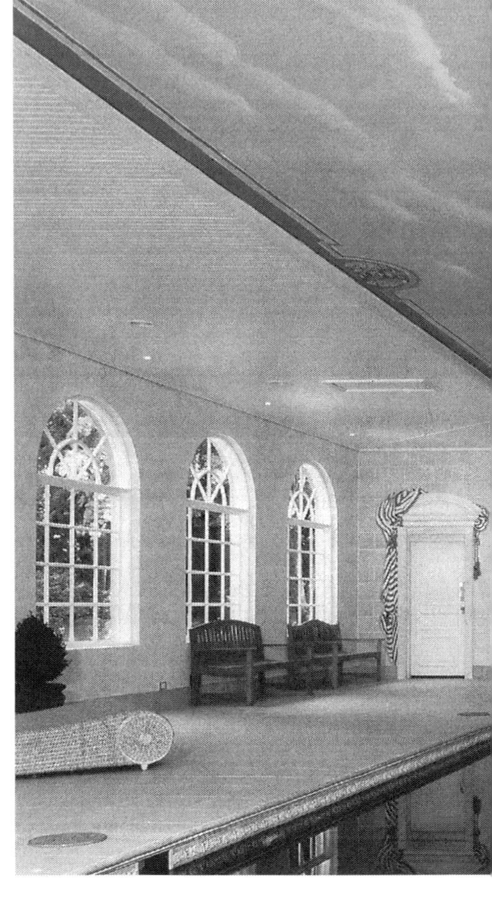

right The French-styled Bath House has an indoor swimming pool with faux sky above for added atmosphere.

a metre or so above ground level after Mary inadvertently shared its waters one night with a black snake. Not wanting to repeat the experience Mary ordered her small army of stonemasons at her disposal to raise the pool and place a 'lip' around it that would cause snakes to fall back on themselves should they attempt to get to the water.

Throughout the garden there is history at every turn. In a courtyard behind the main house there's a bronze fountain that was purchased from the French government, and an urn that cost the family $100 000 to bring out from Wales. In the 'Japanese garden' there's a 100-year old bonsai tree that has to be 3 metres high. Near the tulip lawn the leaves of Australia's oldest variegated elm tree go transparent just for one day before they begin to change colour for autumn, and David the gardener does his best to pick which day that will be so people can be brought out to see it.

Inside in the conservatory there's an old 1776 French butcher's block—a magnificent bench with a rosewood fascia and a surface made up of separate blocks of wood that could be replaced individually if any single one was ever damaged. Back in the garden a rock wall around the 'Wizard Fountain' measuring 2 metres by 2 metres has no joints and was cut from a single piece of rock. Over in the coach house there are two iron griffins sitting in storage that were purchased at auction in France when the owner of a chateau who had 17 of them suddenly realised he only needed 15. It's just

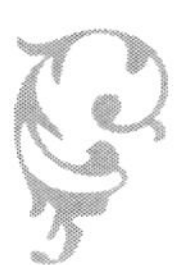

one extraordinary story after another. There are haylofts, 100-year-old workers' cottages for rent, and a fabulous old pin oak tree whose foot-thick branches were partially broken long ago to train it to grow horizontal to the ground, defying gravity and in the process turning the tree into a piece of sculpture.

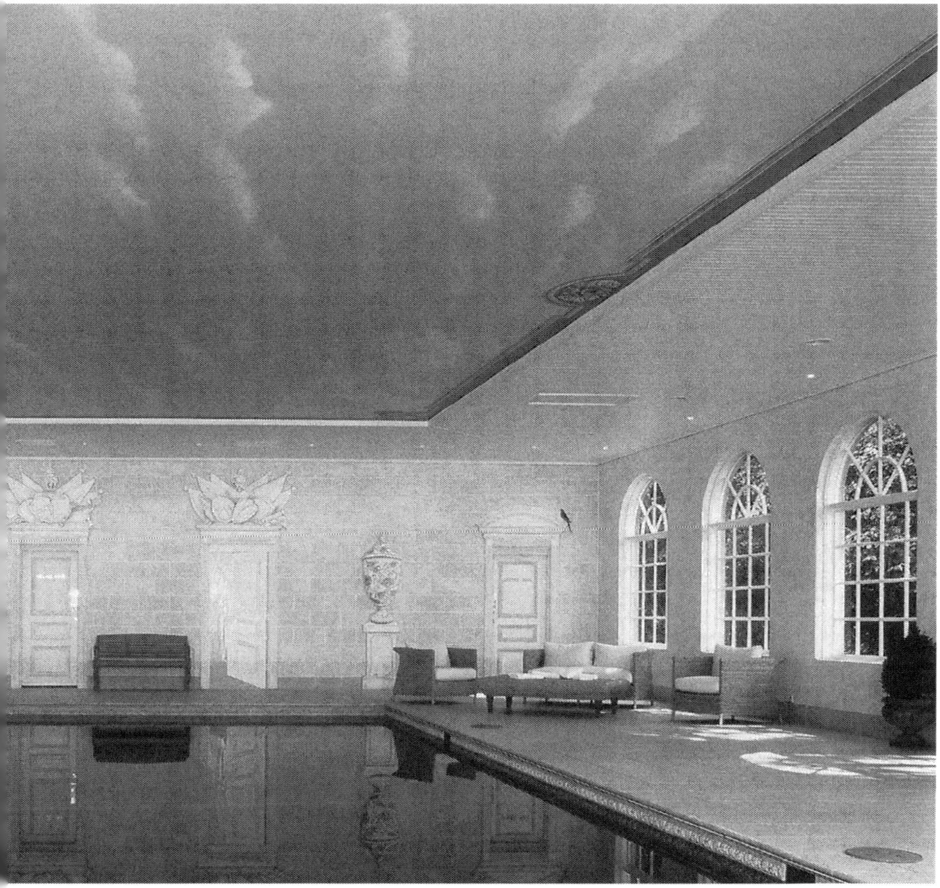

It's surprising just how much you can learn in a day. I was in ignorance of Milton Park when I arrived. It was as though I'd stepped through a secret panel at the back of an old wardrobe and emerged in Narnia. Now, after having spent the better part of a day here, having its treasures explained and its mysteries revealed, I felt a little the wiser. But it still looks like Narnia.

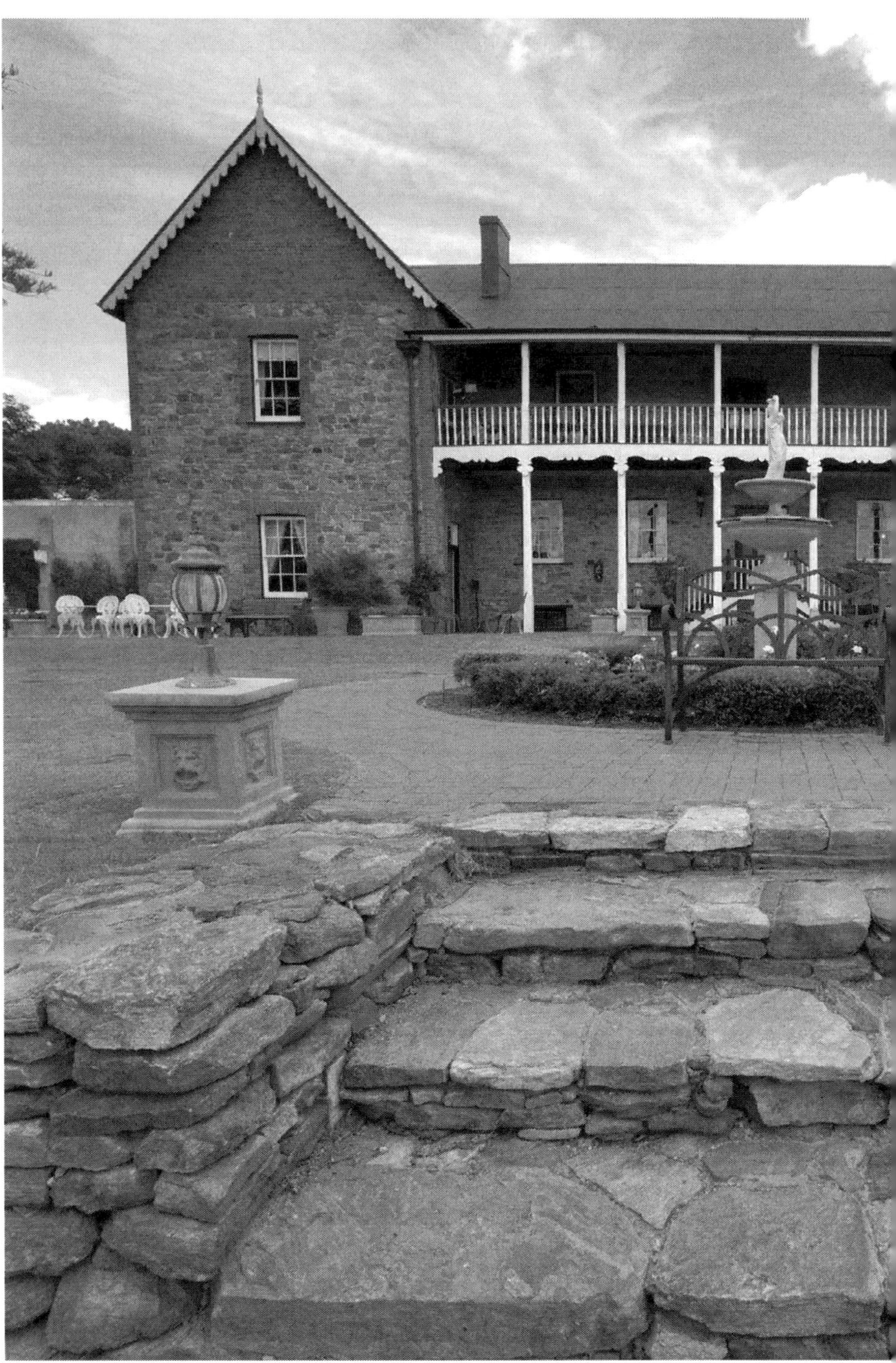

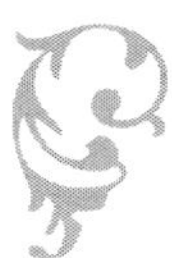

CHAPTER 25

Faversham House

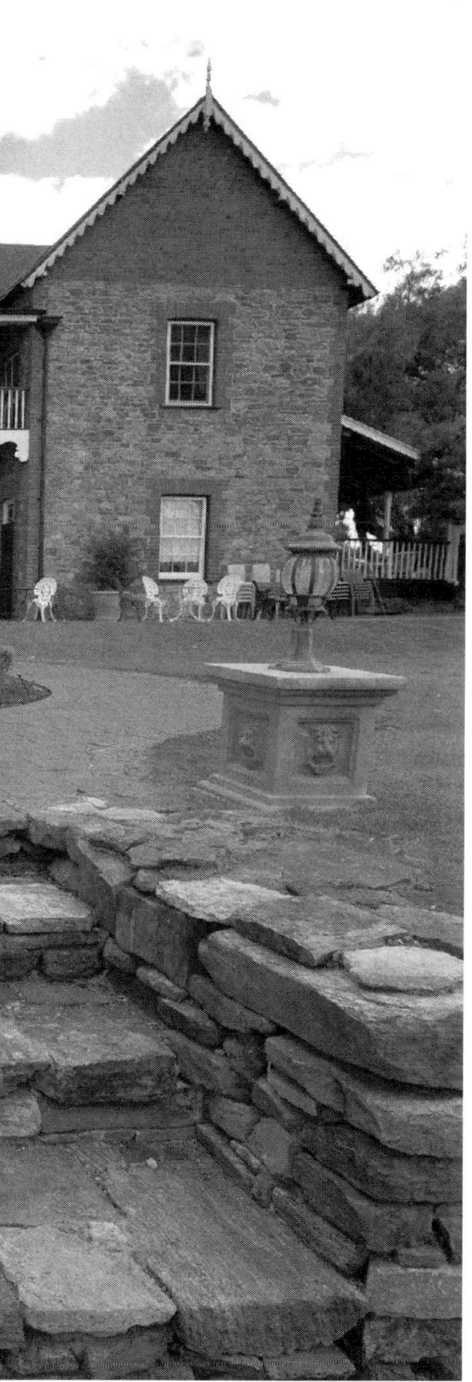

There's an old, apocryphal, antique dealer's story about a woman in England who owned a complete collection of four rare paintings. One day a dealer approached her and enquired if she'd be willing to sell them. She replied that she would, for 20 000 pounds each. The dealer baulked at this and replied that, in his estimation, the four paintings were not worth anything like the figure she had placed on them. The woman then picked up two of the paintings and threw them into her fireplace.

'What in the world have you done?!' he exclaimed. 'See these?' the woman said pointing to the remaining paintings. 'They're worth 50 000 pounds each, now'.

left Faversham House is the proud guardian of Western Australia's oldest Georgian residence, a four-room home below ground level excavated circa 1836 which lies beneath the mansion's foundations.

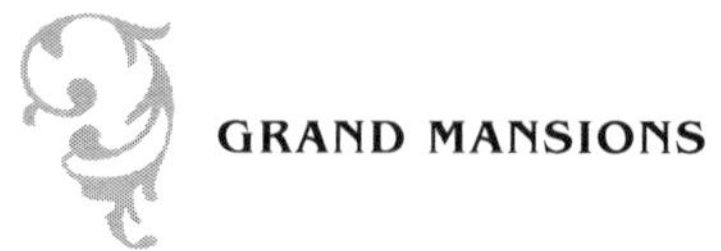

right The balcony at Faversham House provides exceptional views over the historic township of York and to the hills beyond.

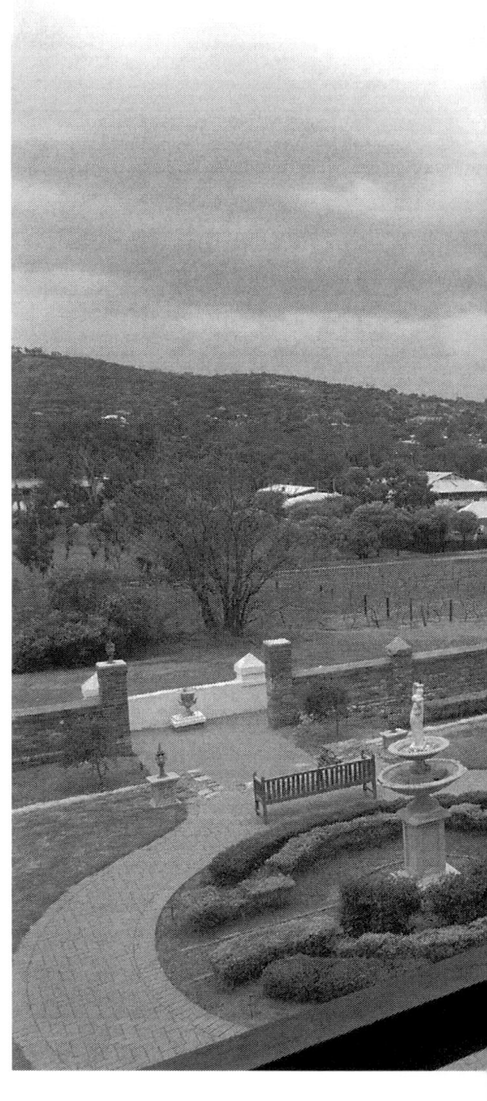

Richard Bliss is an antique dealer who grew up in the Cotswold village of Withington in a small limestone early Georgian cottage purchased by his parents for 400 pounds in the 1930s. It was in many ways a typical example of vernacular architecture, a 'one up, one down' two-room house with a living area, larder and kitchen downstairs, a bedroom upstairs, and set on about a quarter acre. The cottage had no electricity, no running water, and an old dry-stone boundary wall that had long fallen into disrepair and that Richard always promised his father he'd rebuild one day. And when his father, who was a stonemason, passed away in 1995, he did just that. When I asked where Richard's father got his water from, he left the room and returned a moment later with a yoke around his shoulders, a smooth almost sculptured piece of English elm from which dangled two rusted lengths of handmade linked chain at either end with hooks that would close around the handle of a bucket. Richard stood proudly in the doorway of the library of Faversham House and said, 'He brought the water from a nearby stream with these'. It's a pleasurable thing meeting people who, despite their success, never forget their roots.

In 1963–64 Richard left England and came to Australia via a circuitous route through Europe, Turkey, Iran, Pakistan, India, then

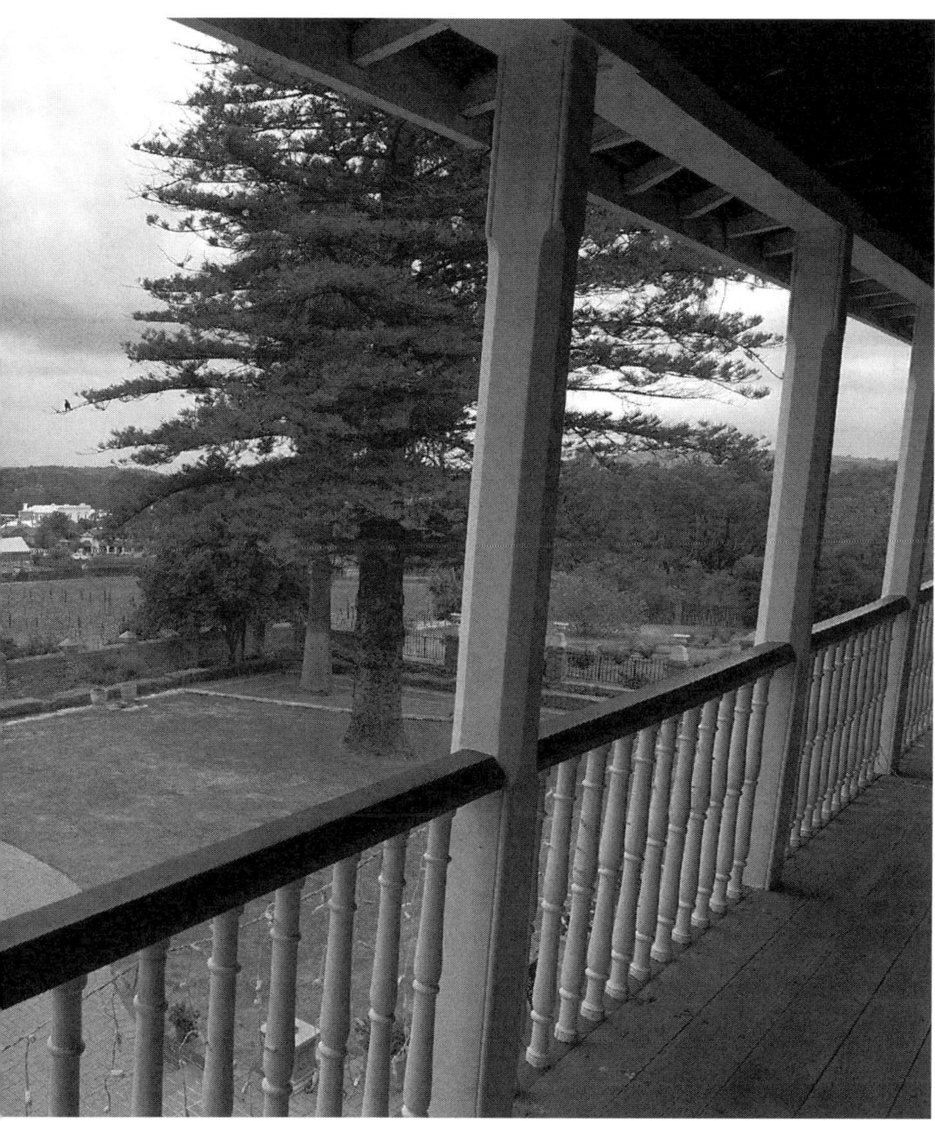

down through Southeast Asia to Singapore and finally to Fremantle with 'two and sixpence' in his pocket. Within 20 minutes of getting off the boat he had a job. He then met Nola, savvy business woman and bawdy, self-deprecating stand-up comedian. They married in 1971 and in 1973 went to live in England, where they did quite well in the antiques trade at a time when the British Empire was shrinking back within the borders of the United Kingdom and

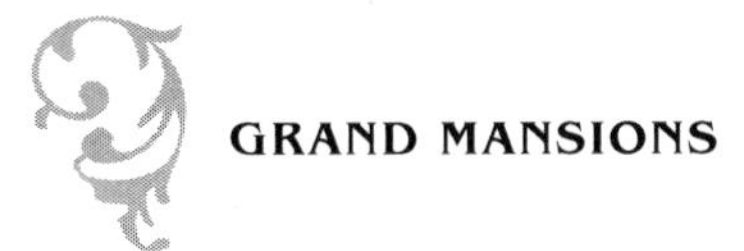

antiques and collectables were flooding into the country from all over the Commonwealth. Richard and Nola returned to Western Australia in 1999 and purchased Faversham House in York, a tranquil hour's drive northeast of Perth, in March 2004, and began transforming the 1840s home built by the pioneering Monger family into the grand guesthouse it is today.

Richard loves constructing dry stone walls, and it wasn't long before he met a local landowner named Tony Boyle, who told him he could have any of the rocks he could find on his 12 000-acre property that might help him to build them. Richard could hardly believe his luck, and to anyone who comes here and walks through Faversham's extensive landscaped gardens, it must seem like he has been building elegant dry-stone walls with considerable aplomb ever since.

In a world where 'how to' books seem to complicate every task to the point of it becoming a science, it's hard to imagine there was a time when the building of a simple dry-stone wall, walls made without mortar and held in place by their own weight, was something that every child in rural England knew how to do. Along with things like hedging and ditching and milking a cow, they learned these things as a child whilst standing by their father's knee. Faversham House is surrounded by dry-stone walls. And they aren't as difficult to construct as you might think, provided you follow certain non-negotiable principles. Start with a widish base, say 800 millimetres, then progressively reduce the wall's thickness to, say, 500 millimetres, at the top. Place your largest rocks at your base and try and ensure there is no 'rocking' of any stone as you go. Always overlap your joints and be prepared to use a geologist's hammer to shape them into submission. Tap the 'rubble' stones in the centre of the wall securely into place. Use smaller, flat stones to slide beneath larger rocks that might have an irregular shape to keep them stable, and employ a string line to maintain your direction and incline. The result of Richard's years of toil is Faversham's beautiful rose gardens and adjacent terraces, crisscrossed by a network of dry-stone walls that are nothing short of inspiring and are unique amongst the hotels in this book. They echo the iconic stone walls of England's Cotswolds and provide an architectural purity and warmth that have been the crucial element in transforming the 5 acres of Faversham House into a handmade haven of peace.

Land in WA's Avon Valley began to be opened up for settlement in the 1830s and York used to be known as Monger's Town. John Henry Monger Snr came here with his pioneering family in 1835–36 and built an inn and a general store before starting work on the family home, which he decided would be built underground. That's right. Underground.

There was a time, not long after the proclamation of Perth's Swan River Colony by the Royal Navy's Captain John Stirling in 1829, when people began to fear that the new colony might have to be abandoned. The sandy coastal plain that characterises the area surrounding Perth was proving wholly unsuitable for growing crops, and most of the good land along the banks of the Swan, Canning and Helena rivers had already been allocated in land grants. New horizons needed to be found for agriculture, but Western Australia was a wild and primitive place in the 1830s, as seen in a letter to the Colonial Secretary from one of York's early residents, R.H. Bland, describing a grizzly murder of a settler and her child: 'The woman was speared with a glass spear which entered the back and came through the pit of the stomach … the child was laying in the centre of the house with its arms and legs extended, in the act of crawling out …'

There were, of course, atrocities on both sides, but this incident helps us understand why a man would build a house that was every bit as much a defensive redoubt as it was a home. John Monger certainly had a siege mentality. Building below ground level was in itself an obvious aid to defence. The iron bars—still firmly in place today on every window that pokes out below the later additions to Faversham House that grew up over Monger's redoubt in the 1850s—not only prevented access but enabled him to shoot at his would-be attackers. But it isn't until you walk down an improvised stairway into the original house that the full enormity of what lies beneath the floorboards of Faversham House today is revealed. It must have been the largest manmade hole in the ground in the west.

In fact, the only sign that there's a previous dwelling below what is now Western Australia's largest inland mansion are the four windows along the base of the east-facing facade and a stairway and door on the west facade that Richard excavated by hand over a gruelling ten-day period in order to expose its west-facing entry.

It is staggering to imagine excavating by hand the amount of earth required to build it. The rooms are large, far larger than one might expect for the time. There was a kitchen, a master bedroom with a

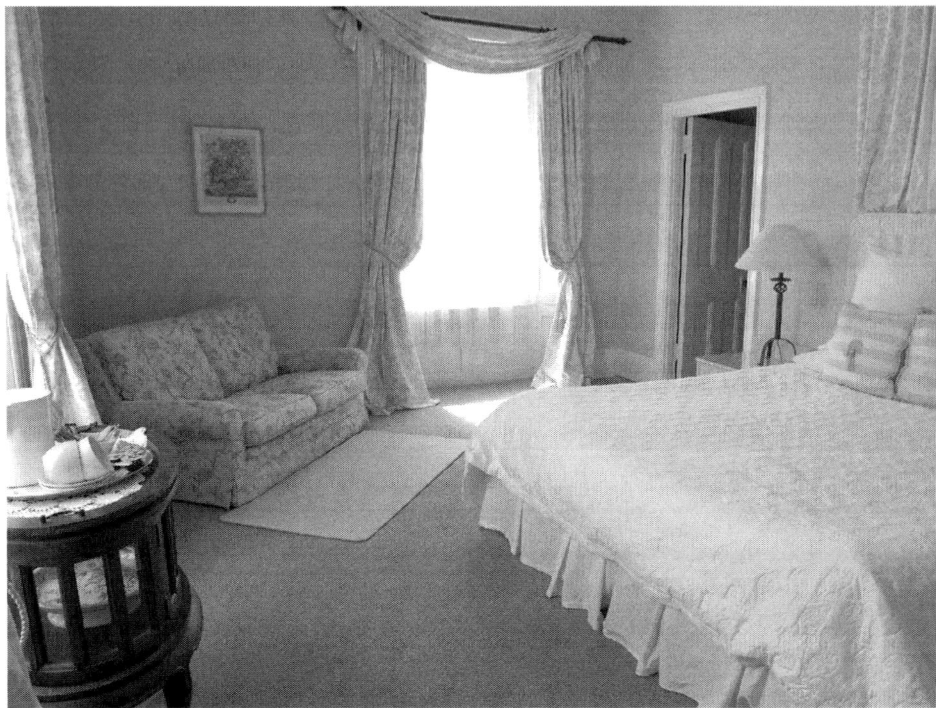

above One of the seven rooms available in the main house. The Pines and Mount Brown rooms open directly onto the verandah.

lovely brick fireplace, a separate room for the children and a large storage room. The only access to the house was via a tunnel that descended from the surface along the northern wall which led down to a double doorway that accessed the storeroom. This was again easily defended because the double entry doors were to the side of the tunnel, not at its end, making it impossible to swing anything in the hope of battering the door down. And it's all still here today, a story in stone that goes back to the earliest decades of white settlement in the state and is, quite simply, the oldest example of a Georgian residence remaining in Western Australia.

Faversham House is full of antiques, and the library at Faversham is filled with books with titles such as *An Illustrated Encyclopaedia of British Pottery and Porcelain, Twelfth Century Decorative Arts,* and *The Tang Potter.* It is impossible to stay here and ignore the wealth of the objects that surround you, and if you're lucky enough to catch Richard dashing to and fro between his various projects, you'll learn more about the antique trade in a half hour than you'd accumulated in your lifetime. What he told me about what happened during the 1940s and 50s to the contents of many English homes, left me gobsmacked.

In the years following the end of World War II, out the back of the great country homes of England, bonfires were burning. Hundreds of them. Possibly thousands, who will ever know for sure? This was the period before the coming of containerisation and the age of the mass transportation of goods across the world's oceans. It was also the age before the development of the English motorway. The first English motorway was the M6, opened in 1958, and prior to that, what the absence of both motorways and containers meant for the contents of grand manor houses across England is that when a deceased estate came on the market, the contents of the house were taken out the back and burned. Why? Well, it was just too costly to transport their contents to London using horses and carts and trucks and then having to crisscross the myriad of England's country lanes, many of them not much wider than a donkey track. It was too costly to transport goods to markets where they could be sold, and as for a worldwide antiques trade, forget it. Even if something got to London and seven or eight individual contractors had already been paid to get it there, which would have amounted to substantially more than the item was worth, where to from there? More shipping costs? Hauling it aboard a freighter in a net and down into the hold? So it never happened.

What *did* happen to it all? It was all burned. All of it. Entire houses full of furniture—Regency furniture, Queen Anne walnut staircases and bookcases, burned in bonfires because it just wasn't worth getting them out of England's rural nooks and crannies. It was a national tragedy, a loss of heritage on a scale that likely hasn't been equalled before or since.

In the world of the guesthouse and the bed & breakfast, the quality of your stay is often dependent upon the personality and charm of your hosts. At Faversham House, you'll get hospitality in spades, and there's no telling where your conversations with Richard and Nola might take you.

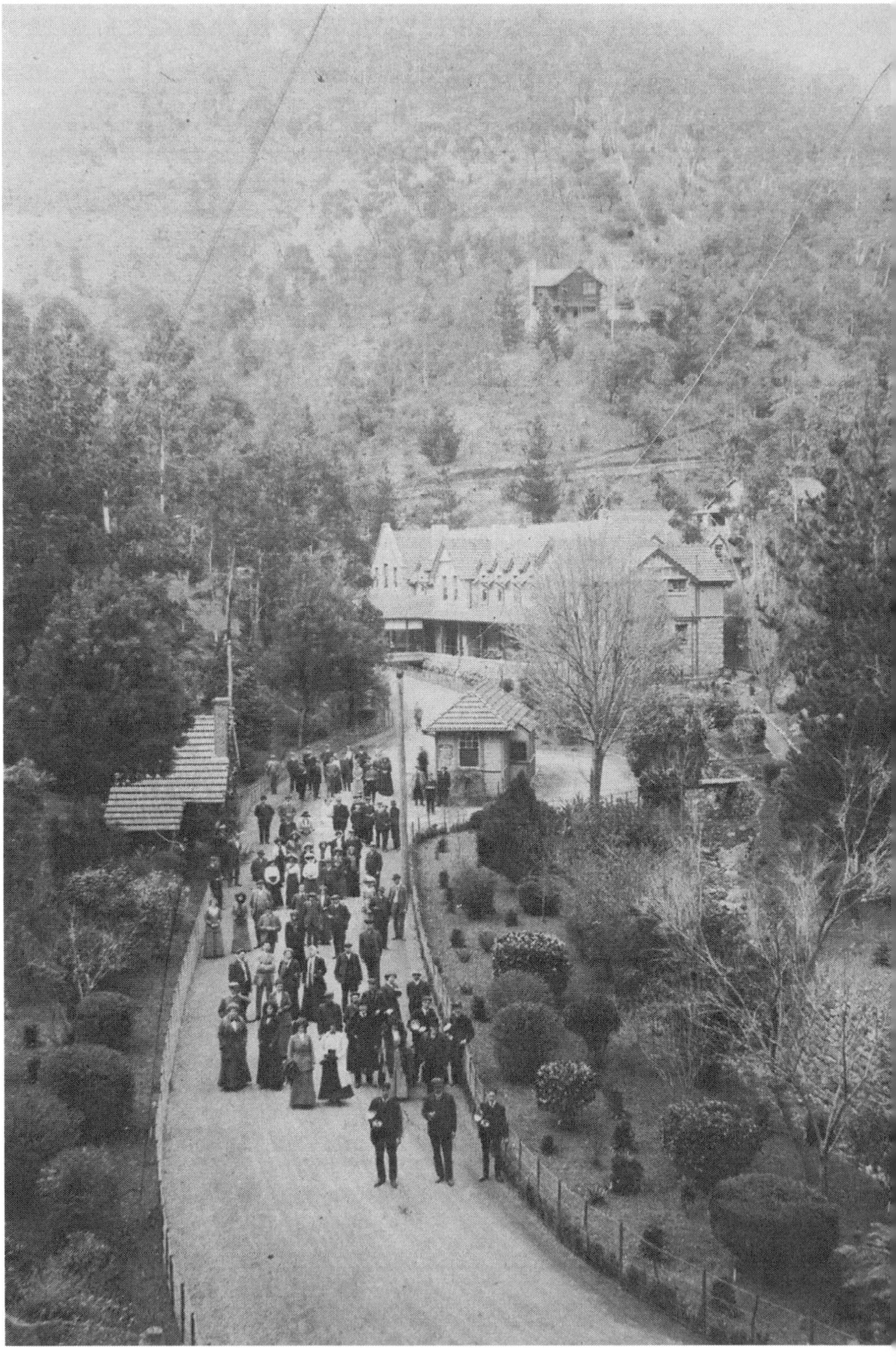

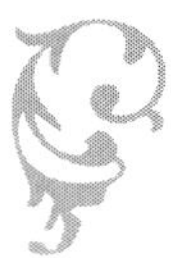

Jenolan Caves House

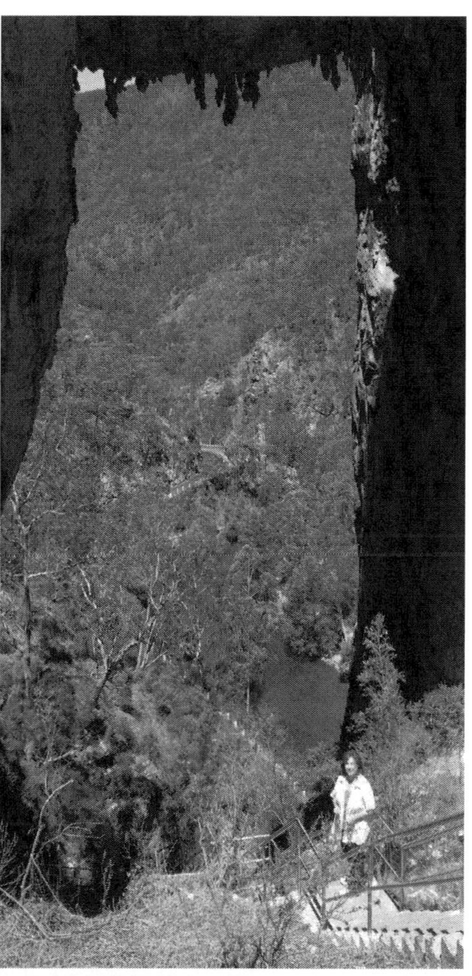

If you're married and have two young boys like I do, there are things you tend to avoid. You don't attend poetry readings. You avoid book signings, fine dining establishments and Woody Allen premieres. And you never, *never*, take them to an afternoon of Hungarian gypsy music. Or so I thought … The musicians Gustaw Szelski and Georg Mertens first met in 1989 when Georg filled in at a recital in the Blue Mountains west of Sydney. The two found they complimented one another so well they decided to form The Paganini Duo, with Gustaw on violin and Georg on guitar, playing traditional gypsy music from Hungary, Russia and Romania. Their numerous CDs have enjoyed worldwide sales.

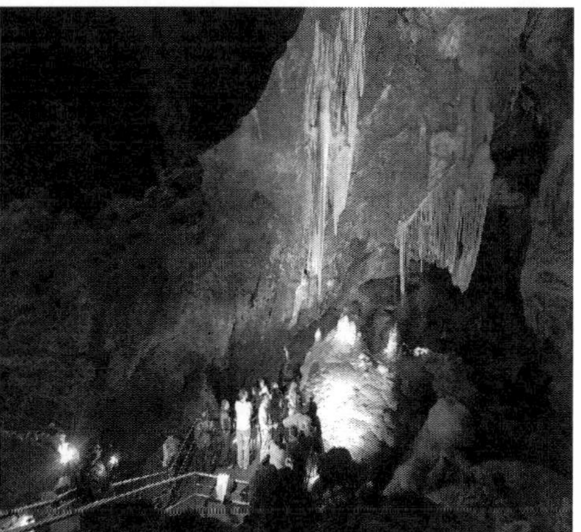

clockwise from left The Caves House was completed in 1898; looking down through Carlotta Arch to Blue Lake; there are over 40 kilometres of passageways at Jenolan.

So what has all this to do with Jenolan Caves House? Well, The Paganini Duo give concerts in the 54-metre-high Cathedral Chamber inside Lucas Cave on the fourth Saturday of every month, a cave which happens to offer some of the finest acoustics to be found anywhere both in terms of its potential to create absolute silence and in the quality of its echo. Joan Sutherland claimed the Cathedral Chamber had the finest acoustics she had ever experienced, and Dame Nelly Melba and even the Vienna Boys' Choir have sung there (yes, it's that big).The purity of the notes struck by Gustaw and Georg will make you forget about the world that exists beyond the caves, and the combination of guitar and violin will resonate with you long after you've been led single file out of the cave to re-emerge, energised and uplifted, beneath Jenolan's Grand Arch.

The other thing you'll remember is how the chords and melodies becalmed both adult and child alike. The programs are varied and the selected pieces are likely to include classical selections such as Bach's *Suite No. 5 in C minor*, Tchaikovsky's *Valse Sentimentale*, or Saint-Saëns' *The Swan*. Our boys sat through the one-hour concert, and their reactions ranged from genuinely impressed and intrigued through to, at the very worst, fidgeting. After all they were boys, and boys love caves. It was the perfect combination for a great night out and afterwards there was a wine and cheese tasting back at Caves House where you can mingle with the artists and even purchase a CD.

Jenolan Caves House is one of those hotels we all 'think' we know. If you live within a day's drive of it, chances are you've been there at least once in your life, very likely as a child, and very likely just for the day. You probably didn't stay overnight in Caves House and you certainly wouldn't have revelled in an evening of Hungarian gypsy music. Sure, to get here still remains a bit of a drive, but its isolation has always been the source of its magic. And there isn't a hotel in this book and few anywhere that can match the way Jenolan Caves House triumphantly reveals itself to you as you emerge from the Grand Arch and drive into its fortress-like 'compound' hemmed in by hills that rise up around it.

The Caves House management have also worked hard to establish a fascinating and informative series of lectures focusing on the area's

right The isolation of Jenolan Caves House doesn't prevent 250 000 visitors a year making it New South Wale's premier regional destination.

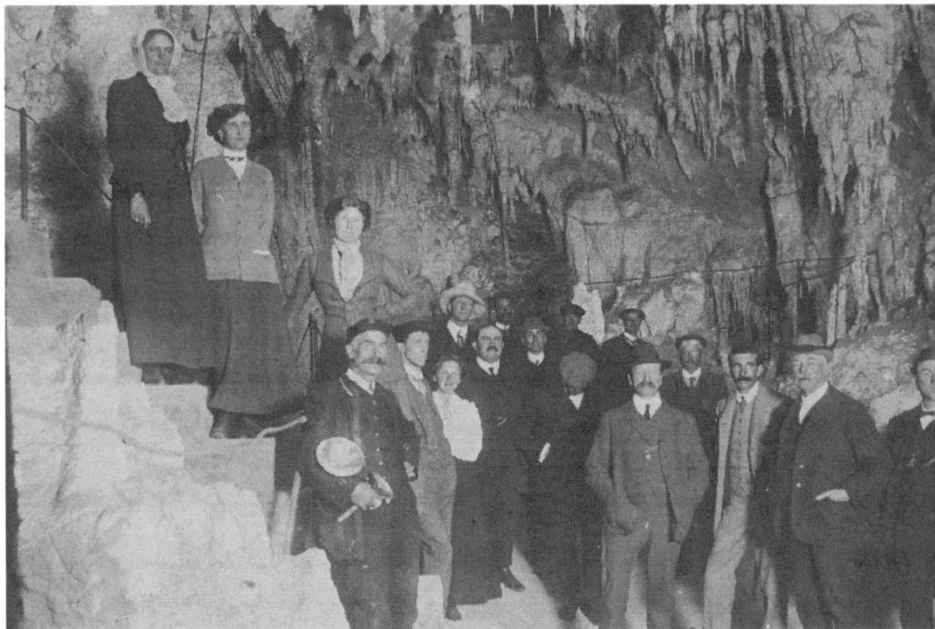

above The early 1880s saw electric lights installed in Chifley Cave, the first of the caves to be lit.

complex geology. Dates and subject matter can be found on the Jenolan caves website but include:

• the many rare bird species that inhabit the surrounding Jenolan Karst Conservation Reserve

• how an ancient marine reef system evolved into the world's oldest cave system (430 million years old when the area lay at the bottom of a warm, shallow sea)

• Dr Anne Musser, an American palaeontologist and illustrator and with a Masters in Biology now with the Australian Museum, talks about the evolution of the platypus, several of which can be seen swimming in the waters of Blue Lake adjacent to Lucas Cave; Dr Musser has a PhD in the study of fossil monotremes (the egg-laying mammals, platypus and echidna)

• Jenolan's own 'Singing Guide', Domino Houlbrook-Cove, a trained opera singer, takes a look at the cave's long association with music and concerts

• Scuba-diving in various caves in the surrounding hills is revealed in depth by Michael Collins, a member of the Sydney University Speleological Society

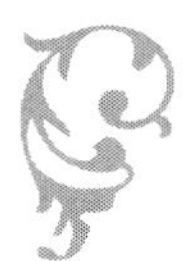

• Naturalist Ian Eddison together with Dr Anne Musser examine the diversity in flora and megafauna that lie above the caves and throughout the Jenolan Karst Conservation Area and the Silurian fossils that have been uncovered.

The point is, what with concerts and lecture series and bushwalking and the architectural splendour and history of Caves House itself, there's a lot more to a visit here these days than just walking through its caves, as fascinating as that undoubtedly is. An overnight stay here is what is needed, to give yourself the opportunity to explore all the wonders, both manmade and natural, that the area has to offer. Like Blue Lake.

Blue Lake, adjacent to Lucas Cave and once certified as 'dead', has been brought back to life by the Jenolan Caves Reserve Trust. If, like myself, you've never seen a platypus in the wild and would like to see at least *one* that isn't in a zoo before you pass on, then you simply must come here. Take the lakeside track that begins at the eastern end of the Grand Arch either early in the morning or late in the afternoon and (I'm tempted to almost guarantee it) your platypus-starved life will be a thing of the past. There are five resident platypuses now living in Blue Lake, an artificial body of water created in 1908 as a reservoir for Jenolan's tiny hydroelectricity plant, but which has, over the past 112 years, sufficiently merged with the surrounding bush as to appear almost natural. The platypuses have *not* been 'introduced' but have appeared there by choice, a testament to the rebirth and continuing good health and management of the lake. My family and I witnessed multiple sightings of all five swimming across the surface, diving and resurfacing again. It was an extraordinary afternoon—from a platypus-less life to five in the space of a few minutes!

The rebirth of Blue Lake (whose brilliant colour is courtesy of dissolved particles of clay and limestone) and its return to a vibrant ecosystem is a restorative process reflected in the recent history of Caves House itself. Allowed to run down whilst under the stewardship of prior owners, Caves House is currently back in the hands of the New South Wales State Government, although a tender has again been put out to return it to private hands.

Caves House is also at the centre of an impressive network of walking trails. Tourists began arriving here by coach as early as 1879, and when the Six Foot Track opened up in 1887 it was possible to make the 45-kilometre trek on horseback in a little over six hours. The

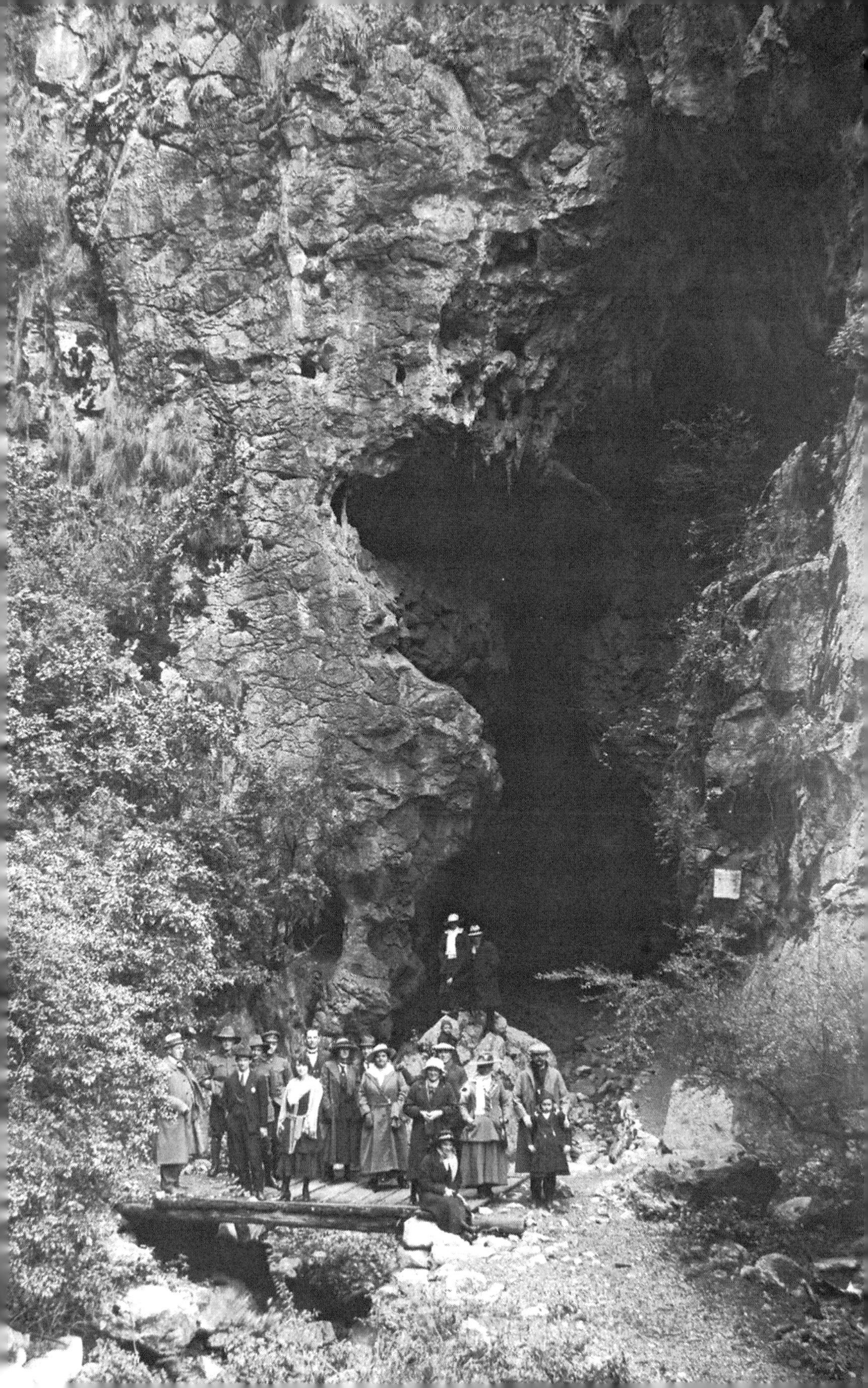

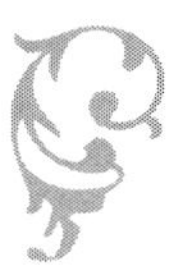

left The Jenolan Caves first began to emerge as a tourist destination in the 1880s.

track begins just outside the hotel's front doors (it's a two-night walk to Katoomba though most hikers prefer to start at Katoomba—from there it's all downhill). For the less adventurous there is the McKeowns Valley Walk, a 3-hour, 4-kilometre walk, that begins at the end of Playing Fields Walk, itself a 1–2-hour, 4-kilometre walk that begins at the Devil's Coachhouse and goes up into the McKeowns Valley.

But, of course Caves House was not built for concerts, lectures, walking trails and the area's flora and fauna. What brings people here is the network of underground rivers, caves and arches, Jenolan's hidden world of limestone karst formations. Over eons, water, together with its constituent mix of organic acids and carbon dioxide brought from plant roots and vegetable matter carried down from the surface, has followed planes of weakness in the soft rocks to give us the spectacular subterranean world we see today.

There are approximately 350 separate entrances to the Jenolan Caves complex, a system so vast and interconnected that it is still to be fully mapped and understood. Two rivers pass through it, the Jenolan River and Camp Creek, both of which flow into Blue Lake and from there into the Cox's River. There are 17 species of bat whose droppings provide food for the cave's micro-organisms, and more than 150 species of invertebrates, almost half of which are endemic to Jenolan, including white albino crickets, scorpions and blind cave shrimp.

Much is often made of the pioneering nature of that other great Blue Mountains institution and eclectic jumble of architectural styles, the Hydro Majestic in Medlow Bath, which opened up the very edge of the British Empire to guests in the midst of a snowstorm on 4 July 1904. However, on that cold July evening Jenolan Caves House, almost a day's ride *beyond* the Hydro Majestic, had already been a haven for travellers for eight years.

Built in 1898 the rambling, atmospheric Tudor-style Caves House was and remains one of Australia's great hotels, resonating all the charm and atmosphere of a European chalet with its broad verandahs reminiscent of St Moritz and a natural, laidback ambience, the product of the overwhelming sense of tranquility you feel the moment you drive in through the Grand Arch into Caves House's cloistered, natural world.

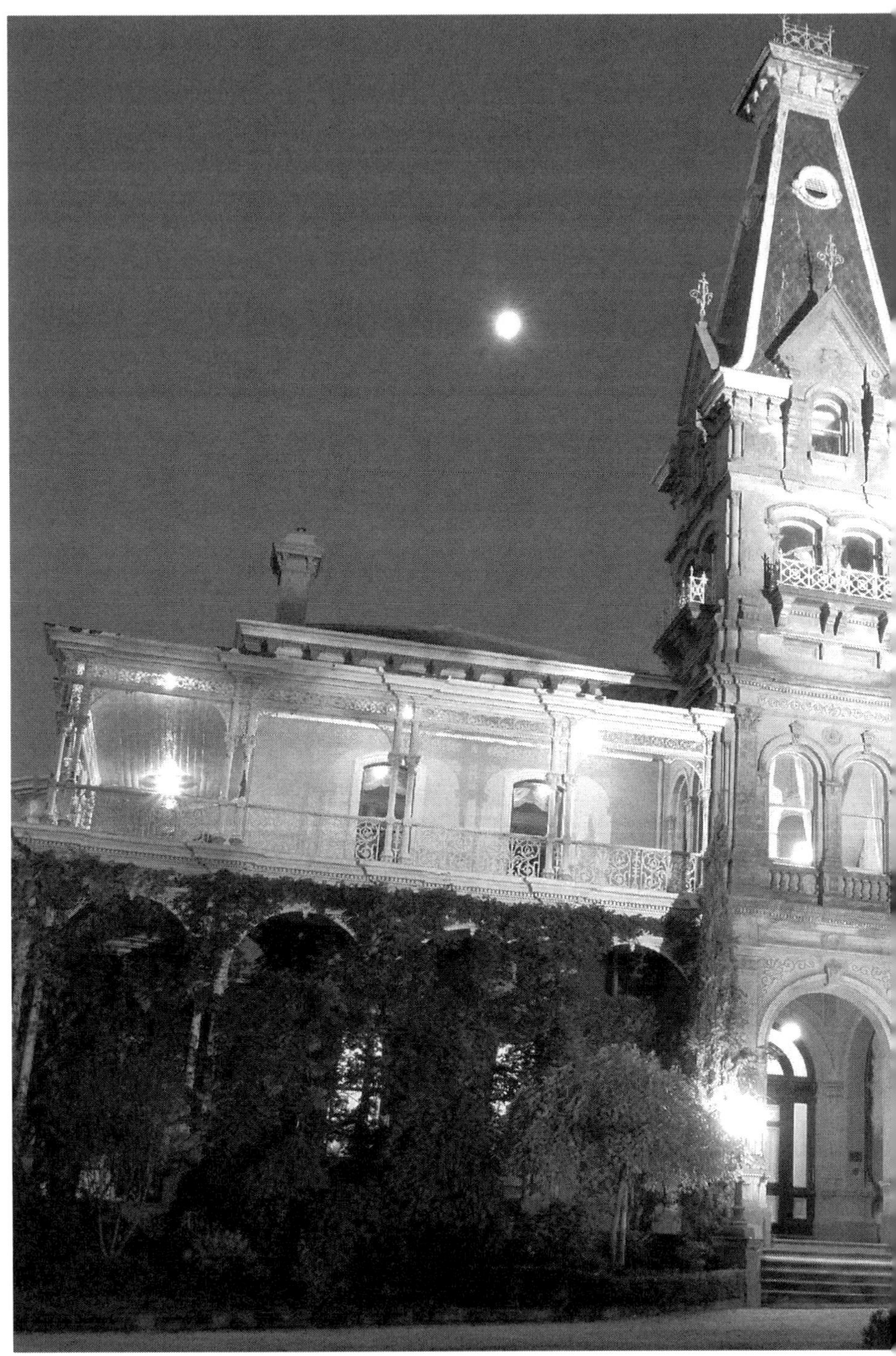

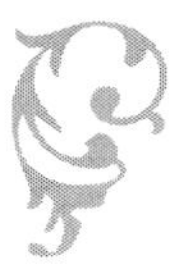

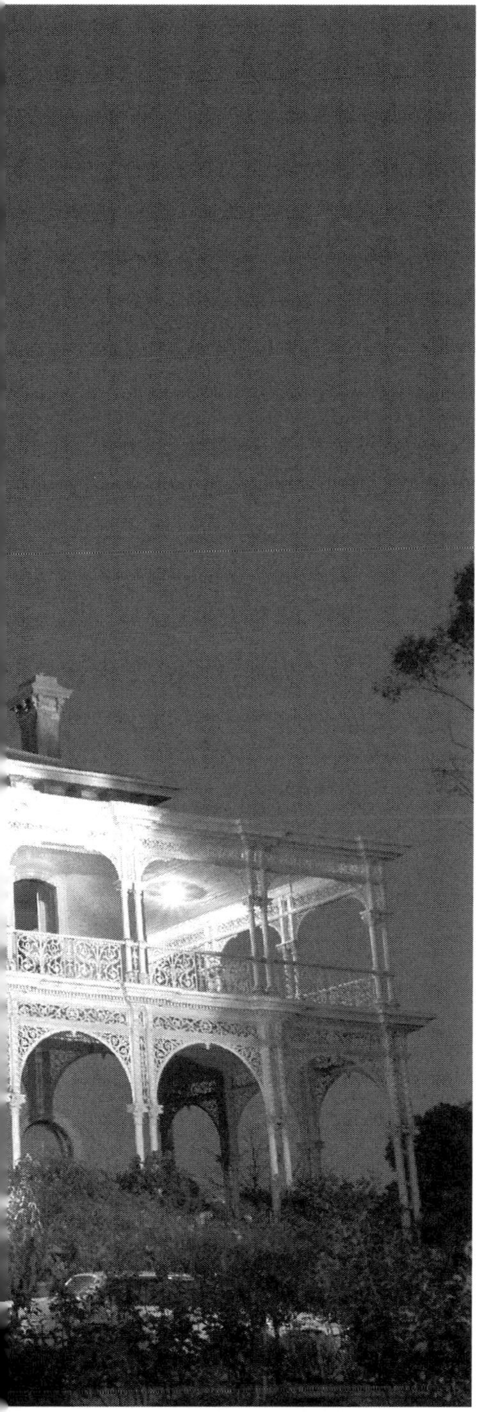

Rupertswood

In the afternoon of 25 December 1882, Christmas Day, an impromptu game of backyard cricket was organised between the touring English cricket team, captained by Ivo Bligh, and a local team. It was played on a slightly sloping paddock alongside Rupertswood, a 50-room Italianate mansion in Sunbury just north of Melbourne. No official scoresheets have ever been recovered (though likely none were ever kept) but it is generally conceded that the English won the game. At dinner that night the owner of Rupertswood, Lady Janet Clarke, presented the English captain, Ivo Bligh, with a tiny urn in which were placed the charred remains of a set of bails that someone had set fire to after the game.

left One of Australia's great houses, the exterior of Rupertswood is dominated by its signature tower, a blend of Italianate and French Second Empire influences.

During the tenure of Lady Janet Clarke's husband, William, the house was at the epicentre of Melbourne high society. After his death in 1927, Ivo Bligh returned the long-forgotten urn over to London's Marylebone Cricket Club, and the legend of The Ashes, the Holy Grail of cricket, was born. What drama! What pathos! How many contemporary hotels, regardless of their reputation or location, must wish they could claim ownership of a story like that?

The story of Rupertswood began with the construction of a two-room cottage in the 1840s by William Clarke's father, William Clarke Snr, who arrived in Victoria and immediately began to purchase vast tracts of land. Clarke Snr wanted land close to Melbourne and bought it at a guinea an acre, throwing nine squatters off their land in the process. He then purchased a further 36 000 acres plus all the properties from Whittlesea to Werribee. He died in 1874 leaving 4 million pounds to his son, William John Clarke, who began building his family home in Sunbury in 1874. It cost 25 000 pounds and was the most modern home of its kind in the colony.

It had speaking tubes to every room, hot and cold water to each bedroom (unheard of at the time), and a gas-producing plant outside that produced power to light the chandeliers. Its gardens were designed by the noted landscape architect William Sangster and still retain many elements of the original design including the entrance and most of the driveways, the rockery and a produce farm. There was also a lake in the shape of Australia. Originally there were to be two gatehouses but when the first one was completed William decided he didn't like it and promptly ordered the second, which was only partially completed, to be pulled down. The remaining gatehouse is now recognised as one of the finest gatehouses of any residence in Australia. It's such a pity there aren't two of them.

The foundation stone for Clarke's 50-room home was laid in 1874 and the mansion was named after William John Clarke's oldest son Rupert, who eventually would inherit it. It was Rupert who brought in the sewerage, built the internal bathrooms (up till then they had commodes) and brought in many of the heavy Victorian decoration in the late 1890s. He stayed until 1910 when he had a reckoning (called people together, worked out who was owed what—many who worked the property never took wages)—then realised he needed to sell it, and did so, to his brother William Lionel Russell Clarke, who

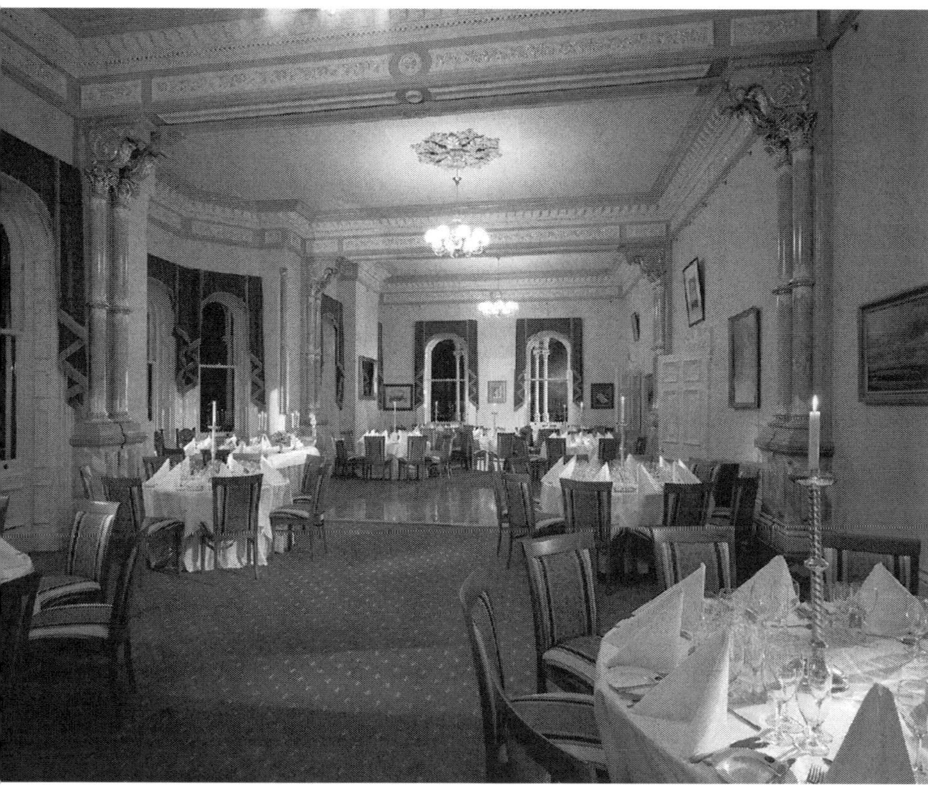

above The scale of the High Victorian Drawing Room is reminiscent of the great manor houses of England and is available for conferences or private dinners.

subdivided the gardens into paddocks for his horses and other areas of the farm.

In 1922 Rupertswood would eventually pass from the Clarke family forever when Lionel sold the house and grounds to Hugh Victor McKay, the inventor of the Sunshine Harvester. It was a lovely slice of serendipity. Hugh McKay used to walk past the house on his way to work as a young man and would often say to himself, 'One day I'll own that house'. But sadly his tenure there would not be a long one.

H.V. McKay died at Rupertswood in 1926 and the mansion was then purchased by William Naughton, a pastoralist who wanted land close to Melbourne to fatten his cattle for Melbourne's markets. One of Australia's great pastoralists, William Naughton's tenure at Rupertswood, however, also proved to be a short one and in 1927 he sold it and 1100 surrounding acres to the Salesian order of the Roman

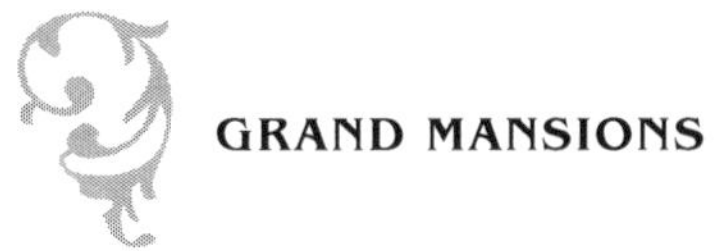

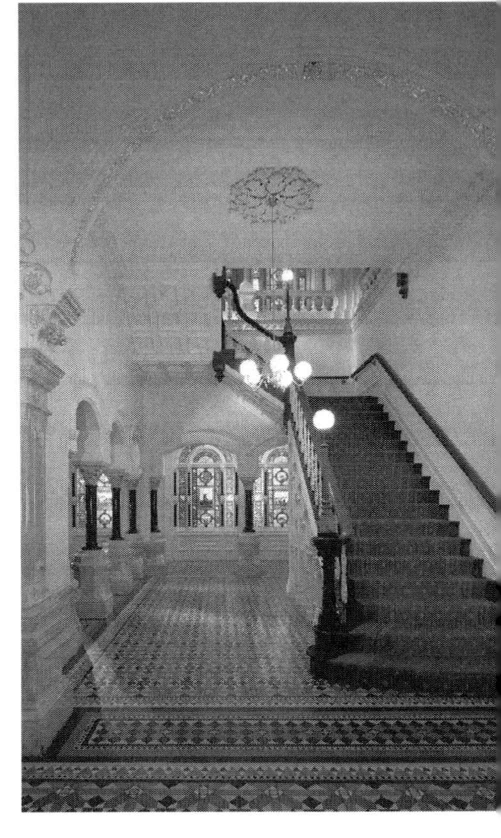

right The foyer is home to the main staircase, and in the background can be seen three of Rupertswood's six priceless Ferguson & Urie stained-glass panels.

Catholic Church who purchased Rupertswood mansion in order to provide accommodation and establish a college in its extensive grounds to educate poor and orphaned boys. The stables were converted into classrooms, but they burned down in 1929 and it was decided to reorganise certain rooms in the mansion into sleeping quarters and classrooms. From 1929 until the 1960s it remained a school for orphans and wards of the state. It started admitting day students in the 1950s and in the 1960s became a college with 500 students—all boys—with an agricultural school attached. Girls were admitted in 1987 and Salesian College soon had 1100 students from Years 7 through to Year 12 with Rupertswood mansion at its centre.

Tony Menhennitt was a student at Salesian College in the 1960s when the mansion was home to priests and various other teachers and members of the Salesian order. Students were *never* allowed to go into the mansion where the priests lived, and Tony never entered the house himself until the close of a Eucharistic festival one year where he was asked to carry some altar boy outfits and banners into the mansion but even then was under strict instructions to follow the laundry staff through to the proper room.

Tony loves to tell the story of an 8-year-old orphaned boy who walked up Rupertswood's driveway early one morning in the 1920s and knocked on its front door. Janet Clarke answered the door, asked him in, gave him something to eat, gave him a job to clean some shoes, and the young boy stayed at Rupertswood under his own volition until he was 16. 'That's the kind of people the Clarkes were,' Tony says. 'They may have been wealthy, but they were good, decent people.'

'I remember 1963 so well,' he went on, 'when my mother and father took me to Rupertswood for the very first time for my interview for admission to the school. I was over-awed by it. It even had its own private railway station back then, that William Clarke had managed to divert to Rupertswood from the Mount Alexander rail line. I was stunned. But then, strangely, after walking around for just a few minutes, I felt completely at home. That's one thing you have to know about Rupertswood—it might *look* like a museum, but it has never *been* one. It was built as a family home, which is why people always feel comfortable here.'

I know what he means. The furniture here isn't roped off, which immediately transmits the message from the mansion's management and staff that you are not only a guest here, but a *trusted* one as well. Rupertswood trusts you. It trusts you to admire the treasures they have here, to walk amongst them, to get up close, and not to abuse the privilege. Its history is accessible.

There are ten guest rooms at Rupertswood today, the most elegant of which is the H.V. McKay suite on the first floor with two rooms overlooking the adjacent dairy farm with access to the first-floor balcony. Less expensive rooms are found in the old servant's quarters, though all have queen beds and ensuites.

Ron is a Sunbury local of 40 years, and when he arrived Rupertswood had been lived in by priests and members of the Salesian order who remained there until 1998 when major restoration works on the mansion were begun. The volunteer group he works for has, over the years, raised enough money to fully fund the restoration of the dining and smokers' halls, and in mid 2010 a permit was lodged with Heritage Victoria for the restoration of the entry hall which, when finished, will match the decor in the main hallway.

The magnificent expanse of ground level stained-glass windows between the grand stairway and breakfast room were installed by Ferguson & Urie, two Scottish plumbers who found, once they had established themselves in the colonies, that they possessed an uncommon aptitude for creating beautiful panels of stained glass. The stained-glass windows in Rupertswood were made specifically for the house and many are signed and dated by the artists. The bluestone

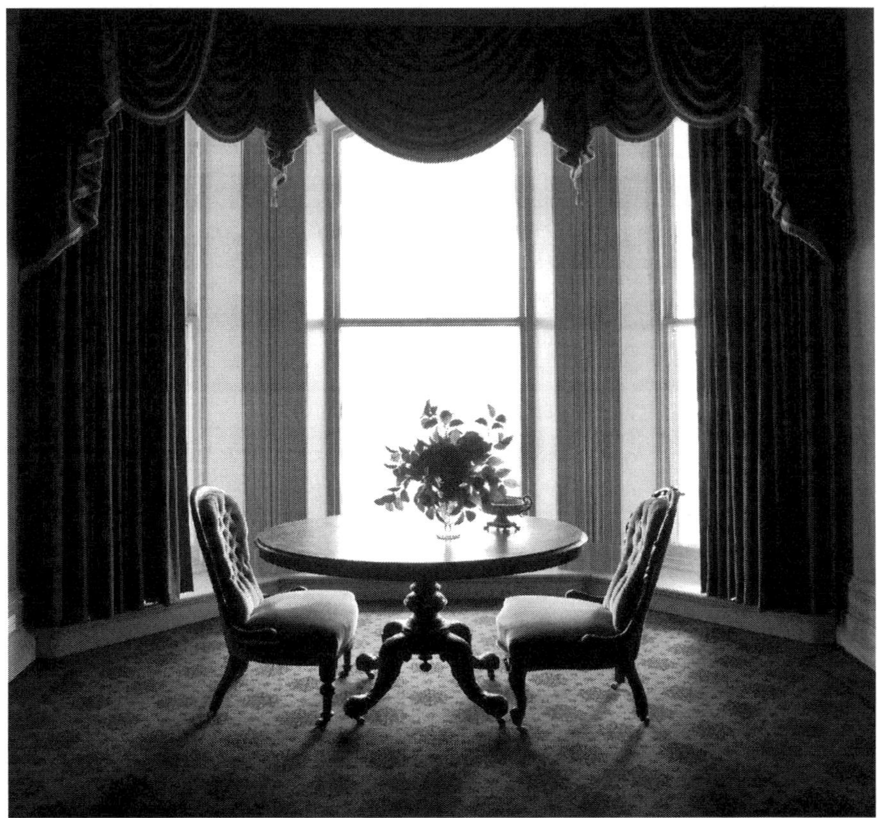

above Quiet nooks can be found everywhere at Rupertswood.

in its foundations is local bluestone, the house is built of bluestone rubble and cement, and Rupertswood's walls are triple brick. The floors are Canadian oregon, but all the metalwork was made in the Melbourne suburb of Brunswick, demonstrating Clarke's avowed determination to invest in the new colony.

If you're a lover of old cellars you'll love Rupertswood's. Built by the Clarke family it is accessed via a flight of sandstone steps that descends from underneath the foyer's grand staircase. The cellar lay undisturbed for more than a century until it was reopened in 2007. I didn't see it in its best light. The day before we arrived in Melbourne, the city was recovering from its heaviest rainfall since 1970 and the floor of the cellar was under 3 inches of water. It still stores the hotel's wines, of course, and is also available for dinner by candlelight should the mood overtake you.

Margaret McClelland gave up a lucrative career with Tourism Victoria to become Rupertswood's General Manager in 2007. Margaret came to Rupertswood for a conference several years ago, fell in love with it, and on Friday 13 April 2007 signed a lease to be its manager—and that night sat up till 5 a.m. cleaning out its fireplaces! When I spoke to her, she had only been home (she has a house in Sunbury) 14 nights in three years. Margaret had clearly fallen under Rupertswood's spell.

No story of Rupertswood would, however, be complete without making reference to the famous Rupertswood Battery, a mounted artillery battery formed by William John Clarke in 1884 during a time when very real fears of an imminent invasion by Russia saw defensive outposts such as Queenstown's Point Lonsdale being built across the colony. The battery was financed by men all of whom had connections to Rupertswood and became admired throughout the colony for their marksmanship and horsemanship. The battery made its first public appearance in 1897, escorting the Governor of Victoria to the opening of State Parliament, and went to England that same year to compete in military tournaments and to escort Queen Victoria during her Diamond Jubilee celebration. The battery was reformed in 1977 in the midst of a resurgence of interest in Australian military history and the increasing popularity of military re-enactments. Aided by a $12 000 grant, the battery was reorganised and supported by Salesian College, with its historical re-enactments teaching the students history, public speaking, etiquette, leadership and teamwork.

Rupertswood is far more than just another boutique hotel. It remains today part of a vibrant, modern college, it casts its eye back over Victoria's pastoral and social development, it keeps alive a proud slice of our nation's military past, and its paddocks gave birth to The Ashes. Not a bad résumé when you think of it.

PART 6

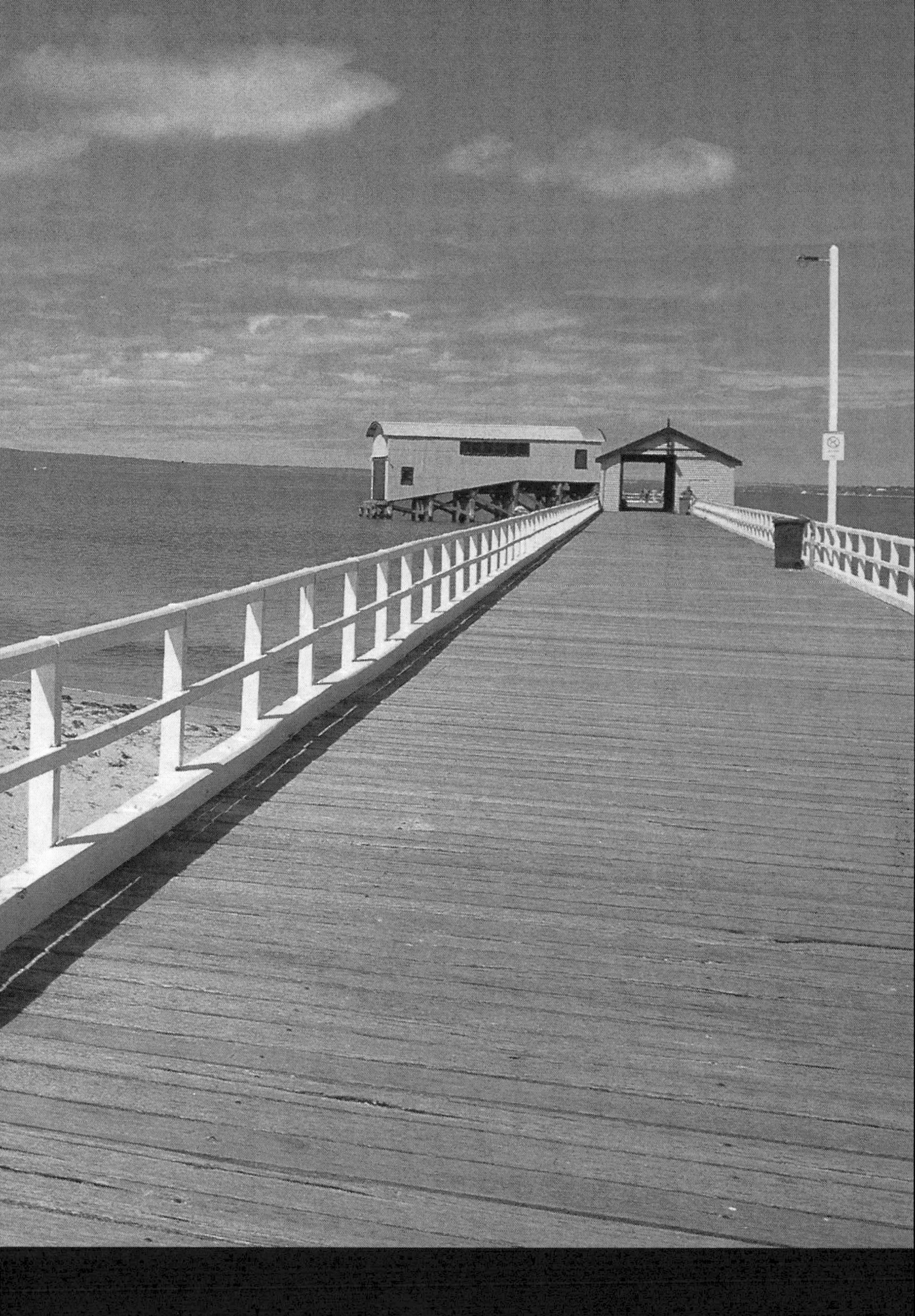

By The Sea

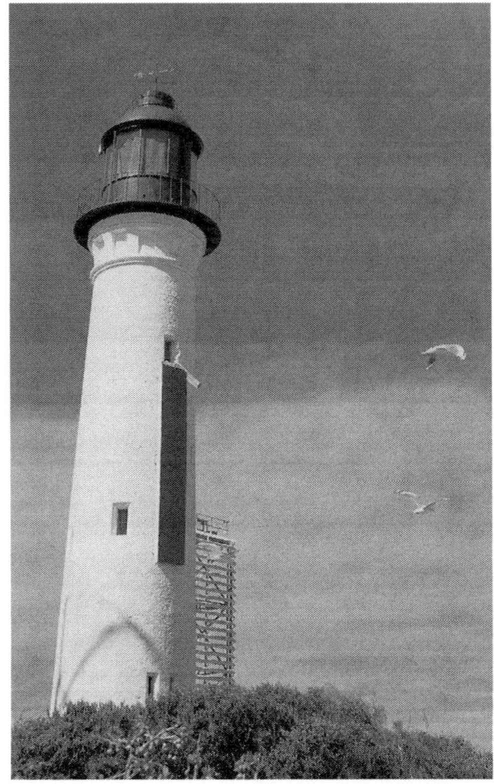

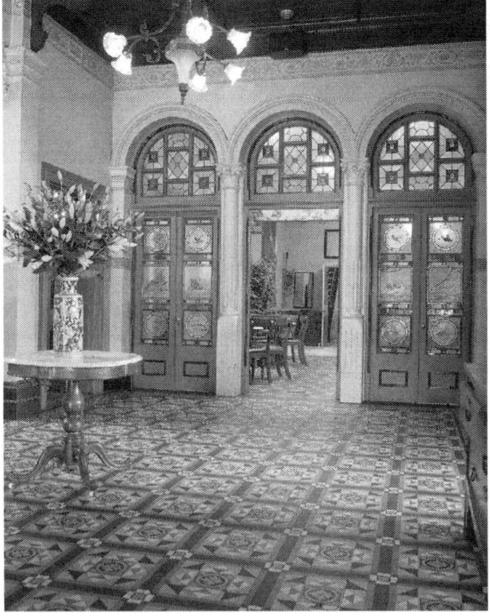

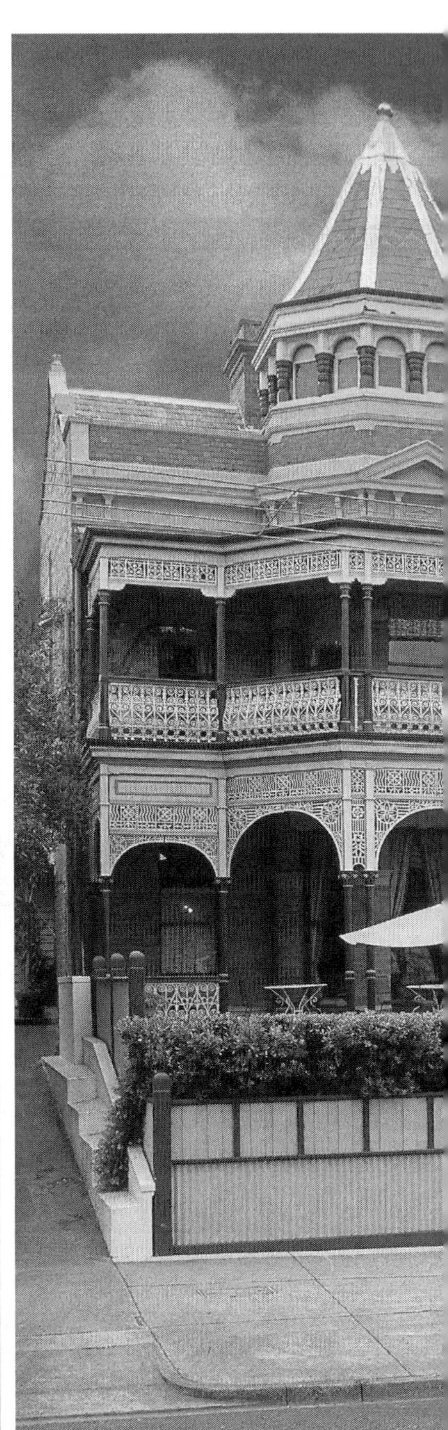

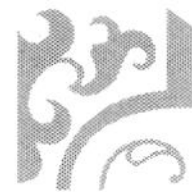

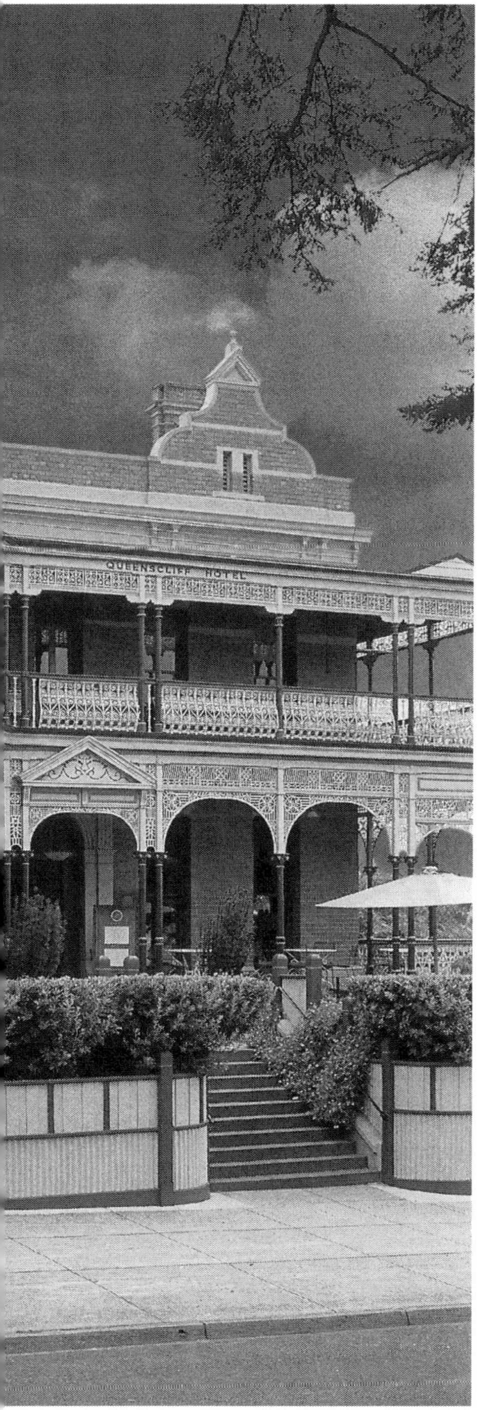

CHAPTER 28

The Queenscliff Hotel

I'll never forget the first time I saw The Queenscliff Hotel. It reminded me that great hotels are living, breathing structures. No two are alike and, just like people, every one of them is 'good' at something, has one particular attribute that will see it through good times and bad, boom times and recessions. It might be a remarkable cellar, or a location other hotels would die for, or the genius of its chef. In the case of The Queenscliff Hotel, that ingredient is its architecture. Ebullient, flamboyant architecture that screams out from behind its manicured hedgerows, 'Look at me—I'm gorgeous!' When it comes to first impressions, this one's hard to beat.

---

clockwise from top left Queenscliff's 'White Lighthouse' was built in 1862; the Queenscliff Hotel is one of Australia's great 19th-century seaside hotels; looking down the foyer towards the dining room.

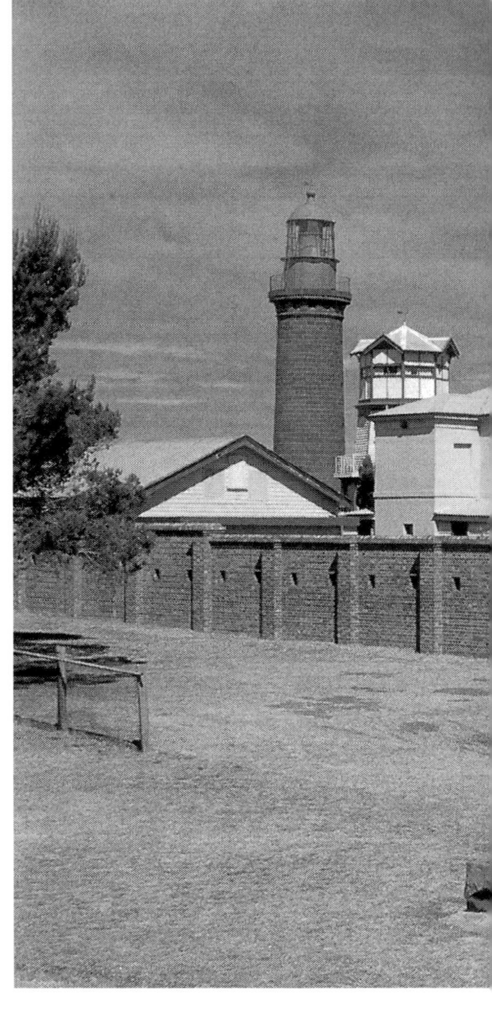

right Fort Queenscliff, a coastal artillery complex dating from 1860, is one of the nation's best preserved historical/military sites.

From the moment its foundation stone was laid by George Admans, the mayor of the Borough of Queenscliff in October 1887, the hotel's architects, Reed, Henderson and Smart of Melbourne, spared nothing. Its facade is a fanciful world of verandahs, lacework, trusses, balustrades, pediments and tuck-pointed cherry-red brickwork, a masterpiece of the Queen Anne era. I love it. Inside, the entry hall floor is paved with encaustic tiles whose colours are the product of the clay itself rather than just glazing, the sort of tiles that can be found in so many of the world's great buildings, including Cleeve Abbey in England and the US Capitol. The hall leads through a leadlight entry hall through to an atrium and into the rear dining room with its exquisitely coffered ceiling highlighted by cast-iron roses, diagonally-set Danzig pine boards and pedimented window cases. The rear doors of the dining room open out into a delightfully private courtyard with a central fountain surrounded by old growth trees that keep out the noise and troublesome onshore winds and is a great place to let children unwind. Upstairs most guest bedrooms have working fireplaces and adjoining sitting rooms, and are reached by a refreshingly broad staircase that makes the carrying of suitcases much less of a trauma than it can be in some turn-of-the-century hotels.

Its distinctive tower was built to provide guests with sweeping

views out to the infamous Queenscliff Rip. It still has its signature polygonal cone roof with its ever-so-slight bell-cast profile, and was built with two small landings and a promenade, which have since been blocked off. The 'rip' can be found lurking in the 3-kilometre-wide stretch of water from Buckley's Cave across to Point Nepean, with the 100-metre-deep chasm of the Yarra bed below, and on the surface the swirling waters of Port Phillip Bay as it wrestles with the incoming currents of the Southern Ocean. Even on days here when the water looks like a millpond, people say you can feel the wheel of your boat tighten in your hands as you cross.

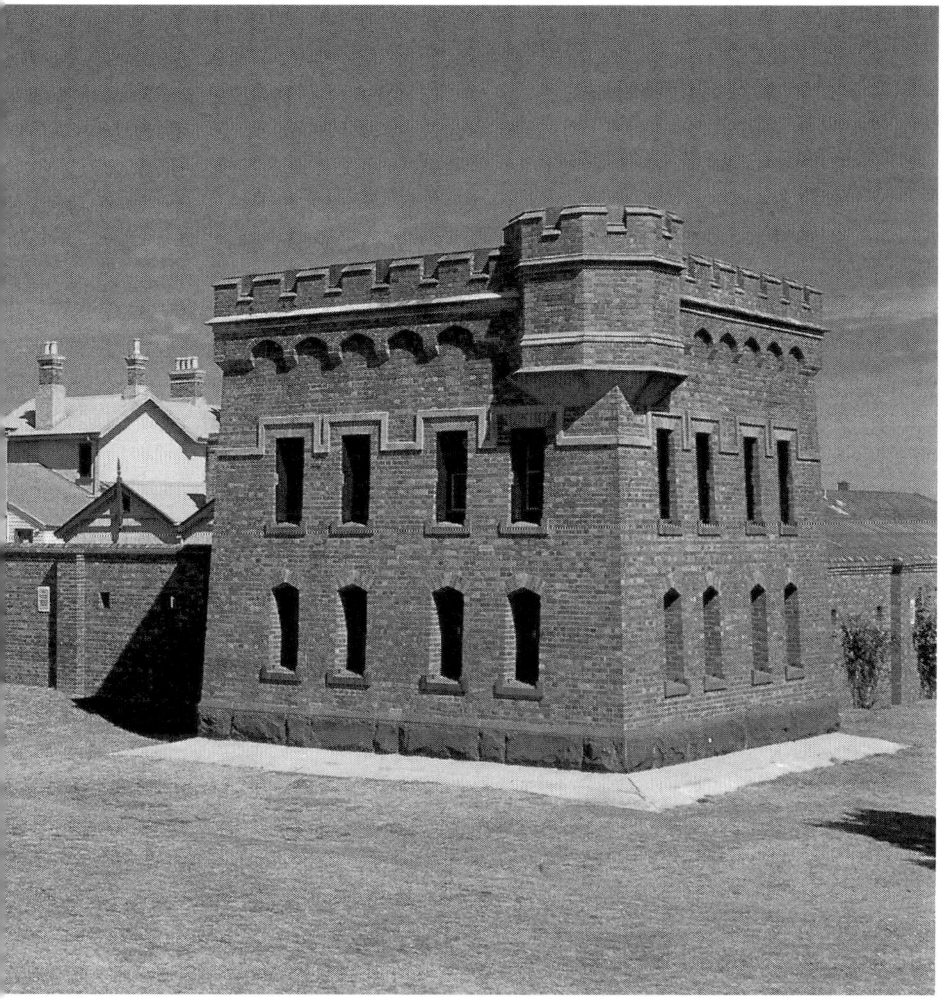

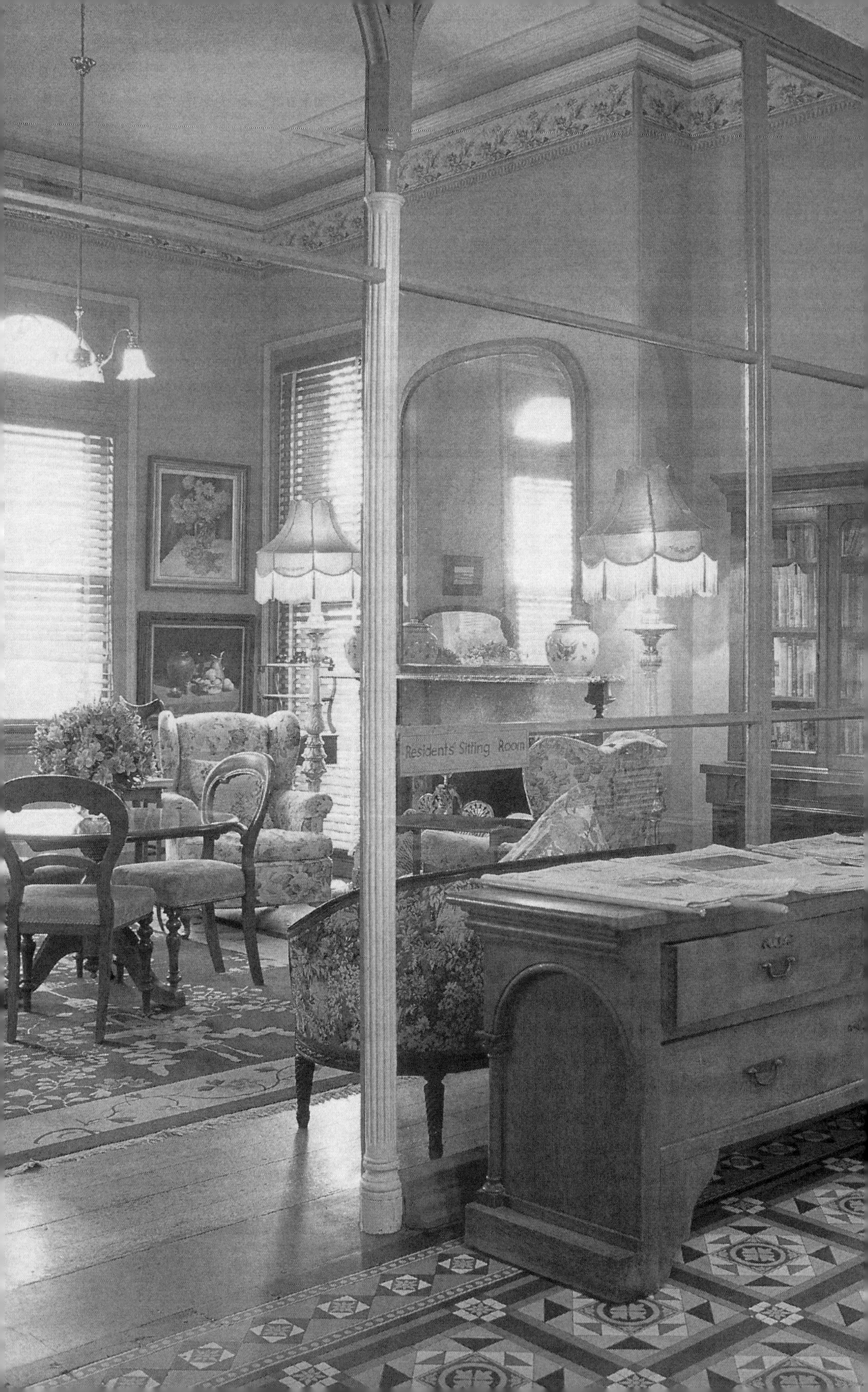

Residents' Sitting Room

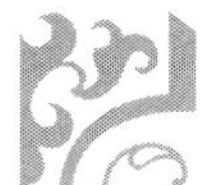

left One of the hotel's three sitting/reading rooms, ideal for a quiet read or a game of chess.

When The Queenscliff Hotel was built, it was lit by gaslight and had lovely glazed airlock entry doors and sidelights which have sadly since been removed. An alley down one side of the hotel took you to a cement pediment over a plain doorway, once the discreet entrance to the hotel's bar and drinking parlours. There are Dutch gables aplenty with their steep slit openings, traditional swag-bellied balustrades and friezes that have been cast flat and look from a distance to resemble delicate fretwork. With all its Dutch and European influences, you might be wondering if there is any nod here at all to Australian vernacular architecture. Well, just take a walk outside and relax on any one of the chairs on the hotel's broad, front verandah and I promise you, you'll feel right at home.

Queenscliff is a rare amalgam of fishing village, traditional seaside resort, and significant maritime centre—a combination unique on the Victorian coastline—and occupies a historically strategic position at the entrance to Port Phillip Bay. It entered into the boom years of the 1880s with a characteristic post-goldrush Victorian frenzy. Mansions and splendid hotels rose up on every block, with mansard roofs and turrets punctuating the skyline. The opening of the Geelong–Queenscliff rail line in 1879 brought tourists from Melbourne and as far away as Ballarat and Kyneton. The pace of construction was so frenetic and bricks were in such short supply that extra trains had to be commandeered to bring them. The introduction of paddlesteamers and the so-called 'Bay Run' brought thousands of tourists a day through the summer months from Melbourne, Port Arlington, Mornington and Geelong. Queenscliff became the resort town of choice for Melbourne's elite and has remained sufficiently removed from the ravages of urbanisation to allow it to maintain its old-world charm.

The Queenscliff Hotel provided us with one of the cosiest 'away' evenings we've ever had, though it had nothing to do with amenities or room size. Unfortunately I neglected to mention that I'd be travelling with my family, so instead of being given a suite we found ourselves in a delightful, though cramped, standard room with one double bed. My fault entirely, I told them, and not to worry. And being a Saturday night the hotel was fully booked, so an upgrade was out of the question. There was just enough space between the end of the double bed and the fireplace for the staff to wheel in a trundle bed while my wife and two boys shared the double. Undaunted we settled down to a night of cards, Cluedo and Scrabble, and, as is often the case when things don't go according to plan, we all had a great night with no television, no distractions, no elbow room, and fabulous views out along the hotel's side verandah to the seaside park across the road and Phillip Bay beyond, with plenty of tea, coffee and hot chocolate courtesy of the communal servery down the hall. It reminded me of my holidays as a child, where a lack of gadgets and comforts were more than compensated for by family fun and simple pleasures. There are larger rooms and suites, I should add, and everywhere an accompanying feeling of nostalgia due in no small part to the philosophy of its owner, Johann.

Johann came to Australia from Germany and settled in the Melbourne seaside suburb of Albert Park before purchasing the heritage-listed 1889 Victorian Hotel on the corner of Beaconsfield Parade and Kerferd Road. He installed ensuites in many of its rooms and breathed new life into the building before selling it to return to live in Europe. When he returned to Melbourne in 2002, the Queenscliff Hotel was on the market. Despite not having had a lot of money spent on it over the previous 25 years and looking a little 'tired', Johann purchased it and has been its proud owner ever since. He again added ensuites where he could and put in a new kitchen. But Queenscliff can be a tough place to do business. From mid-May to mid-September Melbourne's inclement winter weather keeps hotel occupancy rates down and is a tough period for all Queenscliff businesses, an annual downturn that has to be recouped in the warmer months.

Johann spent many of his holidays growing up in Munich, going with his parents to a little place 50 kilometres south of Munich called Tegernsee, a Bavarian spa town on Tegernsee Lake near the border with Austria. Johann was a merchant, but on his arrival in Australia did a three-year apprenticeship as a motor mechanic in Melbourne. Engineering proved his forte and he soon had engineering businesses in Perth and Adelaide, designing differentials among other things. He loved engineering and was reluctant to leave it, but had fond memories of his holidays in Bavaria and had always wanted to try his hand at running a hotel. So he purchased, and later sold, the Victorian Hotel. His philosophy in running a hotel is a simple one: 'Hospitality is similar to engineering—you need precision and thoroughness to make it successful.' It pleases him when he sees people having an enjoyable visit and leave happy and relaxed at the end of their stay. It's not a complicated formula—just provide a great venue with attentive staff in a hotel that encourages you to sit on that lounge, ask someone to light that fireplace, read that book, and do as much or as little as you like. Johann loves Queenscliff but sometimes feels its relative isolation. 'Queenscliff is a great, untouched old town, but it deserves better. We were all hoping the new marina would have made a difference, but so far it hasn't. A lot of people struggle here in winter and don't make enough money and spend the rest of the year getting it back.'

Johann does what he can to keep old traditions alive. A few years ago he went to the offices of the Queenscliff Historical Museum and asked if they had any surviving menus from the hotels and restaurants of the late 1800s. They found what they could, and Johann charged his chef with the task of resurrecting the 100-year-old dishes. Just what *did* Melbourne's well-to-do eat a hundred years ago? Well, in the hotel's fine dining room every Friday and Saturday evening, lit by the glow of antique lamps, candlelight and the original 1880s fireplace, you can find out. Start with an entree of mulligatawny soup, known as 'pepper water' and made with rabbit or a small fowl and thickened with almonds. There's roast quail with herbs, bread sauce and game chips, or poached duck eggs served with roasted field mushrooms and silverbeet. Or why not try pan-roasted duck with celery and chestnuts served with duck-neck sausages?

That's what I liked most about staying here—its palpable sense of nostalgia. And it didn't hurt that Frank Sinatra's 'Songs For Young Lovers' was playing softly as I checked in, either. The fact is, unlike some hotels that might have a problem defining themselves or wondering what their 'essence' should be, the Queenscliff Hotel knows *exactly* what it's there for and knows precisely how to deliver the sort of experiences its guests are looking for. After all, only the staff of a hotel that's been welcoming guests with style for 123 years can wheel in a trundle bed one night, then look you in the eye the very next morning and ask with confidence if you enjoyed your stay.

As Sinatra himself might have said, 'Now *that's* class, baby!'

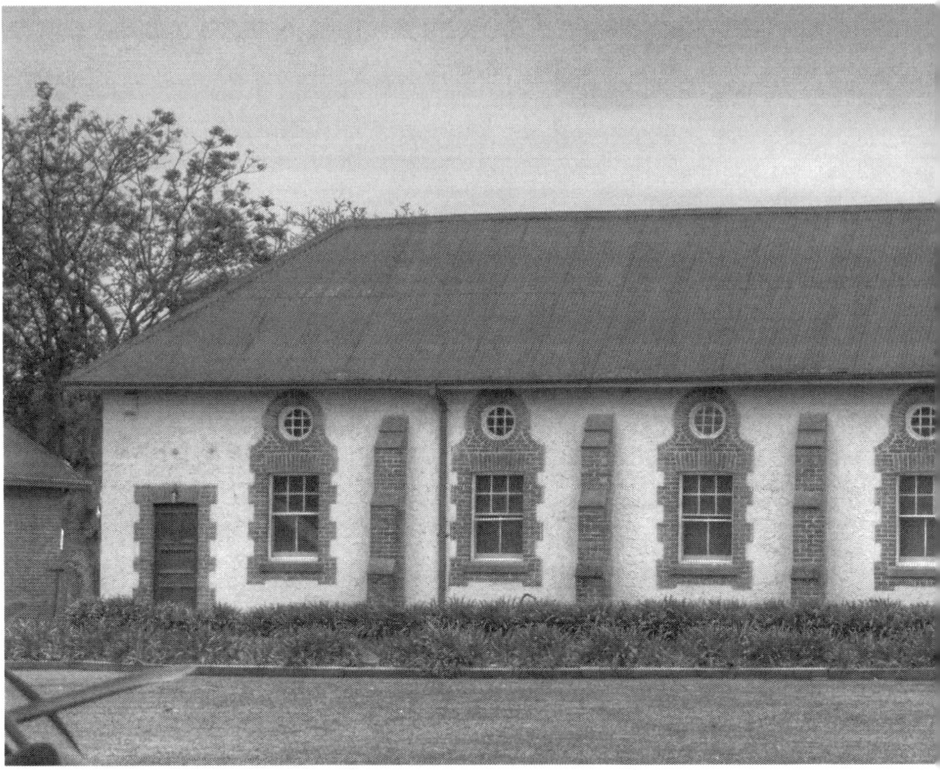

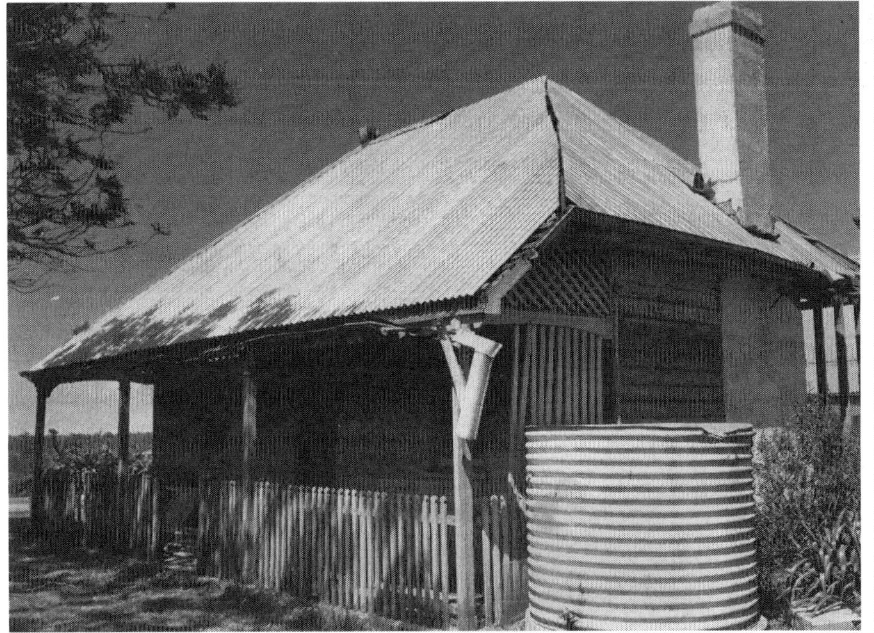

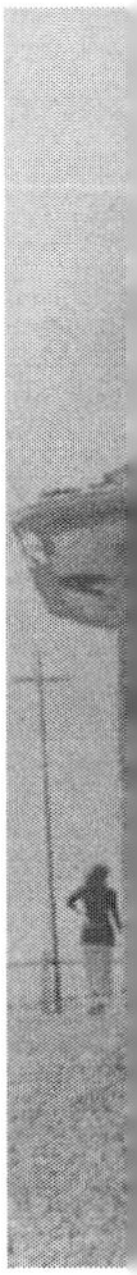

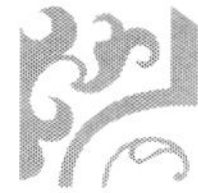

CHAPTER 29

Coolangatta Estate

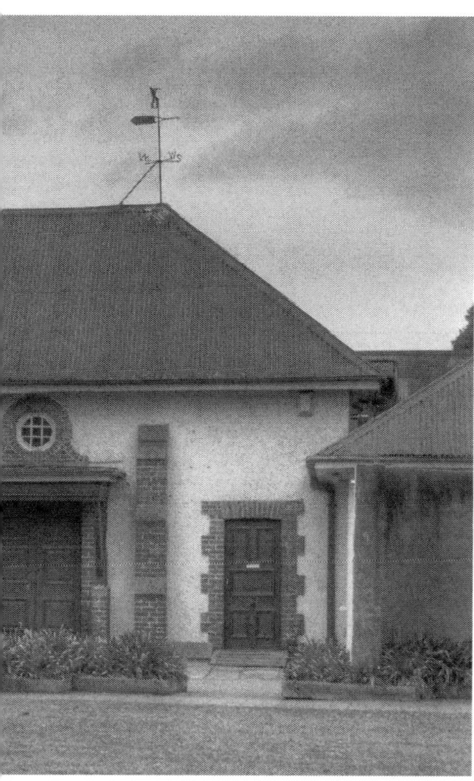

On 20 March 1806, after several days of incessant rain, the waters of Sydney's Hawkesbury River slowly began to rise. But settlers on the low ground along its banks had seen it all before, and when the water level seemed to fall slightly on that first night, they thought nothing more of it. The rain, though, refused to abate, and by the end of the following day the farmlands and communities along the river's banks had become a scene of horror. Police took to their boats and rescued hundreds of settlers from rooftops who signalled their whereabouts by firing musket shot into the air. Remarkably, only five people lost their lives.

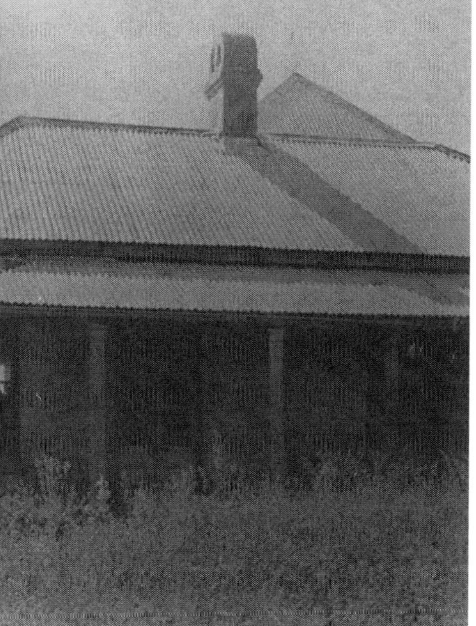

clockwise from top The estate's Great Hall was built in 1832; the billiard room prior to its restoration; the district's last remaining convict cottage prior to restoration.

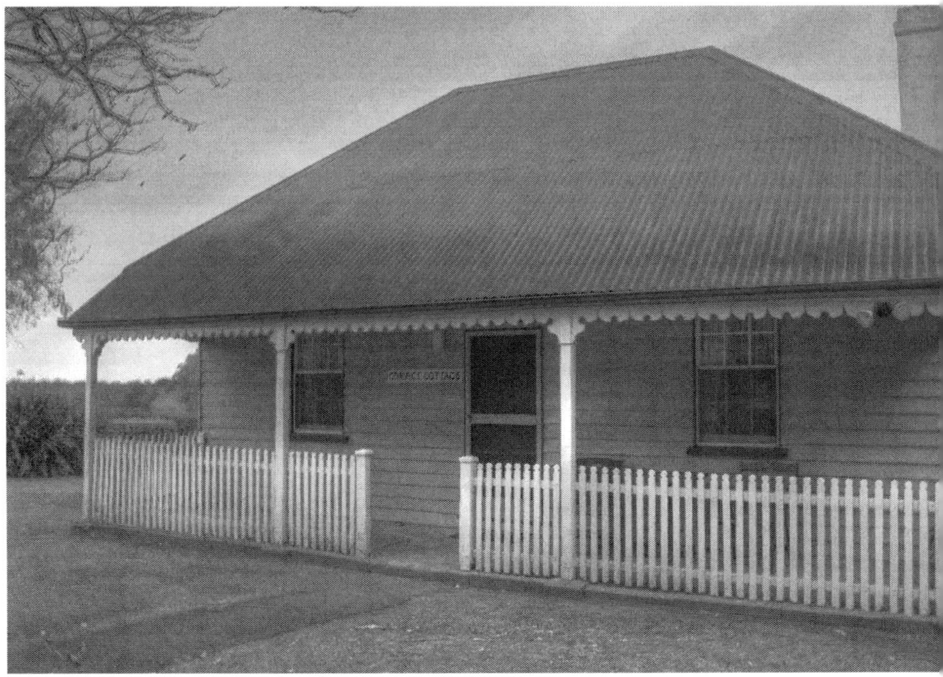

above 'Convict Cottage' has been fully restored and is now available for overnight stays.

At the height of the flood witnesses claimed to have seen hundreds of wheat stacks swept into the river, which were carried downstream to the ocean. When the waters finally abated, labourers from the Parramatta and Castle Hill Public Works were brought in to salvage what food they could, gathering and drying the sodden wheat and shelling the maize. The flood was a disaster for the emerging colony. The farms along the Hawkesbury were the source of virtually all its grain. Its governor, William Bligh, visited the area, inquired after the wellbeing of each settler and promised them the government would purchase any surpluses from their next crops. He also ordered government-owned cattle be slaughtered and given to the settlers so they would have food, which, when the river again flooded with equal ferocity in February 1807, would again be in short supply.

Alexander Berry was born at Cupar in Fifeshire, Scotland, in 1781. He studied medicine at St Andrews and Edinburgh Universities and graduated as a surgeon at the age of 24. Inspired by the exploits of Horatio Nelson, he accepted a commission with the East India Company and became a ship's surgeon. But being a surgeon in an age before either antiseptics or anesthetics was not easy. The suffering and frequent deaths he was forced to watch filled him with disgust, and the young Alexander determined he would pursue a career in commerce instead. He chartered a boat called *The Fly* and set out from England on a commercial venture to the Cape of Good Hope. When he arrived there he heard that the colony in New South Wales was suffering from an acute shortage of food. So he purchased a 520-tonne ship, *The Rappadora*, renamed it the *City of Edinburgh*, and sailed it to Australia, laden with provisions, in September 1807.

Berry arrived in Australia in January 1808 but sold much of his cargo at Port Dalrymple (now Launceston, Tasmania), which earned him the ire of the New South Wales governor, who felt he had sole rights in the purchasing of provisions. Instead of settling down to life on the land, Berry began a period of seafaring that took him to New Zealand and throughout the South Pacific. In 1815 he made his way back to London where he lived for the next three years only to return to Sydney in 1819 and became one of the founding members of the Sydney Philosophical Society. In 1822 he was given 10 000 acres along the mouth of the Shoalhaven River, along with 100 convicts, to help him establish a settlement there:

> For my headquarters I fixed on the north side of the river at
> the foot of a hill called by the natives 'Collungatta'. I located the
> 10 000 acres grant in this locality.

> DIARY OF ALEXANDER BERRY, 23 JUNE 1822

'Collungatta' is an Indigenous word which, roughly translated, means 'fine view' or 'good lookout'. Berry thought it would make an ideal name for the homestead he intended to build, which he named Coolangatta. It grew into a self-supporting community with workshops and mills. The first canal in Australia was cut here in just 12 days, linking the Crookhaven and Shoalhaven rivers, and the estate became a centre for shipbuilding with its first vessel *The Water Mole* launched in January 1824. In the late 1830s Alexander's brother John persuaded him to buy and breed cattle and horses, and the estate would soon develop an enviable reputation for fine stock. When Berry died in 1873, 270 tenant farmers worked his land, which spread over more than 15 000 acres. Alexander's brother David continued to manage Coolangatta until his own death in 1889. More than 2000 people attended his funeral. It was the end of an era, and over the next 40 years the estate gradually fell into disrepair.

Nothing now remains of the original homestead, save for a solitary external brick wall, built by an Indigenous bricklayer named Broughton, that runs along an area of lawn supported by plinths to prevent it from collapsing. The bricks came from a clay pit just 3 kilometres from the estate that is still called 'Brickies Hill' today. A rounded section of the wall at one end is all that remains of Alexander Berry's private bedroom and some foundation work once belonging to the rooms where his servants were housed. The walls at the other end housed the kitchen.

Colin Bishop grew up with his sister and two brothers on the family dairy farm in Nowra and has been familiar with Coolangatta Estate for as long as he could remember, and whenever visitors came to his home his parents would drive them up to the historic estate. In the years after World War II while his sister and two brothers were in the armed services, Colin remained at home helping his father run the dairy farm that was only a mile down the road from the estate he would one day go on to own. He attended Sunday school in Coolangatta Estate's Great Hall, built in 1832 and still standing today, and remembers vividly how, over time, it became so covered in vines that his children would be able to climb over the entire building simply by thrusting their hands and feet into its vast network of branches. In the 1940s the Great Hall was one of the Shoalhaven's most popular dance venues and Colin recalls the local priest, Father Bevan, boiling kerosene tins and making cups of tea and old men playing yuka while the local girls would sit with their backs to the walls, waiting for boys to invite them to come up for a dance. Though now in his late-80s he still remembers playing in and running through the rooms of the original homestead as a child, which ultimately fell victim to fire under 'very suspicious circumstances' in 1946.

The estate was allowed to deteriorate almost to the point of being a candidate for demolition when Colin approached the Hay family in 1947 in the hope of acquiring land for a dairy farm of his own. The Hays sold him an initial 278 acres of Coolangatta Estate in a purchase made possible only after Colin's father approached the Rural Bank, as it was then known, and convinced them to advance his son the entire purchase price of the land against his own personal guarantee. Additional acquisitions soon followed. The old servants' quarters were

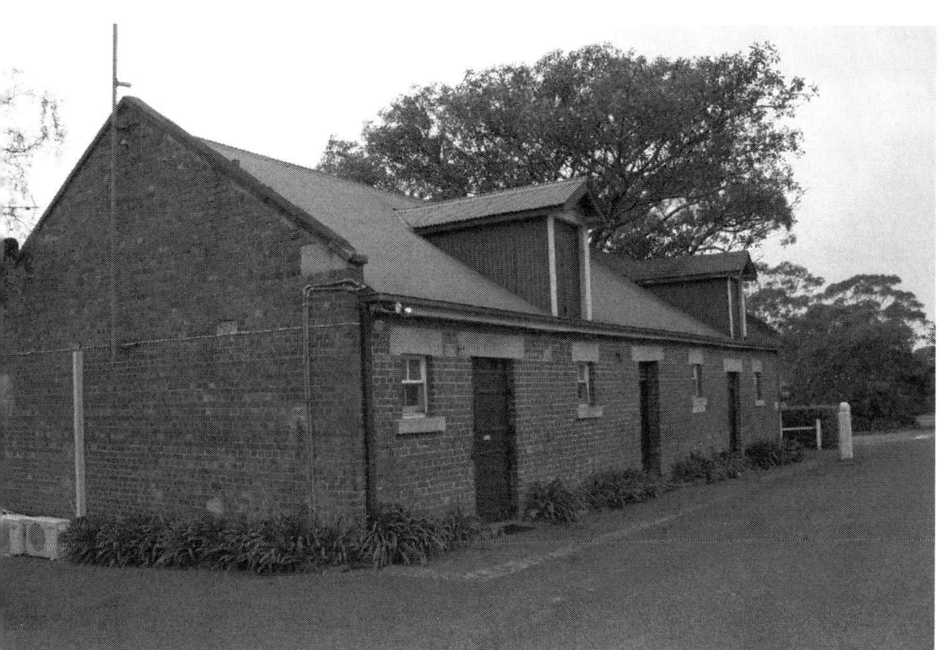

above Once home to several famous horses including 'Archer', the winner of the first Melbourne Cup, the stables have now been converted into comfortable terrace-style accommodation.

purchased in 1950 (the year Colin began dairying on the property) and became the family home. An old convicts' cell was turned into a bathroom, the old laundry was extended and transformed into a lounge room, and an adjoining coachman's quarters became accommodation for a resident employee and his family. An additional six purchases followed as Colin acquired the estate piece by piece. Initially the only concern was how the buildings could be adapted and incorporated into a successful, integrated dairy farm and most were used as farm sheds for years, until increased interest in Australia's heritage saw consideration begin to be given to restoring the various buildings on the property in an attempt to re-create the era of the Berry estate by transforming the farm into a historical village.

The restoration work began in 1971 when, in the absence of any financial assistance from Shoalhaven Council and with personal bank loans stretched to the limit, Colin decided he'd 'go it alone', gradually transforming Coolangatta Estate into what is now the South Coast's finest collection of historic buildings, including the 1840 'Convict Cottage' built entirely of red cedar and the 'Plumber's Shop', the oldest

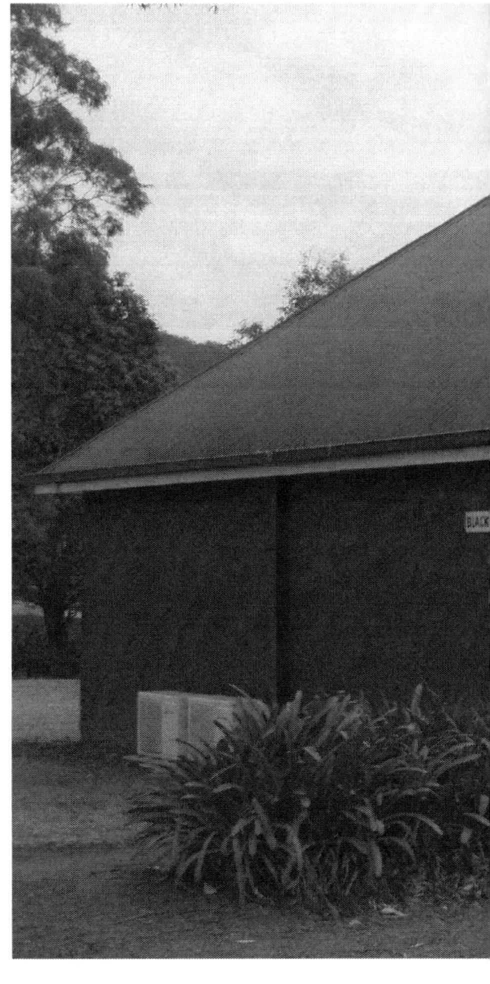

right One of Coolangatta Estate's first buildings, the Blacksmith's Shop now offers three modern, comfortable rooms.

timber building remaining on New South Wales's South Coast, both of which have been refitted internally and transformed into guest accommodation. As has the old dairy, the stables, harness room and blacksmith's shop. Photographs from the late 1800s show a small cluster of buildings around the plumber's shop but these buildings are now all gone. Many ancillary buildings were unnecessarily demolished in the early 1900s during the stewardship of the Hay family who purchased the estate from the Berry's.

Alexander Berry was the first settler to grow vines on the South Coast, on the slopes of Mount Coolangatta in the mid 1800s. In 1988 Colin's son Greg saw the potential for restoring vines to the region and decided he'd take advantage of the Shoalhaven's maritime climate. Coolangatta Estate sends their grapes to the Tyrrell's Winery in the Hunter Valley to be vinified and its whites, fruit-driven and well-balanced, and its medium-bodied reds have together won more than a thousand awards in international and national wine shows. 'For the first three years since the initial planting I could have strangled him,' Colin confided to me. 'There were no returns, and considerable expense. Now the vineyards are a roaring success, of course.' Despite his advancing years Colin still drives tractors in the vineyard for his son whenever he can, and the 10 hectares currently under cultivation produce roughly 5000 cases each year, not to mention creating a very

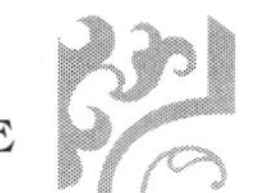

pleasing aesthetic to the estate as a whole.

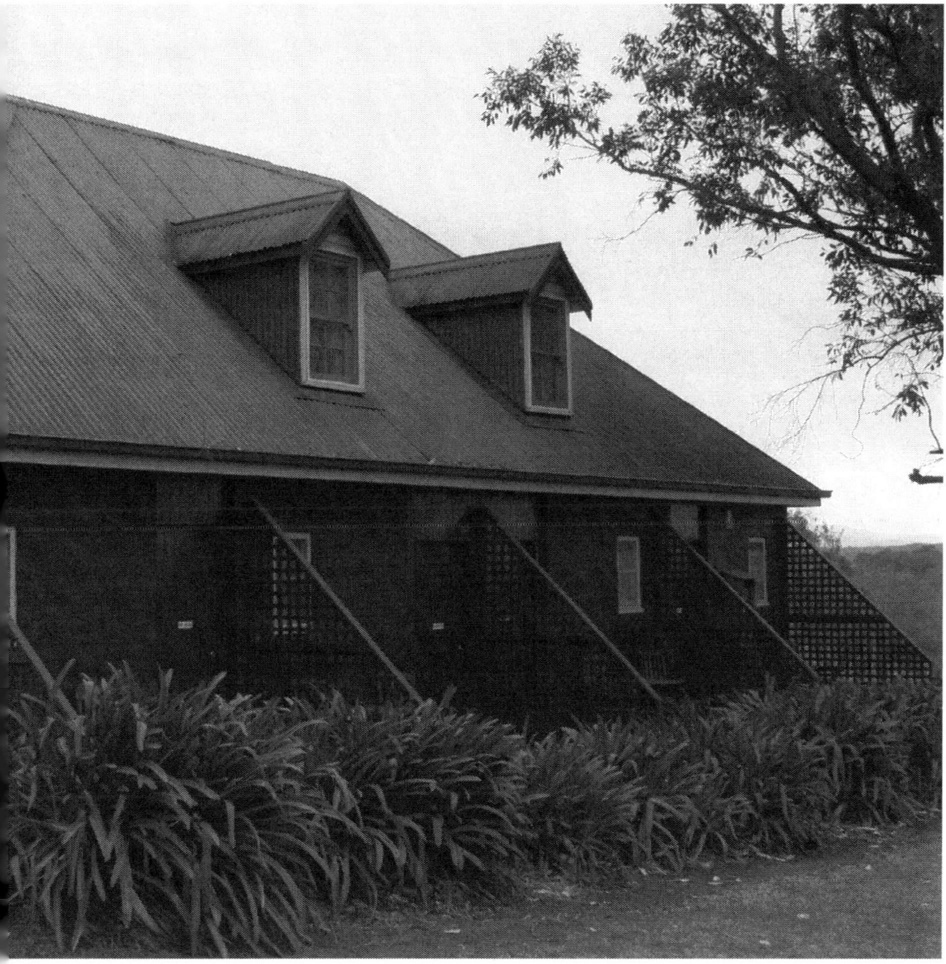

Today Coolangatta Estate comprises 35 guest rooms, has a nine-hole golf course, solar-heated swimming pool, tennis court, croquet lawns, lawn bowls, a cellar door open daily from 10 a.m. to 5 p.m. and a restaurant, all embraced within its award-winning vineyards with elevated views towards the Shoalhaven River and beyond. It is still owned and operated by the Bishop family and continues to be a living monument to Alexander Berry and those who helped establish what was the first European settlement on the South Coast of New South Wales.

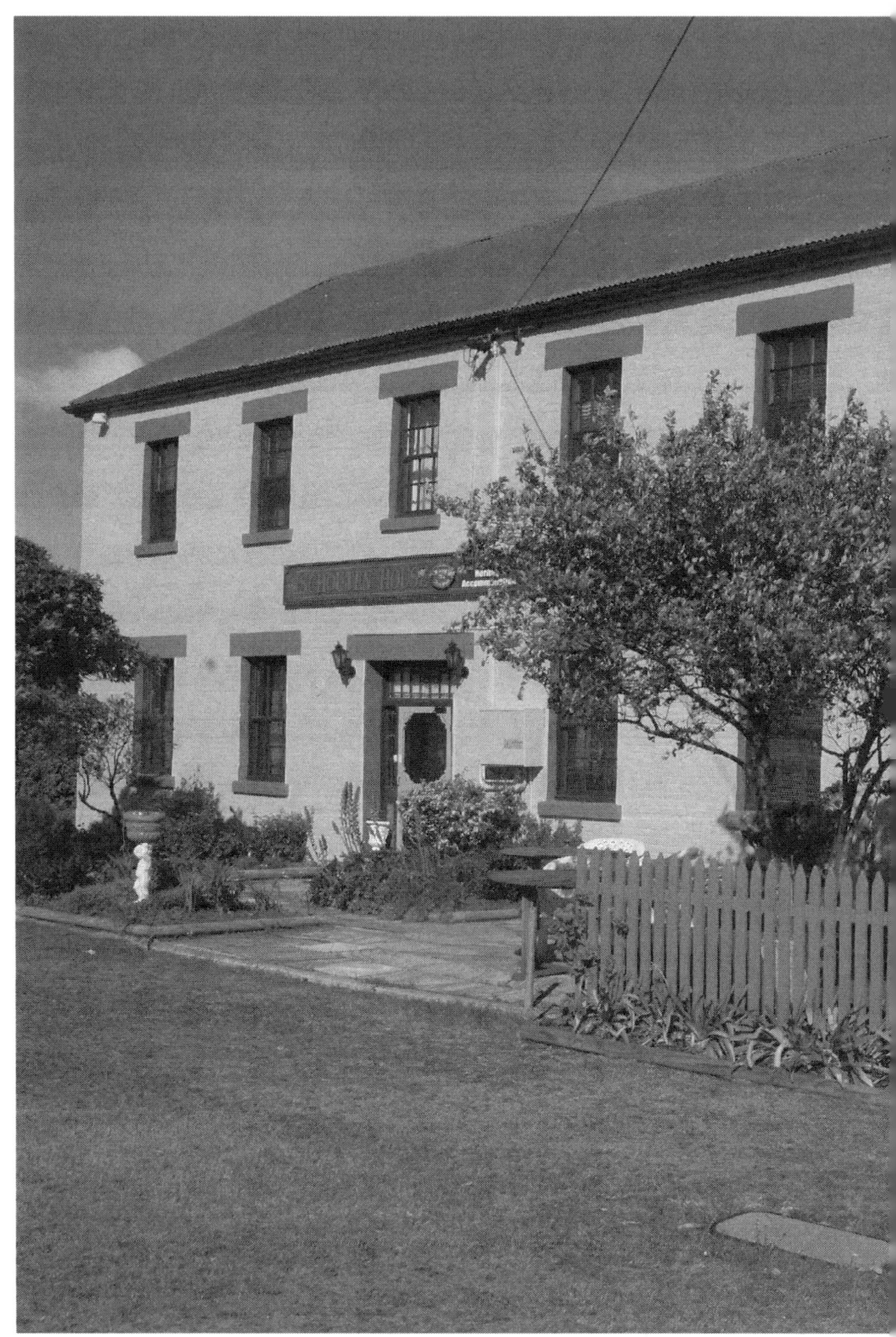

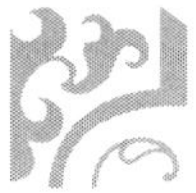

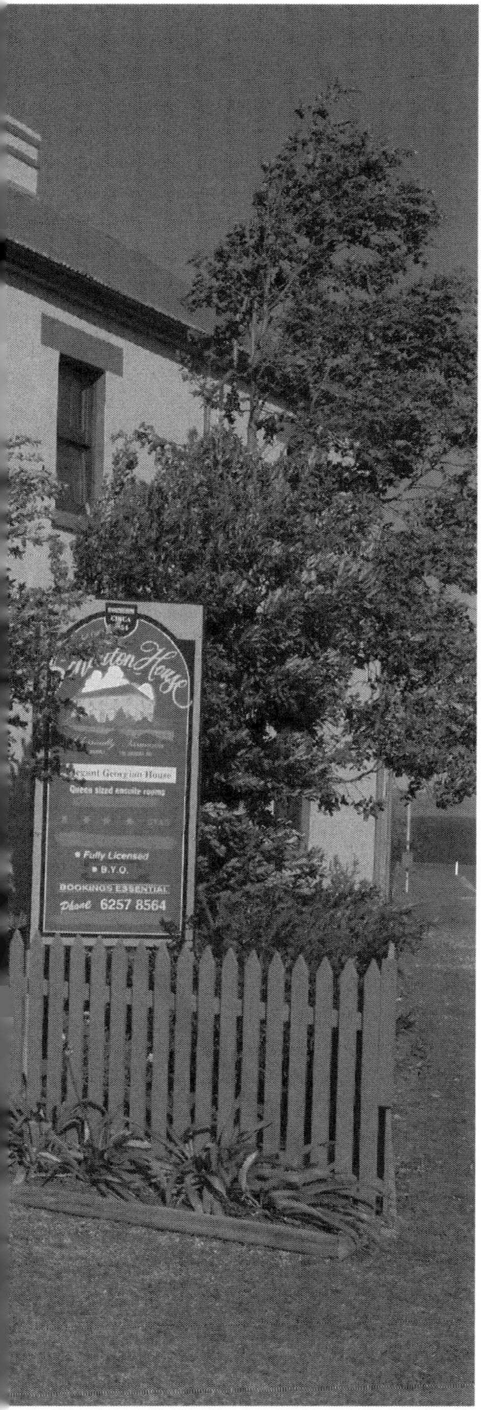

CHAPTER 30

Schouten House

It's funny, the things you can learn over a casual glass of port. Especially the things that you never really thought about, because you presumed there wasn't much to know. Then suddenly someone opens your eyes and you realise there's a whole lot more to them than you ever thought possible. Like bagpipes. I had no idea there were so many different kinds of bagpipes. And if I hadn't stayed at Schouten House on Tasmania's east coast and talked into the night with its owners Jodi and Cameron, who is Scottish and just happens to play the bagpipes, it's likely I'd have gone on supposing that bagpipes were bagpipes and that was the end of it. And that would have been tragic.

left The timeless elegance of Schouten House, built in 1844 in the grand Georgian style.

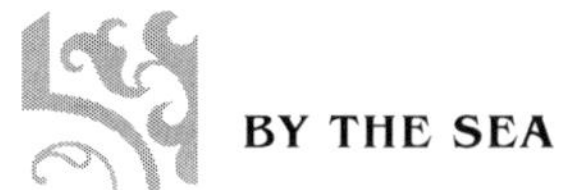

right Typically Georgian, the entry leads directly into the foyer, with the library/sitting room on your left and the breakfast/dining room to your right.

The number of different kinds of bagpipes is staggering. They can be either bellows-blown or mouth-blown, and the internal walls of the chanter, or melody pipe, can be parallel or conically bored. They can have two reeds or one. There are French bagpipes, Lithuanian bagpipes, German and Austrian bagpipes, the Swedish sackpipa, the Hungarian duda and the Polish koza. Bagpipes are found in the Balkans, Iran and across the Persian Gulf. In North Africa there's the zokra in Libya, the ghaita in Algeria and the mizwad in Tunisia with a double chanter that ends in two cow horns! Cameron plays the Great Highland Bagpipe which first emerged in Scotland in the early 15th century, and could play any bagpipe regardless of its origin as apparently it's not too hard to make the transition once you've mastered any one example. He's even had the honour of playing in the Edinburgh Military Tattoo. Of course, running an historic B&B means he doesn't always get the time to practice as much as he would like, but he has played in Swansea's annual 'From France to Freycinet' festival and might occasionally play for guests. If you ask him nicely.

If you're walking over the floor of a house and you feel yourself rising and falling along almost imperceptible inclines, chances are you're walking on a *very* old floor, a floor that's witnessed the comings and goings of generations of families and visitors and events too numerous to mention, a floor that's weathered and contracted and moved and breathed as timber does long after its been secured to its joists. The old cedar floorboards that undulate beneath your feet and the pure wool carpets that protect them throughout the rooms and hallways of Schouten House must be tempting to expose, to pull back the carpet and show off their ageless beauty. But uneven floorboards can be a nightmare to polish, and what's more the carpet that protects them is a treasure in itself. Sometimes it's better just to leave history where it is.

The floorboards of Schouten House are real, unadorned and have withstood the passage of time, and here what is true of the floor is true of the house. Schouten House is *real*. Its fireplaces in the dining room and library can still be lit. Its walls don't sit on a solid foundation but instead were built over the top of rubble deposits.

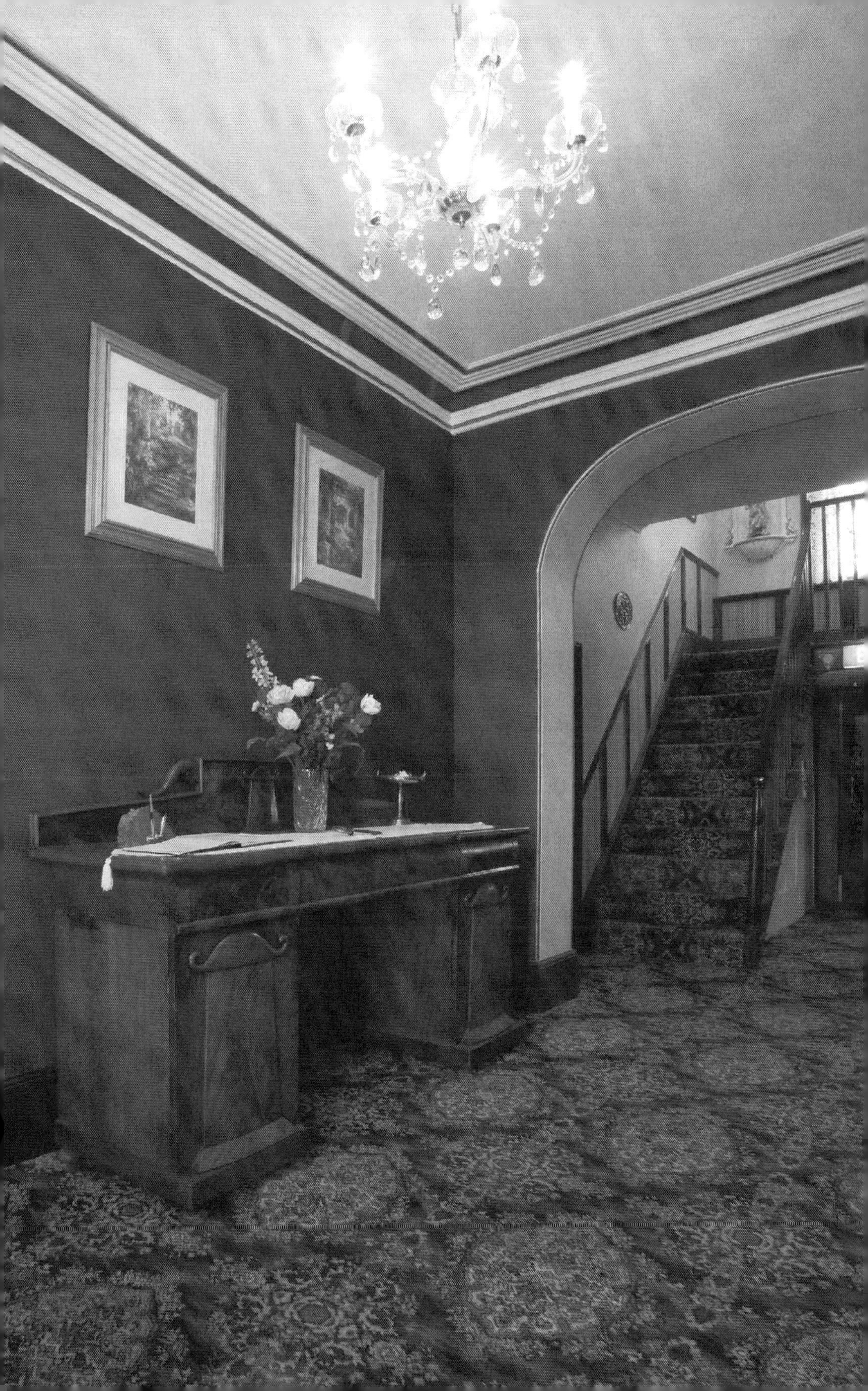

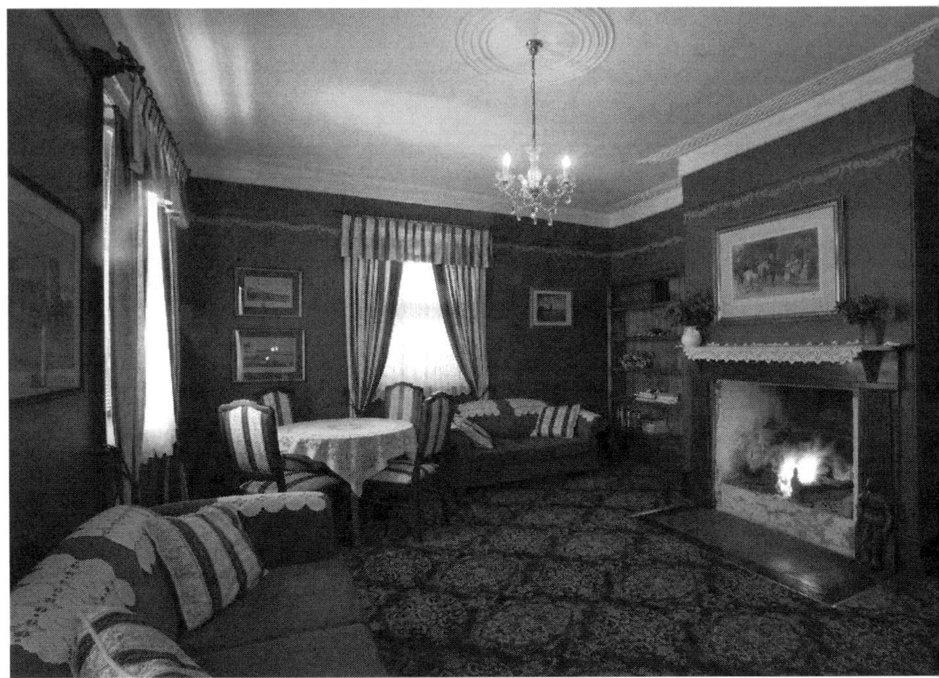

above The library/sitting room is just the right size, an intimate retreat complete with working fireplace and wool carpets will warm even the chilliest Tasmanian winter.

Its shingle roof isn't fastened to the building but is instead held in place simply by virtue of its own weight. Its external and internal walls are not merely double brick but double brick with rubble-filled cavities that together make for some of the thickest walls you'll ever see in a mid 19th-century Georgian house. It was the thickness of the walls and the warmth they impart and the permanency that they give the place that Cameron noticed the moment he walked inside, and Schouten House has not been extensively renewed, nor reinvented, nor has it been a priority to 'tastefully bring it into the 21st century'. It is a rarity—a simple home where the exterior and much of its structural integrity have been left relatively untouched. There are, of course, the usual conveniences, but what makes this little Georgian gem so appealing is its originality, and its relative plainness; a plainness that is, after all, what pure Georgian architecture is supposed to be all about.

Located just metres from the beach, it boasts wonderful views across Great Oyster Bay to the eroded granite islands known as

The Hazards and over to the pink granite mountains that make up Tasmania's stunning Freycinet National Park. Wineglass Bay, likely named because such huge numbers of whales were once slaughtered in its sheltered waters that their blood turned the water as red as wine, is here too. Schouten House's namesake, Schouten Island, sits at the end of the Freycinet Peninsula. It's a rugged island with a fascinating geology, bisected by its own fault line running north–south that's resulted in its eastern side being composed largely of granite and its western side made up of sub-volcanic dolerite; a breeding ground for little penguins, Australian fur seals and Tasmanian native hens.

Originally called the Swansea Inn, Schouten House was built in 1844 by William Champion as a wedding gift to his daughter Theresa. When she died in childbirth a few years later, the house was sold by her husband Samuel Wellard and purchased by a Hobart businessman and publican, Mr Large, who sailed north from Hobart Town in the cutter *Resolution* with his wife and six children in 1850 with the intention of starting a brewery. Upon reaching the waters of Great Oyster Bay, virtually in sight of the house that was to be their home, the heavily laden ship foundered in rough seas. The cutter broke up and sank and all six children perished. Mr Large and his wife survived and were rescued the following day by a small whaleboat, but they never set foot inside Swansea Inn. After burying the bodies of five of their six children in the town's cemetery, the Larges returned to Hobart Town and faded into history.

Samuel Wellard ran the inn as a brewery until the mid 1850s when it was again sold and turned into a grammar school before being purchased by a physician. The house remained a private residence and during the 1940s was renamed Schouten House. In the early 1950s it became a weekend retreat for the boys of Hobart's Dominic College, who slept upstairs at the front of the house in an area that has since been partitioned into two bedrooms with a sitting area in between. The college sold the house in the late 1970s and it was converted into a B&B. It is now owned by Jodi and Cameron, who have brought to the house some interesting culinary twists and traditions. Dinner is preceded by a drink in the library before moving on to the dining room where delicious North Indian dishes and mouthwatering desserts are topped off with a selection of Cameron's fresh, handmade shortbreads.

Jodi and Cameron are very private people. He is methodical and focused with a background in IT, she is spontaneous and always drawn towards artistic pursuits. It seemed at first a peculiar match but the more I talked with them as they shared their passion for the house, the more I saw how perfectly they complement one another. Schouten House is their life, at least for where they are in their lives right now. They live out the back in the old brewery that was built by Samuel Wellard, which means of course the house itself is just for the comfort of its guests, its quiet staircase and hallway encouraging you from your room to relax in the library or discover the house's hidden treasures, like the old iron key now kept safely in a bureau drawer that once was used to lock the house's front door.

The most important ingredient in any B&B experience is the quality of the breakfast. Jodi and Cameron pride themselves on being able to provide their guests with any breakfast request their guests might ask them, but still recall the day they were stumped by a guest's request for eggs 'eyes closed'.

There are more than 100 ways to cook an egg. You can fry it, boil it, scramble it, poach it, they can be soft-boiled, hard-boiled, over-easy or over-medium. You can roast an egg and, some say, even grill one. But how do you cook an egg eyes closed? Well, the first thing you need is bacon fat—*lots* of bacon fat. Once the fat has been accumulated, you then take an egg and crack it gently over the pan before smothering it in the fat by sort of flicking it over the top of the egg until there is no egg white visible. You then pour it over the yolk and continue pouring it over until it becomes smaller and smaller and then, finally, closes its eyes.

Swansea is a nice place. It won the Tidy Towns of Australia Award in 2007 and is steeped in local history. Every year the Swansea Heritage Week draws large crowds and several events have been held in Schouten House, including a performance of 'Grannie Rhodes at Schouten House' by the London-trained dramatist Miriam Cooper. Grannie Rhodes was a real Tasmanian pioneer who lived in the historic town of Richmond north of Hobart and baked bread for the community there till she was almost 100. Today her Richmond cottage is the only cottage in town that still has no electricity or running water. Miriam has composed her own 'Ballad of Schouten House' and performs a recounting of the ill-fated voyage of the Large family in 'The Wreck of the *Resolution* and other local tales'.

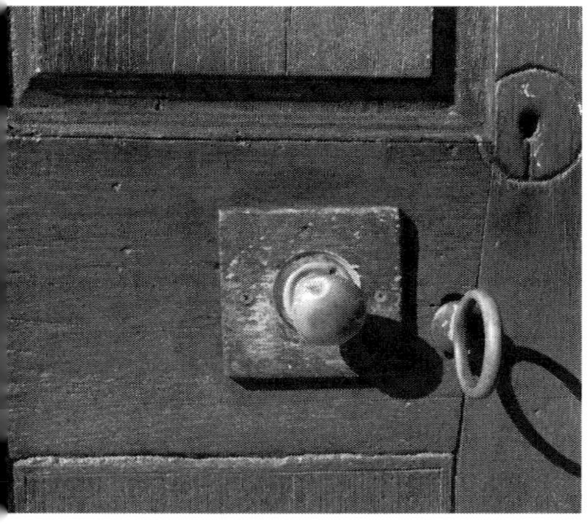

left The unadorned originality of Schouten House is everywhere, right down to the locks in its doors.

As the port continued to be consumed I found out aspects of what it means to be a proprietor of a historic property that I wasn't really prepared for. For instance Mrs Large apparently managed to fall pregnant again after returning home heartbroken to Hobart Town, and as a result Schouten House has rather a large 'family' scattered around the globe, courtesy of the Larges' descendants. Late one night, there was a knock at the door and when Jodi answered it a small group of people told her they were Large family descendants from England who were on a motorcycle trip across northern Tasmania and decided to ride down the coast to Swansea just to have a look at the 'old family home'. An innocent enough enquiry to be sure but also one that left Jodi wondering just how many other descendants might be out there with any veiled claim on the old 'ancestral home!' One day a lady in her 90s from Newcastle in New South Wales came to stay. She'd lived in the house as a child and wanted to see if something she scrawled on an internal wall had managed to survive the decades. Clearly the house has little trouble leaving lasting impressions.

Schouten House is more than just a building. It's been home to people over many generations and its charm elicits long and enduring affection. It's a testament to the genuineness and charm of Schouten House that once you stay here the feeling of 'belonging' stays with you, long after you've left.

ACKNOWLEDGEMENTS

I would like to express my sincere thanks to Simon Westaway,
Andrea Wait, and all those at Jetstar Airways for their cooperation in
not just flying me to five capital cities and arriving on time everywhere
with a minimum of fuss, but for re-arranging departure dates at
a moment's notice and helping me achieve order out of chaos.

Printed in Dunstable, United Kingdom

85050410R00152